ICONIC PLANTS OF INDIA

VOLUME 1

DR. P.N. RAVINDRAN

notionpress.com

INDIA · SINGAPORE · MALAYSIA

Dedicated to:

My life partner, Dr M. Shylaja,

My daughters Neelima and Namitha &

My grandchildren Atheeth and Anika.

They made my life worth living and worth cherishing.

The Inverted Tree.
Mural Painting by Dr. M. Shylaja

In Indian scriptures, the inverted tree symbolises the tree of life and the world. The tree of life has its roots upwards in the unmanifest, rooted in the Divine Being, with its branches spread below as the manifested universe. Likewise, the universe is a tree eternally existing; its roots aloft, and its branches grow towards the earth and spread below. In this analogy, the physical world is rooted in Brahman. Krishna qualified such a tree as the eternal inverted Asvattha tree. The Lord explains that this material world is like a vast *Aśvattha* tree; its roots are growing upwards (*ūrdhva-mūlam*), originating from God, nourished, and supported by Him. The trunk and branches, which extend downwards (*adhaḥ-śhākham*), encompass all the life forms from different abodes of the material realm. In Katha Upanishad, there is the reference: "This is That eternal Asvattha Tree with its roots above and branches below. That root, indeed, is called the Bright One. That is Brahman, and That alone is Immortal. In That, all worlds are contained, and none can pass beyond. This verily is *Tat Tvam Asi* (That art Thou)". (See Chapter on Pipal for details).

Ravindran PN/Dr.

Ravindran PN/Dr was a member of the Indian Agricultural Research Service (ICAR-IARS). He is best known for contributing to Spice's research, development, and documentation. He functioned as Director of ICAR-IISR; National Coordinator for Spices Research (ICAR), founder-director of the Centre for Medicinal Plants Research (CMPR), Kottakkal, and Research Advisor for Tata Global Beverages, Bangalore. Ravindran has authored many globally acclaimed books, such as Black Pepper (Harwood Academic, now CRC Press), Cardamom-the genus *Elettaria* (Taylor & Francis), Cinnamon & Cassia, the Genus *Cinnamomum* (CRC Press), Ginger, the genus *Zingiber* (CRC Press), Turmeric-the genus *Curcuma* (CRC Press) as well as a database volume on Indian spices, Advances in Spices Research. He is the author of the monumental Encyclopaedia of Herbs and Spices (2-volume set, CABI, UK), the most authoritative book on spices. Dr Ravindran is the Chief Editor of the recently published 5-volume, 4400-page – magnum opus, Handbook of Indian Spices – 75 Years of Research and Development (2024) published by Springer Nature.

Dr Ravindran has spent around 20 years since his superannuation from ICAR service studying the heritage plants of India. His study led to the publication of **Lotus – The Cosmic Flower (2017),** the only book that provides a holistic presentation of the lotus flower and its pervasive impacts on Hindu and Buddhist religions, culture, literature, art and architecture. He published the comprehensive **Sacred and Ritual Plants of India (2020)**, which presents a holistic and narrative discussion on all aspects of the sacred plants of India and their impact on the socio-religious and socio-cultural lives of the Indian Hindus.

Dr Ravindran, a man of many accomplishments, resides in Calicut (Kozhikode), Kerala, a place steeped in history and culture. His home, located very close to the landing site of Vaco-Da-Gama, is a testament to his deep-rooted connection to his homeland. He shares this rich cultural heritage with his wife, Dr Shylaja, a botanist, and an accomplished Mural painter. They have two daughters, both living abroad. His contact mail is: *ravinair.pn@gmail. com.*

CONTENTS

PREFACE

The present book, Iconic Plants of India, offers a unique journey through the myths, legends, lore, symbolism, and traditions associated with 20 plants (trees and herbs) that have achieved iconic status. These 20 plants have influenced the socio-religious lives of the people of India from the Vedic or epic time onwards. Some of them are valuable offerings to deities; some are worshipped, and some even attained the status of deities or substitutes for deities.

The book delves into the significant role of plants in the development of Indian culture, from the Vedic and Puranic periods. It explores how the protagonists of Indian culture and philosophy chose a forest life, where plants and groves became part of their belief systems. The Vedic culture and the ritual practices that form the foundations of Hinduism originated and evolved in the forests.

During the ancient Vedic, Puranic, and post-Puranic periods, people held some trees and herbs as particularly sacred, and specific symbolism, philosophy, and traditions developed associated with such plants. Lotus and peepal were the most essential plants during the Vedic period. The epic period saw the appearance of many gods and goddesses in the socio-religious arena of Indians. That was also when many plants got associated with the deities and the worship practices of the people. The concept of the primary deities (the Trinity—Brahma, Vishnu, and Shiva) came into existence, as did many goddesses. The formative years saw the origin of legends and folk tales, which later got included in epics like Ramayana, Mahabharata, and

Bhagavata Purana, as well as other *Puranas* of the later years. Thus, Pipal (peepal) became the *axis mundi* and the tree of Lord Vishnu, Banyan the Akshaya or immortal tree associated with Lord Shiva, the lotus became the cosmic flower having associations with many gods and goddesses (including the Buddhist pantheon), Neem became the tree of the goddess Durga and other Grama-devatas (village goddesses) including the snake goddess. Similarly, Vilva became the tree of Shiva, Thulsi that of Vishnu and so on. All such plants form the Iconic Plants, which played significant roles in the socio-cultural and socio-religious evolution of the Indian people.

The backbone of this book is the previous volume by the same author, Sacred and Ritual Plants of India (Notion Press, 2020), which provides concise accounts of all 85 plants with sacred and ritual associations and usages. The book Iconic Plants of India focuses on the 20 iconic plants intimately associated with Indian (Hindu and Buddhist) socio-religious history and practice. Each chapter is significantly expanded, embellished, and updated to provide a comprehensive and detailed account of each plant, ensuring that the reader gains a deep understanding of the subject matter.

The book begins with an introductory chapter on Tree Worship to provide a springboard for the readers to move through the chapters. I used many quotes from ancient texts (*Puranas, Upanishads*, etc.), which may help the readers connect the past and present writers and thinkers. The references to the Puranas and other ancient texts occur repeatedly in the text, and they do not form part of citations at the end of various chapters but are collated and presented at the end of the book in a separate list.

I am not claiming that the presentations are all-inclusive or that all known legends or traditions are included; there may be many more. However, the more relevant and important ones find a place in the book. This book will help academics and the public to gain insight into the plants that played significant roles in the spiritual, religious, and socio-cultural life of the people of our country, starting from the Rg Vedic period. Such an understanding is an essential requisite for devising effective conservation strategies. Prof. MS Swaminathan, Bharat Ratna and the undisputed doyen of Indian Agriculture and farmers' welfare movement in India commented on my earlier book (in the first edition of Sacred and Ritual Plants of India). His words: "... Books like this may provide an impetus for people to read and assimilate the cultural ethos behind the love of forests and trees and may provide new initiatives for their conservation... I congratulate Dr Ravindran for this narrative on sacred plants; it is a veritable mine of information that is difficult to find elsewhere. Collecting and collating such information from diverse sources is a highly commendable job, and Dr Ravindran· has succeeded. I recommend this valuable book to all people who love nature, plants, and groves and especially to the tree lovers of both India and abroad...". These words of Prof Swaminathan are eminently suited for the present book, too. I hope this book will educate and inspire readers to conserve our natural heritage proactively.

There is a tendency among younger people to dub anything that is from the past as nonsense and superstitious. They forget that we are now here by standing on the shoulders of the past, and the future will be shaped by standing on the shoulders of the present. Knowledge is power; knowing our past will become our power. Without that knowledge, how will we recapture the lost glory of the Arsha Bharat that existed in India? I sincerely hope that books like the present one will help the Indians peep into the past life of our distant forefathers living in unison with nature, a philosophy re-invented by the present lovers of humanity and nature. I hope this book will contribute at least in a small way towards that goal and help our people glimpse into the great significance of plants and plant life in shaping our past thoughts and philosophy, the fruits of which the present generation is enjoying.

There may be shortcomings, both in the matter and the presentation, and I sincerely request the readers bear with them.

It is with utmost humility and gratitude that I present this book, Iconic Plants of India, to the people of India and abroad. I am deeply grateful for the opportunity to share this knowledge and hope it will be of value to you. Your interest and support are greatly appreciated, and I am honoured to contribute to your understanding of Indian culture and botany.

– PN Ravindran
Kozhikode (Calicut),
Jan. 01, 2025

ACKNOWLEDGEMENTS

This book results from many years of study on the diverse aspects associated with certain sacred and ritual plants of India and other South Asian countries. The book contains information collected and collated from the writings of many ancient and modern thinkers and writers from the Vedic and epic times. I have also quoted liberally from diverse sources, from past and present writers and thinkers' writings. The sources of all such quotes are included in the list of citations. *I salute them all and acknowledge with humility the help, knowledge, and wisdom gained from all of them.*

The present book is an offshoot of an earlier book by me, titled Sacred and Ritual Plants of India, published by Notion Press (2020). Twenty of the most important sacred plants that have attained iconic status are included in this volume. The matter is significantly expanded, embellished, and updated in this volume. I thank the Notion press for making use of the earlier publication as the basis for this first and the only book on the iconic plants of India.

The writing of this book would never have happened without the moral and logistical support and help from my wife, Dr. Shylaja former (Associate Professor and HOD, Providence Women's College, Calicut, Kerala). She took a lot of effort to read and correct the draft. She had drawn the mural style picture given on the cover of the book. I thank her from the depths of my heart for the help and assistance she rendered. Many relatives and friends helped me in the preparation of this book by supplying information on various plants, and I place on record my sincere thanks to all of them. Finally, I wish to thank Notion Press for helping me publish this book on the Iconic Plants of India.

I made use of some images from the public domain, the sources of which are indicated below the figures. I am very thankful to all those persons and agencies who hosted these images in the public domain for the benefit of all. Finally let me take this opportunity to thank all my well-wishers and friends who helped me directly or indirectly in the writing of this book.

– PN Ravindran
Calicut (Kozhikode),
Jan. 01, 2025

INTRODUCTION

Forests, Trees & Tree Worship

In the Earth's geological history, there are four periods when forests thrived on this planet. The first was the Carboniferous, ca. 350 million years ago, when land vertebrates started roaming the Earth. The Carboniferous or coal forests, consisting of giant club mosses, tree ferns, great horsetails, and towering trees, occupied the land. The second was the Jurassic, 170 million years ago, when dinosaurs dominated the planet. The forests were mainly composed of cycads, conifers, and ferns. The third, the Eocene epoch, occurred 60 million years ago and witnessed the first primitive mammals. During the early-middle Eocene, forests covered most of the Earth, including the poles. Tropical forests extended across much of modern Africa, South America, Central America, India, Southeast Asia, and China. The last, the Holocene epoch, which began some 500,000 years ago following the ice age, ushered in modern humanity. Early humans and related species had to sustain themselves based on the flora and fauna that existed then. The trees fascinated them, as they provided food and sheltered them from the predatory animals and poisonous snakes that inhabited the forest floor. Ten thousand years ago, forests occupied most of the land mass of the Indian subcontinent. Early human civilization originated in these forests, along the banks of the rivers in the North Indian River valleys. The first such civilization developed in the

Saraswathi-Sindhu River delta, popularly known as the Harappan, Indus Valley, or Saraswati-Sindhu civilization. Such human settlements were a direct consequence of the beginning of agriculture when humans started settling down to grow crops around their homes rather than roaming forests for food.

Studies using ancient DNA have been rewriting prehistory worldwide, and India is no exception. The Genomic Formation of South and Central Asia, a recent study by Harvard Professor David Reich and 92 other scholars, provides specific evidence for two significant migrations to India over the past 10,000 years. The first one originated from the Zagros region in southwestern Iran (which has the world's first evidence for goat domestication) and brought agriculturists, most likely herders, to India. This migration happened probably between 7,000 and 3,000 BCE. These Zagrosian (people from the Zagros Mountain regions, a mountain range extending from Iran, through Iraq to southeastern Turkey) herders mixed with the earlier inhabitants of the subcontinent—the First Indians, descendants of the Out of Africa (OoA) migrants who had reached India around 65,000 years ago – and together, they created the Harappan civilization. (1)

In the centuries after 2000 BCE, a second set of immigrants arrived on the Indian scene. They are the Aryans, originally from the Eurasian Steppe, probably from the region now known as Kazakhstan. They moved to the ancient Bactria-Margiana region (present-day Afghanistan-Iran region), where the Bactria-Margiana Civilization (BMC) blossomed. The BMC people were fire-worshippers and practised rituals like the later-day Indian Soma and Iranian *Hoama* rituals. The Iranian strand led to the Zoroastrian culture, and the Indian strand of the BMC led to the

Vedic Civilization that flourished in the Sindhu-Saraswati River plains. This Sindhu-Saraswati-Vedic civilization (SSC) originated after the decline of the Harappan civilization, which was established by the native Indians inhabiting the land. The BMC people brought the primitive form of Sanskrit, mastery over horses, and a range of new cultural practices, such as sacrificial rituals, which formed the basis of early Hindu/Vedic culture.

Further genetic studies have brought to light more migrations into India, such as that of the speakers of Austro-Asiatic languages from south-eastern Asia. During those times of the SSC, forests covered most of the Indian subcontinent, and the early Indians lived in perfect harmony with the forests. The Indian sages lived in forests, subsisting on tubers and fruits. The sages who lived in the forests wrote all of the ancient Hindu rituals and the philosophical and metaphysical texts and epics. In ancient India, all upper-caste males, after living the life of a youth and then as a family man, were expected to go for a life in the forest (*Vanaprastha*) and finally live in a hermitage as a *sannyasin* or hermit. So, forests formed part and parcel of the life of the ancient Indian people (or Hindus, which initially meant people of the Indus region, hence known as Hindus). The need for land for housing and farming increased as the population increased. Massive destruction of forests followed and continued in the succeeding millennia, and today, India has only about 9.34% of its area as natural forests as of 2021. The Canadian ecologist Munteanu (2019) writes:

> "Since humanity arrived, we have cut down trees for timber, agriculture, and development. Our impact is a matter of scale. When humanity was a mere 300 million in pre-medieval times,

forest ecosystems remained intact. We are now over 7 billion, doing essentially the same thing we did thousands of years ago. What may have been sustainable then is now extirpating entire complex ecosystems and species we may never have known existed. Deforestation releases a massive amount of carbon and sinks it into the atmosphere, driving global warming. It is responsible for reducing wildlife populations by half in the last 40 years and starting the sixth massive extinction event. While too many of us do not understand or appreciate the global consequences of deforestation, we remain intimately and personally connected with trees in ways we don't realize or have forgotten…" (2)

A forest is not just an assemblage of plants but a single complex living organism. In the book The Global Forest: 40 Ways Trees Can Save Us, botanist and medical biochemist Diana Beresford-Kroeger tells us that:

"A functioning forest is a complex form of life. It is interconnected by its own flora and driven by the mammals, amphibians, and insects in it. Fungi, algae, lichens, bacteria, viruses, and bacteriophages are responsible for keeping it in place. The primogenitors of forests are trees. They communicate by carbon-coded calls and mass-market themselves by infrasound. The atmosphere links forests to the heavens and the great oceans. The human family is caught and held in that Web of life." (3).

Tapping into aboriginal wisdom and ancient pagan legend, Beresford-Kroeger invites us into the forest to explore the many beneficial and pharmaceutical properties of trees—from leaves that filter the air of particulate pollution, the cardiotonic property of hawthorn, fatty acids in hickory nuts and walnuts that promote brain development, to the aerosols in pine trees that calm nerves. She further writes:

> "This [global] forest is the environment that drives and fulfils the dream of each leaf in a vast, rhythmic cycle called life. Nothing is outside. We are all of it in a unity that transcends the whole. Maybe, just maybe, this resonates with God. If that is so, then we are all His children, every earthworm, every virus, every mammal, fish and whale, every fern, every tree, man, woman, and child. One is equal to another, again and again."

In 'The Songs of Trees: Stories from Nature's Great Connectors', biologist David George Haskell pens an existentialist poem about life's interconnected network. Haskell's notion of 'listening to trees' arises not from metaphor or metaphysics but from a spiritual understanding of the woven tapestry of life. He writes:

> "We're all — trees, humans, insects, birds, bacteria — pluralities. Life is an embodied network where ecological and evolutionary tensions between cooperation and conflict are negotiated and resolved...Because life is a network, no 'nature' or 'environment' separate or apart from humans. We are part of the community of life, composed of relationships with 'others,' so the human/ nature duality that lives near the heart of many philosophies is, from a biological perspective, illusory...We cannot step outside life's songs.

This music made us; it is our nature to listen to trees, nature's great connectors, to learn how to inhabit the relationships that give life its source, substance, and beauty." (4)

We, humans, form just a fragment, a link, or an inevitable component of this incredible Web of life, this great Web of Nature that encompasses all forms of life. Denise Levertov wrote about this Web:

> "Intricate and untraceable
> weaving and interweaving, the dark strand with light:
> Designed beyond all spidery contrivance,
> To link, not to entrap:
> Elation, grief, joy, contrition, entwined;
> shaking,
> changing,
> forever forming,
> transforming:
> all praise,
> all praise to the
> great web." (5)

Echoing this philosophy, Richard Powers writes in his book 'Observatory':

> "There are no individuals in a forest, no separable events. The bird and the branch it sits on are a joint thing. A third or more of the food a big tree makes may go to feed other organisms. Even different kinds of trees form partnerships. Cut down a birch, and a nearby Douglas fir may suffer... Fungi mine stone to supply their trees with minerals. They hunt springtails, which they feed to their hosts. Trees, for their part, store extra sugar

in their fungi's synapses, to dole out to the sick, shaded and wounded. A forest takes care of itself, and even as it builds the local climate, it needs to survive. A tree is a wondrous thing that shelters, feeds, and protects all living things. It even offers shade to the axmen who destroy it." (6)

Powers further writes about the benefits:

"Tea from infant trees for heart trouble
Leaves from young sprouts to cure sores,
Cold bark brews to stop bleeding after birth,
Warmed galls to pare back an infant's navel,
Leaves boiled with brown sugar for coughs,
Poultices for burns leaves to stuff a talking mattress,
An extract for despair, when the anguish is too much..."

Such a deep appreciation of the tree led a poet (Joyce Kilmer) to write:

"I think that I shall never see
A poem lovely as a tree.
A tree whose hungry mouth is prest
Against the earth's sweet flowing breast;
A tree that looks at God all-day
And lifts her leafy arms to pray;
A tree that may in summer wear
A nest of robins in her hair;
Upon whose bosom snow has lain;
Who intimately lives with rain.
Poems are made by fools like me,
But only God can make a tree." (7)

Yes, a tree is a beautiful organism. Look at a large tree in a tropical forest setting. Below the soil, the root system and its rhizosphere support innumerable life forms, from viruses to bacteria to various flora and fauna, while the portion above the soil supports life forms such as lichens, fungi, algae, parasites, insects, birds, lizards, arboreal mammals, and so on. Numerous herbs and shrubs flourish under the tree in the ideal microclimate it provides. The tree mines nutrients from deep below the soil and brings them to the soil surface through the fallen leaves that form the humus, increasing soil fertility through such activities. The tree and all the life forms that it supports form a 'biome'. When one tree is cut, it leads to the devastation of innumerable life forms. The tree cutter cannot realize the great significance of a tree; the business and selfish interests behind it are insensitive to anything other than profit. Often, this insensibility is also due to ignorance, a lack of understanding of a tree's invaluable role in the sustenance of nature.

The present book is on trees, which in a cultural setting transcends the botanical definition to encompass all forms of plant life—large and small tree forms, shrubs, herbs, aquatic plants, grasses, and even evanescent life forms. Most people across continents remain unappreciative of trees' manifold impact on the rest of life and the earth. They continue to ask the question, "Why plant trees?"

> "Climate change, soil erosion, the destruction of ecosystems and biodiversity, pandemics, and so on and on… By planting trees, we provide a pluralist answer to the planet's multifaceted crisis. Our societies have created a world that urgently needs to be regenerated. Planting trees is part of the answer. It is a multidimensional, ecosystem approach." (Philippe Beau-Douëzy is an ecologist,

environmental consultant, and co-founder of the Plant for the Planet program) (8).

Sacred Groves

"THE groves were God's first temples. 'Ere man learned
To hew the shaft, and lay the architrave,
And spread the roof above them—ere he framed
The lofty vault, to gather and roll back
The sound of anthems; in the darkening wood.
Amidst the cool silence, he knelt down
And offered to the Mightiest, solemn thanks
And supplication. For his simple heart
Might not resist the sacred influences,
Which, from the stilly twilight of the place,
And from the grey old trunks that high in heaven
Mingled their mossy boughs, and from the sound
Of the invisible breath that swayed at once
All their green tops stole over him and bowed
His spirit with the thought of boundless power
And inaccessible majesty. Ah, why
Should we, in the world's riper years, neglect
God's ancient sanctuaries, and adore
Only among the crowd, and under roofs
That our frail hands have raised. Let me, at least,
Here, in the shadow of this aged wood,
Offer one hymn—thrice happy, if it finds
Acceptance in his ear...." (9)

Andrew James Symington writes on this poem:

"The gravity, the dignity, and the solemnity of natural devotion were never before stated so accurately and with such significance. Under the broad roof of the boughs of a vast forest, we are standing in silence and awe of the location's sacred influences. We experience a non-painful gloom as mystery and unseen energy surround us. The shadows are full of worshippers and beautiful things that live in their misty twilights." (10)

The concept of a "God" was born in the minds of primitive humans roaming in the forests in search of food and shelter. The thunder, lightning, torrential rains, and winds probably fascinated and alarmed him. Naturally, in the primitive minds of the first humans, these natural phenomena took the form of some higher power or being sitting in the sky and controlling their future and destiny. The first spark of light dawned in his mind, and he possibly offered part of his daily catch to these forces. Equally likely, the towering trees protected them from rain, scorching sun, wild animals, and reptiles roaming the forests in those days. The trees and plants gave their food, fruits, and roots. Possibly, humans started praying to such towering trees, considering them their saviours and gods; subsequently, this simple concept evolved into a forest god or goddess. John Stewart Collis, in his book 'The Triumph of Trees,' writes:

> "Today the tree is the body, tomorrow the abode of a spirit – animism turns into polytheism. Thus, we see the wild Huntsman of North America known as Heno, riding the clouds, and splitting the forest trees with his thunderbolt; and then we see him later, gathering the clouds together and pouring down warm rains – as a god of agriculture. Many simple spirits developed into a general spirit of vegetation, and often enough in the primitive

mind several misconceptions existed at the same time." (11)

In his celebrated book, The Golden Plough, Sir John Frazer writes:

> "When a tree comes to be viewed, no longer as the body of the tree-spirit, but simply as its abode, which it can quit at pleasure, an important advance has been made in religious thought. Animism is passing into polytheism. In other words, instead of regarding each tree as a living and conscious being, man now sees in it merely a lifeless, inert mass, tenanted for a longer or shorter time by a supernatural being who, as he can pass freely from tree to tree, thereby enjoys a certain right of possession or lordship over the trees and, ceasing to be a tree-soul, becomes a forest god. As soon as the tree spirit is thus in a measure disengaged from each particular tree, he begins to change his shape and assume the body of a man, in virtue of a general tendency of early thought to clothe all abstract spiritual beings in concrete human form. As a result, the sylvan deities appear as humans in classical art, with a branch or another equally clear symbol designating their woodland origin. However, this change of shape does not affect the essential character of the tree spirit. The powers, which he exercised as a tree-soul incorporated in a tree, he still continues to wield as a god of trees...that trees considered animate beings are credited with the power of making the rain to fall, the sun to shine, flocks and herds to multiply, and women to bring forth easily; and, second,

that the very same powers are attributed to tree-gods conceived as anthropomorphic beings or as actually incarnate in living men." (12)

At that point, the whole forest was considered sacred. In due course, the anthropomorphising of the gods gave them human forms, and soon, a stone idol was installed in a forest, and the locals started venerating it. Often, a single or a few stones represent the gods. Those were the beginnings of the religious life of the primitive Indians. From such a level, advanced features of the system gave rise to symbolism, a whole gamut of rituals that persisted for many centuries to the present among the tribal societies. That was also the beginning of the Sacred Groves. (13)

In such a situation, the sacred groves played a vital role. Sacred groves are small patches of forests or groves of trees and associated vegetation, protected by local communities as the residing places of deities. They vary in area from less than a hectare to a few square kilometres, and they are the sites of socio-religious and socio-cultural rituals of associated communities. Such sacred groves are also micro–reservoirs of valuable plant and animal diversity. In the past, sacred groves were maintained in most parts of the world, including Europe. Many studies exist on the famous Mediterranean sacred groves of the past. The ancient Greek and Roman landscapes were dotted with hundreds of sacred groves associated with a grove of trees. Such small woods were the abodes of 'nature spirits' or 'tree spirits.' Pliny (14), the elder who lived in the first century AD, indicated that 'trees were the first temples of Gods, and even now, simple country people dedicate a tree of exceptional height to a god.' Roman mythology has ample indications of the personification of plant spirits. Humans change to trees and vice versa. For the Greeks, the formidable goddess Artemis was the protector of forests, wilderness, and wildlife, and the wilderness itself was then considered sacred. In the centuries that followed, sacred groves vanished from the European landscape for various reasons, such as rapid urbanization, the flourishing timber industry, the use of a large quantity of wood for house construction, and so on. Whatever remained was systematically destroyed by the rapidly growing Christian church. The Christian church, in its formative years and the subsequent Middle Ages, considered anything that was non-Christian as pagan and razed them down systematically.

In India, sacred groves form part of the socio-religious life of the rural population. Many communities practice performing rituals and ceremonies to appease the presiding deity of the sacred grove and ensure the well-being of the community and the families. Such sacred groves often define the cultural and ethnic identity of the associated community.

Estimates indicate that 100,000 to 150,000 sacred groves exist in the Indian subcontinent even now, forming a veritable storehouse of natural biodiversity. Distribution of sacred groves in India is shown in the following figure; the largest number of sacred groves is in Maharashtra (2820), followed by Karnataka (1476) and Tamil Nadu (1275).

The sacred groves started their journey from the pre-agrarian community of primitive humans, and many anthropologists have repeatedly emphasized their importance. They are the storehouses of biodiversity and medicinal plants and provide the water needs of the nearby communities. Many groves are associated with streams and ponds, and the deep tree root system functions as a sponge to absorb and retain water.

In earlier times in Kerala, it was a common practice to earmark and maintain small patches of land with a few large trees as an abode of the mother goddess or serpent goddess (*kavu*). Once, hundreds of such *'kavus'* dotted the landscape of Kerala. It was then a practice to light an oil lamp every evening in front of the *'kavu'*. Naturally, they were the focal points of worship before the temples became popular. In such sacred groves, the conservation of plant and animal wealth was ensured through the imposition of social taboos, which every community member was mandated to obey. In the Western Himalayan region, Singh and colleagues recorded the existence of many such restrictions. All sacred groves are also associated with temples; the temple's deity is the guardian deity of the woods. The close linkage of the forest grove with a deity ensured implicit obedience from the members of the associated community, thereby ensuring the unhindered conservation of the plant and animal wealth of the forest region, albeit incidentally. However, due to the environmental movements' increased awareness, the communities now defend the sacred groves from all forms of encroachment (15).

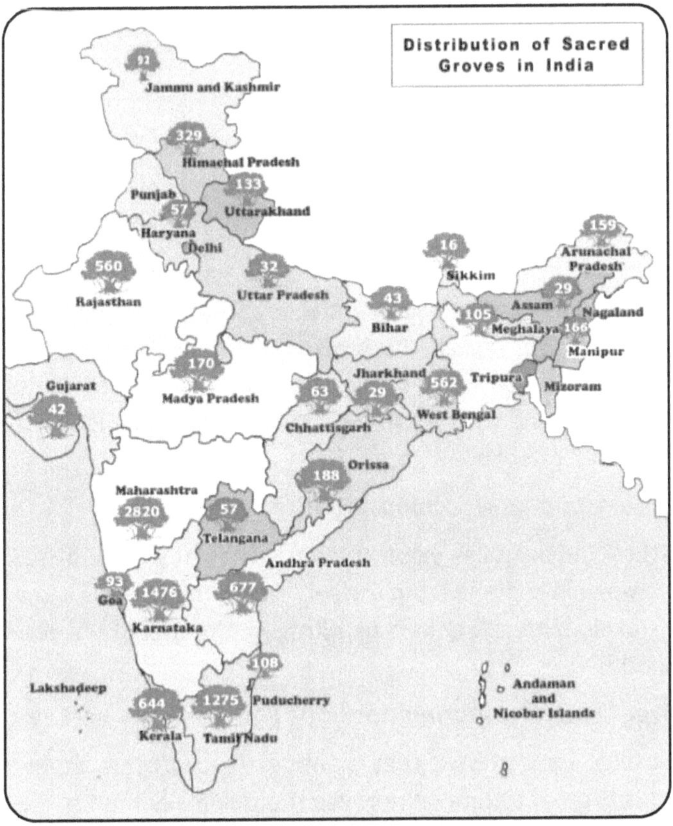

Distribution of sacred groves in India. (Source: C.P.R. Environmental Education Centre, cpreecenvis.nic.in).

A worship place in a sacred grove (Chirakkal Kavu, Kerala)

A Sacred grove in Manipur

Tree benefits

Trees, man's best allies

Trees are our allies. One of the first materials humans used was wood, which they provided. Wood for fire, wood for building, wood for medical uses, and sacred wood: trees have infinite potential for humans.

Tree provides humus

Trees play a significant role in soil production and conservation, one of the most important benefits. Under a bed of leaves, in the shade of a tree, the soil is often rich and soft, holding the promise of farming, which is vital to human existence.

Tree regulates air composition:

Trees' behaviour is extraordinary... They absorb and store carbon...in some cases in the soil, due to the process known as oxalogenesis*. Others fix nitrogen, the fuel of the plant world.

Trees have an amazingly positive effect on our well-being.

Studies have shown that planting trees on the grounds of retirement homes improves the quality of life for their elderly residents and that a stroll through a forest reduces our stress levels. Planting trees in cities enhances air quality and reduces urban violence. "By reconnecting us with nature, trees help us (re)connect with our inner selves: a sacred gift that releases our spirituality..." (16)

Tree triggers aesthetic values and philosophical insights.

Trees are 'markers of time,' they are also beautiful to behold. A majestic tree standing tall in the middle of a field symbolises resistance to time and is a celebration of the mystery of life, which will continue to hold us in its spell for centuries. Planting trees is a virtue that contributes to humanity's subsistence and survival. Planting trees needs to be a conscious act. The goal is not simply constructing rows of some trees, such as the eucalyptus or pines, for carbon offsetting or short-term financial gain. ***The true philosophy behind tree planting is to create conditions that foster a genuine regeneration of the ecosystems we have damaged, thereby providing hope and the promise of new life to the inhabitants of our planet***. Agroforestry, biomimetic forests, life-giving gardens, urban forests, and more can increase these ecosystems' presence and productivity to pave the way for a sustainable future, representing a precious opportunity for humanity – for ourselves and the generations to come.

(*Oxalogenic trees have a metabolic process known as the oxalate-carbonate pathway. This metabolic pathway forms oxalate ions, which, at the soil level, through symbiotic association with bacteria and fungi, form calcium carbonate ($CaCO_3$, limestone), which is one of the most long-lasting types of carbon sink.)

People and Trees

People and trees have far more things in common than many of us think; some such aspects are listed below. We know that humans and trees (plants in general) are mostly water, we share similar physical characteristics, and each of us is unique. In addition, humans and trees are interdependent—we breathe in oxygen and breathe out carbon dioxide, while trees take in carbon dioxide and release oxygen. This extraordinary connection between people and trees is evolving even further as more and more people elect to use a tree urn after they pass. With this, families can grow a beautiful memorial tree to from a living urn containing cremated ashes to honour a loved one and celebrate all they have given us – the joy, the companionship, the love – and keep their memory present in our lives and then give back by growing a living memory with the living urn.

The likeness between a tree and a human was very clearly indicated in the ancient Upanishads. Brahadaranyaka Upanishad has these words:

> "As a mighty tree in the forest, so in truth is the man; his hairs are the leaves, and his outer skin is the bark. From his skin flows forth blood, sap from the skin of the tree; thus, from the wounded man comes forth blood as from a tree that is struck. The humps of his flesh are in the layers of wood; the fibre is strong like the tendons. The bones are the hardwood within; the marrow is made like the marrow of the tree."

Here, we see the case of anthropomorphising of trees, how man's thinking led to the philosophical transfiguration of a tree into a human and vice versa. The 'tree concept' was used very effectively in explaining philosophical issues. In Chandogya Upanishad, sage Uddalaka Aruni, while explaining the mysteries of *ātman* to his son Svetaketu, cites the example of a tree and its vitality.

> "... If the tree is struck at its root, a kind of sap oozes out of it. If it is struck in the middle or at the top the same kind of sap comes out. It suggests that the tree is permeated from top to bottom. If the sap of vitality withdraws itself from any one of the branches, it gets dried up. If it withdraws from the whole of it, the entire tree tries up. Similar is the case with the human body. All the pleasures, all joys, all the vitality..."

Modern thinkers have also argued further for the similarity between man and tree.

Physical Characteristics

Both people and trees stand upright with a crown on top and limbs stemming from a central trunk. In addition, the tubular branching pattern of our lungs resembles the root system of many trees.

Uniqueness and Beauty

Every person and every tree are unique, and no two are alike. With trees, colours can vary, branches can grow and bend at different angles, and buds and flowers occur at various places and seasons. Like people, trees have different growth rates, with variations in height and volume. Some grow tall, while others are short. Some remain skinny, and others grow wide. The uniqueness and diversity in trees and people help make the world more exciting and beautiful!

Reliance on Water

Both people and trees are composed mainly of water and rely on this resource to survive. Most trees are made up of more than 50% water. Similarly, an adult person is made up of approximately 60% water. Without water, life as we know it would not be possible for people, trees, and everything else.

Reliance on Others

Did you know there are just as many microbes in the human body as actual human cells? Even though these microbes are not part of the body, they perform functions essential to human life. Like people, trees rely on other living organisms for survival and reproduction. For example, many trees rely on certain fungi to stick to their roots and to enable them to extract water from the soil sufficiently. In addition, many trees, and shrubs rely on pollinating insects to exchange pollen from their flowering blooms to regenerate.

Love to Live in Communities

According to an article in the Smithsonian in March 2018, researchers have compiled evidence that trees of the same species are communal organisms (like humans) and can even form alliances with trees of other species. The researchers also discovered that forest trees have evolved to live in interdependent and cooperative relationships supported by communication and a collective intelligence akin to an insect colony or a city. (17)

Economic contributions

Around 300 million people, including 60 million indigenous people, are known to live in forests worldwide. According to the United Nations Food and Agriculture Organization (FAO) data, forests provide jobs to more than 10 million people in forest management and conservation. With the production of timber and other forestry products alone, forests constitute 1% of the global gross domestic product (GDP). The total value of forestry product trade is about $250 billion globally, while the total value-added / created by the forestry industry is estimated to be about $500 billion. (18)

How many trees are there on Earth?

A study conducted in 2004 tried to answer this question. This study, based on satellite images alone, led to an estimate of 400 billion trees in the world. The results of another study carried out 10 years later were even more gratifying. This time, the detected figure was about eight times the initial figure. According to a 2015 study published in Nature, our world is estimated to have 3 trillion trees. (19). So, there are 400 trees per person in our world. Around 43% of these trees are estimated to be in the tropics. According to the data supported by field research, there are 390 billion trees in the Amazon alone. Within the scope of the study, sample counts were carried out in more than 400,000 forestry lands in more than 50 countries to detect tree intensity. By comparing this intensity with satellite images, more reliable estimates were made. In 2022, researchers unveiled the world's largest forest database, comprising more than 44 million individual trees at more than 100,000 sites in 90 countries – helping them to calculate that Earth boasts roughly 73,300 tree species. That figure is about 14% higher than previous estimates. Of that total, about 9,200 were estimated to exist based on statistical modelling, but they had yet to be identified scientifically, with a large proportion of these growing in South America. South America is enormously biodiverse. Amazon rainforests and far-flung Andean forests harbour 43% of the planet's tree species and the most significant number of rare species, numbering about 8,200. South America was found to have about 27,000 known tree species and 4,000 yet to be identified. Eurasia has 14,000 known species and 2,000 unknowns, followed by Africa (10,000 known/1,000 unknown), North America, including Central America (9,000 known/2,000 unknown) and Oceania, including Australia (7,000 known/2,000 unknown). This study did not tally with the total number of individual trees globally. One of the co-authors' of the 2015 research put that amount at around $3 trillion. The new study pinpointed global tree diversity hot spots in the tropics and subtropics in South America, Central America, Africa, Asia, and Oceania. It also determined that about a third of known species can be classified as rare. (20). However, the largest forest remains the Russian Taiga boreal forest, which stretches to 4.6 million square miles (11.9 million square kilometres) but is poor in biodiversity. The Amazon rainforest is the largest biodiversity-rich forest on the Earth. This basin encompasses 7,000,000 km2 (2,700,000 sq. miles), of which 6,000,000 km2 (2,300,000 sq. miles) are covered by the rainforest. This region includes territory belonging to nine nations and 3,344 indigenous territories. (Wikipedia, 2024).

According to the State of the World's Forests (SOFO) report for 2020 (SOFO 2020), released by the FAO, more than half of the world's forests are in five countries alone – Brazil, Canada, China, Russia, and the United States. Almost half of the world's forests (49%), which cover 31% of terrestrial areas, are virgin forests. Also, 80% of the forests cover an area of more than 1 million hectares (2.47 million acres).

Sacred Trees & Tree Worship

Tree worship (or dendrolatry, a term not used popularly now), and worship of natural forces evolved gradually along with the evolution of the human species and its social life. It is rather challenging to infer when and where tree worship originated, as we have no historical, anthropological, or archaeological record. Humans probably started worshipping natural forces and trees from the very earliest times. Trees offered them protection from sun and rain and from reptiles and carnivores that abound the forest land of those times. Trees yielded fruits that sustained birds, animals, and humans alike. Probably, the animals, like the squirrels, monkeys, and apes, were man's first tutors; from them, he might have learned to distinguish the edible fruits from the non-edible ones.

In the Indian subcontinent, plant worship probably began in pre-Indus Valley time but as a continuous stream of worship from the Vedic period, which continues uninterrupted even today as a vibrant faith in Indian society. Excavations in Harappa and Mohenjo-Daro provided evidence of tree worship during the Indus Valley civilization (also known as the Sindhu-Saraswati Civilization (SSC). In his classical work on Indus civilization, Marshall mentions two forms of tree worship during that period. One form involves worshipping trees, and the other consists of worshipping the tree spirit. Pandey (1993), in his work on Indian Rock Art unearthed from Adamgarh, mentions the figure of a *Vanadeva*. This figure shows an anthropomorphic form with a lotus crown on his head, an arrow in one hand, a bud in the other, and a flower body. (22) In one of the seals excavated from the Indus Valley, the deity's epiphany is a tree resembling a peepal. In another seal, Mackay has identified a peepal, and in a clay amulet, he found the representation of a neem tree. According to him, the worship of Mother Goddess, the goddess of fertility and crops, seems to be central to the religious practices of that time. The Mother Goddess is represented as rising between two branches of a tree or standing between the bifurcated branches of a peepal tree. (23)

The pre-Vedic worship of trees evolved further and attained new dimensions during the Vedic period and in the post–Vedic times. The number of sacred trees increased considerably in the Puranic period and the centuries following. Such proliferation could be attributed to the increase in the number of deities (gods) that resulted from the polytheistic and iconoclastic worship. During the Vedic period, Soma occupied prime status in worship. In *Rg Veda*, a whole part (*tenth mandala*) is devoted to the extolment of Soma and its worship. In subsequent centuries, elaborate rituals came into the practice for each sacred ceremony, and in every such ceremony, plants and plant products played essential roles. *Puranas* such as *Garuda Purana* and *Agni Purana* mention the different flowers prescribed for offering to various deities. In Hinduism, belief in astrology and the planetary influence on people's lives are deeply rooted. All gods and goddesses, the nine planets, the twenty-seven stars (birth stars associated with people's birth), and the twelve zodiacs are associated with specific plants.

The history of sacred plants in the Indian context can be reconstructed from the *Rig Vedic* period based on the scriptures of that period and the succeeding ones. A. B. Keith wrote in his well-known study on the Religion and Philosophy of the Vedas and Upanishads:

> "...The reference to the worship of trees and plants is very scanty in the Vedic ritual and mythology alike, but they are quite adequate to show that, among all other peoples, these objects were not without their share of reverence. A long hymn in the last book of *Rg Veda* (X.97) is devoted to identifying plants with special reference to their healing properties. In the *Rg Veda* (X.97.18), Soma is already the king of plants, and they are called mothers and goddesses. The Atharva Veda poetically describes a plant as a goddess born of the goddess Earth. On the other hand, plants have the power to hinder childbirth, and in that case, the offering of an animal victim to them is prescribed by the *Taittiriya Samhitha* (ii.1.5.3) to procure their favour..." (24)

The Sage Uddalaka used the seed of the fig tree to prove a metaphysical point, the mystery of *ātman* and its manifestation. There is a famous legend given in *Chandogya Upanishad*. Max Müller has translated it as follows:

The Sage said, looking at his son, who was listening carefully:

> "Bring hither a fig from there."
> "Here it is, sir."
> "Divide it"
> "It is divided, sir."
> "What do you see inside? "
> "These rather fine seeds, sir."
> "Of these, please divide one"
> "It is divided, sir."
> "What do you see there?"
> "Nothing at all, sir."

Then he (the teacher) said to his son:

> "Verily, my dear, that finest essence, which you do not perceive; verily, my dear, from that finest essence, this great *Nygrodha* thus arises. Believe me, my dear', said he, 'that which is the finest essence, this whole world has that as its soul. That is Reality. That is ātman, *tat tvam asi* (that art thou), Shvetakethu.'

This statement, 'that art thou' (*TAT TVAM ASI*), is one of the most remarkable utterances of the Upanishads and one of the most significant metaphysical concepts ancient India gave to the world.

In the *Aitareya Aranyaka*, we get the following reference on seed and its origin:

> "...Next follows the origin of the seed. The seed of Prajapati is the devas (gods). The seed of devas is the rain. The seed of rain is the herbs; the seed of herbs is food. The seed of food is seed. The seed of seed is creatures. The seed of creatures is the heart. The seed of the heart is the mind. The seed of the mind is speech (Veda). The seed of speech is action. The action done (in a former state) is this man, the abode of Brahman..."

In the *Chandogya Upanishad*, we get the following statement:

> "The essence of all beings is the earth, the essence of earth is water, the essence of water is the plants, the essence of plants man, the essence of man is speech, the essence of speech *Rg Veda*, the essence of *Rg Veda* is the *Sama Veda*, the essence of Sama Veda is the *udgitha'*, which is OM and that occupies the highest position..."

The ancient Indian philosophy equated trees with Brahman. In *Katha Upanishad*, we get the famous saying:

> "...There is the ancient tree, whose roots grow upward and branches grow downward – that indeed is called the bright, Brahman, that alone is called immortal. All the worlds are contained in it, and no one goes beyond. That is that..."

Later commentators have interpreted this idea of the inverted tree in various ways. Some interpret the tree as the world and the roots the *Brahman*. The inverted tree is a symbol that depicts the exalted position of the *Brahman*, from which the manifest beings originated and to which they are attached. The inverted tree also symbolises unity in diversity, characterising the Upanishad concept of

Reality. *Brahman* is non-dual (in the form of root), while the manifest world (and the life forms, are entangled in diversity as exemplified by the branches, leaves, flowers, and fruits that occur in diverse stages of development. A tree is the best example to express this concept of unity in diversity — a tree originates from a single seed, the essence of a tree's life. Then, it develops into a gigantic proportion with all the diversities attached. The tree also stands for constancy in change; branches, twigs, leaves, flowers and fruits come and go (like the manifest beings), but the root and the trunk remain constant beyond the memory and span of one's life (hence compared to Brahman). (25).

Yet another step in worshipping trees can be seen in the legends of deities associated with trees and forests. The first references are available in *Rg Veda* itself. In the 146th hymn of the tenth *mandala*, we get the vivid representation of gods and goddesses of trees and forests (*Vanaspati*, the lord of wilderness, and *Aaranya devatha*, the goddess of the forest). The following quote is from Griffith's translation of the Rg Vedic hymn. (26)

HYMN 10: 146

1. GODDESS of wild and forest who seemest to vanish from the sight. How is it that thou seekest not the village? Art thou not afraid?
2. What time does the grasshopper reply and swell the shrill Cicala's voice? Seeming to sound with tinkling bells, the Lady of the Wood exults.
3. And, yonder, cattle seem to graze, what seems a dwelling-place appears: Or else at eve, the Lady of the Forest seems to free the wains.

4. Here one is calling to his cow, another there hath felled a tree: At eve the dweller in the wood fancies that somebody hath screamed.
5. The Goddess never slays unless some murderous enemy approaches. Man eats savoury fruit and then takes his rest even as he wills.
6. I have praised the Forest Queen, sweet-scented, redolent of balm, The Mother of all sylvan things, who tills not but hath food stores.

The point to be noted is that in India, the worship of plants can be traced from the *Rg Vedic* times to the later epic period and through the successive centuries to the modern times and today. Soma was the first plant held sacred. *Satapatha Brahmana* mentions *Aśvattha, Nyagrodha*, and *Udumbara* as the holy trees. In the *Aranyakas*, we get references to many trees and other plants and their usage, including the swings made of wood, which ladies used. This 'phyto-pantheon' became what we see in later *Puranas* and other religious texts." (For details on the *Puranic* references on the origin of plants, please visit the book Sacred and Ritual Plants of India.) (27)

According to *Puranas*, like the *Vishnu Dharmothara Purana*, many ancillary gods and goddesses have trees as their abodes. For example, Jyeshta Devi or Alakshmi, the elder sister of Devi Lakshmi and the seat of all that is unholy, has her abode in *the Asvattha* tree (peepal) except on Saturdays, the day on which goddess Lakshmi visits the tree. The seven divine mothers (*Sapta Matrika* or *Sapta kanya*), created by the various gods, are believed to have their abodes in trees. Brahmani has her abode in the *Palasha (Butea monosperma)* tree, Vaishnavi in *Raja vriksha* (variously interpreted as peepal, Indian laburnum, and *Parijata*), Indrani in *Kalpaka* tree (the mythical wish-fulfilling tree, identity not known – equated with peepal, coconut or *Parijatha*), Chamunda in *Plaksha* (cluster fig or Java fig, *Ficus lacor*), Maheswari in *Pundarika* (white lotus), Kaumari in *Plaksha* (cluster fig, Java fig), and Varahi in *Kalpaka tree* (peepal, coconut or *Parijatha*).

Many ancient texts extolled the blessings one gets from the planting of trees. In *Matsya Purana,* chapter 59 is devoted to the prescription of dedicating trees, planting trees, and their maintenance. Here we get the long-lasting benefits of planting trees:

> "...If anybody plants at least one tree, he can stay in heaven of Indra for thirty thousand years. The planter of trees liberates the same number of his past and future sins, attains the highest perfection and is never reborn on earth..."

The rites and ceremonies connected with the dedication and consecration of trees are also mentioned. This idea is repeated in other *Puranas* too:

Agni Purana says:

> "...The plantation of trees and construction of pleasure garden (for the public) are conducive to the purgation of sin and enjoyment of prosperity...."

Vayu Purana stresses:

> "...He never goes to hell who plants an *Aśvattha,* a *Pitchumanda* (neem), a banyan, ten jasmines, two pomegranates, or five mango trees. Never cut down trees that bear flowers and fruits if you want to increase your family or wealth and future happiness...."

The following interesting quote is from *Padma Purana* (Translation by Santhilal Nagar):

"...O Lord of Kings, he who thus installs (the plants) a tree, would also live in heaven as long as three myriad of Indras (rule there) and would save (from falling into hell), past and future men (i.e. his relatives) equal to the number of hairs on the body. He attains great prosperity, making rebirth difficult. Even that man who listens to this or makes others listen to it (i.e. read it to others) is honoured by gods and in the world of *Brahman*. The tree alone makes a sonless person have a son. They offer libations to plants at sacred places. O, Lord of Kings, plant an *Aśvattha* tree even with great effort. It alone will give you a thousand sons. By planting an *Aśvattha* tree, a man becomes wealthy; the *Aśoka* tree destroys grief. The *Plaksha* (cluster fig) tree is said to bestow the fruit of sacrifice, the *Kshira* tree (latex producing trees) is said to give long life, *Jambuka* (*Xylia xylocarpa*), planting bestows daughters, *Dadima* (pomegranate) gives a wife, *Aśavttha* (peepal) leads to the destruction of diseases, and *Plaksha* (cluster fig) takes one to Brahman. A man who plants a *Vibhutaka (Terminalia bellerica)* tree becomes a ghost. The planting of an *Ankola (Alangium salvifolium)* tree leads to the expansion of the family. Planting a *Khadira (Acacia catechu)* tree gives health. The Sun is ever pleased with *Nimba* (neem) shoots. Lord Śiva is pleased when a *Vilva* (bael) tree is planted, and Parvathi is pleased with planting a red *Lodhra (Simplocos racemosa).* The celestial nymphs are pleased with the planting of *Simsapa (Amherstia nobilis; Krishna simsapa – Dalbergia sissoo)* and the Gandharvas with the *Kunda* (jasmine) plants. One would get a group of servants if one plants a *Tintidika (Diospyros malabarica)* tree—likewise, the planting of *Vanjula (Salix caprea)* leads to the rise of robbers. *Chandana (Santalum album)* and *Panasa (Artocarpus heterophyllus)* also gives religious merits and love. Planting *Champaka (Michelia champaka)* gives good fortune, and that of *Karira (Capparis decidua)* makes one adulterer. Planting of *Tala (Borassus flabellifer)* destroys one's progeny, while planting *Vakula* (Bakula) expands the family. Planting a coconut tree brings many wives while planting a grape-creeper gives one all beautiful wives. Similarly, planting *Kali (Neeli,* indigo plant) causes sexual enjoyment. Planting of *Ketaki (Pandanus odorifer)* destroys one's enemies... Those who have planted trees will attain high position..." (28)

In *Bhavishya Purana,* there is a similar statement. Further, it states that a *Plaksha (Ficus lacor,* Java fig), if planted in a pleasure garden, pleases Brahma and that he would bestow on the planter the highest knowledge and a wife. A *Vilva,* if planted, would give a long life; *Jambu* would bestow wealth; *Tinduka* is the giver of prosperity, while *Dadima* would bestow a good wife. Planting of a *Bakula* and a *Vanjula* destroys sins and gives strength and intellect; planting of *Dhataki (Woodfordia fruticosa)* elevates one to heaven, and *Vata* gives salvation. Similarly, planting a mango tree and *Guvaka* (betel-nut tree) fulfils all one's desires. *Padma Purana* says that if a person plants an *Aśvattha* tree near a pond and the leaves falling in the pond water would be like the offering of *Pindas* (after-death rite), his ancestors would stay in heaven. Similarly, one gets virtue by planting *Champaka, Arka, Nygrodha* and *Nimba*; the benefits of planting ten such trees are equal to planting one *Aśvattha*.

The *Dhanvanthari Samhita* of the *Garuda Purana* lists several medicinal herbs used to cure diseases and mentions the drugs and their recipes. Nagar provided a list of these plants in his book, mentioned earlier. There are some well-known sayings related to trees in Surapala's *Vrikshayurveda:*

> *Dasakupa samavāpi dasavāpi samahrada*
> *Dasahrada samaputro dasaputra samadruma*

> One *vāpi* (tank) is as good as ten wells, one lake is as good as ten tanks, one son is as good as ten lakes, and one tree is as good as ten sons.

In this book, *Vrikshayurveda*, the whole chapter on *Tarumahima* highlights the greatness of planting trees. Plants mentioned include *Thulsi, Vilva, Aśvattha, Amalaki, Vata, Nimba, Amra, Sirisa, Plaksha, Udumbara* etc.

> *Äsvatthamekoni picumandamekom*
> *Nygrodhamekom dasa cincinikom*
> *Kapitha bilvämala thrayam ca*
> *Pancambra väpeenarakom ca paçeyeth*

> A person who plants an *Aśvattha* (peepal), a *Pichumanda* (neem), a *Nygrodha* (banyan), ten *Chinchinikom* (tamarind), one each of *Kapitha* (lemon), *Vilva* (wood apple) and *Amala* (gooseberry) and five *Amra* (mango trees) will never see hell.

These are appeals to the public, and by linking tree planting with the attainment of heaven or *moksha* (Salvation), the ancients successfully implemented very dynamic tree planting and conservation programmes. During the time of Manu, the composer of *Manu Samhitha* (or *Manu Smrithi*), the destruction of plants became a state offence. In his code, Manu provided provisions for severe punishment for those who cut the sacred and fruit trees.

Trees and tree worship have gone deep into the cultural ethos and the iconographic practice of the Indian people. Trees are worshipped as the abode of tree spirits or as the abode of deities and such trees are sculpted on the walls of temples; some of them show garlands hanging from them. Sometimes, such trees are sculpted to be worshipped by humans, celestial beings, and even animals. Such open worship places are known as hyperthereal temples, depicted in the sculptures of Bharhut, Sanchi, Amaravati and Nagarjunamkonda, all Buddhist shrines. The trees sculpted are *Nygrodha, Aśvattha, Bādari, Kadamba, Kathal, Sirisha, Vanni, Vilva, Udumbara, Ashoka, Sala, Naga Kesar, Amra* etc. Saiva temples dedicated to Lord Śiva generally have motifs of *Vilva, Nygrodha* and *Arka* carved on the temple pillars and walls. Vaishnava temples dedicated to Lord Vishnu or his incarnations have carvings of Ramayana scenes or scenes from *Bhagavatha Purana,* such as the *Kadamba* tree and the *Kaliya damana* or *Vastraharana* episodes. (29)

Tree shrines form an essential aspect of worship among ardent believers of Hinduism. Haberman conducted a detailed survey and study of tree shrines and tree worship in North India, which appeared in his book 'People Trees'. In this book, he graphically describes the methods for the worship of pipal, banyan, and neem trees. The procedure includes tying-coloured threads around trees, covering the trunk with clothes, anointing the tree trunk with turmeric powder and vermillion, offering rice, lighting lamps, conducting *arati,* circumambulating the tree, chanting prayers, and so on. Often, the devotees put up a small improvised temple at the base of the trees where a lamp is lit daily morning and evening; the devotees pray to the tree deity, circumambulate, and recite prayers. In such tree shrines, the devotees consider pipal as the manifest form of Lord Hari (Vishnu), while banyan is in the form of Siva and neem that of Devi Durga. (30)

The most important members of the Indian Phyto-pantheon are *Aśvattha* (peepal tree), *Vata (banyan* tree), *Vilva* (bael, wood apple tree), *Thulsi* (sacred basil), *Nimba* (neem tree), *Padma* (lotus), *Aśoka, Amra* (mango), *Amalaki* (Indian gooseberry), *Kadali* (plantain), Khadira (*Acacia*), Badari (*Zizyphus mauritiana),* Sami (*Prosopis*), Kadamba (*Anthocephalus cadamba*), etc. Symbolically, they all represent either incarnations of deities or are considered abodes of gods. In the *Brahma Purana* and the *Padma Purana,* we get the legend that the fierce Hiranyaka, who became invincible due to the boons bestowed on him by Brahma, pursued the gods and that they entered trees to hide. Śiva entered the *Vata* (banyan), Vishnu the *Aśvattha,* (Peepal), Brahma the *Palasha* (*Butea monosperma*), Indra the *Sirisa (Albizia lebbeck),* and the Sun god entered the *Nimba* (Neem). All these trees became very sacred. *Padma Purana* and *Skanda Purana* mention that during the four rainy months (*Chaturmasya*), the gods, goddesses, and demi-gods take their in abodes trees and creepers and fulfil the desires of humans. During the *Chaturmasya* period, the same sources say that the gods took abode in different trees: the Gandharvas in sandal trees, the Gananayakas in

Agaru (*Aquillaria agallocha*) trees, the Yakshas in *Punnaga* (*Calophyllum ionophyllum*) trees, the Guhyakas in *Panasa* (*Artocarpus heterophyllus*) trees, the Siddhas in *Kankola* (*Piper cubeba*), the Nagas in *Nagavruksha (Nagakesar, Mesua ferrea),* the Kinnaras in *Maricha* creeper (pepper, *Piper nigrum*), Kama in *Yashtimadhu (Glycyrrizha glabra)* plant, Agni in *Raktanjan (Pterocarpus santalinus)*, Yama in *Vibhitaki, (Terminalia bellirica)*, Kubera in *Asoka (Saraca asoka)* tree, the Rudras in *Badari (Zizyphus mauritiana)* trees, and the seven sages (*Sapta rishis*) in *Tala (Borassus flabellifer)* trees, *Vasus* in *Priyala (Buchanania lanzan),* *Adityas* in *Japa (Hibiscus rosa-sinensis)*, the two *Aswins* in *Mandāra (Bauhinia variegata), Bhutās* in *Guggulu (Commiphora wightii)* tree, Sun in *Arka (Calotropis)* plant, Soma in *Palāsa (Butea monosperma),* Kuja in *Khadira (Acacia catechu)*, Budha in *Apamarga (Achyrathes aspera),* Brihaspati in *Aśvattha (Ficus religiosa)*, Sukra in *Udumbara (Ficus racemosa),* Sani in *Shami (Prosopis spicigera)* tree and all gods as a group in *Madhuka (Madhuca latifolia)* (31). All such legends and myths are clear indications of the interaction of nature and tree worship with the worship of gods, semi-gods and supernatural powers and the transition and transformation of tree worship into a polytheistic form of worship. (32)

Brahmavaivarta Purana mentioned the maintenance of unique groves of trees and that people circumambulate such groves. The trees in such woods include *Chandana, Champaka, Yuthika* (jasmine), *Madhavi (Hipatage benghalensis), Bakula (bakul, Mimusops elengi),* and *Lavunga (Lavanga latha, Lavunga scandens)* creepers. In ancient times, planting trees around dwelling places was considered necessary, and *Garuda Purana* provided directions on how to grow and where to plant specific trees.

There are taboos, too. *Vata (banyan), Salmali* (Indian silk cotton tree) and *Tintirini* (tamarind) trees were taboo near army camps. *Matsya Purana* mentioned that certain trees should not be used for house construction. They include trees secreting milk, trees with birds' nests, trees felled by an elephant, those struck by lightning, those growing close to temples, burial grounds, the confluence of rivers, half-dried, broken and those growing on the banks of lakes.

Among the trees, the peepal (pipal) or *Aśvattha* is the cosmic tree in Indian culture and the mystic tree of India. Peepal is also the most sacred tree for the Buddhists. We also have a mystic flower, the lotus, which is seldom worshipped, but most widely used in worshipping all Hindu deities and Sri Buddha. Moreover, it is also one of the most sacred for Buddhists, for Chinese, Vietnamese, and Japanese. This flower is the seat of Brahma, of goddesses Lakshmi and Saraswathi, and of Gautama the Buddha.

As time rolled on and centuries passed, many ceremonies and beliefs grew around the sacred trees. In such traditions, plants became the symbolic medium to propitiate a favourite deity for a particular purpose. When one looks at the objectives of such worship and ceremonies, one gets an interesting list:

- to win fertility in women, animals, and land
- for good luck, wealth, prosperity, and fortune
- to drive away ghosts, evil spirits, and demons
- for curing, averting or alleviating diseases
- for securing a place in heaven after death
- for getting a husband, for husband's love, affection, and health
- for relieving labour pains and safe delivery
- to avoid ill luck, curses, and evil influences of others

- to avert widowhood
- for a good harvest and plentiful crops
- to offer oblations to ancestors for the satisfaction and blessings of the departed souls
- for immortality and to avoid ill influences and misfortune
- to satisfy souls and holy spirits that reside in trees
- for any other purpose, such as a happy and peaceful life.

Trees were associated with many omens in the past; such beliefs are still prevalent in the tradition-bound villages in India. Sadashiv Dange, in his Encyclopaedia of Puranic Beliefs and Practices, lists the omens associated with trees planted in the house. A passage from this:

> "The weeping of the tree indicates diseases; laughter indicates confusion in the country; fall of a branch – death of a warrior in war; flowering when underdeveloped – the death of children; fruit or flowers before season–breakage of the nation; milking– all-round destruction; oily substances – famine; the flow of wine (*madya sraava*) – destruction or erosion of vehicles; blood – war; honey– disease; water – lack of rain; and if the fruit or the flowers spoilt while on the tree itself, the indication is the death of the king (*Matsya Purana*)..." (32)

Specific remedies are prescribed in case a tree shows the signs noted above.

> "...The tree should be covered and worshipped with sandal paste and wreaths of flowers; on it, an umbrella should be held for the pacification of the evil; Brahmins should be fed, and the gods

should be appeased with dance, music and songs (*Bhavishya Purana*).,,"

Flowers are also associated with good and evil omens and certain magical rites or sorcery, as mentioned in the *Agni Purana*. White flowers indicate good signs (omens). There is a mention in *Vamana Purana* that a person should go for his daily duties after touching a white flower. For killing a person, flowers of *Karaveera* (*Nerium indicum*), yellow *sapha* (yellow saffron, *Carthamus tinctorius*), and mustard are indicated. Flowers of *datura* (*Datura stramonium, Datura innoxia*) smeared with ghee and offered into the fire would fulfil all desires. The offering of *jati* (*Jasminum grandiflorum*) flowers smeared with ghee into the sacrificial fire would fulfil the desire to get a daughter. For the worship of goddesses, lotuses are to be offered into the fire." (33)

In India, several festivals are associated with plants, and women observe many to remove barrenness, to get male progeny, or for a long-married life with husbands and children. Some ceremonies are simple and consist only of praying, lighting a lamp, or tying a thread; others can be very elaborate and last a few days. The most elaborate one is the *Navapatra puja (Navapatrika puja)*, prevalent in many parts of India, most noticeably in Bengal. *Navapatrika puja* forms part of *the Durga puja* ceremony. Here, nine aspects of Durga, symbolized by nine plants, are worshipped. The nine aspects are:

Brahmani: a benevolent form of Shakthi, considered the female counterpart of Brahma, represented by a plantain (banana plant) with stems and leaves.

Kaali (Kalika): a terrible form that Shakthi had taken while fighting with Mahishasura. There are several legends about her origin and worship. The *kachu* (Colocasia) plant symbolizes her.

Durga: Durga in the form of Mangala (bestower of auspiciousness) is present in *haridra* (turmeric), and so this is the third plant.

Kritika: Durga took this form (also known as *Karttiki*) while fighting Sumbha and Nisumbha and the *Jayanthi* plant (balloon wine or heart seed), symbolizing her, and this became the fourth plant.

Raktadantika: Shakthi took this form to fight the demon Raktabija. The pomegranate (*Dadima*) represents her, forming the fifth plant.

Parashakti, when incarnated as Parvathi, worshipped Lord Śiva with flowers of *Aśoka,* and that the Lord loves this tree, and that Devi made it her abode in the aspect *Sokarahitha*, the remover of sorrow. So, *aśoka* becomes the sixth plant.

Chamunda: An aspect of Durga emanated from the forehead of Karthyayani (an incarnation of Durga who killed the invincible demon Mahishasura) for killing the fearsome demons Chanda and Munda. The arum plant symbolizes her, and this forms the seventh plant.

The paddy plant is humans' source of nourishment. Devi Parvathi as Annapoorna (the goddess of food and nourishment), and Devi Lakshmi, the goddess of prosperity, dwell in this plant, which is the eighth plant.

Finally, a branch of the *vilva* tree bearing two fruits representing Śiva and Śakthi is added. All nine plants are tied into a bundle with a *Girikarnika* (*Aparajita*, butterfly pea) vine, symbolizing Durga. (34).

This bundle is given a ceremonious bath, then dressed in red silk, vermillion is applied, decorated, placed by the side of the idol of Durga, and worshipped as Devi Durga for nine days. Each day, an aspect of the *Devi* is invoked separately to offer pooja. Each plant or leaf is collected ceremoniously, and many formalities exist in bundling them. The whole festival is an elaborate one in which everyone in the neighbourhood participates. Here is an example of the evolution of simple plant worship to a complex and elaborate one with a lot of symbolism attached.

The well-known *Navadurga* tradition is closely allied to the Durga aspects worshipped during the *Durga puja* and the *Navapatra puja*. According to the *Devi Mahatmyam* tradition, the *Navadurgas* are: Śhailaputrī, Brahmachārinī, Chandrakanta, Kushmāndā, Skandamātā, Kātyāyanī, Kālarātrī (Kali), Mahāgaurī and Siddhidātrī. These nine forms of Durga are the major deities worshipped during the nine days of the *Navaratri* festival, and *Navapatra puja* forms part of this nine-day celebration. The *Navadurga* worship is famous all over India, while the *Navapatra puja* tradition is observed mainly in Bengal, Bihar, Gujarat, Rajasthan, and Uttar Pradesh. Even in these places, it is not that popular except Bengal. (35)

Yet another example of such elaborate worship is the *Vriksha – panchayatana puja*. Here, five gods [Śiva, Vishnu, Surya, Ambika (Parvathi), and Ganesha] are worshipped symbolically through the worship of five sets of plants (*Vilva – Aegle marmelos* and *Drona – Leucas cephalotes*) for Śiva, *Aśvattha* and *Thulsi* for Vishnu, *Karaveera (Nerium indicum)* and *Svetarka (Calotropis gigantea)* for Surya, *Khadira (Acacia catechu)* and *Durva (Doorva, Cyanadon dactylon)* for Ganesha, *Aśoka (Saraca asoka)* and *Sankapushpa (Aparajita, Clitoria ternatea)* for Ambika or

Durga). Such a setup is permanent and varies with the type of worship. For example, for Śiva *Panchyatana pooja*, Śiva, symbolised by *Vilva,* occupies the centre. *Asoka* is planted in the northeast corner (representing Ambika); *Asvattha* in the northwest corner (symbolising Vishnu); *Khadira* in the southwest corner (representing Ganesa); *and Karaveera* in the southeast corner (representing Sun). The second one is planted in a circle in each location surrounding the tree: *Drona* is planted around *Vilva, Thulsi* around *Aśvattha, Sankapushpa* around *Aśoka, Svetarka* around *Karaveera,* and *Durva* around *Khadira.* In the Vishnu *Panchyatana pooja, Aśvattha* occupies the centre. Such a *Panchayatana* setup is a joint worship facility in certain villages, often associated with temples. (36)

Related to this is the *Navagraha Vana* or *Navagraha Vatika.* This is a garden of nine planets represented by nine plants. These plants are planted in a particular direction to get the benefits of the nine planets. The nine plants are:

Swetarka representing the Sun, planted in the centre;

Palash represents the Moon, planted in the southeast;

Khadira represents Mars, planted in the south direction;

Apamarga represents Mercury, planted in the north direction;

Peepal represents Jupiter planted in the northeast direction;

Udumbara stands for Venus, planted in the east direction;

Shami tree represents Saturn, planted in the West direction;

Durva grass represents Rahu, planted in the southwest

Darbha grass represents Ketu, and it is planted in the northwest direction. (37)

Perhaps most readers are aware of the *Sthalavriksha* associated with the Indian temples. *Sthalavriksha* (temple tree) is a plant that is held sacred, sometimes even on par with the prime deity in the temple; this is the living relic of the earlier nature worship. In the temples, especially in the South Indian states, three components are considered sacred. They are the deity, the *Sthalavriksha,* and the *Theertham* (holy tank). Some surveys and studies have investigated *Sthalavrikshas* and its associated lore and traditions. (38, 39) In Tamil Nadu, 34 species of plants (primarily trees) were recorded as *Sthalavrikshas*. The most common trees are:

- Vilva and *Vata* (in all Siva temples).
- Peepal (in all Vishnu and Krishna temples).
- Neem (in Durga temples).

Other plants recorded as *Sthlavrikshas* are listed below:

- Indian gooseberry (Asthiswarar temple at Athanur),
- *Shami* (Aavudaiyar temple, Moonusavadi*)*,
- *Mandara* (Amirthalingeswarar temple, Veppilaipatty),
- *Nuxvomica* (Alagambasewarar temple, Kalarampalli),
- *Madhuka* (Arthanareswarar temple, Tiruchengode),
- Indian Laburnum (Maligeswarar temple, Kothapalayam),
- *Asoka* (Pasupathi-Eswarar temple, Karur),

- *Punnaga* (Ponvaratharaja Perumal temple, Rasipuram),
- *Patali* (Suguvaneswar temple, Salem),
- Mango tree (Thantondrieswarar temple, Belur and Ekambaranath temple at Kancheepuram),
- *Vanjula* (Vanjaleswarar temple, Karur),
- *Arjuna* (Marudhamalai temple, Maruthumalai),
- Jasmine or *Mullai* (Garbha Rakshambigai temple, Thirukarugavur; Kodiyidai Nayaki Samedha Maasilamaniswarar temple, Thiumullaivayal; Kodhai Nayaki Samedha Mullaivaneswarar temple of Thirumullaivayil, etc.

In the Murukan temple of Marudhumalai, there is a custom that is still very much in vogue; the newlyweds of the region must visit the temple and offer prayers to the deity and the *sthalavriksham*, which is an *Arjuna* (*Maruthu*) tree. Then, on the fifth or seventh month of the first pregnancy, the couple revisits the temple with their relatives and conducts the *Seemantham* ceremony below the shade of the *sthalavriksha* (Arjuna/Maruthu). The worship of the *sthalavriksha* is more prevalent in the South Indian states of Tamil Nadu, Karnataka, Telangana and Andhra Pradesh. (*Seemantham* is a ceremony usually conducted on the 7th month of a woman's pregnancy, followed mainly in the South Indian states of Tamil Nadu, Andhra Pradesh, and Karnataka). Devotees in India revere and defend many of the *Sthalavrikshas*. (temple trees). (40)

Iconic trees

Kevin Johnson (2019) starts his article featured in National Geographic with these words:

> "A visit to historic or meaningful trees provides a sense of connection to the wonder of the

natural world. Vital parts of their ecosystems and trees also spark our imagination, inspire famous books, receive worship, and bear witness to history. Spending mindful, intentional time around trees—what the Japanese call *'shinrin-yoku'* or forest bathing—can promote health and happiness." (41)

Indeed, these iconic trees are:

"Ancient, majestic and steadfast, these famous trees have witnessed the birth of religions, sheltered famous outlaws, and stood firm in the face of human folly. Visit them while you still can."

Many such trees have been listed from across the continents. Such trees can better be called historic trees or monumental trees. Many such trees have been reported in the public media. They include the giant sequoia tree, General Sherman (Sequoia National Park, California, USA, qualified as the largest living object on earth), the banyan tree known as *Thimmamma maram* (the record holder of world's most extensive single tree canopy, is around 550 years old and having the "greatest perimeter length for a tree", spreading over five acres with a circumference of 846m), and the Bodhi tree in Anuradhapura, Sri Lanka, the oldest, planted tree and many more.

We know about the all-time mystic and mysterious iconic trees like the tree in the Garden of Eden (the Tree of Life and the Tree of the Knowledge of Good and Evil), the banyan tree of Gaya under which Gautama became the enlightened Buddha, the mythical tree *Ygaddril,* the tree of life of the Norse mythology, the wish-fulfilling *Kalpavrikshas* of Indian mythology, the oak tree (the first tree that earned respect, devotion, and worship of man, about 10,000 years ago), the legendary acacia tree of the city of Saosis, under which the gods were born according to the Egyptian mythology and soon. Coming to the modern world, we have monumental trees like the giant General Sherman (the largest tree in the world at 52,508 cubic feet (1,487 cubic meters), and Montezuma Cypress (*Taxodium mucronatum*) standing in the Mexican town of Oaxaca. (Experts believe it is at least 1200 years old – making it the oldest Montezuma cypress in the world. It also has the widest girth of any tree on the planet, measuring a circumference of 42 meters or 137.8 feet; its diameter from its two widest points measures 14.05 m or 46.1 ft.); Himalayan cypress (*Cupressus torulosa*) of Tibet, Mountain ash (*Eucalyptus regnans*) of Australia, the great Baobab (*Adansonia digitata*) of Limpopo, South Africa etc. However, the largest plant so far known is the marine seagrass discovered in Shark Bay, about 800km (497 miles) north of Perth, Australia. This plant, named *Posidonia australis*, covers about 200 sq. km (77 sq. miles) and is estimated to be about 4500 years old. There are also many other trees, like the banyan tree of Sir Jagadish Chandra Botanical Garden, Howrah (India), the Methuselah Tree of California (*Pinus longaeva*, the oldest tree on earth, ca 4655 Years old), Cypress of Abarkuh, also called the Zoroastrian Sarv, is a Persian cypress (*Cupressus sempervirens*) tree in Abarkuh in Yazd Province of Iran; the Rullah Longatyle (*Eucalyptus globulus*-Tasmanian blue gum), the world's most massive eucalyptus tree at 82.3 meters tall (Australia); and so on. They are all the monumental and heritage trees of humanity. (42)

Then there are the historic trees that stood as silent witnesses to certain great events in the history of humanity. Such trees include Anne Frank's Chestnut Tree (Amsterdam,

Netherlands, in the backyard of the house in Amsterdam where Anne Frank and her family were hiding during World War II)., the Liberty Tree (Boston, Massachusetts, On August 14, 1765, a defiant group of American colonists that proclaimed itself the Sons of Liberty rallied beneath the mighty boughs of a century-old elm tree to protest the enactment of the highly unpopular Stamp Act. The young rebels decorated the tree with banners, lanterns, and effigies of the British stamp master and prime minister); Isaac Newton's Apple Tree (at Woolsthorpe Manor in – Colsterworth, Lincolnshire, England), September 11 Survivor Tree (New York City, New York); etc. Recently Natesh has written a book on 72 selected iconic trees from various states of India (Iconic trees, S, Natesh, Rolli books, 2024).

In the following chapters, the discussions are NOT on individual or historical or monumental trees such as the ones mentioned above, but the ICONIC PLANTS from a socio-cultural viewpoint. Here, the stress is not on individual trees, but on certain plant species that are held sacred and are being worshipped or are regularly used for worshipping, and hence played significant socio-religious and socio-cultural roles in the lives of the Hindus of India, from ancient times to the present, as an unbroken line of intimacy and veneration between people and trees. They are also the plants (some are trees, some herbs/shrubs) used from ancient times for worship, and so have an intimate association with deities. Some are even considered to represent the deities they symbolise.

From the socio-religious standpoint, the most famous and the earliest one was the Soma plant, used in the Vedic times for ritual drinks during the Yajnas. The identity of this *soma* plant is still shrouded in mystery. From the time of the Upanishads, peepal and banyan trees became symbols of many religious principles and were also used in the conduct of the *yajnas*. The former (Peepal) became the cosmic tree of India, and the latter is known as the immortal tree (*Akshaya Vata*) of the Indian people. Plants like lotus became very prominent from the time of Mahabharata, and this flower became known as the cosmic flower of India.

Additionally, there are the trees of Lord Siva (Bael, Rudraksha), the sorrowless tree (Asoka), the tree of Prajapati (Mango), and the tree of Devi Durga as well as the Snake Goddess (Neem). We have the holy basil plant, the plant so dear to Lord Vishnu and goddess Lakshmi. Then there is the banana plant (symbolising Devi Sri and Durga), coconut (the *Kalpavriksha*), etc. All such plants are of vital significance to the Hindus of India. Of course, there are others too, like: *Amalaki* tree, *Palasha* tree, *Kadamba* tree, *Parijata, Badari, Sami,* and so on.

This book deals with 20 iconic plants, which the author regarded as of prime importance. The book is built upon the author's earlier work, Sacred and Ritual Plants of India, but is vastly modified, embellished, and updated. The chapters in this book will provide holistic discussions of the above iconic plants. They will surely help enlighten the readers on India's (and of Hindus) great heritage plants. It will significantly help in the conservation of trees; anyone aware of the legends, myths, symbolism, and traditions of the iconic trees (and other sacred trees) will always embrace them as a precious gift of Nature and feel respect and devotion towards them. There was a time when trees were considered sentient beings; modern humans have become insensitive to these descendants of the distant past, more than a hundred times more ancient than the humans themselves.

Citations and Notes

(See the Lists of citations and notes A and B provided at the end of the book for general references – both ancient and modern.)

1. Joseph T (2018) How ancient DNA may rewrite prehistory in India. BBC Newshttps://www.bbc.co.uk/news/world-asia-india-46616574

2. Munteanu N. (2019) How Trees Can Save Us…Five Perspectives on Humanity's Relationship with Our Forests https://ninamunteanu.me/2019/09/14/how-trees-can-save-usfive-perspectives-on-humanitys-relationship-with-our-forests/

3. Beresford-Kroeger D (2010) The Global Forest: 40 Ways Trees Can Save Us. ⌈Viking; First Edition (May 13, 2010)

4. Haskell DJ (2017) The Songs of Trees. Viking Pub. New York.

5. Levertov D. (2002) Web. Selected Poems, New Directions Publishing Corporation, New York.

6. Powers R (2019) The Overstory. Random House, UK.

7. Kilmer J (1915) Trees. https://www.poetryfoundation.org/poetrymagazine/poems/12744/trees

8. Beau-Douëzy P. (2019) The tree, the future of Humanity. Interview with Jean-Philippe Beau-Douëzy. https://www.yves-rocher-fondation.org/sur-le-terrain/larbre-futur-de-lhumanite/.

9. Bryant WC (1824) A Forest Hymn. https://allpoetry.com/A-Forest-Hymn.

10. Symington, AJ (1880). William Cullen Bryant: a biographical sketch: with selections from his poems and other writings. Harper & Brothers. OCLC 10645450.

11. Collis J S (1954) The Triumph of Tree, Sloane Publishing, Cornwall-on-Hudson, NY, 1954

12. Frazer, Sir James George. (1922) The Golden Bough: a study of magic and religion.

   E-edition (e-text by David Reed),, https://www.fulltextarchive.com/book/The-Golden-Bough/.

13. Ravindran PN (2020) Sacred and Ritual Plants of India. Notion press. Chennai.

14. Pliny, The Elder. Cited from http://www.mosmaiorum.org/treehuggers.html.

15. Ravindran PN (2020) See 13.

16. Beau-Douëzy P. (2019) The tree, the future of Humanity. See 8.

17. Grant R (2018) Do Trees Talk to Each Other? https://www.smithsonianmag.com/science-nature/the-whispering-trees-180968084/#:~:text=......20similar%20to%20an%20insect%20colony

18. FAO (2020) FAO: Global Forest Resources Assessment, 2020 Report. FAO, Rome.

19. Ehrenberg R (2015) Global Forest survey finds trillions of trees. Nature,. https://doi.org/10.1038/nature.2015.18287

20. WEF (2022) Scientists count the world's tree species. World Economic Forum, https://www.weforum.org/agenda/2022/02/world-tree-species-forest-deforestation-climate-change/.

21. SOFO (2020) FAO (2018-2022) The State of the World's Forests 2020. https://openknowledge.fao.org/items/d0f20c1c-7760-4d94-86c3-d1e770a17db0.

22. Pandey SK (1993) Indian Rock Art. New Delhi: Aryan Books Internationa

23. Nagar S (2000) Botanical and Medicinal Plants: As depicted in Ancient Texts, Art and Archeology From Dawn of Civilization to the Modern Age, Vol. 1.

24. Quoted from Ravindran (2020) See 13.

25. Ravindran PN (see 13)

26. Griffith RTH (1889) The Hymns of the Rigveda. E.J. Lazarus, https://archive.org/details/hymnsrigveda02grifgoog.

27. Ravindran PN (see 13)

28. Nagar S (see 23)

29. Hawkes S and Goswamy K (2004) Sacred Trees and Indian Life: A collection of photographs on sacred trees together with brief notes. Aryan Books International, New Delhi, 2004.

30. Haberman D L (2013) People Trees. Oxford University Press, New York, 2013.

31-32. Dange S A (1986) Encyclopaedia of Puranic Beliefs and Practices, Vol 1-5, Navarang Pub., New Delhi.

33. Sengupta S (2013) *Navapatrika*: Worship of nature's creative force, http://www.prabashipost.com/n-61-kolabou.aspx#. V4Ocgrh97nE

34. Ravindran PN (see 13)

35-36. Harshananda, Swami (2008) *Panchayatanapooja*, A Concise Encyclopedia of Hinduism, vol.2, RamakrishnaMath, Bangalore.

37. Ravindran PN (see 13)

38. Gunasekaran M and Balasubramanian P (2012) Ethnomedicinal uses of Sthalavrikshas (temple trees)

in Tamil Nadu, Southern India. Ethnobotany Research & Applications, 10: 253 – 268.

39. Prabakaran R and Sabari Lakshmi G (2017) Studies on Sthalavrikshas of various temples in Tamil Nadu, India. Bioscience Discovery, 8: 64 – 72.

40. Gunasekaran M and Balasubramanian P (2012) (see 36)

41. Prabakaran R and Sabari Lakshmi G (2017 (see 37)

42. Johnson K. (2019) 19 Iconic trees around the world. National Geographic https://www.nationalgeographic.com/travel/article/iconic-trees-around-the-world

02

AŚVATTHA (BODHI, PEEPEL)

The Cosmic Tree of India

Namaste āsvatha – rajaya brahma – viśu-ṣivatmane
bodhi-drumaya kartranam pritrunām taranaya ca
ye asmatkule mātruvamse bandhavadurgatim gatah
ṭat darsanat sparsanac ca svargatimyantu sāsvatim
ratnatrayammayādattam ġayāmāgatyavrikaharath
ṭvatprasadan ṁahāpapat vimuktoham bhavārnavāt||
(Vayu Purana)

The Indian Peepal or Bodhi tree is a deeply revered spiritual entity, eulogised as the cosmic tree of India, and the *axis mundi* that connects heaven, earth, and the netherworld. In Indian cultural traditions, the peepal tree is the seat of the Trinity; for the Vaishnavites, the tree is a manifest form of Lord Vishnu and so worshipped. The most remarkable historical aspect is the connection between Peepal and Gautama Siddhartha. Gautama became the enlightened Buddha through meditation under the peepal tree, and after that, the tree became famous as the Bodhi (or Bo) tree. The peepal holds immense symbolism in Indian philosophical thoughts; it symbolises spiritual enlightenment, cultural heritage, and ecological resilience. Many myths and legends have been woven around the Bodhi tree, which are still popular with the Indians.

At least some of the readers might have sat under a peepal tree, listening to the rustling leaves' music, and seeing the leaves dancing in the breeze. I do so often, and then, usually, I experience a strange exhilaration filling my mind and spreading to the limbs. Look at the leaf. It gives the impression of a human standing with outstretched hands to the sky as if praying to the Almighty. Peepal (spelt variously as peepal, pipal, pipul, peepul) is the cosmic tree of India, known in Sanskrit as *Aśvattha,* later became more famous as *Bodhi (Bodhi* tree, *Bodhi vriksha, Bodhi druma,* and *Bo* tree). The pipal tree became the *Bodhi* tree when Gautama Siddhartha sat under it in meditation and attained enlightenment. Asvattha is the most sacred tree for Hindus and Buddhists. It was also the basis of a profound metaphysical doctrine during the Vedic and post-Vedic times. The Peepal tree represented the zeitgeist of ancient India and of Hinduism itself. The peepal tree was the symbol of the cosmic tree and was considered in the past to be the *Axis Mundi*. This aspect is discussed in detail later. Man has established an intimate, unbroken relationship with Peepal; the history of this relationship goes back many millennia. This relationship started at the shadowy dawn of the human past, and through centuries, it has evolved into a relationship, symbolically and metaphysically bonded.

However, the biological history of Peepal is much older and started probably at the beginning of the Tertiary period (Paleogenic period, about 66 million years ago.) The period began immediately after the Cretaceous-Paleogene mass extinction event at the beginning of the Cenozoic era. It extended to the Quaternary glaciation at the end of the Pliocene Epoch. Fossil leaves that belong to *Ficus religiosa* (peepal tree) have been discovered in the Tertiary rocks of the Kasauli range in the Western Himalayas. From the beginning of the earliest civilizations on the Indian subcontinent, the peepel (pipel) tree caught the attention of humans, and early man has come to respect and offer reverence to this tree. Slowly, the peepal (the earliest name is *Asvattha*) became intimately associated with the philosophical, religious, and ceremonial lives of the early Aryans who established the ancient Vedic civilization, which was also the beginning of Hinduism.

One may raise the issue of why, of all the trees, the ancient Aryans chose the peepal tree for their worship and as a sheet anchor for their philosophical ideas. Many other trees, including the mango tree, are equally impressive and more functional. Some academics have suggested that the Aryans chose the peepal tree for a specific reason. The plausible explanation is that the peepal resembled the poplar tree, which the ancient Aryans revered in their native Central Asian homeland. Another possible reason is that peepal is a tree that vanquishes other trees. Seeds of peepal seldom sprout and grow on the ground. However, they sprout and grow quickly on other trees (especially on trees like Khadira or acacia). The peepal tree starts its life as an epiphyte; the roots grow downward and touch the earth, and when they penetrate the soil, gradually, the tree becomes independent. In this process, the peepal breaks and kills the host tree. In this habit of peepal, the Aryans saw the symbol of a vanquisher of enemies. In those ancient times, the Aryan community lived constantly in fear of attacking enemies, like all other communities in the ancient world. So, they saw a symbol of an enemy killer in the peepal and started respecting and worshipping the peepal tree. We find references for such a conclusion in Vedas, mainly in the Atharva Veda (III.6):

Atharva Veda (III.6):

> 1. The male sprung from the male, from the khadira;
> may it slay my enemies whom I hate and who hate me!
> 2. Break them, O Asvattha! the pertinacious foes,
> O you born of the repeller (the Khadira)!
> In alliance with Indra the demon slayer, with Mitra and Varuna!
> 3. As O Asvattha, you have broken the Khadira
> within the great ocean (of air), so break all
> those I hate and who hate me!
> 4. You who go conquering like a conquering bull,
> with you here, O Asvattha! May we conquer our rivals!
> 5. May Nirrti, O Asvattha, bind in the indissoluble
> fetters of death, my enemies whom I hate
> and who hate me!
> 6. O Asvattha! climbing the forest trees, you
> put them below you, so split apart the head of
> my enemy and vanquish him!
> 7. Let them (the enemies) float down like a boat
> out from its mooring! There is no return
> for those pushed away by one born of the repeller.
> 8. I push them away with my mind, away with my
> thoughts, and with the incantation. We push
> them away with the branch of the *Asvattha* tree.

The Aryans, in their competition for land, power, and domination of the native inhabitants, adopted the Asvattha, "vanquisher of rivals among forest trees," as a symbol of strength and destruction of the "enemy," and imbued it with power through a symbolic interpretation of the botanical facts. In all the phraseology of this charm, reference to the growth habits of the Asvattha is quite apparent. This hymn accompanies a ritual in which an amulet made from the wood of an Asvattha growing on a Khadira tree (*Acacia catechu*, Willd.) is used with the hope of destroying enemies. (1)

> "I bow my head in obeisance to thee, O, *aśvattha*, the lord of trees, standing as a living form of the holy triad of our pantheon with thy high fame as *bodhi druma*, the renowned *Bo*, for the release of the dead forefathers, the makers of the line of descent. Those in my direct line and those connected with the mother's line the kith and kin who have gone into the state of woe, may they, from thy holy sight and touch, pass into an eternal state of heavenly life. The triple debts have I paid, Oh! King of Trees, by coming on pilgrimage to Gaya. By thy benign grace am I rescued from the awful ocean of existence and liberated from deadly sin".

Asvattha (Peepal): Legends on the Origin

References to the Peepal tree can be found from ancient times in the scriptures, like Vedas and epics. In the *Danastuti*, which occupies a position intermediate between religious and secular hymns of the *Rg Veda (Rig Veda)*, there are about forty hymns classified as *Danastuti*. In one of the hymns, the word *Asvattha* was indicated as the name of a king. *Rig Veda* mentions that Asvattha wood is essential to making vessels for sacrifices. In *Yajurveda, Asvattha* was the residence of Gandharvas and Apsaras (YV, 3.4.8). In *Maitrayani Samhita (Maitrayaniya Samhita, MS)*, there is an episode associated with the origin of peepal. When Agni was born in dazzling brilliance, his heat and brilliance were too much for the rest of the creatures. So, Agni entered the *Asvattha* tree and deposited his brilliance in it. Because of this belief, Rishis use the fagots of the *asvattha* tree to kindle fire during ritual practices. They believed that by using

Peepal tree, and many serpents' idols installed below.

Peepal leaves

Unripe fruits

Asvattha faggots in the sacrificial fire, they could bring the splendour of the God Agni into the sacrifice. (MS 1.6.2).

Maitrayani Samhita (MS) of *Krishna Yajurveda* gives one of the earliest myths on the origin of peepal. After creating diverse organisms, the creator, Prajapathi, was desirous of creating something unique. He turned into a horse and, casting his head low on the ground, meditated for a year. In the end, a tree bursts forth from the head of the *asva* (horse), and the new tree becomes famous as the *asvattha*.

MS mentions another legend. Once Agni (the fire god) revealed his sacrificial form to Pururavas, he carried that form in his lap and transferred that to a pan. That fiery form changed into *Asvattha* and the pan into a *Shami* tree (see below for details). The *Taittiariya Brahmana* gives another legend on its origin. Agni, as *Yajna Prajapathi*, once descended from the immortal world and searched for a place to remain in solitude, away from all others. At last, he took the form of a horse and remained concealed in a tree; that tree was named *Asvattha*, literally meaning the place of a horse.

Maitrayani Samhita and the *Mahabharata* mention a story relating *Asvattha,* Urvasi, and the famous King Pururavas. Later, this legend became the theme of Kalidasa's well-known book, *Vikramorvashiyam*. The gist of the story is as follows: Urvashi was the most beautiful of the celestial nymphs (known as Apsaras), and she occupied a position of envy in the court of Lord Indra. However, Urvasi was feeling bored in heaven, and she longed to roam around the earth, enjoying and experiencing the beauty and warmth of the earth. She often came down to earth, in the company of her female attendants, to enjoy and take a dip in the cool waters. On one such occasion, she was leaving the earth before daybreak when an Asura named Kesi blocked her way and tried to abduct her. She cried aloud. It so happened that Pururavas, the mightiest and most handsome of humans, was travelling across the sky in his chariot. He heard the cry of Urvasi and immediately chased the asura and freed Urvasi. Thus, the loveliest woman of heaven and the most handsome man on earth met, and for a brief period, their bodies touched. Urvasi experienced the warmth of a human body for the first time, and for the first time, she experienced the feeling of lightning passing through her body and her blood pounding in her veins. Emotions swelled up, and the charming Pururavas became her passion. Pururavas had seen Urvashi in Indra's court before, and now he saw the most dazzling woman at close quarters, and his heart subdued before her. He left Urvashi with her friends, but when they parted, each was madly in love with the other. Soon after that, Urvasi had to give a dance performance under the direction of Rishi Bharat. She was playing the role of Vishnu's consort, Lakshmi. Urvasi's mind was wandering around Pururavas, and she was making mistakes in the dance. She even uttered the name Pururavas instead of Purushothama (Vishnu's name). Sage Bharat became angry and cursed Urvasi:

> "You will get to live with the person you are thinking about, he said, and you will also give birth to his son. But you will have to choose between the father and the son because the day they see each other, you will have to leave them both and return to heaven."

Urvasi felt internally happy after hearing the curse, while the other Apsaras were aghast with fear. Urvasi was sure to get the love and affection of Pururavas. She located him in the garden of Gandhmadan (hill or mountain of intoxicating fragrance), whining away for his ladylove. Urvashi left heaven and went to the waiting arms of Pururavas.

There are variations in the above story. In the *Devi Bhagavatha Purana*, Brahma cursed Urvasi, while in *Bhagavatha purana* it was Mitra-Varunas who cursed Urvasi. Urvasi had heard about Pururavas's fame and had felt tender love for him. Urvasi met Pururavas; he was in ninth heaven when his dream lady appeared before him. He immediately requested that she be his wife. She agreed but laid down three conditions:

> "First, I have with me two lambs, which I bring up as my sons, and they have to be taken care of. No harm should befall them. Second, I take in only ghee. On no account should you compel me to eat any other food, and the third one, don't come near me in nudity except at the time of our physical union."

The King agreed to all these conditions. From that day on, Urvasi lived in the palace as the queen. They lived happily for a long while without separating from each other.

But Urvasi had to ultimately return to her heavenly abode, as an Apsara cannot live forever with a mortal. Pururavas became inconsolable at his loss, and the Gandharvas took pity on him. Since Urvasi could not live with him on earth, these semidivine beings decided to include Pururavas among them by making him immortal. They told Pururavas that he could become immortal by conducting a specific ritual to unite with Urvasi. They gave him the divine fire (*agnisthali*, a pot holding divine fire) and instructed him to perform the ritual before the sacred fire. Pururavas took the fire and carried it home. He left the fire in the forest and went on to take a bath. On his return, he found the fire, and the pan turned into the *Aswattha* tree and the *Shami* tree, respectively; the *Aswattha* was growing out of the *Shami* plant.

Having lost the fire, Pururavas was in utter despair. He approached the Gandharvas again. They instructed the King to make a fire drill or *Arani,* from the wood of the two trees, make fire, and conduct the stipulated rituals, wishing in his mind for a permanent life with Urvasi. After a few trials, Pururavas finally made the *arani* (fire drill) using *Aswattha* wood for the upper part and Shami wood for the lower part. Pururavas made the fire, conducted the ritual, and attained permanent Gandharva status and eternal life with Urvasi.

There is symbolism associated with this. *Aswattha* is the male, *Shami* is the female, and Agni, thus produced, is the child. *Asvattha* mounts *Shami,* and rotating the *arani* (fire drill) creates friction, and the whole process is akin to the union of a man and woman and, hence, of procreation. The top part is made of peepal wood, and this represents the male phallus, and the bottom portion, made in the form of a close-fitting whole, is symbolic of the female vagina. So, for the first time, Pururavas used the Arani and made fire; hence fire is regarded as his son. Since then, for every ritual, the holy fire (*Paavaman*) has been created by using the *arani.* This is the story behind the origin of the peepal tree. (2)

[**Note:** Lord Agni is Brahma's *manasaputra* (mind-born son), and his consort is Svaha Devi. They had three sons, viz. Paavaka, (*Dakshinagni*), Pavaman (*Garhapatya*), and Shuch (*Aahavaniya*). All three are also known as Agni. However, the three forms differ in their origins. Paavaka is also called *Vaidyut* and is produced from water currents, *Paavaman* is also known as *Nirmathya* or created by *Nirmathana* (friction). Shuchi is *Soura*, purely from Surya's (Sun's) radiation. The fire generated by Pururavas was through friction; hence, it was the type known as *Paavaman or Garhapatya*]. (*Matsya Purana*)]

In *Matsya Purana*, there is another interpretation of the origin of peepal. Once Surya (Sun) was conceived as *Asva,* the cosmic tree as *Asvattha,* and its cosmic energy as *Asva*, the Sun. The cosmos is called *asvattha* because a horse is at the centre, or because it stands like a horse on three legs and the tree is the fourth, or because it depends on the power or movement of the archetypal Horse that is Surya. *Vamana Purana* mentions that trees originated from gods, and *asvattha* came into being from the Sun God. So, the Sun is the father of *Asvattha* tree. *Asvattha* is always depicted as Lord Vishnu's manifestation, and the Sun is his manifestation, too.

Padma Purana gives the legend of the curse of Parvathi (mentioned in the previous chapter also). Once, all the gods decided to visit Mount Kailas to pay homage to Lord Shiva and to plead to him to beget a son who alone can kill Tarakasura. However, the wise rishi Narada (the only rishi who can move freely in all the three worlds), told them that it was an inappropriate time for a visit as the Lord was enjoying private moments with his consort, Devi Parvati, and that they should not be disturbed. But Lord Indra did not like Narada's intervention and assured the rest of the gods that as the King of devas, he would take responsibility and that there was nothing to fear when he was there to protect them. But all the gods were afraid of the consequences. So, they finally decided to depute Agni. Agni had to agree to the request of the gods. Agni, disguised as a Brahmin, reached the abode of Shiva. Shiva and Parvathy were engaged in a romantic dalliance. The heat of Agni disturbed them, and Parvathi became furious and, in a fit of anger, cursed the gods that they, together with their wives, would turn into trees. The gods were in trouble now as no power could prevent or reverse the curse of Devi Parvathi. Gods sought forgiveness and she then promised them that as trees they all would attain fame and do good to humans. Thus, Indra turned into a mango tree, Brahma became a *palash* tree, Vishnu became a peepal tree, and Shiva became a *vata* (banyan) tree.

For the early Aryans, who reached India during the pre-Vedic and Vedic periods, *asvattha* might have provided similarity to poplar, a tree with which they were very familiar and sacred from ancient times in the Central Asian regions. So, they might have started calling it *popla* or *pipla*. The name *asvattha* became prevalent in *Puranic* times. The term peepal originated from the Sanskrit *pipla*.

In some European countries, peepal is called Indian poplar. The meaning of the term *aśvattha,* and its origin has been interpreted differently by commentators of ancient scriptures; this aspect has already been mentioned earlier. Swami Chidbhavananda says, '*aśvattha* means that which is not today's, it was yesterday's'. Another interpretation is that 'which is not for tomorrow only' means that *aśvattha* is permanent or everlasting. (3). Yet another interpretation provided in Praharaj's *Purnachandra bhashakosa* is that the tree whose leaves quiver is always like a horse's ears, is the Asvattha. (4)

The name *Asvattha* has another significance. In ancient times, during the regime of various kings, innumerable peepal trees were planted along the waysides in all regions in present-day north India. Such plantings provided shade for the travellers and harnessed their horses. In those days, kings and nobles were travelling on horseback, ordinary people were on foot, and the shade of the peepal tree was a boon to all. In due course, *Asvattha* became synonymous with a tree for harnessing horses. So, from those days on, the tree became known as *Asvattha*. (5).

There are many other references in the ancient literature on peepal. *Taittiriya Brahmana* of *Krishna Yajurveda* (Black *Yajurveda*), names seven holy trees needed for the *Yajnas* and rituals; *asvattha* is the first among them. *Asvattha* wood was used to construct a pen to tether the sacrificial horse. In *Satapada Brahmana* of *Sukla* (white) *Yajurveda, asvattha* is mentioned as the seat of dead ancestors. In this *Samhita,* there is a mention that the peepal tree issued forth from Indra's skin and his honour after his limbs fell when Tvaṣṭr (Tvoṣṭā, the Vedic name for Viswakarma) exercised him. There are references to several types of vessels made of peepal wood for use in

Yagas and other rituals. There is a stipulation that vessels to serve the offerings (*havis*) to Mitra should be from a peepal branch that broke off naturally, while the one to serve Varuna should hewn from the tree. (6, 7)

Some of the Upanishads refer to the *Asvattha* tree. It is extolled as the "world tree" (*Samsara vriksha*), and the word peepal used to denote the fruits of the past deeds of human beings. In *Kathopanishad*, *asvattha* is qualified as "Brahman", meaning eternal. For one of the questions from Nachiketas, Yama answered like this:

> "This is an eternal *Aśvattha* tree whose root is above, but its branches are downward. It is He that is called the Bright One, the *Brahman,* and immortality. In Him, all the worlds are established. None goes beyond Him. This is what you seek."

In *Mundakopanishad* and *Svetasvasara Upanishad*, we get references to the peepal as a fruit, which is eaten by the bird called *Jeeva*. In this metaphysical sense, Peepal means the deeds of the past, and everyone must enjoy the fruit of one's past deed:

> "Two birds who are always inseparable companions cling to the self – same tree. One eats the sweet fruit, and the other looks on without partaking."

Maitri Upanishad (also known as *Maitrayaniya Upanishad* or *Maitrayaniya Brahmaya-Upanishad,* belongs to the *Krishna Yajurveda*) tries to connect Brahman the *Asvattha* with the syllable '*Om',* and recommends the worship of this *Asvattha* through the word *OM.*

> "The three-quartered Brahma has its root above. Its branches are space, wind, fire, water, and earth. This Brahma is named 'the Lone Fig-tree'. Belonging to it is the splendour, which is you, Sun,

and the splendour of the syllable *Om*. Therefore, one should worship it with *Om* continually. He is the only enlightener of man." (Mait U VI, 4).

A similar idea is also mentioned in the *Chandogya upanishad*.

There are mentions on *asvattha* in *Sutra* literature too (such as *Gobhila Grahya Sutra, Paraskaya Grahya Sutra,* and *Gautama Dharma Sutra*. In *Indra Yanja* (Sacrifices to Indra) peepel leaves are used as symbols for wind gods. *Brahmacharins* (celebates) of the Vaisya caste always carry staff from *Asvattha* branches. *Manu smriti* and *Yajnyavalka smriti* ordain that *asnataka* (one who is taking the ritual bath (*snana,* or *samavartanam*) after the completion of the *gurukula* life or *Brahmacharya*) must circumambulate the *asvattha* tree before proceeding to the ritual bath. *Asvattha* is also stipulated to use as sacrificial faggots to Brihaspati.

Asvattha is the tree of Knowledge (Wisdom)

We find innumerable references about *Asvattha* in epic literature, except in the Ramayana. In the Mahabharata, the *Asvattha* is identified as a deity and given a status like that of other gods like Sun and Vayu. In the Bhagavad Gita, Lord Krishna said he is the *Asvattha* among the trees in his discourse to Arjuna.

> *Asvatthah sarva-vrksanam*
> *devarsinam ca naradah*
> *gandharvanam citrarathah*
> *siddhanam kapilomunih.*

(Of all trees, I am the holy fig tree, and amongst sages and demigods, I am Narada. Of the singers of the gods (Gandharvas), I am Citraratha, and among perfected beings, I am the sage Kapila.)

In Chapter 15 of Bhagavad Gita, the mortal world is compared to an *asvattha* tree.

> *śhrī-bhagavānuvācha*
> *ūrdhva-mūlamadhaḥ-śhākham aśhvatthaṁ prāhuravyayam*
> *chhandānsiyasya parṇāni yastaṁ vedasa veda-vit.*

The Supreme Divine Personality said:

> They speak of an eternal *aśvattha* tree with its roots above and branches below. Its leaves are the Vedic hymns, and one who knows the secret of this tree is the knower of the Vedas.

The Lord explains that this material world is like a vast *Aśvattha* tree for the soul. Its roots are growing upwards (*ūrdhva-mūlam*), originating from God, nourished, and supported by Him. The trunk and branches, which extend downwards (*adhaḥ-śhākham*), encompass all the life forms from different abodes of the material realm. Its leaves are the Vedic mantras (*chhandās*), which describe rituals, ceremonies, and rewards. By performing such rituals, the soul can ascend to the heavenly abodes and enjoy celestial pleasures, though eventually, when the rewards deplete, they must fall back to earth. In this way, the *Aśvattha* tree leaves nourish the soul's material existence and perpetuate the continuous cycle of life and death. The soul cannot experience the beginning or the end because of this continuity. Hence, this tree form of the world is *Avyayam* or eternal. Just like the waters of the oceans evaporate, they form clouds that rain on the earth, creating rivers and eventually flowing back to the oceans. Likewise, the cycle of life and death is also continuous.

The Vedas also mention this tree:

*ūrdhvamūlo 'vākśhākhaeşho 'śhvatthaḥ
sanātanaḥ* (Kaṭhopaaniṣhad 2.3.1)
"The *aśvattha* tree, with its roots upward and branches downward, is eternal."
*Ūrdhvamūlamarvākśhākhaṁ vṛikṣhaṁyo
samprati
nasajātujanaḥ śhraddhayāt mṛityutyur
māmārayaditi* (*Taittirīya Āraṇyaka* 1.11.5)
"Those who know this tree with its roots upward and branches downward will not believe that death can finish them."

The intention of describing this tree in the Vedas was to make us understand that we are beyond the cycle of life and death and should work towards cutting this tree down. For the same purpose, Lord Shree Krishna has mentioned that one who understands the secret (of cutting) this tree of *samsara* is the knower of the Vedas (*Vedavit*). (8)

15.2:

*adhaśhchordhvaṁ prasṛitāstasya śhākhā
guṇa-pravṛiddhāviṣhaya-pravālāḥ
adhaśh cha mūlānyanusantatāni
karmānubandhīni manuṣhya-loke*

The branches of the tree extend upward and downward, nourished by the three *guṇas*, with the objects of the senses as tender buds. The roots grow downward, causing the flow of karma in the human form. Below, its roots branch out, causing (karmic) actions in the world of humans.

Muktananda gives the following comments:

"Similar to how water irrigates a tree, the three modes of material nature or the three *gunas* irrigate this eternal tree of material existence. The sense objects generated by these *gunas* are like buds on the tree (*vishaya-pravālāḥ*), which sprout, causing further growth. These buds sprout, creating several aerial roots of material desires. For example, another tree of the fig family, the banyan tree, has aerial roots that grow straight from the branches down to the ground; as time passes, they turn into secondary trunks. Such a growth makes the banyan tree grow huge, covering a large area.

Likewise, in the context of the material world, the sense objects are like the buds on the *aśvattha* tree, which sprout into aerial roots as they evoke desires of bodily pleasures in a person. To satiate these desires, a living being performs karma. But these desires are unending and keep increasing, like the aerial roots, which nourish this metaphorical tree, causing its unlimited expansion. Eventually, the soul gets further entangled into this web of material consciousness."

15.3:

Narūpamasye hatatho palabhyate
nāntonachādirna cha sampratiṣṭhā
aśhvattha menaṁsu-virūḍha-mūlam
asaṅga-śhastreṇa dṛiḍhenachhittvā
tataḥpadaṁ tat parimārgitavyaṁ
Yasmin gatānani vartanti bhūyaḥ
tam evachādyaṁ puruṣhaṁprapadye
yataḥ pravṛittiḥ prasṛitā purāṇī

The real form of this tree is not perceived in this world, neither its beginning nor end nor its continued existence. But one must cut down this deep-rooted *Aśvattha* tree with a strong axe of detachment. Then, one must search out the base of the tree, which is the Supreme Lord, from whom streamed forth the activity of the universe a long time ago. Upon taking refuge in Him, one will not return to this world again.

Mukundananda gives the following commentary:

> "Shree Krishna says that the mystery of the *aśvattha* tree is not easy to understand for the embodied souls, as they are deeply entangled in the continuous cycle of life and death. The buds of the tree, which are the objects of the senses, lure them into developing desires. Ignorant souls keep working hard towards fulfilling these desires, which only keep increasing and nourishing the tree to grow further. When such desires are fulfilled, they return with double the intensity, forming greed. But when obstructed, it causes anger, fogs the intellect, and further deepens the ignorance.". (9)

In its bodily form, the soul only thinks of itself as the person in flesh and bones. It is forgetful of its origin and its eternal existence. It identifies itself with its human name, family, country, etc. Thus, the living being gets involved in unfruitful endeavours to satisfy bodily needs and material happiness. Sometimes, a human being commits sins to satiate one's desires knowingly or unknowingly. These cause it to move downward and reborn in the lower species and nether regions. Sometimes, it gets attracted to the leaves of this tree, which are the ritualistic ceremonies of the Vedas; this help accumulate pious merits. The propensity for material pleasures drives the human being to be involved in such pious activities. The pious merits help the soul move upward in the celestial abodes; when these merits deplete, it falls into the lower forms, and this cycle continues. Thus, Chaitanya Mahaprabhu said:

kṛishṇabhuli 'sei jīvanādi-bahirmukha,
ataevam āyātāredeya samsāra-duḥkha
kabhuswargeuṭhāya, kabhunarakeḍubāya,
daṇḍya-jane rājāyenanadītechubāy. (10)

Since the soul is forgetful of God for eternity, the material energy is subjecting it to worldly miseries. Sometimes, this energy lifts the soul to the celestial abodes; at other times, it drops it down to hellish regions. Such an action is akin to the torture meted out by kings in olden times. In the olden days, some kings ordered a very torturous punishment, wherein a person's head was immersed into the water almost till suffocation, then released for a few gasps, again pushed into the water, and the process repeated. The condition is similar for a soul trapped in the tree of material existence, being pushed back and forth between the upper and lower regions according to its merits. When born in the celestial forms, it enjoys some temporary relief, which fades soon, and the soul falls back into the human realm.

Several lifetimes have passed, and the soul continues to work towards material enjoyment. Such a situation has caused the tree to expand its roots of desire further and has become huge. Yet, one can cut this tree with dispassion, says Lord Krishna. The remedy for the soul's never-ending suffering is *asaṅg*, which means detachment. The axe of detachment can cut the roots of desires nourished by the three modes of material nature. The Lord further explains that this axe of detachment can only be developed with the knowledge of the self. One must realize that:

"I am not this material body, but an eternal spiritual being. The everlasting happiness that I pursue cannot be achieved with material things. My endeavours towards gratification of the material desires of this material body have no satiation; they are only getting me further trapped in the *samsara* or the web of life and death."

With detachment, one can stop further growth of the tree roots, and due to lack of nourishment, the tree starts to wither.

The next step is to look for the base of this upside-down tree, which, in real terms, is on the top and much higher than everything else. It is here that the Supreme Lord of all creation resides. As Lord Krishna had earlier mentioned, "I am the origin of all creation. Everything proceeds from Me. The wise who know this perfectly, worship Me with great faith and devotion." (Verse 10.8) Therefore, to find the ultimate source, we must surrender to God, as this verse explains: "I submit unto Him from whom the universe came into being a long time ago."

This way, the unfathomable tree can be conquered and axed. However, in an earlier verse, Lord Krishna also said: "My divine energy, Maya, consisting of the three modes of nature, is very tough to overcome. But those who surrender unto Me cross over it easily." (Verse 7.14) Therefore, the only way to cut down the *asvattha* tree is by surrendering to the Supreme Lord and taking refuge under Him. By doing this, we will not return to this material world, and after death will go to His divine Abode.

Peepal (*Asvattha*) as a World Tree

Throughout human history, most cultures described their homeland as "the centre of the world" because it was the Centre of the universe known to them. For example, the name 'China— Middle Kingdom' expresses an ancient belief that the country stood at the Centre of the world. In India, the mythical Mount Sumeru was considered the Centre of the earth. Instead of a mountain, a tree can also form the axis mundi. The tree provides an axis that unites the three planes:

- Its branches reach for the sky.
- Its trunk meets the earth.
- Its roots reach the underworld.

In India, the peepal tree became the cosmic tree and forms the *axis mundi*. In Norse mythology, the Yggdrasil, or World Ash, formed the cosmic tree where Odin found enlightenment. Odin was a highly revered god in Germanic and Norse mythology. According to the beliefs that existed in the Ancient and Middle Ages, Odin was the bestower of wisdom, healing, death, royalty, the gallows, knowledge, war, battle, victory, sorcery, poetry, frenzy, and the runic alphabet, and portrays him as the husband of the goddess Frigg. She was the goddess associated with foresight and wisdom in Norse mythology. According to the Slavic, Finnish, and Baltic people, the oak tree was the cosmic tree in the Celtic nations. Celtic nations are a group of six geographical regions that share the Celtic language. The six regions are Ireland, Scotland, Wales, Brittany (now a part of the French Republic), Cornwall (now a county in southwest England), and the Isle of Mann (a self-governing territory under the British Crown). They have an international league to promote cooperation) The *Jian-mu tree (Kien-mu)* was the cosmic tree for the Chinese. The tree of knowledge and the tree of life in the creation myth story is known to everyone. This myth in Genesis, in the Old Testament of the Bible, represents another aspect of the cosmic tree. Each of these trees is said to stand at the Centre of the paradise garden, from which four rivers flow to nourish the whole world.

Though this concept of *Axis mundi* and the cosmic tree had arisen in many cultures, it is in India that this cosmic tree attained such profound metaphysical dimensions through the peepal tree. The cosmic tree was held as the great Universal Mother, the goddess of nature. Many cultures believe that the cosmic tree stands for the sacredness of the world, its creation, continuation, and fertility. The peepal tree is also known as the 'tree of life' and the 'tree of knowledge'. During the *Rg Vedic* (*Rig Vedic*) times, the peepal tree formed the symbol of the cosmos. During the *Atharva Veda* period, people worshipped peepal for victory over their enemies and the birth of male progeny and regarded it as the abode of gods and goddesses. Later, in *the Puranas,* the peepal became the abode of the goddess Lakshmi. It is also sacred to the sun god. In *Maha Bharatha,* there is a reference that worshipping *aśvattha* (peepal) is worshipping the cosmos. This tree is a constant presence in all temples, especially in Vishnu temples. Devotes worship the tree daily during their evening prayer. Devotees circumambulate the tree, chanting the prayer:

> *moolatho brahmarupaya*
> *madhyatho vishnuroopaya*
> *āgratho ṣivaroopaya*
> *vrikṣarajayathe nama*

I bow to the sacred peepal tree, the king of all trees; I bow to Brahma in the roots, Vishnu in the trunk, and Śiva in the branches. The above four lines form the first stanza of the *aśvattha stothram (hymn* on *aśvattha*).

Apart from the *axis mundi* aspect, *asvattha* is also considered the world tree (*samsara vriksha*). In this statement, Swami Chidbhavananda compares the *Asvattha* with the phenomenal world that is perishable but not constant and steady. (11) Like the tree, *samsara* originated in Brahman, and as it branches out, it gets more and more materialized, and roots grow down to earth, back to the *samsara*. In other words, the functioning of *samsara* is like that of the peepal tree. Both receive their sustenance from the earth, grow tall, and grow out, receiving the external world's stimuli (such as air and water). Then, the life force flows back to the roots, thus making them grow more profound and more robust. What appears in the manifest world (branches. leaves, fruits, etc.), while behind the manifest world, there is an unmanifest world that propels the life force from the roots to the treetop and then back to the root tip. This unmanifest world is the Brahman that controls all the manifest world.

The deification of the tree *Asvattha* during the Puranic period is best exemplified in the story of the birth of the renowned Sage Vishwamitra, whom many people consider the National Sage of India. This story serves as an example of the fertility-granting power of the *Asvattha* tree. *The Mahabharata* and *Vishnu Purana* provide this legend in detail. King Dadhi's daughter Satyavathi was the consort of the famous Sage Hrichikan (name given as Ruchika in some versions) and grandson (son according to some versions) of Sage Bhrigu. Satyavathi requested that Sage Bhrigu bless her and her mother with sons who have great qualities and power. Bhrigu prepared two vessels of porridge and instructed Satyavati:

"You and your mother partake of these two *Carus* (porridge)...For having a male child, your mother should take the red porridge after embracing the *Asvattha*, and you should take the white one after embracing the *Udumbara*."

Saying thus, the Sage went away. But some confusion occurred, Satyavathi took the red porridge and embraced the *Aśvattha,* while her mother took the white one and embraced the *Udumbara.* Over time, Satyavathi gave birth to Jamadagni and her mother to Vishwamitra.

There are several variations of the above myth in different epics. According to one version, it was sage Hrichikan who gave the porridge. Another version is that Sathyvathi's mother deliberately exchanged the porridge. The *Skanda purana* provides the details as follows: The bride's (Sathyavathi's) mother advised the daughter to ask the Sage (Hrichikan) for an excellent boy full of Brahmana's virtues for herself and a brave Kshatriya boy for the Queen. The Sage performed '*Putreshtu Yagna'* to fulfil the desires of the daughter and her mother, viz., a boy of great Brahmanik radiance and another boy with unusual Kshatriya vivacity, respectively, and gave away two seedlings (sprouts), one for herself and another for her mother. After consuming the respective seedlings, he instructed his wife to embrace an *Asvattha* tree and her mother to embrace a *Udumbara* tree. But the daughter and the mother wanted to test the Sage and thus exchanged the seedlings and the trees. The Sage discovered the exchange of seedlings and trees and got quite angry, but the young wife sincerely begged the husband to conceive a boy with Brahmanic qualities, although he might have a Kshatriya background. The Sage replied that there could not be a reversal of the situation, yet the boy born of Kshatriya origin might be an illustrious Sage or a Rajarshi. Thus, Vishwamitra was born to Sathyavati and Jamadagni to the Queen. Whatever the variations in the legend, the fact remains that *Asvattha* and *Udumbara* could grant offspring, according to belief. This belief in fertility became a significant point of worship of *Asvattha* from ancient times onwards.

According to the Atharva *Veda,* gods sit under celestial trees. On earth, the rishis (sages) sit under the *aśvattha.* Its shade is said to confirm miraculous powers, like understanding the language of animals or remembering previous births. The presiding deity of the peepal tree is the Sun; in some texts, Śiva is the presiding deity. Goddess Lakshmi resides in the Peepal tree. It is also very sacred for the Buddhists; for them, it is the *Bodhi* tree, the tree of knowledge. While meditating under the tree, Gautama attained enlightenment and became the enlightened Sri Buddha. In Sri Lanka, it is called the *Bo* tree. The terms bodhi, peepal, and *asvattha* are used interchangeably.

Asvattha Becomes the Bodhi Tree

The *bodhi* tree is the tree of wisdom, the tree of enlightenment; we know wisdom precedes enlightenment. The *bodhi* tree is visualized as having its roots immersed in or drinking deep from the waters of infinity and its branches and leaves reaching the void and lit by clear light. As the Buddhists say, it is the tree of refuge, the abode of security from the 'raging dragons of desires'. The leaves are bright green, indicating the youthfulness of spring; the bark has the darkness and fragrance of the forest, indicating the outward life moulded in the crucible of experience. It has the fruits of knowledge; they are not forbidden fruits. Instead, they are fruits intended for all the seekers; the fruits on the lower branches bestow knowledge of good and evil;

those of the upper branches give wisdom and immortality. The *bodhi* tree unites all worlds; there are no sentinels or guardians, and all seekers can take its fruits and gain insight as much as their minds can. However, the seeker must travel a long path, not a royal road; they must devote many years or even an entire life to undertake this journey. Very few people have tried to tread this difficult path; only a few have reached the destination, like Gautama the Buddha.

The *bodhi* tree is a symbolic representation of the individual's journey into enlightenment and infinity. Like the seed of the *bodhi* tree, which is so minute but grows into such a mighty tree, so is the mind. The tree is rooted in the ground and nurtured by the soil and water, just as the mind is rooted in ego, nurtured by desires. As the tree grows beyond the ground, it grows upward, leaving the ground and reaching towards heaven. Yet the sap must flow back to the trunk, to the ground; the roots grow deep, drawing from the deep waters; the more profound it grows, the stronger the tree becomes. Just like that, as we are trying to reach heaven, our mind is constantly being drawn back to the ground, and we grow strong only by going deep into the depths of our mind to tap the forces lying deep within us. Such is the state of humankind, constantly being pulled in two directions. One is the direction of freedom and ultimate liberation, transcending all boundaries. The other is rootedness, security, comfort, and the ego that will not leave hold on the ground and is satisfied being on the ground throughout one's lifetime. The *bodhi* tree and Sri Buddha are models. Buddha showed the path to liberation and the means of achieving it. Sri Buddha is the most remarkable human being to have ever walked this earth.

The most revered tree on earth is the Bodhi tree, also known as the Bo tree, located in the Buddha Vihar in Anuradhapura, Sri Lanka. Worship of *the Bo* tree is widespread in all Hindu and Buddhist countries, from Sri Lanka to Japan. The history of the *bodhi* tree is deeply intertwined with the enlightenment of Gautama while meditating under the peepal tree in Gaya, in Bihar. Two aspects connect the *bodhi* tree of Gaya with Sri Buddha. The first is that Buddha sat under this tree when he got enlightenment. The second, he spent a whole week—the second week after the enlightenment— gazing at this tree with motionless eyes. To fully appreciate the episode of Buddha's enlightenment, it is essential to follow his life for a while. The bodhi tree, as the sacred tree of knowledge, holds a significant place in Buddhism, serving as a powerful symbol of spiritual enlightenment and rebirth, and connecting us to our rich spiritual heritage and traditions.

Buddha's enlightenment under the Bodhi tree.

There is a general understanding that the spiritual rebirth of the world starts in the mind of man/woman, and the tree of life grows out of his own heart, the centre of his being, the axis of his world. As they go through different planes of life, the tree of life sprouts and develops within them and spreads its branches in ever-new infinities; in fact, they can (potentially) turn into a tree of life, into a tree of enlightenment. One of the finest expressions of this spiritual rebirth is the life of Gautama, the Buddha. In Buddhism, each of the 28 successive Buddhas is equated with a particular tree of life or tree of enlightenment, a *Chaitya vriksha (vrksa)*. The names of the various *Chaitya vrikshas* are listed in the *Buddhavamsa* and equated with the presently known trees. Buddhists revere the *bodhi vrkisha* or *bodhi druma* (tree of knowledge), under which every Buddha achieves enlightenment (bodhi). The Bodhi Tree of each Buddha is taken from the local vegetative milieu; for example, Kakusandha Buddha's Bodhi Tree is the Sirissa or Sirish (*Albizia lebbeck*), Konagamana Buddha's is the cluster fig (*Ficus glomerata*), Kassapa Buddha's is the banyan (Indian fig, *Ficus bengalensis*), the *chaitya vriksha* of the future Buddha (Maitreya) is *Naga Pushpa (Messua ferrea)*, and so on. The *Asvattha* (*Ficus religiosa*) is the sacred tree of knowledge (*samyaksam bodhi*) associated with the last historical Buddha, Sakyamuni. All such trees and others related to later events, particularly in Sakyamuni Buddha's life, would have been familiar within the biogeographical limits of early Buddhist activity in North India. (12, 13)

The *Lalitavistara*, a Buddhist epic, tells how Queen Mother Mahamaya came to an *Asvattha* tree "which [had] supported the mothers of the previous Jinas": all the previous Buddhas had been born under the same tree. At the time of birth, a branch of the *Asvattha* tree bent down towards her; she grasped it in her right hand, and the infant sprang forth from her right side: the Buddha was born at the foot of the World Tree. (*Note:* There is controversy over the tree under which Gautama was born. See the next section). Haldar (1977) and Burkill (1946) suggested that this description owes its origin to the belief that the foot of this tree (or the tree itself) is a fertility symbol. Coomaraswamy (1971) believes that the tree had originally been a *Chaitya-vriksha* (the abode of a tree spirit) when Mahamaya halted beneath it and that the tree's spirit bent down the branch.

The peepal tree (*Ficus religiosa*) appears again in connection with another significant event in the life of the Sakyamuni Buddha, namely the enlightenment. Having passed through 43 previous incarnations as a tree spirit, he finally attains the highest knowledge (Enlightenment) 'sitting under the sacred tree of Brahma. With this event, which is assumed to have taken place on the banks of the Niranjana River at Bodhgaya (in Bihar, south of Rajgir in the northern Gangetic Plain) in the year 528 B.C., this already sacred tree acquires a historical dimension as a monument with a specific place not only in the sacred story but also in the development of Buddhist religion. The pipal tree relates to the Buddha's Enlightenment. It has been adopted as the specific sign of that event and has since been worshipped as the symbol of that pivotal event. (Snodgrass 1985:183). At this stage in its evolution, the sacred tree becomes the Tree of Knowledge of Good and Evil. It also becomes vocal in the light of divine wisdom, given expression by Sakyamuni. The Tree of Life is also the Tree of the Knowledge of Good and Evil. In the Buddhist view, the tree as cosmos, as the procession of continuous life, yielding all the fruits of existence, is simultaneously the Wisdom Tree (*jnana-vriksha*) and the Tree of Life (*jiva vriksha*). However, the two aspects are inseparably joined in non-duality: they are two aspects of the same truism that transcends all dichotomies. The peepal tree was already an object of miraculous efficacy in pre-Buddhist times and, therefore, worthy of worship (as indicated earlier in the Atharva Veda). Thus, peepal became essential to the new Buddhist cult, as the Bodhi Tree of the Sakyamuni Buddha. Then, the tree was first enclosed in a sanctuary and, later, a temple-like edifice with an overhanging platform built around the tree.

Buddha's awakening

From the Vedic times to the Buddha's time, there is a gap of about one and a half millennia. This period saw the growth of Brahmanical Hinduism come to prominence, and the caste system took its stronghold in all spheres of ancient Indian life and activities. Before the birth of Buddha, Hinduism was at its worst. The traditions, religion, and philosophy developed by the Aryan invaders as they spread along the Indo-Gangetic plains have undergone much degeneration; most people were ignorant of the lofty ideals of the Upanishads. The philosophical ideas of the Upanishads were adulterated with much that was inconsistent with them; its' monotheism stood against Vedic polytheism. The Brahmanical priests evolved all types of ritual practices for exploiting innocent people while maintaining their sway over the entire population. The priests urged the laity that they could appease the angry gods by singing hymns, sacrificing animals, offering prayers, fasting, and so on. The people were made to believe that the gods could be made to grant petitions using certain ceremonies, which only the priests could perform. Under this system, a sinner was he who failed to pay for praise, prayer, and sacrifice. The priestly cast, therefore, gained social supremacy and wielded immense power over its followers. At the same time, there was widespread resentment among the young, thinking people and such feelings led to the establishment of new schools of thought. Some six systems of Indian philosophy are said to have originated at that time. However, the laity believed the Brahmans, and for them, ceremonies were the crux of the religion. The commons lived in terror of demons and spiritual gods, and they thought these forces needed to be pleased through worship and sacrifices, for which they had to depend on the Brahmins and pay them through their noses. Amidst such conditions, there was a need for a great personality to show the proper way of life.

Opinions differ as to the dates of Siddhartha Gautama's life. Historians have dated his birth and death as circa 563-483 BCE, but more recent research suggests that he lived later than this, from around 490 BCE until circa 410

BCE. (17). The Buddha at his birth was called Siddhartha. His family name was Gautama. His parents were King Suddhodana, ruling raja of the Sakya clan, and Queen Maya, daughter of Ankara, also a Sakya king. Legend tells us that for twenty years, the Queen had no children; then, after having a strange dream of a white elephant entering through her side, she became pregnant. According to the custom of the time, the Queen returned to her own home for the delivery, and while on the way, in the beautiful spring sunshine, she rested in the flower garden of Lumbini Park. All about her were Asoka blossoms, and in delight, she reached out her right arm to pluck a branch and the prince was born precisely at that time, from her right side. Everyone in Heaven and Earth extolled the glory of the Queen and her princely child and danced joyfully. This memorable day was the eighth of April in ca. 563 BC. The joy of the King was extreme as he named the child Siddhartha, which means "every wish fulfilled." (18). There is a controversy as to the identity of the tree under which Gautama was born. The alternative trees indicated are Asoka (*Saraca asoka*), Sirisa (*Albizzia lebbeck*), Sal (*Shorea robusta*), and Peepal (*Ficus religiosa*).

In the palace, however, delight was quickly followed by sorrow, for after seven days, lovely Queen Maya suddenly passed away. Fortunately, her younger sister, Prajapati Gotami, became the child's foster mother and brought him up with loving care. According to the legends, a hermit who visited the palace predicted that the prince would become either a great spiritual teacher or a king of kings, and his father, anxious that he should be the latter, had him trained in material exercises, riding, and martial arts.

As Siddhartha grew up, his curiosity could not be contained. He felt that his life of luxury was empty. At 29,

Siddhartha persuaded his chariot driver, Channa, to take him out of the palace to the city. There, he encountered the Four Sights that changed his life and outlook forever. The four sights were:

An old person: Siddhartha had never seen an old person before. He asked his chariot driver, Channa, what he was looking at. Channa explained that when people get older, they physically decline.

A sick person: When Siddhartha saw an ill person by the side of the road, he was upset, as he had never before seen anyone who was sick and helpless. Channa explained that people get ill during their lives and become powerless.

A dead person: The third sight was a dead person being carried. Channa explained that everyone dies eventually.

The fourth sight was a holy man (an ascetic) who lived a self-denial life. This person made Siddhartha curious because the holy man looked totally at peace. After Channa explained the first three sights, Siddhartha was shocked. Then, when he encountered the holy man (the fourth sight), he was struck by how calm and serene the holy man seemed amid the crowds and noise. From that point, Siddhartha knew that his path would be understanding, not the privilege and responsibility of royalty.

The mental struggle went on in the mind of the prince until his twenty-ninth year when his only child, Rahula, was born. The birth of a son seemed to bring things to a climax, and he decided to leave his palace, where he was virtually a prisoner, and to seek the solution of his mental unrest in the homeless life of a mendicant. This plan he carried out one night by leaving the castle with only his attendant, Channa, and his favourite horse, snow-white Kantaka, and even these he left behind him when he had crossed the river that marked the boundary of his father's kingdom. It is essential to bear in mind the fact that this great renunciation was made, not in old age but in youth, nor from a satiety of worldly pleasures but with a fuller power to enjoy them, not from poverty and therefore having no worldly loss to sustain, but with plenty and the means of satisfying all cravings, and that it was made more from sympathy with the sorrow of others than from any personal sorrow within himself. (20, 21)

From the scriptures, we learn that Siddhartha left the boundaries of his kingdom and went eastward to Rajagriha, the capital of King Bimbisara of Maghada. Two noted Brahmins, Arada Kalama and Udraka Ramaputra, dwelt in the neighbourhood. Gautama went to them to quench his thirst for knowledge, but these teachers could not satisfy him, even though he had mastered their philosophy. Then he resolved to leave them and betake himself to Uruvilva, near the present Mahabodhi temple of Buddha Gaya, to practice severe asceticism, which was prevalent among the hermits of his day. Gautama practised many varieties of it for six years, thinking that perhaps the soul might spring free from all earthly ties and become united with the God of Eternity, Brahma. He underwent the severest discipline in the mortifying of his body, sitting mute and motionless, controlling even his breath. So still, he sat in meditation, and birds and beasts moved about him unafraid. He took less and less food and water until, it is said, he ate scarcely more than one grain of rice or sesame seed each day. He grew thinner and thinner in body and fainter in strength (22, 23)

At last, one day, when he could no longer think, a dumb instinct awoke in him; he crawled down to the water and lay in warm, shallow water, utterly done. The five ascetics with whom he had held counsel and who expected great results from this incredible suffering said, one to another: "He will die now. The ascetic Gautama will die." At last, supporting himself by a bough, he crept up the bank. A little refreshed and able to think again, he perceived that divine knowledge would not be found by such means. He realised that asceticism was not the means to genuinely noble insight and deliverance. (24)

Every spring, a sparrow came and built its nest on his shoulder. Then, one spring, it did not return. Tears of loneliness filled his eyes. "All these years, I have spent in unspeakable pain, and still there's sadness in my heart," he said. "What's the point? "

Suddenly, what was that? The sound of singing and the vibration of dancing feet roused him from his sadness. Words of a song drifted up to him from the road where a group of girls was singing on their way to the village:

> "With the strings too loose, the lute does not sound.
> With the strings too tight, they will break apart.
> Not too loose, not too tight, the lute sounds just right!" (25).

'What a fool I have been! I have tightened my strings of life too tight," he said. "How can I find Truth in a body so lean and wasted? One cannot find true happiness in too much pleasure or pain but in the Middle Path.'

Leaning on his staff, Siddhartha went to the river and washed away the filth on his body. The water was cool and refreshing, and the sandy bottom felt pleasant under his feet. But after bathing, he was so weak that he almost fainted. Tired and weary, he rested on the riverbank under an old Banyan tree. According to legends, on that morning, on the forest's edge, a lotus flower sprang up from the ground bearing a jewelled bowl of rice – milk (rice porridge). The gods watching over Siddhartha sent Sujata, a heavenly maiden, to offer him rice milk. He ate silently and then, looking at the maiden, said, "If you had not given me food, I would have died without finding Truth. May happiness come to you." With renewed strength, Siddhartha stood up, put the empty bowl afloat in the river, and declared, "If I am to become a Buddha, may this bowl float upstream." And it did. As the bowl cut its way against the current, it got into a whirlpool and whirled down, down to the jewelled chambers of the Dragon King, Muchalinda. Catching the jewelled bowl, Muchalinda held it up and announced, "Siddhartha will become a Buddha. Let us rejoice!" The sky darkened and the great Garuda bird swooped into the swirling water. Snapping up the bowl, he took it to the Tushita Heaven. Then, the river spirits came and sprayed Siddhartha with showers of emeralds, sapphires, and diamonds that fell in a sparkling heap at his feet. (26)

On a full moon day in May, Siddhartha waded across the river on his way to Gaya (in the present Bihar). On the road, he met a poor young boy named Svasti, sobbing bitterly. On his back was a bundle of kusa grass. When he saw Siddhartha, he ran to hide, but Siddhartha blocked his way. Svasti stood dumbstruck.

"Why are you crying, my friend?" Siddhartha asked.

"O Holy One. Stay back! I'm untouchable," Svasti cried.

Siddhartha put his hands on Svasti's shoulder. "I asked not what caste you are, but why you are unhappy?"

Never had Svasti been treated with such understanding. A strange feeling came over him. No longer afraid, he dried his tears and asked, "Have you seen my cows? They ran away while I was cutting grass. Their owner will surely beat me for this!"

"Come, I will help you," said Siddhartha. They walked down to the river, where Siddhartha cut a reed and made a flute, upon which he played. Sweet notes filled the quiet forest. By and by, they could hear cowbells.

Look, the cows have come back," cried Svasti. Picking up a stick, he began to beat them. "I'll teach you to run away, dumb beasts!" The eyes of the cows widened, and the woods echoed with their loud cries as they felt the sting of Svasti's stick. Again, they ran away from him.

Siddhartha said, "Beating animals turns them away from you and fills them with mistrust and anger."

Svasti thought for a moment. Filled with shame, he took Siddhartha's flute and played. Hearing the music, the cows calmed down and returned.

Then Svasti handed a bundle of the sweet-smelling grass to Siddhartha. "Here, this is for you and the lesson you taught me." (27)

When the sun spread the soft, glorious evening rays on earth, Siddhartha spread the sweet kusa grass under the boughs of a lovely peepal tree and sat down with his legs crossed. He then made an irrevocable vow:

> "Even if my blood dries up and my muscles shrink, leaving skin and bones only, I will not leave this seat until I finally and absolutely achieve the goal of finding, for myself and all mankind, a way of deliverance from the suffering of the cycles of life and death."

In short, Siddhartha sat under the Bodhi tree and vowed not to quit the spot until he had attained Enlightenment. (28)

Now Mara, the Evil One, heard this vow and boomed! "I've got to stop Siddhartha! If he wins, I'll be doomed." And calling his armies of demon sons and daughters around him, he mounted a magnificent elephant and made war on the silent figure. Mara tried all the magical powers at his command to stop Gautama, but failed. All Mara's weapons turned into flower petals and floated on the ground. (29)

> "One by one, Siddhartha met Mara's armies and defeated them with his goodness. The night became still and peaceful. A full moon crept over the horizon, and a mist of tiny red blossoms dropped on the prince's golden shoulders. He went into deep meditation. Like an eagle soaring to the sun, his mind passed beyond the limits of human understanding. He saw the world as it is, not the way it appears. As his mind soared higher, he saw the rounds of birth and death that all living beings undergo: one birth, ten births, a zillion births. It was the same for everyone – from a tiny ant to the greatest king. All living beings are born, live, and die, not once but repeatedly. The cycle is like a wheel that spins round and round. It is called the "Wheel of Rebirth." Those who do good deeds are reborn into happiness, and those who do evil are reborn into misery, as a beggar, an enslaved person, or even a mouse. That is known as the law of "*karma*." He saw that suffering was due to selfish desire. The more one has, the more one wants. But when desire ends, suffering vanishes like night. The light of true happiness shines forth, bringing Enlightenment. Then, one need never be reborn and suffer again." (30)

On the 49th day, according to legend:

> "The Buddha entered a state of concentration so deep and clear he began to see the nature of his mind and that of the universe. During three phases or "watches" of the night, he apprehended how suffering and unhappiness are caused by our actions and our clinging to an illusory sense of self. And he became aware of how to let go of all that. As the morning star appeared in the sky, Siddhartha opened his eyes and looked at the world through the eyes of a Buddha. He was perfect in wisdom and found the path that leads beyond all the sufferings and difficulties of this world. 'Wonder of wonders!' he exclaimed. 'All living beings have the Buddha nature and can become Buddhas. I will show them the Way.' And on that glorious morning with its glorious light, gods and humans rejoiced. The blind could see. The deaf could hear. The lame could walk. Dry rivers flowed with water, and flowers bloomed out of season. The animals hushed their cries, and people stopped quarrelling. A wonderful fragrance filled the air. Encircled in a wreath of ever-changing colours- now blue, now orange, now green, now pink – the Buddha sat in perfect peace. His hair curled to the right, and a flesh mound appeared on his head. A soft breeze lifted the Bodhi tree leaves, and the world was peaceful." (31, 32).

The Mahabodhi Temple at Bodh Gaya, in Bihar, India, marks the traditional place where the Buddha attained Enlightenment under the *bodhi* tree. The temple was first constructed during Ashoka's reign in the third century B.C.; the present structure—built entirely of brick—dates from the fifth century A.D. According to the Pali canon, Buddha had given several discourses. In the Longer Discourse to Saccaka, the Buddha describes his Enlightenment in three stages:

During the first watch of the night, the Buddha discovered all his past lives in the cycle of rebirth, realizing that he had been born and reborn countless times before (retrocognition).

During the second watch, the Buddha attained the use of the third eye and discovered the Law of Karma and the importance of living by the Eightfold Path.

During the third watch, the Buddha discovered the twelve-fold chain of causation and the principle of interdependent co-origination. He realised that if there are no independent substances, then everything must be dependent on every other thing. The Buddha passed through the eight stages of Dhyana (Pali: Jhana) and reached Nirvana, "with substrate" – i.e., while still occupying a body. He also discovered there was "no self," i.e., no ATMAN, a substantial enduring self, the "Higher" Self, which the Buddha rejected. (33)

Fourth watch (happened at daybreak):

> "The Fourth Watch of the Night is the breakthrough to Enlightenment, the direct and unambiguous awakening to the Buddha's mind, and the entrance into Nirvana. It occurred at dawn when the Buddha's long night of *samsara*, and his countless lives of darkness, struggle, and suffering ended. The new day's dawn was that of enlightened awareness and the great awakening from sleep. The Fourth Watch is the reunion of all worlds. The first three-quarters of the night are exploration,

learning the limits of the ego, species identity, and of consciousness itself. We also call these states as self-consciousness, group consciousness, and absolute consciousness." (34)

In the words of the Buddha himself:

"My heart, thus knowing, thus seeing, was released from the fermentation of sensuality, released from the fermentation of becoming, released from the fermentation of ignorance. With the release, there was the knowledge, 'Released.' I discerned that 'Birth is ended, the holy life fulfilled, the task done. There is nothing further for this world." (35)

Gautama Siddhartha became the Buddha. He received Enlightenment; ignorance dispelled, knowledge arose; darkness dispelled, light arose. He attained the highest consciousness and received it with a cry of "light!" He reached the goal and won the highest insight. He became the perfect one, a Buddha. He obtained the "pure, spotless eye of the truth", and beheld his many former existences with their unique character and details. He understood the cause of suffering and the means of ending all sufferings and reaching Deliverance, the perfect peace of Nirvana. For a while, illuminated with all wisdom, sat the Buddha, lost in contemplation of the universe as it is. And at least, lifting his voice, he cried aloud in triumph his song of victory:

"...Through many of Samsara's births
I hasten seeking, finding not
The builder of this house:
Pain is birth again, and again.
O builder of this house you're seen,
You shall not build a house again,
All your beams have given away,

Rafters of the ridge decayed,
Mind to the unconditioned gone,
Exhaustion of craving has it reached..." (37)

This memorable day was the *Vaishakha Poornima* (full moon day of Vaisakha; April – May), 623 BC. He was thirty-five years old. The Buddha's Enlightenment was not the result of miraculous or mystic occurrences caused by the influence of extramundane, divine power, but the direct apprehension of the truth; not a "revelation," but a "self-realization."

Fisher (1993) quotes Asvaghosha, the famous Buddhist Scholar:

> "At that moment of the fourth watch when the dawn came up, and all that moves was stilled, the great seer reached the stage that knows no alteration, the sovereign leader, the state of omniscience. When the Buddha knew this truth, the earth swayed like a person drunk with wine. The four quarters shone bright with crowds of Siddhas, and mighty drums resounded in the sky. A pleasant breeze blew softly, and heaven rained moisture from a cloudless sky, and the trees there dropped flowers and fruits out of due season as if to do him honour. At that time, just as in paradise, the *Mandāra* flowers, lotuses, and water lilies of gold and beryl fell from the sky and bestrewed the place of the Shakya sage." (38)

Gautama, now the Buddha, stayed at the same spot for a few more days. One week, he sat there gazing at the tree that gave him Enlightenment with un-winking eyes. The peepal has now become the Bodhi. He thanked the peepal tree and went away to find his five friends. After days of walking, he crossed the Ganges River and came to Deer Park near Benares. The park, long adorned with flowering trees, was filled with the songs of birds and the scent of Sala flowers. The five friends, seeing him, whispered among themselves, "Here comes Siddhartha, that luxury-loving fellow. Let's ignore him."

But as the Buddha slowly approached, they saw his radiance and glory. Before they knew it, they were preparing a seat for him and washing his feet. Then the Buddha spoke to them, saying, "I have discovered the Path to true happiness. If you listen and practice yourselves, you will know that what I say is true. (Daneuse Murty 1892, and others that appeared in www; Bodhi tree or *Bodhi – druma*, Chapter 8, in Alexander Cunningham's book, Mahabodhi or the great Buddhist temple under the Bodhi tree at Buddha Gaya,1892.)

As the full moon rose that July night, the Buddha gave his first sermon, "Turning the Dharma Wheel." He spoke the Four Noble Truths. In life, there is suffering. The cause of suffering is selfish desire. Cutting off desire leads to the end of suffering. The path to ending suffering is to follow the Eightfold Path: right views, right thoughts, right speech, right action, right livelihood, right effort, right mindfulness, and right concentration. (39, 40).

The five friends realized that Siddhartha had become a Buddha, and they became his first disciples. They formed a community known as the Sangha. The Sangha grew, and soon, there were sixty monks. The Buddha taught them meditations to purify their body, speech, and mind. He gave them rules about wearing their robes and eating their daily vegetarian food. He made a rule at once whenever a wrong was done so it would not happen again. These rules later became the Precepts of Buddhism.

After three months, the Buddha said, "O monks, go forth for the happiness of the many. Teach this Dharma, which is wonderful in the beginning, in the middle, and wonderful in the end. Let each go a different way." Joyfully, the disciples set out in all directions, walking from village to village, sleeping under the stars, and braving all sorts of weather and hardship. All they asked for was a little food on the way. Their lives were extremely simple: owning a bowl, a robe, a sitting cloth, a needle, a water strainer, and a razor. They turned the Dharma Wheel everywhere they went, giving people comfort and happiness.

Peepal and Buddhism

The earliest records on the peepal tree are the *Kalinga Bodhi Jataka,* which gives vivid details of the tree and its surroundings before Buddha's Enlightenment, and the *Asoka Vadana,* which relates the story of Emperor Aśoka (of the third century BC) and his conversion to Buddhism. King Ashoka's second wife, Tisayaraksita, jealous of her husband's love for the Bodhi (or perhaps the nymphs she believed it harboured), had the tree cut down. Ashoka then piled earth around the stump and poured milk on its roots. The tree miraculously revived and grew to a height of 37 meters. Ashoka subsequently built a three-meter-high stone wall to protect the tree. However, King Pushyamitra Shunga destroyed the tree within a half-century while persecuting Buddhism. The tree planted to replace the Bodhi, possibly at that stage, was a scion from the original. In 600 A.D., Sesanka, a fanatic Saivite (follower of the Siva cult) King, once again destroyed the Bodhi tree. Hiuen Sang, in his travelogues, recorded this event. In 620 AD, King Purnavarma planted a sapling, believed to be of the original *Bodhi* tree, in the same spot. There is also a view that the King arranged for a branch of the Mahabodhi in

Anuradhapura to be bought in for the above re-planting. Hiuen Sang recorded that on the day of the *Vaishakha* celebration, thousands of people from far and wide would come to anoint the base of the holy tree with scented water and milk. This tree survived for hundreds of years till 1876, when it fell over during a storm. The present bodhi tree is a seedling raised from the former tree.

However, some people also doubt whether the present tree of Bodh Gaya is even a scion of the original Bodhi. The current tree, which a British archaeologist named Alexander Cunningham planted in 1881, most likely represents the last in a line of replacements. Such doubts over the provenance of the Bodhi tree at Bodhi Gaya look up to the Jaya Sri Maha Bodhi at Anuradhapura as the closest authentic link to the living Buddha and hence preferred as the scion wood for establishing Bodhi trees that are central to the many Buddhist temples in Asia. (41, 42)

The Bodhi tree of Gaya with Mahabodhi temple in the background. (Believed to be the third-generation tree propagated from the original bodhi). (Courtesy Krishna Prasad)

In the *Mahabodhi* temple of Gaya, pilgrims must pay homage to the *bodhi* tree. The *Gaya Mahatmya* mentioned that before offering the funeral rites on the *Vishnupada* (footprints of Vishnu, a place with the footmarks of the Buddha), the pilgrim should go to the *bodhi* tree and pray, reciting the hymn from *Vayu Purana* and given in *Gaya Mahatmya,* which means:

> "I Salute, repeatedly Salute thee, *asvattha* tree, the tremulous leaved, the *Yajna swarupa* (sacrifice personified), the Bodhisattva, the eternal source of penance. O Peepal tree, the noblest among trees, thou art the eleventh among the Rudras, Pavaka among the Vasus and Narayana among the Devas. O, noble peepal tree, since Narayana always resides within thee, art thou the most benevolent among trees. Thou art blessed, thou destroyer of bad dreams, I Salute the God who has assumed the form of *asvattha* tree, who is the holder of conch-shell, the discus, and the mace. I Salute Hari, the lotus-eyed, who has assumed the form of a tree." (43)

The Bodhi Tree (Mahabodhi) of Anuradhapura, the most worshipped tree on earth:

The most worshipped tree on earth is the Mahabodhi tree in the Mahabodhi Vihara at Anuradhapura. During the time of Ashoka, he sent out Buddhist monks far and wide to spread the message of the Great Master and to convert people to Buddhism. Among them was Asoka's son, Thera Mahinda (Mahindra in Sanskrit), who travelled to Sri Lanka. There, King Devanampiya Tissa was receptive to the teachings of Sri Buddha and, in due course, embraced Buddhism. Mahinda ordained the King and many noblemen and commoners on the Island. Then, the queen got attracted to the Buddhist teachings, and she, along with 500 women, went to Thera Mahinda seeking admission to Buddhism. But Thera Mahinda couldn't ordain them, as according to the stipulation of Sri Buddha, a woman Buddhist *Bhikkuni* (a female monk) could only ordain women. Therefore, the Thera requested the King to depute an envoy to Emperor Asoka, asking him to send his younger sister, Theri Sanghamitta (in Sanskrit, Sanghamitra), for this purpose along with a branch of the sacred Bodhi tree., under which the great one attained supreme Enlightenment and became the Buddha. The King accordingly sent an envoy named Aritha, who sailed by ship to Pataliputra (present-day Patna in Bihar). He arrived at Asoka's palace and placed the request from the King of Sri Lanka. Asoka was not happy about sending his daughter to a distant land. But his daughter, Theri Sanghamitta (Sanghamitra), prevailed upon the emperor and got his permission. Soon, Asoka arranged to obtain a branch of the bodhi tree to carry to Sri Lanka.

The Pali chronicle *Mahavamsa* describes how Emperor Asoka acquired a branch of the bodhi tree.

> "...The King thought, 'The great Bodhi tree should not be injured with a knife. How would I take a branch?'...The King went to the great Bodhi tree, decked with various ornaments, adorned with different precious stones, garlanded with various flags, strewn with different flowers, and resounding with varying music... The army was surrounding and enclosing the Bodhi tree with a curtain. With his hands clasped in salutation, the King gazed upon the great Bodhi tree and prayed for a branch.... A stem from the southern branch

that was about four hands long cut itself off, descended, and set itself in the bowl of fragrant earth...Roots sprang forth from the cut stem and got themselves firmly set in the vase. Upon seeing this miracle, the King was greatly gladdened and uttered a cry of joy. Thus, with a hundred roots there, the great Bodhi-tree set itself on the fragrant earth, pleasing the people. At that moment the great Bodhi tree set itself in the bowl, the earth quaked, and there were various miracles.". (44)

In Mahavamsa, we get the following passage:

"At the moment that the great Bodhi tree set itself in the vase, the earth quaked, and wonders of many kinds came to pass. By the resounding of the instruments of music (which gave out sound) of themselves among gods and men, by the ringing-out of the shout of Salutation from the hosts of Devas and Brahmanas, by the crash of the clouds, (the voices) of beasts and birds, of the yakshas, and so forth, and by the crash of the quaking of the earth, all was in one tumult. Beautiful rays of six colours from the fruits and leaves of the Bodhi tree made the whole universe shine. Then, rising in the air with the vase, the great Bodhi tree stayed invisible for seven days in the snow region." (45)

In short, the description says that when Asoka prayed to the Bodhi tree, a branch severed itself, came down, and sat in the golden bowl filled with soil. The King and the Nobles carried the Bodhi sapling to the port of Pataliputra, from where a ship took the Bodhi tree down the Ganges and to the Bay of Bengal to its final destination, Lanka. Mahavamsa says that to watch over the Bodhi tree:

> "... the King appointed eighteen persons from royal families and eight from families of ministers, and eight persons from brahman families and, eight from families of traders and persons from the cowherds likewise, and from the hyena and sparrow hawk-clans, and also from the weavers and potters and all the handicrafts, from the nagas and the yakshas; then the most exalted prince had given them eight vessels of gold and eight of silver and had brought the great Bodhi-tree to a ship on the Ganges.....likewise the Theri Sanghamitta, who was barely eighteen years old at that time, with eleven *bhikkhunis* entered the ship"...the ship set sail to the distant Island of Sri Lanka.(46)

The King of Sri Lanka, Devanampiya Tissa, received the sacred object with great reverence. Accompanied by the Nobles, he descended neck-deep into the water, taking the Bodhi branch upon his head and placing it in a pavilion at the seashore. The King worshipped it for three days and acted as doorkeeper, bestowing the kingship of Lanka on the sacred Bodhi. On the tenth day, the King placed the bodhi tree upon a beautiful chariot, and he accompanied it to Anuradhapura to be planted in the Maha Megha Park at the very spot, according to the chronicle Mahavamsa, where the Bodhi trees of the Buddhas of the previous time cycles had grown. According to the chronicle, Mahavamsa, eight saplings that arose from the seeds of the branch and thirty others that occurred in the same manner were planted at various places on the Island.

The tree brought by Sanghamitta and planted in Anuradhapura by King Devanampiya Tissa became famous as the Jaya Sri Maha Bodhi, and it is in the Mahamewna gardens. The Buddhists also hold it as the Southern Branch of the historical Sri Maha Bodhi at the Buddha Gaya in Bihar, India. Gautama sat under this tree and meditated and attained Buddhahood. The planting of the Jai Maha Bodhi Tree in Anuradhapura dates to 288 BC, and it is the oldest living human-planted tree in the world (with a known planting date). The tree is now 2312 years old. All people on the Island of Sri Lanka venerate the Jai Maha Bodhi, and so do all Buddhists all over the world.

How this tree yielded its first saplings is given in the records of Mahavamsa as follows:

> "Amidst that great assembly, which was amazed at the miracle, a fruit on the east branch became ripe even as they gazed and fell unspoiled. The Thera (an elderly monk) picked it and gave it to the King to plant. The ruler planted it in a golden bowl... Even as all were looking at it, eight shoots sprang and grew into eight Bodhi-saplings and, with his mind amazed, honoured them by offering the white parasol and bestowed on them royal consecration." (47)

Tera Mahindra and Their Sanghamitra remained in Sri Lanka for the rest of their lives. The King Devanampiya Tissa built separate viharas for them. The Buddhists of Sri Lanka still remember them with great respect and gratitude.

Worship of Bodhi in Sri Lanka.

King Devanampiya Tissa, the first Buddhist King of Sri Lanka, is said to have bestowed the whole country upon the Bodhi tree and held a magnificent festival after planting it with a fabulous ceremony. For this festive occasion, the King ordered decorating the entire country. The Mahavamsa refers to similar ceremonies held by his successors as well. The rulers of Sri Lanka performed elaborate rituals to worship the tree every twelfth year of their reign. King Dutugemunu (2nd century B.C.) conducted such a ceremony for 100,000 pieces of money. King Bhatika Abhaya (1st century A.C.) held a ceremony of watering the sacred tree, which seems to have been one of many such special pujas. According to the Mahavamsa, other kings also expressed their devotion to the Bodhi tree in various ways.

During Devanampiya Tissa, forty Bodhi saplings grew from the seeds of the original Bodhi tree at Anuradhapura. They were sent to other monasteries on the Island for planting. The local Buddhists saw to it that every monastery on the Island had its own Bodhi tree, and today, the tree has become a familiar sight. The saplings derived, most probably, from the original tree at Anuradhapura through seeds (it is only an assumption).

The ceremony of worshipping this sacred tree in Sri Lanka was first begun by King Devanampiya Tissa and followed by his successors with unflagging interest. It has continued up to the present day. The ceremony is still as famous and meaningful as at the beginning. For the commoner, the worship of the tree fulfils the emotional and devotional needs of the pious heart in the same way as does the veneration of the Buddha image and, to a lesser extent, of the dagaba (stupas in Sri Lanka). Moreover, its association with deities dedicated to the cause of Buddhism, who can also aid pious worshippers in their mundane affairs, contributes to the popularity and vitality of Bodhi worship. (48).

Today, the main centre of devotion in Sri Lanka is the ancient tree at Anuradhapura. Ordinarily, pilgrims are not allowed to go near the foot of the tree on the upper terrace. They must worship and make their offerings on altars provided on the lower terrace so that no damage is done to the tree by the multitude that throngs there. The place is closely guarded by those entrusted with its upkeep and protection. In contrast, the daily rituals of cleaning the place, watering the tree, making offerings, etc., are performed by *bhikkhus* and laypeople entrusted with the work. For the Buddhists, these rituals are of great merit, and such rituals are organized on a lesser scale at other important Bodhi trees on the Island. Today, the Jai Mahabodhi tree receives worship and respect as a symbol of the Buddha himself. According to *The Vibhanga Commentary** the *bhikkhu* who enters the courtyard of the Bodhi tree should venerate the tree, behaving with all humility as if he were in the presence of the Buddha. One of the main items of the daily ritual at the Anuradhapura Bodhi tree (and at many other places) is offering alms as if to the Buddha himself. A unique ritual held annually at the shrine of the Anuradhapura tree is the hanging of gold ornaments on the tree. Pious devotees offer valuables, money, and various other articles during the performance of this ritual. (49). (* The *Vibhanga* is, the second book of the *Abhidhamma-pitaka*, in which specific topics central to the Buddha's teachings are analysed. English translation of the *Vibhanga* Commentary is available under the title, Dispeller of Delusion).

Mahabodhi temple at Anuradhapura, Sri Lanka. Above: Jaya Mahabodhi now; below: picture indicating the former appearance – a dead stem, and a surviving branch, which has grown and the present view is shown in the first picture.

Another popular ritual connected with the Bodhi tree is lighting coconut oil lamps as an offering (*pahan puja*), especially to avert the evil influence of inauspicious planetary conjunctions. A person may go for a bodhi-puja during a troublesome period. A central item of Bodhi puja is lighting several coconut oil lamps around a Bodhi tree in a temple. The person will accrue much merit if coconut oil lamps are offered at the Maha Bodhi. The other puja items involve offering milk, scented rose water, flowers, fruits, betel leaf and nuts, medicated oils, coins, and valuables. Before the offering, the coins are to be washed in saffron water. The offering of coins is an act of merit acquisition and has assumed ritualistic significance with the Buddhists of the Island. Every temple has a charity box into which the devotees drop a few coins to contribute to maintaining the monks and the monastery. All the other offerings are arranged methodically on an altar near the tree, and the devotees recite the appropriate hymns. (50) Another part of the ritual is the hanging of flags on the branches of the tree in the expectation of getting one's wishes fulfilled. Bathing the tree with scented water is also necessary for the ritual. So is the burning of incense, camphor, etc. On completion of the offerings, the performers would circumambulate the tree once or thrice, reciting an appropriate stanza from the sacred book. The commonest of such stanzas is as follows:

Yassa mule nisin nova
Sabbari vijayam aka
Patto sabbannutam Sattha
Vande tam bodhipadapam.
Imeete mahabodhi
Lokanathena pujita
Aham pitenam
asshami
bodhi raja namatthute.

The prayer means:

"I worship this Bodhi tree seated under which the Teacher attained omniscience by overcoming all inimical forces (both subjective and objective). I, too, worship this great Bodhi tree, which the Leader of the World honoured. My homage to thee, O King Bodhi."

The devotees believe that the usual transference of merit to the deities after the ritual protects the Buddha's Dispensation." (51).

There is yet another widespread prayer. Devotees spread flowers (mostly lotus and water lily flowers) and recite the prayer given below (translation):

This spread of flowers, fresh-hued and fragrant,
I offer at the sacred lotus Feet of the Noble Sage.
With flowers in great variety, the Buddha I adore
And by this merit may I gain release.
Even as these flowers must fade, my body, too, will pass away.
With lights brightly shining, dispelling the gloom,
I honour the Fully-Awakened, that Light of the Triple World,
Who dispels the gloom (of ignorance).
Perfumed with infinite qualities, the Tathagatha,
fragrant of face and form, I revere with incense, sweet and penetrating.
To the Buddha, the Dhamma, the Sangha,
in the relics of His body,
enshrined at Lanka, Jambudvipa,
Naga loka and the Heaven of the Thirty(-three) –
in stupas there:
I give honour.

To all the images of Buddha, in all ten directions,
to even hairs and other relics,
I give honour.
To the Ten Powers of the Buddha,
To the Cairn of Bodhi, I give honour.
Greetings to every Stupa that may stand in any place,
The relics, the Great Bodhi, and Buddha forms everywhere!" (52)

However, such elaborate bodhi worship is now impossible at the Mahabodhi tree at Anuradhapura, as the devotees are not allowed to go near the tree to pour milk or scented water.

The new form of Bodhi Puja:

Around 1976, a new form of Buddhist ritual came to public notice. It was a form of Buddha pūjā devised and, at that time, generally conducted by a young monk called Panadure Ariyadhamma. The Venerable Ariyadhamma is a forest-dwelling monk who began his meditation training, while still a layman, at Kanduboda and received his higher ordination there. His *Buddha pūjā* system revitalized the traditional form of *pūjā*. In the new system, offerings of the kind is made usually at 6 P.M. – flowers, lamps, incense, etc. – were made before images of the twenty-eight Buddhas (twenty-seven former ones and Gautama) to the recitation of a few Pali verses. Another traditional element the ritual revives is honouring the bô or Bodhi tree as a symbol of the Buddha's Enlightenment. The latter element led rapidly to the new ritual's becoming known as *Bodhi pūjā*. In this form of Puja, the followers worship all the previous Buddhas along with the worship of Gautama Buddha and the Bodhi tree. (53)

The Buddhists believe that there are many Buddhas and that they lived in the previous times from an unimaginable time. Gautama Buddha who lived in our times, or during the present historical time is 28th. So, there were 27 Buddhas who lived and guided the humans of those times to achieve Salvation. In Theravada Buddhism, 'Buddha' refers to one who has become enlightened through one's efforts and insight. A Buddha has realized the Enlightenment that ends the cycle of birth and death and brings liberation from suffering. The Pali canon states that Buddhas have appeared in the past and will also appear in the future. Numerous enlightened Buddhas also arose in earlier world cycles and preached the very same Dharma that gives deliverance from suffering and death to all mature beings. The names of these 28 Buddhas are religiously preserved by Buddhists, together with their age, stature, the trees under which they attained Enlightenment, their country, and the names of their father and mother. They all have two chief disciples to assist them in their mission. Every Buddha has always obtained supreme intelligence under the shadow of a particular tree. All these 28 Buddhas were born into royal families or affluent Brahmin families. When they had seen the four signs – an older man, a sick man, a corpse, and an ascetic – they renounced worldly life and left home. They engaged in meditation on mindfulness until they attained Enlightenment. At the request of God Brahma, they preached their first sermon to those who followed them. (54)

Gautama Buddha is the fourth and current Buddha of the present Kalpa. He was born as a son of King Suddhodana and Queen Mahamaya in Kapilvastu. Prince Siddhartha (Siddhatta) Gautama married Princess Yasodharā and had a son named Rāhula. Prince Siddhartha finally arose fully enlightened as Gautama Buddha under the shade of the Peepal Bodhi tree, which according to belief, grew up spontaneously when he was born. Kolita and Upatissa were his chief disciples who assisted him in his mission. He delivered his first sermon, *Dhamma cakkappavattana Sutta* (The Setting in Motion of the Wheel of the *Dhamma Sutta* or Promulgation of the Law *Sutta*), in a deer park at Benares. The Buddha spent the rest of his life teaching *Dhamma* (*Dharma*, the path of righteousness). His teaching was reasonable and practical, as he never taught what he had not seen and known. In his eightieth year, when he was in Kusinara (Kusinagara – a town in the Kushinagar district in Uttar Pradesh, an important pilgrimage centre of Buddhists), he had a severe attack of dysentery. Buddha consoled Ananda, who was weeping, then called his disciples together and addressed them to work on their Salvation diligently. Then he entered *Parinirvana*, from which there was no return. (*Parinirvana* is the final nirvana, "complete nirvana," "nirvana-after-death," etc. Parinirvana occurs upon the death of the body of someone who has attained nirvana during his lifetime. It implies a complete release from samsara, karma, and rebirth as well as the dissolution of the skandhas [Skandhas are the five psycho-physical aggregates, which according to Buddhist philosophy are the basis for self-grasping (attachment to the concept of a self that is unique). They are *rupa-skandha* – aggregate of form; *vedana-skandha* – aggregate of sensations; *saṃjñā-skandha* – aggregate of recognition, labels or ideas; *saṃskāra-skandha* – aggregate of volitional formations (desires, wishes and tendencies); *vijñāna-skandha* – aggregate of consclousness. (55)]

The auspicious ceremony of Buddha Puja is held to pay homage to the 28 enlightened Buddhas who taught

Dhamma at different times. Such practice reminds Buddhists to strengthen their devotion, and many Buddhists also pay tribute to the future Buddha, Metteyya (Maitreya) (53).

Some puranic Legends

An interesting legend is associated with peepal or *Pipla,* the Sanskrit synonym for *aśvattha. Skanda Purana* has the story of Rishi Dadhichi, who sacrificed his body so that Indra could make the weapon *vajra* out of his spine to kill the demon king Vritra. At that time, his wife, Suvarachas, was pregnant. Overcame with grief, she cut open her womb when the foetus from Dadhichi came out. She kept the foetus under an *aśvattha* tree and then committed suicide (*sati).* The foetus was an aspect of Rudra (a synonym for Śiva). Animals and birds raised the child under the peepal tree. He ate only the fruits of the peepal tree; later, he became the renowned sage Pippalada, one brought up by the *pipla* (*aśvattha*) tree. The term *peepal* came from *pipla.* Then there is also a legend in *Brahma Purana* that Aśvattha and Pipla were two demons, sons of the demon Kaitabha. Aśvattha was in the form of a tree, while Pipla, in the guise of a Brahmin, advises people to go and touch the *Aśvattha* tree. When they go to the tree and touch it, the tree demon kills them. Later, Sani (the planet god, Saturn) killed them.

According to puranic legends, *aśvattha* is the permanent abode of Alakami (also known as Alakshmi or Jyeshta), the elder sister of Goddess Lakshmi, and Lord Vishnu granted this tree as her abode, except on Saturdays when goddess Lakshmi visits the tree. Both *Padma Purana* and *Linga Purana* give the story associated with Alakāmi. The legend given in *Padma Purana* is as follows:

> Alakāmi was the elder sister of Goddess Lakshmi; both originated from the *Parāśakthi*; Alakāmi

from the left side and Lakshmi from the right side. Alakāmi had qualities opposite in all respects to those of Lakshmi; she was the personification of everything unholy, and hence, none accepted her in marriage. At the behest of Lakshmi, Lord Vishnu arranged sage Uddālaka to marry her (sage Dushsaha as per *Linga Purana*). Alakāmi was unhappy with Uddālaka in a hermitage and used to nag her husband for another residence. Once, Uddālaka took her to a peepal tree, left her there, and vanished. She waited in vain and then wept bitterly. Lakshmi took pity on her plight, and at her request, Lord Vishnu, along with Lakshmi, appeared before her and assigned the peepal tree as her permanent abode, except on Saturdays when Lakshmi visited the tree. In the *Linga Purana,* this legend seems to have some variations. According to this Purana, Sage Markhandeya advised the sage Dushsaha to make the peepal tree his abode with his spouse Alakāmi. Through this legend, the composers Puranas gave the people reasons for worshipping the tree. By making the *aśvattha* the abode of both Alakami and Lakshmi, a proper reason was provided to the public to believe that by worshipping this tree, they can conquer Alakami and propitiate Lakshmi. All legends associated with sacred trees were clever ways of propagating the idea of protecting the trees and, in turn, protecting Mother Earth.

Padma Purana tells the story of a very poor, pious Brahmin who was an ardent devotee of Lord Vishnu. He was so poor that even his wife left him and went to her parents' home. One cold winter night, he did not even have a rag to get protection from the cold, so he decided to make a fire from the branches of the peepal tree near his house. He went out and made one cut on a branch. Suddenly, Lord Vishnu appeared out of the tree. On His body, there was a red line of a cut. The poor Brahmin was in utter shock. Lord Vishnu asked him, "Why have you given me a cut by the knife?" The poor Brahmin had no answer; he fell at Vishnu's feet and wept. Lord Vishnu comforted him and told him to ask for a boon, which would be granted. The Brahmin was in great agony; he replied, "O, God. If you are pleased, grant me this boon. Allow me to attend upon you forever so that my mind will remain at your lotus feet forever. Except this, I want nothing more". Lord Vishnu was immensely pleased. He granted him the boon and immense wealth and blessed him with many years on earth with his family, and then he would reach Vaikunta and live there eternally. After that, his wife returned, and they had many children. They started worshipping the peepal tree ardently as the embodiment of Lord Vishnu.

In *Puranas* (*Vishnu Purana, Vayu Purana, Maha Bhagavatha Purana*) there are descriptions of the last moments of Sri Krisha before he departs from the earth, after completing all the purposes for which he (Vishnu) took the incarnation. On the eve of the ascension, Krishna meditated under an *asvattha* tree. "Beholding his own *Maya*, Lord Krishna sipped the water from the river Saraswati and sat down under the foot of the peepal tree. He placed his lotus-like right foot on his left thigh and reclined against an *asvattha* tree. Krishna was radiant, filled with joy, and was in absolute peace. He was ready to depart the earth and ascend to the divine realm of Vaikunta (the abode of Lord Vishnu).. At this time, a hunter mistook the lotus feet of Krishna for the eye of a deer and shot an arrow that pierced

Krishna's foot. The moment for his departure arrived. So, the peepal tree was the witness for the last moments of Krishna, whom the scriptures proclaim as the complete incarnation of Vishnu. (According to *Bhagavatha Purana*, this hunter was the rebirth of Bali, the great Monkey king Rama killed by sending an arrow while hiding behind a tree. Krishna repaid this last debt, too, before his final departure from the world.)

Vamana Purana mentions a gigantic golden *asvattha* tree on the west side of the mythical Gandhmadan mountains. At that tree's root was an altar made of gold and jewels. The branches are very long and very large. On that tree lived all types of beasts and birds. The fruit of that tree was as large as pitchers and was very sweet. All gods and demigods attended to that tree constantly. According to *Linga Purana*, there was a gigantic *asvattha* tree on top of the Vipula (Vipula, Vepulla) mountain, one of the seven hills located around the ancient Rajagriha, in the ancient Magadha, the present-day Bihar). This tree was known as the *Chaitya Padapa*. *Kurma Purana* mentions yet another gigantic peepal tree and adds that mountains like Mandara, Gandhamadan, and Vipula had colossal trees of *Asvattha, Vata* (banyan), *Jambu* and *Kadamba*.

According to Puranic legends, the peepal is the abode of goddess Bhavani and is considered the female counterpart of the banyan tree by many ethnic groups. Gopinatha Rao, in his book on *Hindu Iconography*, mentions that the *asvattha* tree is the abode of *Bhutamata* and goddess Kumari. (57) Macdonell, in his classic work on *Vedic Mythology* mentions that *Apsaras* (celestial singers and dancers) inhabit this tree in which their cymbals and flutes resound. (58) Lord Krishna tells Arjuna that among trees, he is *asvattha,* indicating that it is the most sacred and the noblest. *Bhagavata Purana* tells that *aśvattha* is that which is not the same tomorrow; perhaps it shows the fast-growing nature of the tree or the ever-moving nature of its leaves. *Mahabharata* tells us that a person who worships this tree daily worships the whole Universe, thereby indicating its cosmic nature. *Asvattha* is also the tree of fertility. Cutting the tree was and is still considered taboo by the Hindus and Buddhists. It is also the abode of the Sun god and many other deities such as Indra, Ganesha, Brihaspathi, Agni, Dharma, and demigods like Gandharvas and Apsaras. Some communities believe that Lord Vishnu was born under the *aśvattha* tree (the cosmic tree!) and that Lord Krishna was shot at by a hunter while resting under an *aśvattha* tree. At the end of the world, during the great deluge (*Maha pralaya*), when everything in the Universe will come to an end), Lord Vishnu transforms himself into a baby and lies on an *aśvattha* leaf *(vata* leaf, in another version of the legend), that will float on the eternal waters for an infinite period till another cycle of creation begins by the *Parāsakthi* (The Ultimate force, this word defies translation).

In a tribal legend, Lord Śiva married a beautiful twiner climbing on an *aśvattha* tree, and out of this union, an obstinate black son was born. The Kol and Bhil tribes consider themselves descended from this son of Śiva, born of a twiner. (59). *Aśvattha* is the totem tree of the Rathod, Nonama and Maira clans of Bhils. Bhils and Garacia tribes believe that evil spirits inhabit the tree, especially at night, and they do not permit ladies and children to go near the tree at night. The tree is not grown near their houses as they believe there would be quarrels. The people of the Garacia tribe place *aśvattha* leaves on the heads of ladies in labour pains to facilitate an easy delivery. A garland made of peepal leaves is hung at the entrance of a patient's room suffering from skin disease, and the belief is that as the leaves dry up, the patient gets cured. The members of the Bhopas tribe present a miniature bed to this tree after worshipping before marriage, believing that the couple may at least have a bed to rest on as their property. Among the Garacia tribe, after the cremation ceremony, the site is covered by a big basket of bamboo containing seven cups made from the leaves of a peepal tree, having in each a dish favourite to the deceased; the belief is that the spirit of the dead would eat and drink during the night. The people of the Damor tribe place under the tree a clay pot containing bones and ash collected from the cremation site till an auspicious day for plunging it into a river. (60)

Aśvattha trees sometimes grow on other trees like mango, acacia, neem etc (peepal starts its life as an epiphyte). *Aśvattha* tree, growing on a *khadira* tree (*Acacia*), is believed to have the power to defeat enemies with the help of Indra, Mitra, and Varuna as *aśvattha* overpowers and breaks *khadira* as it grows. Hence, the enemy is overpowered and vanquished. In the past, branches of such trees were carried to the battlefields with the belief of winning the war. On the battlefield, *aśvattha* was invoked along with *khadira* by reciting the *piplastuti* (hymn on peepal) for helping in subduing the enemy. *Aśvattha* and *Khadira* are offered in the sacrificial fire to ward off demons and enemies. (61)

The Asvattha tree is a fertility symbol, as mentioned in the legend on the birth of Vishwamitra. This fertility aspect of the bodhi tree is a subject of many folk songs in Sri Lanka. To give an example, hear this one:

ape gamen bat baendagenatisavaevateyantayi tisavaevaeratunelume bat da genakantayi etanasitanpevipeviudamaluvataentayi udamaluvebodishamipirimiputekdentayi '

Let us come to the Tisa Vaeva bringing rice from our village

Let us eat this rice, on red lotus leaves, from the Tisa Vaeva

And from there, pure in body and soul, let us go to the Bodhi on the upper terrace,

And may the Lord, the Bodhi, bless us with a boy-child.

If a woman gets a child after making such a vow, she will come back, with the baby and a tender coconut plant, to fulfil that vow.

Aśvattha – role in religious rites.

Aśvattha has played a significant role in the religious rites of ancient India and the Hindus. *Aśvattha* is the first among the *'panchadruma'* (five great trees) used in rituals; the others are *nimba, champak, bakula,* and *narikela. Aśvattha* is also the first of the *'panchapallava* (five *great leaves)* used in rituals, the others being *amra, vata, udumbara,* and *palasa.* Tantric texts (such as the *Tantrasara* of Abhinava Gupta, translation of HN Chakravarthy, 2012), speak about *kula vriksha* (trees of a community) that are to be held sacred, and all members of the community pay their homage to such trees every day. *Aśvattha is* the first of these trees. (Abhinavagupta, in his *Tantrasara,* quotes the *Kameshara Tantra,* according to which the *kulavrikshas* are: *aśvattha, vata, aśoka, vilva, nimba, kadamba, sleshmataka,* and *karanja,* and then adds three more, namely *udumbara, dhatri,* and *chincha.*).

Historically, *aśvattha* wood was an essential item for all the *yajnas. Yajna* or *yaga* is part and parcel of the ancient Indian culture and religious practices of the Hindus. Before performing any *Yajña*, a sacrificial shed with four doors had to be put up for conducting the *Yajña* rites. According to the *Agni Purāṇa*, the four entrances to the sacrificial shed had to be decorated respectively with the branches of *plakṣa, udumbara, aśvattha,* and *nyagrodha* trees. From the east, they are respectively named the door of peace, the door of prosperity, the door of strength, and the door of good health. For *Yajna,* the sacrificial fire had to be created using an *arani* (a close-fitting fire drill or mortar and pestle). By rotating the pestle inside the *arani,* fire sparks are produced through friction; usually, the base is made of peepal wood, and the top is *Shami* wood. The sacred *yupa* (a post for tying the sacrificial animal) is made of peepal wood (or a thick stem from the tree). The *panchadruma kashaya* needed for *yajna* is made of *asvattha, vata, palasha, madhuka,* and *nimba.*

There is also the type of *deva pooja* or worship of deities known as *Vriksha panchayatana pooja*, for which five trees are used. Here, five gods [Śiva, Vishnu, Surya, Ambika (Durga), and Ganesha] are worshipped symbolically through the worship of five sets of plants (*vilwa* and *drona* for Śiva, *aśvattha* and *thulsi* for Vishnu, *karaveera* and *svetarka* for Surya, *Khadira* and *doorva* for Ganesha, and *aśoka* and *śankapushpa* for Ambika or Durga). Such a setup is permanent and varies with the type of worship. For example, for Vishnu *Panchyatana pooja*, Asvattha and Thulsi occupy the centre. (62). (Also see Chapter 1).

There is a ceremony known as *Aśvattha Prathishta,* or the consecration of *aśvattha.* It is an elaborate ceremony by which, the tree is believed to be transformed into Lord

Vishnu. *Bhavishya Purana* gives the details of this ceremony. Chapters 3 and 4 of this *Purana* prescribe the procedure. Closely related is the peepal marriage festival. Here, a peepal tree and a neem are planted close together, and after about eighteen years, a marriage ceremony is performed between the two trees growing together. In this ceremony, the peepal is treated as the bridegroom (the symbol of Lord Vishnu), and Neem is the bride (emblematic of Devi). This marriage will be conducted on *sukla paksha* (waxing phase of the moon) during *the Utharayana* period (January 15 to June 15), avoiding the moon's first, fourth, eighth, and ninth phases. There was a press report (Times of India, June 10, 2007, report by TS Sreenivasa Raghavan) about such a peepal-neem wedding celebrated in Palghat in Kerala.

> "The wedding was on May 27. Between 6:21 am and 7:21 am, the sacred thread wound around the *peepal* tree. Later, at the *shuba muhurt (auspicious moment)* between 8:30 am and 9:30 am, he was married to the *neem,* four years younger than him (the peepal). The bride is wrapped in a traditional Kancheepuram silk sari, which cost Rs 20,000, and a gold *mangal sutra,* looking innocent and elegant as she flushed with tender green leaves. The groom (peepal) wore a silk *veshti, angavasthram* (traditional attire for male members in South India), and sacred thread made of silver and gold. There was a sumptuous feast for the guests. Chellappa Vadhyar, the priest who conducted the sacred thread ceremony and the wedding, is certain that the *peepal* is male and the *neem* is female...." (63, 64).

A legend prevalent in Karnataka connects the two trees (*asvattha* and *nimba).* According to this, neem represents seven beautiful daughters of a malignant spirit. One day, while proceeding to the river for a bath, Lord Krishna appeared before them and requested that they marry him. But the sisters refused, and to escape from Krishna, they took the form of neem trees. Immediately, Krishna transformed into a large peepal tree and held the neem trees warmly. After that incident, it became a custom to perform a marriage ceremony between the two trees, which are worshipped together (65). Chettiar, in his book Folklores of Tamil Nadu, describes such peepal-neem marriages and mentions the widespread belief that a person who performs such a marriage and then installs a *naga* (snake god) idol under the tree would be blessed with children and prosperity. In rural India, three weddings between peepal and banyan are also celebrated. In such cases, the peepal is the bride (symbolizing the Mohini aspect of Vishnu), and the banyan is the groom (symbol of Lord Śiva). (66)

In rural Bengal, married women observe a *vrata* known as *Aśvattha patra vrata* for the house members' well-being and prosperity. In this *vrata* ceremony, observed on the *Chaitra Sankranthi* (last day of the Bengali calendar), a woman uses peepal leaves in five stages: young, fully opened green, old, and yellowing, dried and withered. Each leaf signifies a stage of a woman's life and desire. A young leaf is the symbol of new life (and hence stands for a new son). A mature green leaf leads a woman to the goddess of beauty and is to get attractiveness and beauty. Old and yellowing leaf stand for the long life of a woman's husband, and the dry leaf is believed to lead her to greater happiness. According to belief, the withered and torn leaf will lead her to wealth. (67)

Peepal worship is common all over India. In most temples devotees circumambulates the banyan tree, which is often the *stahlavriksha,* and then light a lamp at its base. In most temples, the peepal will have a raised platform around the tree base, and with serpent idols installed on it. Devotees light their lamps (mostly small earthen lamps) on this platform.

Peepal-tree associated worship places are also common in many parts of India. Such worship places consist of a small often improvised structure below a peepal tree and a local priest light lamps and carry out the pujas. Such "peepal temples "are regularly visited by the local believers.

A peepal tree-associated worship place with an improvised 'temple'

Circumambulation of the *Aśvattha* tree is considered a very pious act of devotion. *Skanda Purāṇa* says that a woman devotee should circumambulate an *aśvattha* tree a hundred thousand times in the month of *Kārttika* (Oct. – Nov.). On Saturdays, she should worship Rādhā and Krishna beneath it. She should then feed a couple symbolizing Rādhā and Krishna. After feeding the couples, she should preferably observe *mouna vrata (vow of silence).* By observing this *vrata,* even a barren woman will get a son.

Haberman's book *People Trees* describes in detail the worship of peepal (pipal) trees by women in Varanasi; he also discusses at length the socio-anthropological and socio-cultural aspects connected with this worship. Let me quote a few lines from this book.

> "...I watched a woman dressed in a turquoise blue and magenta sari, her long shiny hair tied neatly into a bun, remove her sandals and approach one of the trees reverently. Standing near the tree, she looked up into its branches for a few moments with her hands joined together in prayer. She then bent down and made a water offering, pouring it slowly onto the tree's roots from a small copper pot while chanting *"Vasudevaya namaha"* (All honour to Vasudeva !; O Vasudeva, I bow before you). She lit a few sticks of incense and pressed them into the ground at the base of the tree and then took some marigold flowers from a plastic wicker basket and placed these carefully near the incense. Once she had finished this, she took out a small piece of orange cloth and spread it on the ground before the tree. She hung a garland of flowers just above the bright cloth, hooking it to a rough piece of bark on the tree trunk and then

offered two green guava fruits, some white sugar crystals, and several red bangles on her cloth altar. Next, she got up, tied a red and yellow string around the tree, walked around it clockwise seven times, and wrapped the tree trunk to honour and establish a mutually protective relationship with it. Returning to her altar, she laid out a leaf bowl containing bright orange *sindu*r paste and a bag of uncooked white rice. Taking a small amount of the rice in her right hand, she joined the colourful swirl of women encircling the tree. Each time she returned to her altar she sprinkled the rice onto the orange cloth. She then reached down into the leaf bowl, took some *sindhur* paste on the ring finger of her right hand and stretched up to dab this onto the upper trunk of the tree. Taking up another handful of the rice, she repeated this ritual process 108 times. Once she had finished her revolutions of the tree, she returned to her altar, crouched down, and began massaging the foot of the tree with evident tenderness for several minutes. After this, she stood up and, placing both her hands lightly on the sides of the tree, hugged it while touching her forehead gently to its trunk. Gathering her instruments of worship into the plastic wicker basket and taking one last look up into the tree's upper branches, she turned and walked away..." (68)

Such elaborate worship is only on the *Somavati Amavasya vrata,* and many women participate in the ritual ceremony. Women observe this ritual mainly for blessed family life and the health and prosperity of their family members. In such rituals, the people do not worship peepal per se, but they worship Lord Vishnu in the form of the peepal tree, as the believers consider this tree to be the manifest form of Vishnu. In shrines associated with peepal trees, people offer worship daily, and they also circumambulate the tree, usually thrice, and sometimes even 108 times. All over India, peepal tree shrines are held in great respect, and the *navagraha* (nine planetary deities) idols are installed in such shrines. Occasionally there are also snake idols installed under peepal tree shrines. People offer worship in these shrines daily, along with the worship of the principal deities of the temple. While circumambulating, devotees recite the *Pipalastuti* (hymn on Peepal), as follows.

> *"āśvattha hutabhukvasa ġovindasya ṣadapriya*
> *āsesham hara me papam vrikśaraja namosthuthe*
> *ṁule brahma tvaci Vishnuhsakhayam*
> *ṣankaraeva cha*
> *patre patre sarva devaya vasudevayate namaha|*

> ('O *aśvattha*, the Lord of Trees, I offer my obeisance to you. You are the refuge of the fire (the devourer of oblation) and the pet of Govinda. I prostrate the form of Vasudeva, where Brahma resides in your roots, Vishnu in your trunk, Śiva in your branches, and all the deities are in your leaves. You, O, Lord of trees! Destroy all of my sins.')

In *Brahat Sthotra Ratnakarah* there is an *aśvattha sthothram,* which, according to legends, was given by Lord Brahma to Rishi Narada. There is also an *Aśvattha pranama mantra:*

> *om, agre brahma mule Vishnu sakhayam*
> *ṁahesvarah*
> *patr edevaganahsarve vrkśaraja namostute|*

According to this, Brahma occupies the top, Vishu the roots, and Śiva the branches; all other devas occupy the leaves. In *Padma Purana,* it is also indicated as an incarnation of Vishnu and Bodhisattva, as mentioned earlier. There is also an *asvattha stotram* given at the end of this chapter. Bhishma, the grandfather of the Pandavas, advised Yudhishtira to go to a peepal tree and conduct the *vrata* ritual on the *Somavati Amavasya* day (a new moon falling on a Monday), to appease Lord Vishnu. Bhishma told him that such a *vrata* under the peepal tree, followed by the circumambulation of the tree 108 times, would get Yudhishtira absolved of all the sins of killing his kith and kin. Moreover, Parikshit would be revived from the curse Asvadhama inflicted on the Pandavas, and he would continue the lineage. Yudhishtira observed the *vrata* as per the prescribed procedure and ensured the blessings of Lord Vishnu. Moreover, as advised by Bhishma, Yudhishtira taught Droupadi the importance of the *Somvati Amavasya vrata* under a peepal tree and how to observe the *vrata.*

Haberman arrived at the following conclusions from his study of the rituals connected with the peepal tree:

1. It provides a blueprint and rationale for a special ritual like the circumambulation of the tree 108 times.
2. The peepal tree itself is worshipped as the king of trees and as the manifest form of the *Trimurtis.*
3. The peepal tree represents Lord Vishnu's manifest form.
4. The peepal tree is a powerful presence and a vital sentient being.

It can be approached with reverence to yield significant benefits for domestic life, such as good health, well-being, longevity for family members, happiness, wealth, and overall abundance for the worshipper (69). The worship of Peepal continues as a vibrant faith among the women of India.

The Jains also consider *aśvattha* as the *bodhi* tree, a significant sacred tree. The Jain religious text *Samavayanga sutra* gives a list of pasts, present and future *Thirthankaras*, and *aśvattha* is the *'Chaitya vriksha' of* the fourteenth *Thirthankara*, Anantanada, according to both *Digambara* and *Svetambara* sects of Jainism. According to *Tiloyapaannathi*, the *Chaitya vriksha* of Asurakumara, one of the ten *Bhavanati* gods is *aśvattha*, according to both sects.

Despite the religious importance, *aśvattha* is scarcely sculpted in Hindu temples. The reason probably is the belief that peepal is the abode of Brahmins' ghosts. However, it is represented widely in Buddhist shrines. *The Bodhi* tree is sculptured extensively on the Buddhist *stupas* at Sanchi, Barhut, Amaravathi, Nagarjunakonda, Mathura, Sarnath and Nalanda. The representations include Gautama Buddha sitting under the *Bodhi* tree in a meditation pose or in a pose of giving benediction. In fact, before the worship of Buddha in the anthropomorphic form, he was symbolically worshipped as a throne under the Bodhi tree. One of the sculptures in Barhut represents an *aśvattha* tree worshipped by guardians of the four quarters. In Sanchi, a sculpture depicts monkeys offering honey to an *aśvattha* tree, and men and women worship it. Some Amaravathi sculptures also depict *bodhi* trees being symbolically worshipped as Buddha by men and women. (70)

For many centuries, the peepal has been the spiritual life-giver to the Hindus and the Buddhists, and it continues to be so even today. For the poor, uneducated villagers of India, it is God incarnate. The Peepal Tree has also gone deep into the cultural ethos of Indian society. Randhawa gives many folk songs having references to peepal tree:

> 'Tell me, O Peepal tree
> Which is the path to heaven?'
> O silent peepal tree,
> Do open the knot of my soul' (71)

Local Traditions

There are many local traditions associated with the *asvattha* tree. Despite India's diverse socio-cultural setting, there is a lot of commonalities in the beliefs and practices related to the *asvattha* tree (for that matter, with other sacred trees). In most regions, people worship peepal as the manifest form or abode of Lord Vishnu. In Rajasthan, women devotees water *asvattha* daily, and men devotees water them on Sundays. Today, they believe that Devi Lakshmi makes the tree her abode. Some believe Lord Vishnu and goddess Lakshmi make *Asvattha* their abode on Sundays. In Rajasthan, Uttar Pradesh, Madhya Pradesh, and Bihar, people think that gods and goddesses' dwell under the peepal tree. Some unpolished granite stones are often kept around the trunk for people to sit under. Ordinary people also worship these stones. In Orissa and Bihar, people consider *Asvattha* to be the abode of Buddha, whom many regard as the ninth incarnation of Vishnu. They circumambulate the tree, reciting the *asvattha stotram* (given at the end of this section). In Orissa, in a place known as Tritol, in Cuttack District, there is a temple for the deity *Peepala-Madhava*. Here, devotees conduct *Panchavriksha pooja* with the help of priests. In this pooja, five sacred trees are worshipped as the embodiment of five of the most important deities (same as the *Panchayatana puja* mentioned earlier). In Orissa, people observe *naga-*

panchami and *naga-Chaturthi* under peepal trees with the hope of getting good sons and the long lives of their husbands. In many parts of Orissa and Bengal, the bride and groom are first married to an *asvattha* tree before the real marriage. (72)

There is also a prevalent belief in Bengal, Orissa, and other north-Indian regions that *Asvattha* leaves are the abode of gods and semi-gods. Devotees worship the tree as the manifest form of Vasudeva (Sri Krishna); after bathing, they pour water at the tree's base and pray, reciting the *asvattha storm* (Hymn on *Asvattha*). The people in those regions also believe that Goddess Sashthi (Saṣṭhi) (a Hindu village goddess worshipped as the protector of children; she is also the deity of vegetation and reproduction and bestows children and aids in childbirth). In rural Bengal, Sashthi is revered for the welfare of daughters and their families. (73, 74).

In many parts of India, there is a belief that worship of the peepal tree is stipulated to achieve marital happiness. In Punjab, on a Sunday, Tuesday, or a festival day, a barren woman is advised to take a bath under a peepal tree and then carry out the *Chaukapurna vrata* under the tree to receive the blessings of the peepal tree to get offspring. In most parts of India, married women worship the peepal tree to win the tree's blessings for a happy married life. (75).

Lord Vishnu, lying on the peepal leaf as an infant, is a widely known motif in innumerable art forms. (The same legend appears in the case of Banyan, too). After the green colour has been removed, peepal leaves could be used to paint the Krishna motif. Such peepal-leaf Krishna pictures are known as Peepal-Madhava (*Aalila Krishna*).

In more recent times, peepal leaves have been used widely as a substratum for painting a variety of deities and other subjects. Peepal leaf paintings of Bala-Krishna (Krishna as a baby) are often kept as a treasure in many upper caste Hindu houses among the Vaishnavites and by the Hindus in Kerala). This motif is used in gold ornaments and *mangal sutra* (*Aalila-thali*) used by many ladies in Kerala. Lockets depicting "*Alila-Krishna*" are among the most widely used, especially by young girls. (76). Offering the peepal leaf is mandatory in some ritual worships (*vrata pujas)* such as *Siddhivinayaka puja, Sankastha chathurthi vrata puja, Shri Uma-Mahesvara vrata puja* and Narasimha Jayanthi *vrata puja.* (77).

Skanda Purana ordains that if a person does not have any one of twelve types of sons (like own, adopted, purchased etc. as stipulated in *Manu smriti* and *Yajnavalkya smriti*) to give emancipation to his ancestors, he should then plant an *aśvattha* tree, considering it as his son. He should tend this tree well and then get it married to a *Shami* tree, and if it survives, his family will prosper. Rishi Gaalava advised the sonless Vidura (Vidhura), the stepbrother of Pandavas and Kauravas, to plant an *asvattha* sapling, tend it properly, and then consecrate it as his son, and install a Vishnu idol below the tree. Vidura raised a peepal sapling and consecrated it as Rishi Gaalava advised. According to another legend, Vidura planted the *asvattha* tree in a place now known as Vidhurashwatha, in the Karnataka state. The associated legend is as follows:

After the Kurukshetra war, Vidura (Vidhura, son of Sage Vyasa, and step brother of Pandavas and Kauravas, a very righteous person, and a devotee of Krishna) felt miserable about the war between the cousins and the bloodshed that ensued. He approached Krishna for advice, who in turn asked him to proceed on a pilgrimage. Accordingly, Vidura travelled across the land and finally reached the hermitage of Rishi Maithreya, on the banks of the river Uttara Pinakini (now more commonly known as River Penna, or Pennar, that originates in the Chenna Kesava hill of the Nandidurg range, in Chikkaballapura district of Karnataka and flows towards east eventually draining into the Bay of Bengal.). On realising the issues tormenting Vidura, Sage Maitreya suggested that Vidura should consecrate an *aśvattha* sapling and the bring it up as his son and then install a Vishnu idol below the tree and worship, to get salvation. The next day morning while offering morning prayers in the river, Vidura saw an *aśvattha* sapling floating in front of him. Vidura took it as a good omen, collected it and based on the advice of sage Maitrya, planted it and then brought it up as his son. He then installed an idol of Vishnu and worshipped. Pleased by his devotion, Brahma, Vishnu, and Shiva appeared before him, blessed him, and granted salvation. As Vidura planted the *aśvattha* tree and attained salvation here, this place got its name Vidurashwatha, and the *aśvattha* tree there was believed to be the one planted by Vidura. The tree got destroyed in 2001, during a heavy storm and rain. The stump of the tree is still preserved at the site. A new peepal has taken its place, adjacent to the original tree. Devotees have installed hundreds of snake idols below the tree. The temple there is dedicated to Brahma, Vishnu, and Shiva, and the *aśvattha* tree was considered the embodiment of the Trinity. [Vidurashwatha is also known as the "Jallianwala Bagh of South India". On April 25, 1938, a group of villagers congregated in front of the temple to hoist the swadeshi movement flag and to organize *satyagraha*, as part of the freedom struggle of India. The police fired indiscriminately at the group, resulting in the death of around 35 people.

This is like the incident at the Jallianwala Bagh in Amritsar. A memorial was built in 1973 at this place as a respect to the martyred.]

In the *Skanda Purana,* we get the reference that if a sonless woman circumambulates *aśvattha* tree one lakh times on a Saturday in the month of K*arthika* (Oct.Nov.) after worshipping the idols of Radha and Krishna placed under the tree, will be blessed with a noble son. But, to touch the tree on other days is taboo because, on those days, Alakāmi inhabits the tree. Installation of idols of various deities under the *aśvattha* tree was common practice throughout the ages, and Puranas stipulate it. *Skanda Purana* advises worshipping this tree during the *Chathurmasya* (the four rainy months). Kicking the tree or touching it with a foot is regarded as equal to killing a Brahmin. For the Hindus, cutting an Aśvattha tree is unthinkable; the belief is that the one who cuts this tree would go to hell. Peepal bark is one of the many items required for the purification ceremony of idols before the consecration and installation. (78, 79, 80)

Some Related Legends

In a Zen Buddhist school, the Master wanted to choose his successor. So, he addressed the gathering of disciples:

> "Day after day, instead of trying to free yourselves from this bitter sea of life and death, you seem to go after tainted merits, which cause rebirth. Merits will be of no help if your Essence of Mind gets obscured. Go and seek *Prajna* (wisdom) in your mind, and then write me a stanza about it. He who understands the essence of mind will be made the Sixth Patriarch."

Most of the disciples felt that the one to inherit the Patriarchy would be their instructor, Shen Hsiu, so they left it to him to write the stanza. But Hsiu himself was worried about his merit. So, he wrote a verse on the wall for the Master to see.

> "Our body is a *bodhi* tree
> And our mirror bright
> Carefully, we clean them hour by hour
> And let no dust alight."

On enquiry, Hsiu admitted that he wrote it. The Master told him:

"Your stanza shows that you have not yet realised the Essence of Mind. So far, you have reached the 'door of enlightenment', but you have not yet entered it."

Subsequently, another illiterate disciple, Hui Neng, managed to write a stanza that read:

> There is no *Bodhi* tree,
> Nor stand of a mirror bright.
> Since all is void,
> Where can dust alight?

The Master greatly appreciated this verse and declared that Hui Neng would be the next patriarch. (81)

Judith Beveridge (2003) wrote a poem in her book Between the Palace and the Bodhi Tree that won the Josephine Ulrich National Poetry Prize in 2003. The poem is entitled "Ficus religiosa," and the quote below is from that poem.

> "Under the *bodhi* tree
> I vow with all beings
> to sit until I become one with
> all the heart-shaped leaves.
> Under the *muchalinda* tree –

I vow with all beings
to sit until the moon, a bowl,
is almed only by the Good.
Under the *goatherd's* banyan –
I vow with all beings
to sit until, at the root, every
snake becomes an acolyte.
Under the *rajayatana* tree –
I vow with all beings
to sit until the nests of all the birds
are given gifts by the cuckoo.
Under the red-blossoming aśokas –
I vow with all beings
to sit until the clouds
reissue the seeds of knowledge.
Under the thin mulberry –
I vow with all beings
to sit until the silk-worms eat
all greed-driven life cycles. "(82)

The poem needs some explanation:

There are four trees associated with the Enlightenment of Buddha. They are the *Bodhi* tree, the *Ajapala Nygrodha* tree, the *Muchalinda* tree and the *Rajayātana* tree. In the Gaya bodhi tree complex, name boards with inscriptions describing each tree's significance serve as a reminder of its location. The first one is the *Bodhi Pallanka*, the place of Enlightenment. The inscription erected here says:

'Prince Siddhartha attained Buddhahood (Full Enlightenment) in 623 BC on the *Vaisakha* full moon day, sitting under this peepal (*bodhi*) tree. The *Vajrayana* or diamond throne, under this *bodhi* tree, is the central place of worship.'

Another name board announces:

> 'Animesalochana ('the place of unwinking gazing'). After Enlightenment, Lord Buddha spent the second week in meditation here, gazing unwinking at this *bodhi* tree.'

The second tree is the *Ajapala nygrodha* tree (banyan tree). Here, the signboard reads:

> "Lord Buddha spent the fifth week under this tree in meditation after Enlightenment. Here, he replied to a *brahmana* that only by one's deeds one becomes a *brahmana*, not by birth."

To quote from the ancient Buddhist text *Maha-Vagga:*

> "...Then The Blessed One, after the lapse of seven days, arose from that state of exalted calm, and leaving the foot of the Bo-tree drew near to where the *ajapâla* (that is, the goatherd's) banyan-tree was; and having drawn near, he sat cross-legged at the foot of the *ajapâla* banyan-tree for seven days together, experiencing the bliss of emancipation."

The third tree is the *Muchalinda* tree on the bank of the Muchalinda Lake (the abode of the snake king). There is an opinion that this was also a peepal tree under which this great Naga king lived). The inscription erected here reads:

> "Lord Buddha spent the sixth week in meditation here. While he was meditating, a severe thunderstorm broke out. To protect the meditating Buddha from the violent wind and rain, even the creatures came out for his safety. The legend is that Muchalinda encircled the Lord seven times and spread out its hood over him like an umbrella to protect him from the storm and rain.'

Maha Vagga has these words:

> '...Then The Blessed One, after the lapse of seven days, arose from that state of exalted calm, and, leaving the foot of the *Ajapâla* banyan tree, drew near to where the *Muchalinda* tree was, and having drawn near, he sat cross-legged at the foot of the *Muchalinda* tree for seven days together, experiencing the bliss of emancipation. (83)

Now, at that time, a great cloud appeared out of season, and for seven days, it was rainy, cloudy weather, with a cold wind. Then issued Muchalinda, the serpent-king, from his abode, and enveloping the body of The Blessed One seven times with his folds, spread his great hood above his head, saying:

> "Let neither cold nor heat nor gnats, flies, wind; neither sunshine nor creeping creatures come near The Blessed One!".

Once the storm had passed, the *Naga* monarch unwound his coils, changed into a young man, and bowed low to the world saviour with hands respectfully joined together.

The fourth is the *rajayātana* tree (a kind of forest tree). Here, the inscription reads:

'After Enlightenment, Lord spent the seventh week here in meditation. Two merchants – Tapussa and Bhallka – offered rice cake and honey to the Lord and took refuge under him – *Buddham Saranam Gacchami; Dhammam Saranam Gacchami.*' (*Sangha* was not founded then).

Under the Muchalinda tree, Śree Buddha uttered the words:

"How blest the happy solitude
Of him who hears and knows the truth!
How blest is harmlessness towards all,
And self-restraint towards living things!
How blest from passion to be free,
All sensuous joys to leave behind!
Yet far the highest bliss of all
To leave the pride which says, *I am*." (84)

Asvattha Titbits:

- *Aśvattha* wood is used for brushing teeth in the months *Mārgaśīrṣa* (Nov.-Dec.) and *Pauṣha (Pausa)* (Dec.-Jan) for the *Kṛṣhṇāṣhṭamī-Vrata*, according to the 10th century *Saurapurāṇa,* one of the various *upapurāṇas* depicting *Śaivism.* In the month of *Pauṣa (Pausha),* the toothbrush is that of *aśvattha,* food is ghee, and the deity to be worshipped is Śaṃbhu (an aspect of Siva); the merit accrued is eight times that of *vājapeya (a name of a Vedic yajna).* Aśvattha wood is also used for brushing the teeth in the month *Jyeṣhṭa* (May-June) or the *Anaṅgatrayodaśī-Vrata,* observed in honour of Siva. In *Jyeṣhta,* the toothbrush is that of *aśvattha*-wood, the food taken is *lavaṅga,* the deity to be worshipped is Pradyumna (an aspect of Siva), the flowers used in worship are *mallika* (jasmine), and the *naivedya* offerings is *sohalikā.* The result accrued equals *vajapeya* yajna.(85)
- *Aśvattha* is one of the thirty-six sacred trees, according to the *Ṣaṭsāhasra saṃhitā,* an expansion of the *Kubjikāmata tantra*: the earliest popular and most authoritative Tantra of the *Kubjikā* cult. Accordingly, *Aśvattha* trees are the most

excellent *Kula* trees with accomplishments and liberation. They are full of *Yoginīs, Siddhas*, Lords of the Heroes and hosts of gods and demons. One should not touch them with one's feet, urinate and defecate on them, or have sex, etc., below them. One should not cut or burn them. Having worshipped and praised them regularly with their flowers and shoots, one should always worship the *Śrīkrama* with devotion with their best fruits and roots...".

- *Aśvattha* is one of the nine *kulavṛkṣhas* (*Kula* trees) in which the *Kula Yoginīs* reside, according to the *Kulārṇava-tantra* verse 11.66-68. Accordingly, *Kula Yoginīs* always live in *kulavṛkṣas* (*Kula* trees). Therefore, one should not eat on the leaves of such trees, and they should be especially worshipped. The cultural prohibitions associated with Aśvattha (*such* as not sleeping under the *Kula Vṛkṣhas)*, carry significant weight in these traditions. *Aśvattha* represents one of the four types of *Kṣīravṛkṣha* (milk-tree), according to the *Netratantra* of Kṣhemarāja, a *Śaiva* text from the 9th century in which Śiva (Bhairava) teaches Pārvatī topics such as metaphysics, cosmology, and soteriology (the study of religious doctrines of salvation.). They are used in rites of pacification and prosperity. (86)

- *Aśvattha* is one of the eight trees (*vṛkṣha*) of the *Gunachakra*, according to the 10th century Ḍākārṇava chapter 15. Accordingly, the *guṇachakra* refers to one of the four divisions of the *sahaja-puṭa* ('innate layer'), situated within the *Padma* (lotus) in the middle of the

Herukamaṇḍala. *Aśvattha* is associated with the charnel grounds (*śmaśāna*) named *Gahvara*; with the direction-guardian (*dikpāla*) named Kubera; with the serpent king (*nāgendra*) named Takṣaka and with the cloud king (*meghendra*) named Ghūrṇita. (87).

- *Aśvattha* is the *chaitya tree* under which the parents of Ananta are often depicted in Jaina iconography, according to both the *Śvetāmbara* and *Digambara* traditions. The term *chaitya* refers to "sacred shrine," an important place of pilgrimage and meditation in Jainism. Sculptures with such *chaitya trees generally show* a male and a female couple seated under a tree, with the female having a child on her lap. (88)

- *Aśvattha* is one of the five *udumbara* fruits considered forbidden to eat for Jain laypeople, as listed under the *khādima* category of forbidden food (*āhāra*), according to *Amitagati* in his 11th century *Śrāvakācāra*.

- *Aśvattha* is the *chaitya vṛikṣha* (sacred tree) associated with the Asurakumāra class of the *bhavanavāsin* species of Devas (gods), according to Jain cosmology. (89)

One must appreciate and marvel at the fact that the worship of the peepal tree that started over 4500 years ago continues in Indian society uninterruptedly, despite the foreign occupation, sociocultural changes, and scientific advancements that swept through the Indian subcontinent during the past centuries. However, the current pace of changes that the younger generations confront is rather corrosive and may strike deep into the sociocultural setup of our country, and in the years to come, many religious beliefs and practices of the present may undergo sweeping changes and even extinction. "Beyond its historical context, the Bodhi Tree holds a universal message of wisdom and compassion. Its teachings transcend cultural and religious boundaries, inviting people of all backgrounds to explore the depths of their consciousness. The Bodhi Tree's shade becomes a refuge for seekers from all walks of life, asking them to rest in its wisdom and contemplate life's profound mysteries...The Bodhi Tree serves as a profound reminder that true enlightenment begins within. Just as the tree's growth is nurtured from the inside out, our spiritual journey requires introspection, self-awareness, and a willingness to let go of attachments that hinder our progress. The Bodhi Tree encourages us to explore the depths of our minds, confront our fears, and transform ourselves from within." (90)

The Asvattha stotram:

The *Stotram* is in Sanskrit and the translation given is by Sri PR Ramachander, a Sanskrit scholar and translator of many Sanskrit prayers to English.

> *moolatho brahma roopāyamadhyatho*
> *Vishnu roopine*
> *āgrathaṣivaroopāyavrikśharajaya the namaha*
> My Salutations to the king of trees.
> Whose root is the form of Brahma,
> Middle is the form of Lord Vishnu,
> And top is the form of Lord Śiva.
> *Aśvattha sarva pāpānasatha janmaarjithanicha*
> *ṇudhasva mama vrakśendra*
> *sarvaaisvaryapradho bhava|*
> The holy banyan tree pushes away, all sins earned,
> In several hundred births, and Oh king of trees,

Please grant me all different types of wealth.
Āyurbalam yasovarcha prajapasuvasooni cha
brahma prajnam cha medham ca
thvamnodehivanaspathe
Would you not give me, Oh product of the forest.
Long life, fame, splendour, children,
cattle and riches,
As also knowledge of God and
intellectual wisdom.
ṣathatham varunorakśheththvam
aradvruṣtirasrayedh
parithasthvamni śhevanthamthrunani
sukhamasthu the|
Varuna always protects you as you are
rain dependent,
And you do not allow any grass to grow in
the shade round you.
ākśhispaandhambhujaspaandhamdu
svapnamdhur vichinthanam
ṣathroonam cha samuthanamhy asvastha
samaya prabho|
Oh Lord Äsvatha, please control pain in the eye,
Pain of hands, bad dreams, bad and evil thoughts,
And help me in destruction of my enemies.
Aśvatthā yavarenyāyasarva aisvaryapradāyine
ṇamo dusvapnanasāyasusvapnaphaladāyine|
Oh aśvattha who blesses us and grants
all type of wealth,
My Salutations to you, who destroys
bad dreams and grants good dreams.
Yām druśtvamucytherogai
ṣpruśhtva papa paipramuchyathe
yad aśhrayathchiranjeevi

ṭham aśvatthamnam āhmyaham|
I Salute that aśvattha,
Seeing which diseases flee,
Touching which sins are destroyed,
And surrendering to which,
You get long healthy life.
Aśvattha sumahabhaga subhagapriya darsana
īśhtakamam cha may dehiśatrubhyasch
aparābhavam|
Oh great Lord Äsvatha, who is pretty and looks
pretty,
Please fulfill all my desires and give
disappointment to my enemies.
Āayuprajam dhanamdhānyam soubhagyam
sarvasampadam
ḍehi deva mahavrikśhathvam aham
saranamgatha|
I surrender fully to you and,
So be pleased to give, oh great tree,
Long life, sons, wealth, cereals,
Great luck all types of wealth.
rig yajusamamanthrathma sarvaroopiparathpara
aśvattho vedamooloasouriśhibhi prochyathesada|
Great sages go in search of Äsvatha,
As it is the soul of Rig, Yajur and Sama Vedas
And takes all forms, greater than the greatest,
And is the root of all the three Vedas.
Brahmahaguruhachaiva daridhro vyadhipeeditha
Āavarthyalakśhasankhyamtham sthothram
yedath sukheebhavth|

If this prayer is repeated one hundred thousand
times,
Even those cursed by Brahma or the teacher,

And those who are poor and diseased,
Would get cured of all ills and lead a pleasant life.
Vyakthaavyakthasvaroopaya
sruśtisthithyanthakarine
Ādhimadhyanthsoonyaya viśtara sravasenama|

Salutations to the very stable one,
Who has clear and unclear forms,
Who creates, looks after and destroys,
And who does not have beginning, middle and end.

ravim ravavadharaogye
ṣivam some ṣhivaya cha
ṣakthim bhoumejayarthi ca
vanijyarthibudhe saran|
ġurougurum cha vidhyarthi
ḍhanarthi bhargavesriyam
ṣarvadukha vimokśharthee
ṣarve sammandhavasare|
ṣarvada sarvadevamscha
viśeśhanmada somayo
aśvatth aroopinodevan
vrikśharajo prapoojayeth

Go round on Sundays and worshipping
Sun to get heath,
Go round on Mondays and worshipping
Śiva to get pleasant life,
Go round on Tuesdays and worshipping Parvathy
to get victory,,
Go round on Wednesdays and worshipping devas,
to get luck in business,
Go round on Thursdays and Worshipping Guru to
get good knowledge,

Go round on Fridays and worshipping Goddess Lakshmi to get wealth,
Go round on Saturdays and worshipping the greatest god, to get rid of all sorrow.
Always all gods, especially Saturn and the moon,
Worship the God in the form of *asvattha,*
And offer prayers to this Lord of all trees.

Description and uses:

Peepal*: Ficus religiosa* **Linn. (Ficus family – Moraceae)**

[Peepal, sacred fig (English); pipal, peepal, peepul (Hindi); Rangibasri, Aśvatthamara, Aralimara (Kannada); Arayal (Malayalam); Arasumaram, arrayal, arasan (Tamil); Äsvathamu, bodhi (Teungu); Bawdi nyaung, Lagat, Mai nyawng Bur, Si weishu Chi, Pu tishu (Taiwan); Piguier-ou-arbrepagodes (French); Reliugioser Fiegenbaum (German); Bo, Bodhi (Sinhala) Pho (Thai); Pho simaha pho (Central Thailand)]

The peepal is a large and handsome tree without prop roots, distributed in South Asian countries, including Burma, Thailand, China, Cambodia, etc. The peepal tree is often grown as an avenue tree and planted in extensive ornamental gardens. The leaves have long-petioles, cordate, and shiny, with an apex drawn into a tail. The flowers are minute, highly reduced, and organized into an inflorescence known as hypanthium. The fruit of the peepal tree is an enclosed infructescence, a syconium, and an urn-like structure lined with fruits, often mixed with flowers and pollinator wasps. The tree exudes latex when cut.

In traditional Ayurveda, peepal is known mainly as *pippala* or *pipla*. Charaka and Susrutha indicated bark decoction in haemorrhages, leaves as a poultice for covering wounds, and root paste for treating skin afflictions and urinary disorders. Rice cooked in milk with peepal bark, fruit, buds, root, honey, and sugar is reportedly an aphrodisiac.

The classical Ayurvedic text *Bhavaprakasha describes pippala's properties*:

> "*Pippala* is difficult to digest, cold in potency, cures diseases of *pitta, sleshma,* and *rakta,* and heals ulcers. It is heavy in action, astringent in taste, promotes complexion, and cures the diseases of female external genitalia."

Dhanwanthari Nighantu indicates peepal for *rakta dosha* and *kapha dosha.* It is a very good urinary astringent. Khare gives the following properties: "Bark is astringent, antiseptic, alternative, laxative, haemostatic, vaginal disinfectant. Leaves and twigs are laxative. Aerial roots have the quality of promoting conception in women. Dried fruit is a uterine tonic. In folk medicine, bark decoction controls whooping cough and asthma. (91)

The fruits contain 4.9% protein, with two essential amino acids (isoleucine and phenylalanine). The seeds contain phytosterols such as β-sitosterol and its glycosides, albuminoids, carbohydrates, fatty matter, colouring matter, and a natural type of rubber (caoutchoue 0.7–5.1%.). The fruits contain flavonols like kaempferol, quercetin, and myricetin. Leaves and fruits contain carbohydrates, protein, lipids, calcium, sodium, potassium, and phosphorus.

The major constituents of the bark are:

Different kinds of phenolics, fibre, lignin, saponins, wax, lupeol, ceryl behenate, leucoanthocyanidin, leucopelargonidin-3-0-β-Dglucopyranoside, leucopelargonidin-3-0-α-L-rhamno pyranoside, lupeol acetate, α-amyrin acetate, leucoan thoc yanidin, and leucoanthocyanin. The bark extract has antioxidant, anti-convulsant, anti-ulcer, anti-diabetic, proteolytic, etc. (92, 93). In Ayurveda, a combination of barks of four fig trees, known as *nalpamara,* is used for treating skin ailments. They are Peepal (*Ficus religiosa*), *Vata* (*Ficus benghalensis*), *Udumbara* (cluster fig: *Ficus racemosa*) and *Plaksha* (Indian laurel: *Ficus lacor, F. virens*). They have similar properties and composition and are prescribed in cases of diarrhoea, dysentery, various skin afflictions, urinary disorders, vaginal disorders, etc. Ayurvedic formulations such as *aśvatthamūladi modaka, nalpamaradi tailom*, and toiletry articles like *nalpamaradi* soap are the widely used products containing peepal bark.

Citations and notes

(General references are listed at the end of the book)

1. The Life of Sakyumuni Buddha, Jodo Shinshu Buddhist Temples of Canada – Living Dharma Centre, http:// www.bcc.ca/ Buddhism/sakyamuni.htm, accessed on 20 June, 2010.

2. Fischer, R. E, Buddhist Art and Architecture, 1993; quoted from E.B.Findly.

3. Swami Chidbhvananda, The Bhagavad Gita, 1975 (Cited from Ojha, 1991)

4. Purnachandra Bhasha Kosa. Cited from Ojha PC (1991) Asvattha in everyday life. Sundeep Prakasan, New Delhi.

5. Ojha, PC (1991) Asvattha in everyday life as related to puranas. Sundeep prakashan, Delhi.

6. Story of the Bodhi tree by Daneuse Murty and various other articles that appeared in www; Bodhi tree or *Bodhi druma*, Chapter 8, in Alexander Cunningham's

book, Mahabodhi or the great Buddhist temple under the Bodhi tree at Buddha Gaya, 1998.

7, Adikaram, E.W.: Early History of Buddhism in Ceylon, 1946 (Reprint 1994).

8. Dhamma – Puja, Bodhi vandana (Salutations to the Bodhi tree), also available at: http://www.buddhistpilgrimage. info/puja_-_all.htm.

9. Mukundananda Swami (2014) Bhagavad Gita The Song of God. https://www.holy-bhagavad-gita.org/publishers-note.

10.Chaitanya Charitāmṛit, Madhya Leela 20.117-118, Cited from Mukudananda (9),

11. See (3)

12.Mingun, S ed. (1992). Appendix: List of the Mahabodhi Trees of 24 Buddhas. The Great Chronicle of Buddhas. Vol. 1, Part 2. Yangon, Myanmar: Ti=Ni Press. pp. 316–317, 322.

13. Halder 1977

14. Burkill 1946

15.Comaraswamy 1971

16. Snodgrass, A (1985). The Symbolism of the Stūpa. Motilal BanarsidassPublishe,New Delhi.

17. Anonymous (2010) The Life of Sakyumuni Buddha, Jodo Shinshu Buddhist Temples of Canada – Living Dharma Centre, http://www.bcc.ca/ buddhism/sakyamuni. htm, accessed on 20 June, 2010.

18. Fischer, R. E, Buddhist Art and Architecture, 1993; quoted from E. B. Findly.

19. JSBT (2010) Jodo Shinshu Buddhist Temples of Canada, The Life of Sakyumuni Buddha– Living Dharma Centre, http://www.bcc.ca/ buddhism/sakyamuni.htm;

20. JSBT (see 19)

21. The White Lotus (Ch.7, the Lion Budha). Osho on-line library. www.osho.com/online library-ad infinitum-bodhidharma.

22. JSBT (2010) (see 19)

23. Murty D (2003) Biography of Sakyamuni Buddha. The Corporate Body of the Buddha Educational Foundation, Taipei, Taiwan.

24. See 23.

25. See 23.

26. Adikaram, E. W.: Early History of Buddhism in Ceylon, 1946 (Reprint 1994).

27. JSBT (2010) Jodo Shinshu Buddhist Temples of Canada (2010) The Life of Sakyumuni Buddha,– Living Dharma Centre, http://www.bcc.ca/ buddhism/sakyamuni. htm, accessed on 20 June, 2010.

28. Murty D (2003) (see 23)

29. Murty D. (1982, 1998) Story of the Bodhi tree by Daneuse Murty and various other articles that appeared in www; Bodhi tree or Bodhi druma, Chapter 8, in Alexander Cunningham's book, Mahabodhi or the great Buddhist temple under the Bodhi tree at Buddha Gaya, 1892. Digital edn. 2009.

30-31. See 29.

32. Anonymous (2023) Bodhi Tree. Wikipedia, https:// en.wikipedia.org/wiki/Bodhi_Tree#cite_note-GCB1P2-29

33. Anonymous (2023) The Buddha's enlightenment. Uni. Idaho, https://www.webpages.uidaho.edu/ngier/307/enlight.htm.

34. Anonymous (2006) The Practice of the Fourth Watch of the Night.https://wisdom-tree.com/wisdom/thefourthwatch.html.

35. Anon (2023) Four stages of awakening. https://en.wikipedia.org/wiki/Four_stages_of_awakening.

36. Mihita, Bhikkhu (2019) Night of Buddha's enlightenment. Sumeru books, Ottawa, Canada.

37. Anon. (2012) The Illustrated Dhammapada. Buddha Dharma Education Association Inc., https://buddhanet.net/dhammapada/d_oldage.htm.

38. Fischer, R. E, Buddhist Art and Architecture, 1993; quoted from E. B. Findly.

39. Haberman, D., People Trees, Oxford University Press, UK, 2013

40. BBC (2021) The Buddha and his teachings in Buddhism: The Noble Eightfold Path. https://www.bbc.co.uk/bitesize/guides/zr3sv9q/revision/3.

41. Adikaram, see 26.

42. Murty D, see 29.

43-47. Mahavamsa, 17, 18: The Receiving of the Great Bodhi-Tree. https://mahavamsa.org/mahavamsa/original-version/18-receiving-great-bodhi-tree/.

48-49. Ravindran PN (2020) Sacred and Ritual plants of India. Notion press, Chennai.

50. Adikaram (see 26)

51. Kariyawasam AGS (1995) Buddhist Ceremonies and Rituals of Sri Lanka, Buddhist Publication Society, Kandy, Sri Lanka.

52. Buddha puja, t www.thebuddhistcentre.com/translations.

53. Seneviratne HL et al (2009) Bodhipuja: collective representations of Sri Lanka youth. American Ethnologist,7(4):734 – 743. DOI:10.1525/ae.1980.7.4.02a00080.

54. *Dhamma – Puja, Bodhi vandana* (Salutations to the Bodhi tree), also available at: http://www.buddhistpilgrimage.info/puja_-_all.htm

55. Five *skandhas*, Buddhist Encyclopedia, https://www.encyclopediaofbuddhism.org/wiki/Five_skandhas.

56. May SS (2015) 28 Buddhas. Asian and African studies blog, https://britishlibrary.typepad.co.uk/asian-and-african/2015/06/28-buddhas.html.

57. Gopinatha Rao, T. A. Elements of Hindu Iconography, 2 Vols., 1914. The material cited is taken from Bansi Lal Malla, Trees in Indian Art, Mythology and Folklore, 2000.

58. Macdonell A.A. Vedic Mythology, 1971.Quoted from Ravindran 2020. (see 48.

59-61. Ravindran (see 48)

62. Harshananda Swami (2008) A Concise Encyclopedia of Hinduism, vol.2, Ramakrishna Math, Bangalore, 2008.

63. Nair P T (1965) Tree marriages in India. In: Gupta, S. N. (ed.), Tree Symbol Worship in India, Indian Publications, Calcutta.

64. Anonymous (2024) Marriage with Trees & Plants, Indian Wedding, http://www. indianetzone.com /27/

marriage_   with_trees_plants_inanimate_objects_ indian_custom.htm., 2-14.

65. Kabiratna S. MeyedorVratakatha. Quoted from Ojha, see (29).

66. Chettiar, S.M.L. Folklore of Tamil Nadu, 1980.

67. Dwivedi, D. (2017) Aśvattha related rituals: a study, http:// www.academia.edu/26961811/   a%c5%9avattha_ related_rituals_a_study_e-learning_document.

68-69. Haberman D (2013) People Trees, Oxford University Press, UK.

70. Gupta S M (1996) Plants in Indian Temple Art, B. R. Publishing, New Delhi.

71. Randhawa M S (1957) Flowering Trees In India, 1ICAR, New Delhi.

72. Swami Chidbhvananda, The Bhagavad Gita, 1975. (Cited from Ojha, 1991)

73. Dwivedi (see 67).

74. Ojha, PC (1991) Asvattha in everyday life as related to puranas. Sundeep Prakashan, Delhi.

75-77. Ravindran (see 48)

78. Chettiar (see 66)

79. Dwivedi (see 67).

80. Ojha (see 74)

81. Anon. (2022) Vidhurashwatha—connecting Mahabharatha and freedom movement of India. https://adventourer. in/vidhurashwatha/.

82. Anon (2004). This legend is given in the Buddhist studies of the Buddha Dharma Education Association, The Chan (Jap. Zen) School of Buddhism).

83. Beveridge, J. 'Between the Palace and the Bodhi Tree' "The poems (in this book) are an imaginative depiction of Siddharttha Gautama, who later become the Buddha, as he wanders the towns and forests of north India in around 500 BC, before he achieved enlightenment," Beveridge.)

84. Mahavagga: The Mahavagga consists of several sutra-like texts, including an account of the period, immediately following the Buddha's awakening, his first sermons to the group of five monks, and stories of how some of his great disciples joined the Sangha and themselves attained Awakening. Also included details of various rituals and rites for the monks.

85-89. Anon. (2024) Ashvattha, Aśvattha, Āśvattha: https://www.wisdomlib.org/definition/ashvattha.

90. Anon. (2024) The Significance and Spiritual Symbolism of the Bodhi Tree. https://plantsinformation.com/... Buddhists%20worldwide.

91. The minor anthologies of the Pali Canon: Buddhavamsa and Cariyā-Piṭaka, translated by Bimala Churn Law. London: Oxford University Press, 1938.

92. Khare CP (2004) Encyclopedia of Indian medicinal plants. Berlin Heidelberg, New York: Springer-Verlag.

93. Chandrasekar SB et al. (2010) Phytopharmacology of *Ficus religiosa*. Pharmacogn Rev. 2010 Jul;4(8):195-9. doi: 10.4103/0973-7847.70918.

03

BANYAN (*VATA, NYGRODHA*)

The Tree of Immortality

"It was a godly sight to see
The venerable tree
For over the lawn, irregularly spread
Fifty straight columns propt its lofty heads
And many a long depending shoot
Seeking to strike a root
Straight like a plummet grew towards the ground
So like a temple did it seem that there
A pious heart first, impulse would be prayer...." (1)

The Banyan, the national tree of India, is revered as sacred in Hinduism. Banyan has played a significant role in the social and religious life of the Indians from ancient times to the present. For centuries, the banyan tree has been a central point for the village communities of India, the focal point of human interactions and socialisation. The banyan hosts the local market, as the village traders use the shade to sell their merchandise. The tree is often a symbol of the fabled *'Kalpa Vriksha'* or the 'Tree of Wish Fulfilment.' It is also the tree of immortality (*Akshaya Vata*), associated with longevity. The banyan tree itself is an ecosystem and supports several life forms. Banyan trees can grow to massive proportions; in terms of canopy spread and volume, banyan occupies the first position in the plant kingdom. The tree is also known as *bahupada* (having many legs) because, as the tree spreads, many roots grow down from the main trunk and branches, establishing in the ground and becoming trunk-like. They support the weight of the growing branches of the banyan tree. A large banyan looks like a forest. Some of the giant banyan trees occur in India, and the topmost position goes to the tree named *Thimmamma* in a village in Andhra Pradesh, which occupies an area of more than five acres of land.

The banyan tree, like the peepal, is considered the seat of the Trinity: Brahma in the root, Vishnu in the trunk, and Śiva in the branches. The banyan tree is described as the 'crested one', because of its widespread overhanging canopy. Śiva is the presiding deity of the tree, and devotees believe the tree is his incarnation, following a curse of Parvathi (see the chapter on peepal). Dakshinamurthi, an aspect of Śiva as preceptor, is depicted as seated under a banyan tree (the tree of knowledge) and imparts knowledge or *vidya* to the seekers. The tree also symbolises Brahma and grows in Pushkaradwipa, his abode.

In *Rg Veda* and *Sama Veda,* there is no mention of *Nygrodha /Vata.* But in *Rg Veda,* there is mention of a tree named *Pischel,* which, from its characteristics, can be equated to *Vata/ Nygrodha (RV* I-24-7). It is frequently mentioned in *Atharvaveda* and later literature. *Sukla Yajurveda* mentions vessels made from *Vata (nygrodha)* wood for use in *Aswamedha yaga* (horse sacrifice). *Atharvaveda* gives some hymns and incantations to drive away the demigods (*Apsaras* and *Gandharvas*) occupying the *nygrodha* tree. In *Adharva Veda,* there is a statement that *Gandharva* and *Apsaras* won't be present where *nygrodha* grows. There is also a recommendation to grow *vata* trees to purify air.

Vayu Purana mentions that *Vata/Nygrodha* symbolises prosperity; the fruits are food for *Durga,* and *Yaksa* worships the tree. According to *Kurma Purana, Padma Purana,* and *Mastya Purana,* whoever dies under the *Vata* tree goes directly to heaven. In *Vishnu Purana*, the *Vata* tree is equated with Vishnu.

> "All this world was derived from thee. As the wide-spreading *Nygrodha* tree is compressed in a small seed, the whole universe is comprehended in thee as its germ at the time of dissolution. As the *Nygrodha* germinates from the seed and becomes first a shoot and then rises into loftiness, the created world proceeds from thee and expands into magnitude. As the bark and leaves of the Plantain tree are to be seen in its stem, thou art the stem of the universe, and all things are visible in thee. The faculties of the intellect that cause pleasure and pain abide in thee as one with all existence; but the sources of pleasure and pain, singly or blended, do not exist in thee, who art exempt from all qualities." (VP, I.12.2).

According to the *Vamana Purana,* the *vata* tree arose from Manibhadra, the chief of Yakshas. In *Markhandeya Purana*, while describing the *Jambudvipa,* it is stated that a *Vata vriksha* (a great Banyan tree) stands on Suparva mountain. In conclusion to the description of Earth, we get the statement that "at Mount Meru, there is a green-leaved *Nygrodha,* and the people drink the juice of its fruits, and the men who eat its fruits live for a thousand years, free from old age and illnesses."

In *Ramayana,* Valmiki mentioned many trees in *Ayodhya, Aranya,* and *Kishkinda kanda.* (Kanda= part).

Among them, the most vividly described is the *Vata vriksha,* five banyan trees in the *Panchavati* forests. In *Mahabharata,* Rishi Veda Vyasa mentioned that Pandavas, during their life in forests (*Vanavasa*), spent about four months under a *Vata vriksha.* In *Bhagavata Purana,* Krishna, as an infant, is described as sleeping on a Banyan (the tree of eternity) leaf. According to *Manu Smrti, Kshatriya* warriors are eligible to keep the *gada* (wooden weapon) prepared out of Banyan wood. Either Vishnu or Siva occupies the *Nygrodha* trees planted in front of the temples (of Vishnu / Siva). The trees planted in public places like crossroads, village squares, or open grounds are tenanted by lesser divinities such as Yaksa, Kinnara, or Gandharva. During the universal deluge at the end of a *Kalpa,* Lord Vishnu sleeps on a leaf of *Nygrodha* that floats on the eternal waters. (2)

About the great trees *Rig – Veda Brahmana* makes a mention (Keith's translation):

> '*Nygrodha* is the lordly power of the trees
> *Udumbara* is the paramount ruler of trees
> *Aśvattha* is the overlordship of the trees
> *Plaksha* is the self-rule and sovereignty of the trees.'

These four trees mentioned above are considered the greatest of the Indian trees from the Vedic times and were intimately associated with the Vedic rituals of the past in various ways. The real identity of the *udumbara* tree is still doubtful, though the Ayurvedic experts equated it with the cluster fig, *Ficus racemosa.*

Banyan tree with several prop roots.

A banyan tree in a park

| Banyan fruits | Banyan leaves |

Banyan tree as a metaphor

Banyan and its fruit and seed were proof for illustrating one of Hinduism's most profound metaphysical principles: the mystery of the *ātman* and its manifestation. There is a famous legend given in *Chandogya Upanishad.*

> "Sage Uddalaka had a son called Shvetaketu (Svetaketu). When he was twelve, his father told him, "It is time for you to find a spiritual teacher. Everyone in this family has studied the holy scriptures and the spiritual way." So Shvetaketu went to a teacher and studied the scriptures for twelve years. He returned home very proud of his intellectual knowledge. His father observed him and said:

> "My boy, you seem to have a high opinion of yourself; you are proud of your learning. But did you ask your teacher for the spiritual knowledge that enables you to hear the unheard, think the unthought, and know the unknown?"

> "What is that knowledge, Father?" asked Shvetaketu.

> Uddalaka said:

"Just as by knowing a lump of clay, everything made of clay can be known, since any differences are only words, and the essential Reality is clay. In the same way, by knowing a piece of gold, all that is made of gold can be known since any differences are only words, and the Reality is only gold."

Shvetaketu responded, "My teachers must not have known this, or they would have taught it to me. Father, please teach me this knowledge."

"I will," replied his father, and he continued, "In the beginning, there was only Being. Some people claim that there was nothing at all in the beginning and that everything has come out of nothing. But how can this be true? How can that which is come from that which is not? Initially, there was only one Being, and that Being thought, 'I want to be many so that I will create.' Out of this creation came the cosmos. There is nothing in the universe that doesn't come from that one Being. Of everything that exists, this Being is the innermost Self. He is the truth, the Self Supreme. And you, Shvetaketu, you–are that!"

Shvetaketu asked, "Please teach me more about the Self, Father."

"Let's start with sleep. What happens when we sleep? When a person is absorbed in dreamless sleep, he is one with the Self, although he does not know it. We say he sleeps but we mean he sleeps in the Self. 'A tethered bird grows tired from flying in every direction, finding no rest anywhere, and settles down at last on the very same perch on which it is tied.

In the same way, the mind, tired of wandering around here and there, settles down at last in the Self, its life and breath, to which it is bound. All creatures have their source in that Being. He is their home; He is their strength. 'When a man is dying, speech folds into mind, mind folds into life, life dissolves into light, and his light merges into that one Being. That Being is the seed, the truth, the Self, and you, Shvetaketu, you—are that! "

"Please tell me more, Father."

"My son, bees make honey by gathering nectar from many flowers to make their honey, so no one drop of honey can say that it came precisely from one specific flower. You can't identify the juice of one particular flower in the honey. And so, it is with creatures like us who merge in that Being, whether in sleep or death.

And as the rivers that flow from the east to the west merge in the sea and become one with it, forgetting that they were ever separate rivers, all creatures lose their separateness when they merge into pure Being. Whatever creature it may be – tiger, lion, wolf, boar, mosquito, worm – it only becomes aware of a particular life when it is born into it or is awake.

If you strike at the root of a tree, it bleeds but still lives. If you strike at the trunk, the sap oozes, but the tree lives on. The Self as life fills the tree and supports it; it flourishes in happiness, gathering food through its roots. However, if life departs from one branch, that branch withers, and when life leaves the whole tree, the entire tree withers.

Remember, my son, your body dies, but your Self does not."

Uddalaka told Shvetaketu to bring him a fruit from a nearby banyan tree and to break it open.

Shvetaketu did and said, "There are seeds inside, all tiny."

"Now, break one of the seeds and tell me what you see."

"Nothing, Father."

Uddalaka said, "'My son, this great banyan tree has grown from a seed so small that you cannot see it. Believe me, the Spirit of the whole universe is an invisible and subtle essence. Now, take this Salt, put it in some water, and bring it to me tomorrow morning."

The following day, Shvetaketu looked for the Salt but could not find it because it had dissolved. Uddalaka asked his son to taste the water. "Salty," he said, adding, "The salt will always remain in the water."

"That's right. The Salt permeates the water, just like the Self. Even though we cannot see it, the Self is within all things, and there is nothing that does not come from Him. This invisible and subtle essence is the Spirit of the whole universe. That is Reality. That is truth. And you, Shvetaketu, you— are that, "and he continued:

"verily, my dear, that finest essence, which you do not perceive; verily my dear, from that finest essence this great *nygrodha* thus arises. Believe me, my dear', said he, 'that which is the finest essence, this whole world has that as its soul. That is Reality. That is *ātman, 'Tat Tvam Asi.'– that art thou,* Shvetaketu."

(*Tat* = that; *Tvam* = thou or you; *Asi* = art or are; *Tat Tvam Asi* = That thou art, or thou art that, or you are that)

This statement *'That Art Thou' (tat tvam asi)* is one of the most remarkable and profound utterances (*mahavakyas*) of the *Upanishads*, one of the most significant metaphysical concepts given to the world by ancient India, and the banyan tree figures in it as a unique example, how the manifest universe emerged from the unmanifest essence. [There are four *Mahavakyas, fo*ur sutras, great utterances, in the Upanishads, each representing a Veda. They guide one from the gross Reality of *annamaya kosha* or physical body, to *manomaya kosha*, the astral body, and then to *pranamaya kosha*, the causal body. The soul, free from the entanglements of the body, attains the *jivanmukhta* state. The awakened Self is now a part of the all-pervasive *Brahman.* These *Mahavakyas* convey the essential teaching of the Upanishads: Reality is one, and the individual is identical to it. The four *Mahavakyas* are:

- *Prajñānam Brahma – Brahman* is *Prajñānam –* knowledge is truth; *Aitareya Upanishad* 3.3 of the Rg Veda.
- *Ayam ātmā Brahma –* This Self (Atman) is Brahman *– Mandukya Upanishad* 1.2 of the Atharva Veda
- *Tat tvam asi –* "Thou art that," *Chandogya Upanishad* 6.8.7 of the Sama Veda
- *Aham brahmāsmi –* "I am (part of) Brahman", or "I am the Divine; *Brihadaranyaka Upanishad* 1.4.10 of the Yajur Veda.]

The banyan is one of the most sheltering trees in our tropical country; its shade is dense and soothing, and from ancient times, many travellers have found solace under its cool shade. It gave shelter to countless oxcarts, horses, and cattle as the tree was abundant on the waysides and open places. From ancient times, the riders and messengers travelling for days from one place to another took refuge under the banyan tree. Under the banyan tree, the local chieftains held the assembly of the people, and under its shade, the merchants sold their merchandise. The very name banyan is derived from the term *baniya*, meaning merchants. The banyan tree was once the focal point of the assembly of people for celebrations, and the old and jobless assembled under the tree in the evenings to talk, laugh and spend time. The Pandya King Adhiveera Rama, who was known for his didactic verses in chaste Tamil, is known to have wondered:

> "A single seed from a little fruit of the Aal tree (Banyan) is not even as big as the egg of the smallest fish in the pond. It is able, however, to grow into a mighty tree, which can shelter a royal entourage, complete with giant elephants, chariots, and elegant horses apart from all the royal attendants!"

Respect for this and other trees of this nature is thus linked to their use and sacred associations. The banyan was a part of the daily life of the Indians till almost recent times when TV and cell phones usurped our lives. (3).

Vata tree— Mythology

The mythology of *Vata* and that of *Aśvattha* are entwined, and many myths and legends are common to both. For example, in *Matsya Purana*, we read that during the universal deluge at the end of four *yugas* (aeons, Kalpa), Lord Vishnu, in his infant form, sleeps on a *vata* leaf. In the *Bhagavatha Purana*, we get a story. The deathless Rishi Markhandeya was wandering through the watery abyss during the *Maha Pralaya* (great deluge) when he encountered a child sleeping on a *vata* leaf. Amazed, Markhandeya questioned the child and asked about his identity. The child replied that he was Narayana, the universe's creator, sustainer, and destroyer. Here, the *Vata* leaf is representative of the Tree of Life. The same *vata* leaf was mentioned as the abode of the Sun also. This very same legend is also given in the case of the peepal tree. In the *Vishnu Purana*, the *nygrodha (vata)* tree is compared to Lord Vishnu: identical words are used for *asvattha* (peepal) also (see the lines given at the beginning of this chapter).

Brahma Purana tells the legend that when the demon king Hiranyaka entered the sacrificial arena of Priyavrata, all the gods attending the function ran away or disappeared. Śiva entered the *Vata* tree, Vishnu the *Aśvattha,* and Brahma the *Palāsha* tree (see the previous chapter). In *Skanda Purana,* there is a legend that Brahma, along with the other gods, created the *Saptha Devathas** to kill the demon king Andhaka near a *Vata* tree. On the new moon day of *Srāvana*, worship of *Saptha Devathas* is ordained in certain places, such as Avanti. As in the case of *Aśvattha,* Banyan is also an abode of *Bhutamata*, who is worshipped from the first day of the dark fortnight till the 14th day. Chandika, an aspect of Durga, is said to occupy the root of the banyan tree. (Chandika is a fierce aspect of Durga, who assumed this form for killing the invincible Mahishasura. (See notes for details.)

[*There is more than one reference about the seven divine mothers (female deities, *Sapta Devatas* or *Sapta*

Mathrukkal), given in various epics and other religious texts, and one comes across differences in their names and their origin. Such differences probably mean the creation of the *Sapta Mathrukkal* took place more than once to fulfil more than one task. They are the manifestations of the divine, creations of various gods, all combining the powers of the respective gods and that of Durga Devi (also known as Sakthi, Parvathi, or Gauri). The earliest reference of *Sapta Matrika* is found in *Markandeya Purana*. The Seven devatas (mother goddesses) according to the puranas are: Brahmani, Vaishnavi, Maheshwari, Kaumari, Varahi, Indrani and Chamunda. Their description in ancient Puranas, such as *Varaha Purana, Matsya Purana, Markandeya Purana* etc refers to their antiquity. Each of the mother goddesses (except for Chamunda) had come to take her name from a particular God: Brahmani form Brahma, Vaishnavi from Vishnu, Maheswari from Shiva, Kaumari from Skanda, Varahi from Varaha and Indrani from Indra. Chamunda is an emanation from Devi Parvati. According to *Devi Bhagavatha*, nine female forms emanated from the gods; they are Brahmani, Vaishnavi, Sankari (Maheswari), Kaumari, Yamya, Narasimhi, Varahi, Kauberi and Varuni. They were created to help Durga for the elimination of Darika, the invincible asura, and to establish peace and righteousness in all three worlds. Brahmani, Vaishnavi, Maheswari, Kaumari, Indrani, Varahi and Chamundi are also known as the seven mothers *(Sapta Mathrukkal)*]. (4, 5)

Legends on Panchavati

The readers may be familiar with the name *Panchavati* of the Ramayana fame, located on the southern bank of Godavari. References to this place were plenty available in the Ramayana. Rama, Lakshmana, and Sita lived there for a few years, and some of the most crucial events, such as the abduction of Sita, took place there. Panchavati is the present-day Nasik. In ancient times, five large *vata* trees stood in a circle, hence the name *Pancha Vati (Panchavati)*, which was the place of five *vata* trees. There are two well-known legends associated with the five *vata* trees.

The first legend is about the Sun god and his consort Usha. Usha had a tough time with her husband because he was so dazzling, and it was difficult for her to even look at him. So, she came down to the earth and began to live in the hermitage of Kanwa Muni, one of the great *rishis* of the Puranas. Surya was anxious to meet his wife, so he came down to earth and went to the hermitage of Kanwa Muni. Usha saw Surya coming, and she wanted to escape. She took the form of a female horse and began to run away. Surya spotted her and pursued her in the guise of a male horse. He caught up with her, and they started making love in the form of horses. Five young inmates of a nearby hermitage were witnessing the scene, and they started laughing and shouting at the two disguised horses. Surya got angry and cursed them to be *vata* trees on the spot instantaneously. The boys sought forgiveness, and Surya told them that the curse would be lifted when Rama, the incarnation of Vishnu, came there along with his brother and wife and constructed their *ashram* on the spot. The place subsequently became known as *Panchavati,* the place of five *vata* trees.

The second legend is related to five Gandharva youths and the Rishi Agastya. Once, around the Panchavati, five Gandharva youths came across the renowned sage Agasthya. The boys decided to have some fun with the *rishi*. So, they encircled the *rishi* and did not allow him to move or proceed in any direction. After some time, the rishi got enraged and cursed the Gandharva youths to remain in the same spots as *vata* trees. The youths begged the sage for forgiveness and deliverance from the curse. Agasthya said that one day, Śri Rama, with his wife and brother, would come and stay in an *ashram* built amidst the five trees, and then they would get Salvation from the curse. (6, 7)

References to banyan in the ancient texts

Several references to banyan are found in ancient texts, particularly in the Maha Bhagavatha Purana (BP), which is believed to have been written by Rishi Ved Vyas. (Source: The essence of Vedic knowledge; https://vaniquotes.org/wiki/The_essence_of_Vedic_knowledge.)

BP. 1.6.15: ... After that, under the shadow of a **banyan tree** in an uninhabited forest, I began to meditate upon the Super soul situated within, using my intelligence, as I had learned from liberated souls.

BP. 1.10.21: ...The seeds of universes develop into gigantic forms like seeds of a **banyan tree** develop into numberless banyan trees.

BP. 2.5.11: ...Just as the tiny seed of a **banyan** fruit has the potency to create a giant **banyan** tree, the Lord disseminates all varieties of seeds by His potential *brahma-jyotir* (*sva-rociṣā*), and the seeds are made to develop by the watering process of persons like Brahmā.

BP. 2.7.29: Uprooting a gigantic **banyan** or arjuna tree and extinguishing a blazing forest fire simply by closing one's eyes are impossible by any human endeavour.

BP. 3.4.8: The Lord was sitting, taking rest against a young **banyan tree (or *asvattha* tree)**, with His right lotus foot on His left thigh, and although He had left all household comforts, He looked pretty cheerful in that posture.

BP 3.6.39: A small **banyan** fruit contains thousands of tiny seeds, and each seed holds the potency of another tree, which again has the potency of many millions of such fruits as causes and effects.

BP 3.33.4: As the Supreme Personality of Godhead, you have taken birth from my abdomen. Oh my Lord, how is that possible for the supreme one, who has all the cosmic manifestation in His belly? The answer is that it is possible, for at the end of the *Kalpa** You lie down on a banyan tree leaf and lick the toe of Your lotus foot just like a tiny baby. (**Kalpa*: A *Kalpa* is equal to 4.32 billion years, which is a "day of Brahma" (12-hour day proper) or one thousand *maha yugas*. A *Kalpa* is followed by a pralaya (dissolution) of equal length (a night of Brahma), which together constitute a day and night of Brahma.)

BP 4. 6.17: Mount Kailāsa is also decorated with trees such as *kata*, jackfruit, *julara*, peepal, *plakṣas*, **nygrodha**, and trees producing asafoetida. Also, there are trees of betel nuts and *bhūrja-patra*, *rājapūga*, blackberries, and similar trees.

BP 4.6.31: They also saw that the bathing ghāṭs and their staircases were made of *vaidūrya-maṇi*. The water was full of lotus flowers. Passing by such lakes, the demigods reached a place with a majestic **banyan** tree.

BP 4.6.32: That **banyan** tree was eight hundred miles high, and its branches spread over six hundred miles. The tree cast a shade, which permanently cooled the temperature, yet there was no noise of birds.

BP 4.18.25: The trees made a calf out of the **banyan** tree; thus, they derived milk from many delicious juices. The mountains transformed the Himalayas into a calf, milking various minerals into a pot made of the peaks of hills.

Bp 4.24.50: The Lord's abdomen is beautiful due to three ripples in the flesh. His abdomen resembles the leaf of a **banyan** tree, and when He exhales and inhales, the movement of the ripples appears very, very beautiful. The coils within the navel of the Lord are so deep that it seems that the entire universe sprouted out of it and yet again wishes to go back.

BP 5.14.41: As a monkey takes shelter in the branch of a **banyan** tree and thinks he is enjoying, the conditioned soul, not knowing the reality of his life, takes shelter of the path of *karma-kāṇḍa,* fruitive activities.

BP 5.16: On the side of Supārśva Mountain is a *Kadamba* tree with streams of honey flowing from its hollows, and on Kumuda Mountain there is a ***nygrodha*** tree named *Śatavalśa*, from whose roots flow rivers containing milk, yoghurt, and many other desirable things.

BP 5.16.12: Standing like flag staffs on the summits of these four mountains are a mango tree, a rose apple tree, a *kadamba* tree, and a **banyan** tree. Those trees have a width of 100 yojanas (800 miles) and a height of 1,100 yojanas (8,800 miles). Their branches also spread to a radius of 1,100 yojanas.

BP 5.16.24: Similarly, Kumuda Mountain has a marvellous **banyan** tree called *Śatavalśa* because it has a hundred main branches. From those branches come many roots, from which many rivers are flowing. These rivers flow down from the top of the mountain to the northern side of *Ilāvṛta-varṣa* for the benefit of those who live there. Because of these flowing rivers, all the people have ample supplies of milk, yoghurt, honey, clarified butter (ghee), molasses, food grains, clothes, bedding, sitting places, and ornaments. All the objects they desire are sufficiently supplied for their prosperity, so they are pleased.

BP 7.9.33: This cosmic manifestation, the material world, is Your body. This total lump of matter is agitated by Your potent energy known as *kāla-śakti*; thus, the three modes of material nature manifest. You awaken from the bed of Śeṣa, Ananta, and a tiny transcendental seed is generated from Your navel. From this seed, the gigantic universe's lotus flower is manifested precisely as a **banyan** tree grows from a tiny seed.

BP 8.2.9-13: In a valley of Trikūṭa Mountain, there was a garden called Ṛtumat. This garden belonged to the great devotee Varuṇa and was a sporting place for the damsels of the demigods. Flowers and fruits grew there in all seasons. Among them were *mandāras,pārijātas, pāṭalas, aśokas, champakas, chūtas, piyālas, paanasas, amras, āmrātakas, kramukas*, coconut trees, date trees, and pomegranates. There were *madhukas*, palm trees, *tamālas, asanas, arjunas, ariṣṭas, uḍumbaras, plakṣas*, **vata trees**, *kiṁśukas* and sandalwood trees. There were also *picumandas, kovidāras, saralas, sura-dārus*, grapes, sugarcane, bananas, *jambu, badarīs, akṣas, abhayas* and *āmalakīs*.

BP 10.18.22: ...Thus carrying and being carried by one another, and at the same time tending the cows, the boys followed Kṛishṇa to a **banyan tree** known as Bhāṇḍīraka.

SB 10.30.5: (The gopīs said:) O *aśvattha* tree, O *plakṣa*, O **nygrodha (banyan),** have you seen Kṛishṇa? That son of Nanda Mahārāja has gone away after stealing our minds with His loving smiles and glances.

BP 10.39.46-48: Akrūra then saw the Supreme Personality of Godhead lying peacefully on the lap of Lord Ananta Śeṣa. The complexion of that Supreme Person was like a dark blue cloud. He wore yellow garments and had four arms and reddish lotus-petal eyes. His face looked attractive and cheerful with its smiling, endearing glance, lovely eyebrows, raised nose, finely formed ears, and beautiful cheeks and reddish lips. The Lord's broad shoulders and expansive chest were gorgeous, and His arms were long and stout. His neck resembled a conch shell, His navel was deep, and His abdomen bore lines like those on a **banyan leaf (peepal leaf).**

BP 11.30.42: Upon seeing Lord Kṛiṣhṇa resting at the foot of a **banyan tree**, surrounded by His shining weapons, Dāruka could not control the affection he felt in his heart. His eyes filled with tears as he rushed down from the chariot and fell at the Lord's feet.

BP 12.8.2-5: Authorities say that Rishi Mārkaṇḍeya, the son of Mṛkaṇḍu, was an exceptionally long-lived sage who was the only survivor at the end of Brahmā's day when the entire universe disappeared in the flood of annihilation. But this same Mārkaṇḍeya Ṛishi, the foremost descendant of Bhrigu, took birth in my own family during the current day of Brahmā, and we have not yet seen any destruction in this day of Brahmā. Also, it is well known that Mārkaṇḍeya while wandering helplessly in the great ocean of annihilation, saw in those fearful waters a wonderful personality—an infant boy lying alone within the fold of a **banyan leaf**

BP 12.9.20: Once, while wandering in the water, the Rishi Mārkaṇḍeya, discovered a small island, upon which stood a young **banyan tree** bearing blossoms and fruits.

BP 12.9.22-25: The infant's dark-blue complexion was the colour of a flawless emerald, His lotus face shone with a wealth of beauty, and His throat bore marks like the lines on a conch shell. He had a broad chest, finely shaped nose, beautiful eyebrows, and lovely ears resembling pomegranate flowers and inner folds like a shell's spirals. The corners of His eyes were reddish like the whorl of a lotus, and the brilliance of His coral-like lips slightly reddened the nectarean, enchanting smile on His face. His splendid hair trembled as he breathed, and His deep navel became distorted by the moving folds of skin on His abdomen, which resembled a **banyan leaf.**

Other beliefs and traditions

There is a common belief that *vata* trees planted near temples are the abodes of Vishnu and Śiva. At the same time, demi-gods, and spirits like Yakshas, Kinnaras, Gandharvas, etc., occupy the trees in public places. Another belief is that Chamundi occupies the banyan trees growing on funeral grounds. (Chamundi is a very fearsome aspect of Durga, originating from Katyayani (Durga), who killed the fierce demons Sumbha, Nisumbha, and Rakthabija). Because of this belief, *vata* trees are planted on funeral grounds. In Tamil Nadu, there is the belief that Aiyanar, the village's guardian deity, sits under the *vata* tree. The South Indian goddess, Pidari (a localized version of Durga or Kali), has four manifestations associated with the *vata* tree. Indra, the king of gods, was portrayed in ancient times as sitting with his queen under the shade of a *Vata* tree, from the branches of which people gathered clothes, food, and drink, symbolizing its aspect as *Kalpavraksha.* In *Matsya Purana*, *vata* is the *'Kalpavraksha'* (wish-fulfilling tree). According to belief, Goddess Lakshmi visits *the Vata* tree on Sundays, and in earlier days, women folk used to worship the tree on that day. (8). According to another legend, the *Vata* tree was initially situated in Vasuki's (the king of serpents) garden. Amba, Mother Earth, wanted it for her children, but Vasuki was not willing to spare the tree. Amba fought with Vasuki and, with the help of Śiva, took the tree and gave it to her children on earth (9).

The story of Savitri and Sathyavan

The legendary story of Savitri and Satyavan occurred under a banyan tree when Savitri's devotion won her husband's life from Yama, the god of death. In Hindu mythology, the story of Savitri and Satyavan is well-known and unparalleled. The great sage Markandeya narrated this story, which forms part of the *Aranyaka Parva* (*Vana Parva* of *Maha Bharata* (*Pativrata Mahatmya Parva* in chapters 291-297 of the *Aranyaka Parva*). The story occurs as a multiply-embedded narrative in the Mahabharata as told by sage Markandeya. When Yudhishthira asks Markandeya whether there has ever been a woman whose devotion matched Draupadi's, Markandeya replies by relating this story. The climax of this story takes place under a *vata* tree. The story and the associated *vrata pooja* are famous all over India among the Hindu community. For Indian women, Savitri is the role model and embodiment of all feminine virtues, and they worship her during the *Vata-Savitri Vrata*. The gist of the story is as follows:

Aswapati was the king of Madra, who had no children. He undertook many years of penance, praying to Goddess Savitri to win a boon for a son. The goddess appeared before the king but refused to give the boon of a son. Instead, she bestowed on him a boon that he would get a daughter who would be equal in virtue and courage to many sons. Eventually, the queen gave birth to a daughter, and the king named the child Savitri. She was exceptionally beautiful, brave, and virtuous. When she attained marriageable age, the king tried to fix up her marriage. But she did not like the suitors the king brought to her. So, the king asked her to find out someone of her choice. She went to the forest as if propelled by unknown hands and met a handsome young man, Satyavan, the only son of the exiled blind king of the country Dyumatsena, who was leading the life of a hermit. Satyavan and Savitri fell in love almost at the very first sight itself. She returned to the palace and announced who her future husband was to be. The great sage Narada, who arrived there then, foretold the death of Satyavan one year after the marriage. But this news did not deter Savitri from marrying Satyavan.

When Satyavan proceeded to the forest to cut firewood on the fateful day, Savitri followed him. Satyavan, while cutting the wood, suddenly fainted and fell from the tree. He died lying in the lap of his beloved wife, Savitri. Soon, Yama's servants appeared to take his soul away, but they could not approach Satyavan's body because of the protection offered by Satyavati's chastity and love. Soon, Yama, the God of Death himself, appeared and carried away the soul of Satyavan from his body.

The remaining part of the story quoted below is from the book 'The Triumph of Love by Shivdutt Sharma (10).

> "Overwhelmed with grief and with faltering steps, Savitri started walking behind Yama's retreating form as his mount lumbered southwards – the direction in which lay the abode of the dead. After they had gone some distance, Yama, hearing the footsteps of someone following him, turned around to look. Reining in his mount, he saw Savitri following him with a determined expression on her face and a new resolve in her eyes. Yama was aghast. Leave alone and stand in his presence; no human had had the courage or dared to follow him

before this. He was both astounded and enraged. But noticing Savitri's heartbroken, forlorn look, his eyes softened. Halting his mount, he admonished her in a gentle voice.

"Thus far and no further, Savitri. You cannot accompany your husband to the land of the dead. Return to your husband's body lying inert under the tree. Take him away to his parents so that they may lay him on the funeral pyre with appropriate prayers and rituals. Observe the mourning period and then pick up the threads of your life again."

"I have no intention of mourning, Yama-dev, as long as I walk behind my husband. My place is by his side, dead or alive."

"Savitri, you have been freed from all your obligations to Satyavan by his death. You have come as far as it is possible to come. Now, I suggest you return."

"Yama-dev, I have led the life of an ascetic this past year in the hermitage, in the service of rishis and sages and my husband's parents. I have observed my vows religiously, and I have loved and served my husband with my whole heart and entire being. The wise sages told me that walking only seven steps with another establishes a bond of friendship with one's companion – as I have done with you. I have walked this far, and I shall keep walking behind you and the soul of my husband, which you have secured with your noose. You, Yama-dev, are the mighty son of Vivasvan, who deals with everyone fairly and upholds the laws of dharma. My place is by my husband's side –

by scriptural mandate, social custom, and the injunction of dharma. Therefore, I cannot go back without him, as that would be against my dharma," Savitri answered.

Yama rubbed a hand over his chin and looked thoughtful. Savitri had a point, and she made it well. Yet, there was no way he could release Satyavan's soul. No way! But how could he get around this improbable situation where he found himself? Then, an idea struck him.

"Savitri, I am impressed with the argument you have put forth. For that, I will grant you a boon. Ask me for anything except the life of your husband."

Savitri paused to think. She knew that she had to think this out carefully to accomplish what she had set out to do. So, she said,

"Yama-dev, my father-in-law, bereft of his eyesight and subsequently his kingdom, has been living in exile in the refuge of Rishi Dalbhaya's hermitage. He has suffered hard and long. I wish you to end his suffering by granting him eyesight and strength so he can reclaim the kingdom of Salwa that is rightfully his."

"It shall be as you ask, Savitri. Now, please turn back. You are weary and tired; return to the hermitage."

Having granted the boon, Yama prodded his mount and began to move on through the wooded forest. But Savitri's reply made him stop again.

"How can I feel weary in the presence of my husband, Yama-dev?" asked Savitri. "The fate that is my husband's is certainly mine as well. I shall follow him wherever you take him. Among the vows we had exchanged during our marriage was the vow to always remain by his side. By following you, I am only observing that vow."

Yama smiled and said: "'These words that you have spoken, Savitri, gladden my heart. They would enhance the wisdom of even the most learned of men. Ask me another boon, except for Satyavan's life, and I shall happily grant it."

"My father, King Aswapati, had done a rigorous penance for eighteen long years in the forest and a great yagna after that to beget a son. However, in her wisdom, the Goddess Savitri bestowed on him this daughter you see standing before you today," said Savitri. "For my father, I ask the boon of a hundred worthy sons, born from the seed of his loins, so that his line may be perpetuated."

"May every father have a wise, caring, and loving daughter such as you, Savitri, who even in her misery can wish for her father's happiness. I will happily grant this boon. Go now; do not persist in following the soul of your dead husband."

"My father's happiness you have granted Yama-dev, and for that, I am truly grateful," said Savitri. "But as for asking me to return, to what shall I return – the corpse of my husband? "

"What lies there is just the shell of your husband, Savitri. His soul, which is pure, will rest comfortably in my kingdom until the record of his deeds, which no doubt has been that of a noble, obedient son and a loving husband, shall be weighed in the balance. Then, accordingly, it will be sent onwards to reside with the gods in heaven. You can rest happy with that thought," Yama assured Savitri.

"I know he will be comfortable in your kingdom, and since you are also known as the Lord of Justice, I am confident you will dispense absolute justice while evaluating his deeds. On the one hand, by granting the boons I have asked for, I know you want me to fulfil my responsibilities towards Satyavan's parents and use my remaining life on earth for some good purpose," Savitri answered. "But, how can I be happy when you are carrying away that which was the source of my happiness and the love of my life with you?"

Yama took a deep breath and then let out a long sigh and said:

"Even love must bend to the will of Fate, Savitri. Yet, I am truly amazed at the extent of your devotion and commitment to your husband. Never have I encountered such courage, determination, and intense love in a woman. It is so rare that I gladly grant you one last boon to honour it. Ask for anything, but don't ask for..."

At that moment, a doe crossed their path with a young faun in tow. It froze for a few moments to gaze at the buffalo. It was now or never, Savitri thought. Seizing the moment, Savitri quickly said:

"Dharmaraja, I ask for the boon of a hundred sons born to me of my husband."

Although the doe and her faun distracted Yama's attention momentarily, Yama automatically said, "Granted!"

The doe leapt across the path gracefully while the young faun ambled across. Savitri's heart leapt with joy, and a smile wreathed her face.

"Thank you, Yama-dev. You are indeed compassionate and benevolent."

Yama's eyes widened as he realized the implications of the boon he had just granted. Wonderstruck, he stared at Savitri and said slowly:

"You did not ask for Satyavan's life! Yet how will the boon see fruition unless I release his soul? In the face of adversity, Savitri, you have displayed a remarkable force of will and an astounding presence of mind."

"So now I request you, Dharmaraja, for the boon of life for Satyavan. For by your words alone will he be restored to me."

"So be it!" Saying this, Yama gently removed the noose in which Satyavan's soul was trapped. The spirit of Satyavan flew north and quickly vanished from sight.

Yama said: "You have won the day! Return now, go to him and wake him from his sleep."

Her heart filled with joy; Savitri ran back to the forest where Satyavan lay. On approaching her husband's still form, she saw a king cobra with its hood flared, which had been guarding over him. Savitri folded her hand and bowed with reverence, acknowledging its protective presence. Uncoiling itself, the cobra slithered away into the grass.

Kneeling, Savitri gently lifted Satyavan's head and placed it once again in her lap. She noticed that his chest no longer appeared to be collapsed and caved in. It was fuller now, rising and falling with the breath of life. Stroking his hair, she bent over to kiss his forehead. At the touch of her soft lips, Satyavan's eyelids flickered, and he stirred awake. Tears of joy flowed down Savitri's eyes and fell over his face. She quickly wiped them away before Satyavan could notice her crying.

"That's the best sleep I have had in a long, long time," he said, looking up into Savitri's eyes. "But you should have woken me up earlier. The sun is low in the sky. My parents will be wondering why we have not yet returned home. What will we tell them?"

When Savitri and Satyavan returned, they found Dyumatsena's eyesight and strength had returned. Savitri narrated what happened in the forest. Soon, Satyavan's father got back his lost kingdom, and all was well and ended well.

This event occurred under a *vata* tree and formed the basis for observing the Vata Savitri Vrata. Married women observe this vrata to celebrate the triumph of love over death, conquering death through love and devotion. Every Saturday in the month of Jyeshta, women offer prayers to this tree for the long life of their husbands.

Savitri's devotion to her husband is the key theme of this myth. Even before they are married, she is unshakeable in her conviction to stand by Satyavan despite his impending death, and this devotion is what impresses her father so much that he allows the wedding of the two. She also shows devotion towards her husband's family, who essentially become her new primary family in the Hindu tradition. Her requests to Yama to grant her father-in-law's sight, strength, and kingdom exemplify this ideal. Lastly, her devotion to Satyavan, even in death, is impressive. She follows Yama, the god of death, and he grants her multiple divine boons, eventually even giving her back Satyavan's life.

Savitri is the ideal *Pathivrata (role model of chastity).* Indian women believe in *pathivratyam* (chastity or purity, defined as the ascetic dedication to the woman's husband), the highest *vrata,* or ascetic observance that Hindu women follow. The *pativrata* is closely related to *Sakti,* the spiritual power conceived as the consort of Shiva, and the husband was dependent on this spiritual power for his survival and strength. The story of Savitri exemplifies this, as Savitri's devotion is very closely tied to her husband's strength and survival, literally bringing him back from death. She follows Yama, an extraordinary display of ascetic devotion, and her spirituality is a critical factor in convincing Yama to bring Satyavan back. (11)

Worship of Vata

Vata Savitri Vrata

Married women observe the *Vata Savitri Vrata,* also known as the *Vata Purnima Vrata,* to ensure their husbands' longevity and prosperity and enjoy a happy marriage. This sacred *vrata* is dedicated to Goddess Gauri (Devi Parvathy) and Savitri (often known as Sati Savitri.) The *Vata Purnima vrata* is commemorated with great pomp and show in the states of Maharashtra, Gujarat, Uttar Pradesh, Bihar, Orissa, Karnataka, West Bengal, and Tamil Nadu. In the southern states of Tamil Nadu and Karnataka, it is known as *'Karadaiyan nombu'.* The womenfolk observe it with great zeal, as it symbolises womanhood. The *vrata* is observed for three consecutive days, from *Trayodashi* (13th day after the new moon day) to Purnima (the full moon), throughout India; However, in some places, people observe the ritual only on the primary day. On this day, women wake up early in the morning and take a bath after applying sesame oil and turmeric paste. They then dress like model wives using necessary adornments, which are also considered sacred by the married women. Such adornments stipulated for married women include vermillion spots applied on the parting of the hair, bangles, kohl (collyrium or kajal), bindi marks on the forehead, henna, and new clothes. Throughout the day, women observe a strict fast for the wellbeing of their husbands. They eat only the young roots of the banyan tree along with water.

In the morning, they worship Goddess Savitri and the holy Banyan tree with full fervour and dedication. In large numbers, married women gather around a banyan tree (the oldest and most prominent in the locality). They pour water on the tree trunk and tie yellow or red threads 108 times around the tree trunk to get blessings for their husband's long life. Fruits like banana, mango, jackfruit, lemon, sprouted pulses, and rice are distributed as prasad. Often, priests of the nearby temples help in the puja and recite the 'Savitri-Satyavan' story to the women. After completing all the rituals, women seek blessings from their husbands and other family elders. The fast is broken only on the following day by eating the prasad. Special delicacies are prepared too and eaten along with family members and relatives.

Vata-poornima (Vata-Savitri) Vrata celebration

According to the prevailing belief, the *Vata Savitri vrata* (also known as *Vata Poornima vrata*) strengthens the bonds between married couples. The *vrata*, more than that, honours the spirit and power of the womanhood. It is observed with absolute faith, which makes this *vrata* sacred, irrespective of the educational or financial status of the devotees. They know that before the *Vata* tree, everybody is equal, and universal womanhood prevails in such celebrations. Even pregnant women and women suffering from ailments can perform this puja, although they may skip fasting. By devotedly offering their prayers, they can seek the same benefits as those who dutifully keep the fast, the devotees believe. For the women devotees, the *Vata* tree embodies the Almighty.

In his book *People Trees*, Haberman provides details of the *Vata Savitri Vrata* as he observed this function at Varanasi. The following extended quote is from Haberman.

> "… I reached the Dharma Kup compound just before sunrise on the morning of the Vata Savitri

ritual. The weather was unusually cool and pleasant …Women were already busy in the dim morning light making their offerings to the goddess in the temple, worshipping the banyan tree and wrapping it with string. The temple offerings included ornate red cloth, flowers, coconut, cucumbers, other vegetables, and various fruits. Offerings to the tree took different forms but always included a water offering. I watched one woman offer water to the roots of the tree from a brass pot. After setting down her pot, she applied dots of *sindoor* (vermillion) powder to the trunk and offered marigold flowers incense, uncooked white rice, and a clay *arati* lamp at the base of the banyan. She then tied a red and yellow string to the tree and wrapped it while going around clockwise nine times.

In conclusion, she placed a hand on each side of the tree and bowed her head to its trunk. All the women I observed made their offering directly to the tree and afterwards circumambulated five or nine times, wrapping the trunk with red and yellow thread. By the end of the day, the tree was ornately clad with strings.

The tree worship continued throughout the day, ending sometime in the mid-afternoon. Hundreds of women came to break their fast here and worship the banyan. The majority were dressed in bright red saris; many dressed in lavish red wedding saris and wore their auspicious wedding jewellery…I observed a group of women offering the tree water, inserting sticks of incense in the ground beneath it, and laying out an orange-cloth altar at the base of the tree. They placed flowers, uncooked white rice, sweets, and balls of cooked whole wheat flour in the cloth altar. After worshipping the tree in this fashion, they wrapped it with string while circumambulating it seven times. They ended the circuit by touching the tree affectionately and putting their heads on the trunk. ...one of the women then took out a booklet and proceeded to read the story of Savitri to a small group of women as they all sat beneath the tree...One woman (from another group of women) laid them out a green cloth for her altar and offered red bangles, white sugar crystals, and packets of red *bindis* to the tree..." (12)

In another location, Haberman found similar procedures but assisted by a temple priest beneath the banyan tree. He read out the story of Savitri and concluded:

"It was by the power gained from worshipping a banyan tree that Savitri herself brought her husband back to life. Therefore, these women also worship the long-living banyan tree to get the tree's blessings for the long life of their husbands. They also do this for their happiness and the wellbeing of their families...."

Haberman also quotes Bhagavathiswara Misra to stress the significance of the ritual outlined above.

"This *vrata* is performed by encouraging women to keep their marital auspiciousness (*soubhagya*) firm. The devotees performing the *vrata* said they performed the vrata for *Suhag* (*soubhagya*), which means a long, happy married life and a long life for their husbands. However, young girls, too, worship the banyan tree, and they do it to get a good husband and a future happy married life. Women believe that the "god of the banyan (*vata-devata*) has much power (*shakti*) to give the blessings of a happy marriage."

Haberman also recounts his conversation with a temple priest under the *vata.* The priest was sure that the *vata* tree was male that the tree was sacred and that it was the husband of Savitri. Some women believe that the tree is Brahma and the husband of Devi Savitri, while others say that the *Vata* tree itself is Savitri Devi. However, most women generally agreed that the tree represents the God who helped Savitri get back her husband's life. Some believe that the tree is a manifest form of Lord Vishnu, while others think it is in the form of Lord Shiva. Haberman summed up by saying that scholars, priests, and tree worshippers today believe that it was the power of Savitri's worship of the banyan tree itself that restored her husband to life.

> "The banyan tree – long known for its endless life and control over death – is now the central feature of the *Vata Savitri vrata* …the banyan tree is not only regarded as a powerful being who can bless the worshipper and her family members with long and happy lives but is ritually available for worshipful influence". (13).

Krishna and the Banyan tree – Vamshi Vata

Krishna has a variety of flutes, which He plays to attract the hearts of His devotees. Based on the length and the number of holes in the flute it is called *Vamshi, Venu,* or *Murali. Vamshi Vata* is the celebrated Banyan Tree in Vrindavan, where Krishna plays His Vamshi to attract the heart of Vrindavana's young maidens (Gopis). Under this tree, Krishna, as Gopinath, the Lord of the Gopis, performed the *Rasa* dance with the Gopis of Vrindavan. When Krishna played on His *Vamshi* in the fifth note, sitting below the *Vata* tree, on the full moon night of the *Sharad* (autumn) season, the ambrosial nectar of the sound vibration of Krishna's flute filled the entire atmosphere. The *Vamshi Vata* was one of Radha and Krishna's preferred meeting places. When Chaitanya Mahaprabhu first came to Vrindavan, he only sat under the Vamshi Vata. Soordas has written a *'pad'* (*padam*a love poem*)* on the divine place:

> *"...kahaan sukh brajkausosansaar !*
> *Kahaan sukh adbasheebat jamuna, yah man*
> *sadavichaar..."*

which means, "There is no happiness anywhere in the world except in the *Banshi Vat* Vrindavan at the bank of Yamuna Ji." It is located on the Bank of Yamuna on *Parikrama Marg* in Vrindavan, near *Keshi Ghat*.

The Banyan tree is often grown near the neem tree. To the Hindus, the intertwined branches of the two trees are the holy union of Siva and Shakthi, and such trees are never cut. Such a tree is considered a symbol of fertility, and childless women used to embrace such banyan trees to fulfil their wishes. The legend of the birth of Visvamithra and Jamadagni has already been given under the peepal. The same legend is mentioned in the case of *Vata* also. (Visvamithra/ Viswamitra is regarded as the National sage of the land of Bharat that is India).

Hattipala Jataka of Buddhists narrates the story of a woman blessed with sons due to the blessing of the *vata* tree. This story relates to a local king, Esukārī, who daily prayed to God for getting a son. His chaplain, hearing that the deity of a specific banyan tree had the power of giving sons, went to the tree and threatened to cut it down unless Esukārī had a son. The tree deity consulted Sakka (Sakro, the ruler of the Trāyastriṃśa Heaven according to Buddhist cosmology, same as Lord Indra in Hindu scriptures), who persuaded four devas to be born as the sons, not of Esukārī, but his chaplain. On the day when the chaplain came to cut down the tree, the deity told him of Sakka's decision and warned him that the sons would not live the household life. In due course, the sons were born and were named Hatthipāla, Gopāla, Assapāla and Ajapāla. But when grew up all of them left home and became ascetics. Indirectly, this story was related to Buddha's great renunciation.

Buddha was telling this story to his disciples. He ended with these words:

> "Thus, Brethren, the Tathāgata made the Great Renunciation long ago, as now"; which said he identified the Birth:

> "At that time, King Suddhodana was King Esukārī, Mahāmāyā his queen, Kassapa the chaplain, Bhaddakāpilānī his wife, Anuruddha was Ajapāla, Moggallāna was Gopāla, Sāriputta was Hatthipāla, the Buddha's followers were the rest, and I was Hatthipāla." (14,15).

The Banyan tree is sacred to Buddhists, too. There are four trees associated with Buddha: the tree of enlightenment (peepal), the tree of the goatherd (banyan), the tree of the serpent king, Muchalinda, and the *Rajayatana* tree (see the previous chapter on *aśvattha* for details). Banyan is the tree of enlightenment of Kasyapa Muni, one of the earlier Buddhas (27th Buddha according to Theravada Buddhism). In Jain mythology, spirits connected with tree worship are known as *Vyantara* gods. As per the *Svetamabra* tradition of Jainism, Banyan is the tree symbol of the Yakshas. It is also the *chaitya vriksha* of the Thirthankara, Risabhanatha. (16, 17)

In Thailand, the banyan tree is considered sacred. *Mae Thapthim* is the goddess of the banyan tree. Thai girls wear phallus-shaped amulets made of banyan wood, known as *dokmai cao* − meaning the flower of the spirit. They offer prayers and offerings to the banyan tree to get the husbands of their dreams. The offering of phallus made of banyan wood to banyan tree is popular in Thailand; people believe such an offering enhances fertility, and the childless will be blessed with children. The wishing trees of Hong Kong are banyan trees; they are commonly known as Lam Tsuen Wishing Trees. Praying for good luck before these trees are one of Hong Kong's most charming and well-preserved traditions. During the first few days of the Lunar New Year, locals and tourists flock here to write down their wishes for the new year, before tying the paper to orange and throwing it high up into the tree's branches. Legend has it that if the orange successfully lodges in the tree's branches without falling back to earth, the wish will come true. Sometimes, the worshippers inscribe their name, birthdate, and prayer or wish on a piece of coloured joss paper and hang it from the tree. Over time, the trees acquired a mythic status among locals. (18, 19)

According to one legend, there was once a Tanka (an ethnic sect) woman who fell mysteriously ill. In a dream, a deity appeared and told her to go to Lam Tsuen, where she needed to throw a piece of joss paper at a great tree as an offering to the gods. After the woman followed the instructions, she magically recovered. The story of this strange tale spread, drawing worshippers to Lam Tsuen.

Another story is about a man who came to Tin Hau Temple to pray for his son, who was struggling in his studies. After he prayed in front of the tree by the temple, his son's academic performance improved spectacularly, and thus, the legend of the Wishing Tree was born. According to local superstition, the banyan trees of Lam Tsuen hold the magical ability to make wishes come true. In addition, the whole village is a carnival of activity during Chinese New Year, with festive decorations and Chinese folk performances on full display. In 2005, a collapsing branch led to two injuries. Nowadays, throwing oranges at the original tree is discouraged for the safety of the worshippers and the trees. Instead, replica trees and wooden racks are used, allowing the tradition to continue. (20).

In many stories of Philippine mythology, the banyan (locally known as *balete* or *balite*) is said to be home to a variety of spirits (*Diwata* and *Engkanto*) and demon-like creatures (among the Visayans, specifically, the *Diliingonnato*, meaning "those not like us"). *Maligno* (evil spirits, from Spanish for 'malign') associated with it include:

- The *Kapre* (a giant).
- *Duwende* (dwarves).
- The *Tikbalang* (a creature whose top half is a horse and whose bottom half is human).

Children at a young age are taught never to point at or go near a fully mature banyan tree for fear of offending the spirits that dwell within them. Filipinos always respectfully address the spirits in the banyan tree when they are near one, walking near or around it to avoid any harm. Filipinos believe that provoking the spirits in a banyan tree can cause great harm, illness, misfortune, untold suffering, and death. In Guam, the Chamorro people believe in tales of *taotaomona*, *duendes*, and other spirits. *Taotaomona* are spirits of the ancient Chamorro that act as guardians to banyan trees. In Sabah, formerly North Borneo, *Nunuk Ragang* or Red Banyan is traditionally considered to be the site of the long houses, sheltering the ten families (immigrants from Taiwan or Southern China) who were the ancestors of the present-day *Kadazan-Dusun* population. (21).

Vata trees of enormous sizes—Super banyans.

Banyan trees are the gigantic trees on the face of the earth based on their canopy size, coverage, and spread. They are the landmark or iconic trees of India. Several such super banyans are known and described by travellers and botanists. Recently, detailed aerial surveys and studies were carried out to assess the size and spread of such trees correctly. These super banyan trees are often destinations for tourists and pilgrims in India but are poorly known outside the country. Several competing claims for the enormous banyan, publicized in botanical, travel, and historical literature, are available. Research workers catalogued, measured, and compared the giant banyan trees to resolve the issues. By employing the possibilities of the Google Earth software, the workers measured the candidate trees and compared them in 2-dimensional space for the area and maximum extent. The workers shortlisted and ranked eight banyan trees as the super banyans in the Indian territory. The first ranked tree is the banyan tree from Andhra Pradesh, known in the name of an old lady, Thimmamma. The tree has become famous as *Thimmamma marimanu (Thimmamma tree)*; its canopy area is 19107 square meters, based on aerial measurements. The signboard below shows that the tree covers a land area of 2.5 ha. A cyclone caused substantial damage to the tree; more damage was due to human-caused clearance of 1 082 square meters of its gross area for building activities. This tree is known as the most gigantic banyan to botanists and enthusiasts in India, but it is little known to the public and practically unknown to the outside world. (22-24). This banyan tree carries a legend behind it. According to a local myth, *Thimmamma marrimanu* came into being in 1434 when a widow named Thimmamma committed sati, a custom among the high-caste Hindus of India. She immolated herself in the pyre of her dead husband. According to local legend, the northeastern pole erected at the site of the pyre miraculously sprung to life. It grew, eventually becoming the present-day tree named after the lady Thimmamma. (25, 26)

Thimmamma banyan tree – the largest banyan in the world, and the world record holder in canopy area and spread

The *Kabir Vad* ranked second despite clearing its 20985 square meter area for the temple inside. This tree is a pilgrimage destination. When British historian Thomas Maurice wrote about Kabir's banyan in 1794, he said it had more than 350 false trunks, each thicker than an English oak tree and another 3000 smaller stems. He noted that locals said the tree was 3000 years old, suggesting it existed long before Kabir. This fact raises the possibility that it is the same banyan Alexander the Great and his army encountered on the Narmada River bank when they arrived in India in 326 BCE. Alexander's men were the first Europeans to have seen a banyan. They were amazed. The vivid descriptions they wrote down would inform Theophrastus, the father of modern botany, back home in Greece. An earlier report (27) says a flood heavily damaged the tree but still had 29,254 square meters. Had it not been damaged or cleared for temple purposes, this tree would have covered the largest gross area of any known living tree. This tree is of additional interest, as the possibility it is more than two thousand years old would make it one of the oldest known banyan trees. (28).

The Kabir Vata.

The third rank holder is known as the Giant Banyan of Majhi, and it is located near Lucknow, almost hidden by mango orchards, and hence is mostly unknown to the world outside. There is also no reference to this tree except for a newspaper report by Shukla (29).

Earlier reports often claimed that the Great Banyan tree of Calcutta, situated in the Jagdish Chandra Bose Botanical Garden, was the largest. The signpost indicated that this tree occupied an area of 1.5 ha, and the measured canopy area was 16534 square meters. The prop roots, which resemble trunks, hold up the tree even though its main trunk has long since vanished. The whole assemblage looks more like a forest of many individual banyan trees. *Pillalamarri*, near Hyderabad, is a giant banyan with the fifth-largest net area (12,267 square meters) and the fifth-largest crown spread (154 meters). Near Bangalore city, there is a popular tourist destination with a vast super banyan known as the *Doda Aladamara*. It has an area of 10,305 square meters). It is the sixth largest by crown spread. Like other superlative banyans, this one has had three per cent of its gross area removed to construct a temple. (30 – 32).

The Theosophical Society of Chennai campus had a banyan tree, often claimed to be one of the most giant trees in the world, with a designated area coverage of 59,500

square feet, or 5,527 square meters. However, this tree fell over in a cyclone and no longer exists. The Ranthambore banyan, at the Jogi Mahal at Ranthambore National Park, is the eighth largest banyan. Of the trees outside India, the largest net area covered is the Lahaina Banyan in Hawaii, covering 4,225 square metres. (33).

.Apart from the above, some Vata trees are famous due to the religious traditions and beliefs associated with them. One such Vata tree is the *Kalpa Vata* of the Jagannath temple of Puri. There is a huge banyan tree called *Kalpa Vata* in the inner enclosure. The Puranas describe this tree as being there when the earth sank under water. The popular belief is that if a devotee prays for anything, the tree will fulfil it; hence, it is a *Kalpavriksha*. The image of Sri Jagannath installed here is named after this ancient Banyan Tree, *Vata Jagannath*. Also, many other deities like *Vata Krishna, Vata Ganesh, Vata Mangala,* and *Vata Markandeya* have been installed near this shrine and named after the Banyan tree. *Kalpa Vata* is worshipped as a god with the spiritual aura of Lord Vishnu. The devotees believe that *Kalpa Vata*, worshipped with profound faith and devotion, is graced to fulfil their wishes. *Sweta vata,* Garoi Ashram, Jagatsingpur, is another famous banyan tree whose leaves and flowers are white, unlike the usual green leaves and red flowers.

The *Krishna vata* at Jagannath temple, Anugul, Orissa, is yet another banyan tree of legendary interest. This *Krishna vata* or Krishna Fig is a large, fast-growing, evergreen tree up to thirty metres tall, with spreading branches and many aerial roots. The unique feature of the tree is that the leaves have a pocket-like fold at the base. The plant is also known as Krishna's butter cup. As with most things in India, there is a mythological story of Krishna related to the leaves of this tree. The story says that Lord Krishna was fond of butter and would even steal it. He once attempted to conceal the butter by rolling it up in a tree leaf when his mother, Yashoda, caught him. Since then, the leaves of the tree have retained this shape.

In Jajpur, Orissa, a banyan tree is known by *Chhatiavata*, popularly known as the second Neelachal Dham. People believe that Lord Jagannath, Balabhadra, and Devi Subhadra will someday visit the Dham. People here also believe Satya Yuga will begin after Lord Jagannath comes here. There is an ancient Banyan tree here, known as *Chhatiavata*. Kendrapara in Odisha state has a 500-year-old banyan tree, a mute witness to times gone by. Following frequent visits from tourists in the area throughout the year, the state government granted the enormous tree, which occupies 1.3 acres of land and has about 600 trunks and sub-trunks, tourist spot status. (34, 35)

In Bali (Indonesia), a divine banyan tree is regarded as a symbol of unity and power. The tree is depicted on Indonesia's national coat of arms with its sturdy trunk and far-reaching roots. The sacredness of the tree comes from the belief that Lord Krishna rests on its leaves. The banyan is integral to every Balinese village's *Pura Dalem*, a temple for the dead. *Pura Dalem* includes the cemetery. The banyan tree represents the eternal cycle of death and rebirth and protects the spirits after death. The leaves of a Banyan tree are large, leathery, glossy, green, and elliptical and are used in cremation ceremonies. The Balinese Hindus believe that after Krishna devoured the universe (destroying it), he turned himself into a tiny child, wrapped himself up in the banyan leaf, which floated on the eternal waters for an infinite period until Krishna (Vishnu) chose to re-create the universe.

(36) Hindus believe that gods and spirits of deceased ancestors inhabit the banyan trees and emit immense spiritual energy. So, the banyan tree trunks are covered with checkered cloths, and temples are built around them to appease the gods and spirits. The locals believe the sacred banyan tree's spiritual energy attracts demons, so cleansing ceremonies are performed routinely, especially near cemeteries, and special shrines are built to ward off demons.

There is a marvellous banyan tree in the small town of Lahaina in Maui (Hawaii), well known as the Lahaina Banyan tree. It is the largest in the USA and is a majestic tree covering an area of about two acres. Spanning about two acres over a city block—and rising more than 60 feet, Lahaina's banyan attained fame all over the region and in the USA. (Fig.)

There are giant banyan trees in many other Indian and Pacific Ocean Islands, too, but they do not belong to the species of Indian Vata tree (*Ficus benghalensis*).

Religious rites associated with the banyan tree

The Banyan tree is associated with various religious rites. Leaves are used in *poojas* and offered during *Satyanarayana vrata pooja* and *Narasimha vrata patra pooja*. (37)

According to the *Brahmavaivarta Purana*, the worship of Chandi and Sakthi (aspects of Durga—both manifestations of Devi Parvathi or Gauri, the consort of Lord Śiva) is to be performed under the *Vata* tree. The goddess Matangi (another aspect of Durga, also considered the mother of all tribes) Is worshipped under a *Vata* tree after her idol is installed. Goddesses Mangala and Vimala (manifestations of Devi Parvathi) are worshipped under the Vata tree after their idols are installed. *Agni Purana* mentions that on the new moon day (*Amavasya* day) in the month of *Jyeshta* (July – August), Mahasati (daughter of Daksha and the first consort of Śiva; an incarnation of *Parāśakthi,* the ultimate power), stay at the foot of *vata*. Women whose husbands are alive are advised to worship the Vata tree with seven types of sprouted cereals, offering threads (a symbol of *mangal sutra* worn by married women) and observe fast for three nights and days. The following day, she should touch the *Vata* tree, sing and dance, eulogizing Sathi Devi. According to some beliefs, Śiva, Parvathi, and Ganesha also stay under the *vata* tree.

Matsya Purana mentions that in Prayag, Śiva stays as a *Vata* tree, *Akshaya Vata*. This tree originated from a sacrificial post that Lord Brahma planted there. Then, the Sun god also made the vata his abode. According to *Vamana Purana*, there was a Vata tree in the middle of the lake in Kurukshetra, in the form of Śiva himself, from which various *varnas* originated.

In any Vedic sacrificial ritual, many different types of utensils are needed. Most are made from *vata* wood, and a few are from *Udumbara* and *Bilva* woods. For example, in the Vedic ritual known as *Athirathram* (*Saagnikam Athirathram*), vessels and utensils such as *ritu, maitravarunam, aidravāyavam, antheryāmam, āswinam, ādityaupashyam, ukthyaupashayam, upāmshu, athigrāhyam* and *dronakalasam* are made from *vata* wood. Besides, the cart used for transporting *soma* is made of *vata* wood. (38). Buds of *the vata* tree are one of the many items needed for the purification and consecration of idols and for many rituals like *Mruthyujaya hoama*. Dry twigs are used as *shamidhas'* (firewood used in *Havana* and *yajna*), for producing sacrificial fire.

Hindu ladies in most parts of India worship the tree with the flowers of marigold and by tying a thread around the trunk, seeking blessings to have a son, and for prosperity and long life for their husbands. A similar ceremony is performed for the peepal tree, too. The villagers believe that by smearing the trunk with vermilion and adorning it with stones, they can win matters related to litigation. The tribals in Rajasthan do not plant this tree near their houses or in their compounds, as the tree is considered the abode of evil spirits, and they fear quarrels in the family, as in the case of peepal. *Vata* trees are to be planted only in public places. Its use as firewood is also taboo. The rural public attaches a supernatural penumbra for the banyan tree, as in the case of the peepal. A folk song from Punjab has this reference, which indicates the faith with which people consider the Vata tree:

> "Under the banyan tree
> I happened to see God Almighty' and then
> 'The banyan knows the secrets
> No good telling a lie in its presence." (39).

Wish fulfilling Vata trees (*Kalpavriksha*) are reported from many locations, which are always associated with certain temples. There is a well-known *Akshaya Vata* in the Kattil Mekkethil Devi (Bhadrakali) temple at Ponmana (Kollom district, Kerala state). Believers throng to the temple every day. The devotees believe their wishes will be fulfilled once they tie bells on the banyan tree in front of the temple (the *sthalavriksha*), and it is the *Akshaya Kalpa vata* (Immortal wish-fulfilling banyan). After circumambulating it seven times, devotees tie bells (as many as they wish) on the tree near the sanctum sanctorum. The sight of hundreds of bells hanging from the tree is a testament to the devotion and belief of the people. The authorities regularly remove the bells, lest the weight of which may break the branches, and to make space for tying bells by the daily devotees visiting the temple.

The wish fulfilling banyan tree: a portion showing the bells and mini-cradles hanging from the branches, all tied by the visiting devotees at the Kattil Mekkethil Devi temple.

A banyan is a vast umbrella of dark green leathery leaves that blocks out the sun or rain showers. These trees form the centrepiece of many villages. Entire cities have even grown up around these trees. Vadodara in western India is one example. Its name is derived from the Sanskrit word *vatodar*, meaning 'in the heart of the banyan tree'. Asia's oldest stock exchange, the Bombay Stock Exchange, was also born beneath a banyan in Mumbai, where stockbrokers would gather in the 1850s.

Banyan, the most giant tree on earth (in terms of spread of foliage), has incited the imagination of many poets and artists. Of all the trees on earth, the banyan tree has the most extensive and farthest-reaching root system. Banyan is sometimes compared to the Indian diaspora; the Indians have spread so far and wide to every nook and cranny of the world. Tagore wrote:

> "To study a banyan tree
> You not only must know
> Its main stem in its own soil
> But also trace the growth
> Of its greatness in the further soil
> For then, you can know the true nature of its vitality." (40)

The idea is true of the Indian diaspora as well. Wherever they go, the Indians retain their Indianness, their roots remain in India, and time and again, they keep coming back to Indian soil, keeping the cultural traditions of their society intact in their minds.

Tagore has written a simple poem on a banyan tree, included in the book *Crescent Moon*.

> "O you shaggy-headed banyan tree standing on the bank of the pond,
> have you forgotten the little child,
> like the birds that have nested in your branches and left you?
> Do you not remember how he sat at the window and wondered at the tangle of your roots and plunged underground?
> The women would come to fill their jars in the pond,
> and your huge black shadow would wriggle on the water like sleep, struggling to wake up.
> Sunlight danced on the ripples like
> restless, tiny shuttles weaving golden tapestry.

Two ducks swam by the weedy margin above their
shadows,
and the child would sit still and think.
He longed to be the wind and blow through your
resting branches,
to be your shadow and lengthen with the day on
the water,
to be a bird and perch on your topmost twig,
and to float like those ducks among the weeds and
shadows."(41)

The poem is a simple one full of imagery. A person who
returned to the banyan tree of his childhood reminisced
about those days. He asks the tree if he remembers a child
who used to rest on his branches but has now left. He then
asks if the tree remembers the women coming near to fill
up their water pots, the sunlight dancing on the water, and
the animals playing as the child would sit and watch. The
child in him wanted to play on the branches of the tree and
be a part of the nature and wildlife of the area.

There is a beautiful poem on a banyan tree in the
ancient storybook, the *Pancha Tantra* of Vishnu Sharma.
Pancha Tantra is an extensive collection of fables, each with
a moral, by the Kashmiri scholar, a member of the King's
court. The poem is reproduced below:

"...Deer reclines in its shade;
Birds in multitude gather to roost
Darkening its dark-green canopy of leaves;
Troops of monkeys cling to the trunk;
While hollows hum with insect-throngs
Flowers are boldly kissed by honeybees.
O! What happiness its every limb showers
An assemblage of various creatures;

Such a tree deserves all praise,
Others only burden the earth." (43)

Maybe, inspired by the above words, the modern poet Robert Southey (2012), the poet laureate of UK, calls the banyan a venerable tree. The sight of the banyan is godly; on seeing it, the first impulse would be to pray.

"It was a godly sight to see
The venerable tree
For over the lawn, irregularly spread
Fifty straight columns propt its lofty heads
And many a long depending shoot
Seeking to strike a root
Straight like a plummet grew towards the ground
So, like a temple, did it seem that there
A pious heart's first impulse would be prayer...." (44)

Reginald Heber (1823), who was the Bishop of Calcutta, exclaimed when he saw the banyan tree for the first time: "What a noble place of worship". Travellers' tales inspired the great English poet Milton to describe the banyan tree in Paradise Lost in the following lines:

"The fig-tree at this day to Indians known
In Malabar or Deccan, spreads her arms,
Branching so broad and long, that on the ground
The bended twigs take root, and daughters grow
About the mother tree, a pillared shade,
High over-arched and echoing walks between..."

Ruskin Bond (2018) depicts the memories of bygone days in the Banyan Tree poem.

"I remember you well, old banyan tree
As you stood there, spreading quietly,
Over the broken wall.

While adults slept, I crept away
Down the broad veranda steps, around
The outhouse and the melon-ground
Into the shades of the afternoon.

....

I must have known that giants have few friends
(The great lurk shyly in their private dens.)
And found you hidden by a dark green wall
Of aerial roots.
Intruder in your pillared den, I stood
And shyly touched your old and rugged wood.
And as my hands explored you, giant tree,
I heard you singing!" (Bond, 2018)

It is somewhat of an autobiographical poem. The author remembers an old banyan tree on the campus where he stayed as a boy in Dehra Dun. The poet reflects on those days after many years of visiting the place; he recalls the moments of his bygone boyhood and remembers that though the house and grounds belonged to his grandparents, the magnificent old banyan tree was his. Its spreading branches, which hung to the ground and retook root, forming several twisting passages, gave him endless pleasure. Among them were squirrels, snails and butterflies. The tree was older than the house, older than Grandfather, and as old as Dehra Dun. He could hide behind thick green leaves in its branches and spy on the world below. In the spring, the banyan tree was full of birds. During the fig season, the banyan tree was the noisiest place in the garden. Halfway up the tree, the boy built a crude platform where he would spend the afternoons when it was not too hot. He could read there propping against the tree with a cushion from the living room. ...The banyan was the lonely tree there, and the poet says that giants have few friends. He stood among the pillared roots as an intruder, shyly touching the old, rugged wood.

In Hindu mythology, the tree is called *Kalpavriksha*, the tree that provides fulfilment of wishes and other material gains. The worship of the tree is represented in a Buddhist sculpture with its long-hanging roots, which drop gold pieces in vessels placed below. As the tree of immortality, banyan cannot be cut according to the Indian scriptures. Cutting the base of a banyan is like cutting at the base of one's own family. However, old beliefs are swept aside, and many a banyan is felled to pay the way for the march of modernity and civilisation, expressed in expressways, railway lines, and high-rise buildings.

Dilip Chitre is a respected poet who wrote an autobiographical poem titled The Felling of the Banyan. As a boy, he witnessed the cutting down of an ancient, huge banyan tree standing on the ancestral farm where he was staying. This was a decision taken by his father, against the wishes of the elderly members, and as a boy, he felt immense pain as he witnessed the slaughtering of the banyan and he wrote:

> "...The banyan tree was three times as tall as our house
> Its trunk had a circumference of fifty feet
> Its scraggy aerial roots fell to the ground
> From thirty feet or more so first they cut the branches
> Sawing them off for seven days, and the heap was huge
> Insects and birds began to leave the tree
> And then they came to its massive trunk

Fifty men with axes chopped and chopped
The great tree revealed its rings of two hundred
years
We watched in terror and fascination this slaughter
As raw mythology revealed to us its age..." (46)

The shape of the banyan symbolises the family itself, and the great rooted tree represents centuries of living and the connection between earth and heaven. The great banyan, helpless to resist, is hacked at by dozens of men. It's like something out of a battle or war...in fact, this feeling does seem to foretell the coming environmental struggles that are still ongoing globally, especially in countries like India, so used to the wilderness but now having to cope with industry, new economics, and expanding populations. The banyan tree is a metaphor for the speaker's family history. In another realm, the poem also symbolises the Indian men and women, cutting off their roots and their cultural moorings and destined (or cursed) to live in an alien society as uninvited guests, silently swallowing the insults and deprivations imposed on them by an alien social set up. Perhaps the poet might also have a religious tone, how a tree looked up as the seat of the trinity cut down by man, severing himself from the spiritual traditions and beliefs prevailing in his family and, in a broader context, society. About this poem, Andrew Spacey writes:

> "The imagery is clear. The great banyan, helpless to resist, is hacked at by dozens of men. It's like something out of a battle or war...in fact, this felling does seem to foretell the coming environmental struggles that are still ongoing globally, especially in countries like India, so used to the wilderness

but now having to cope with industry, new economics, and expanding populations." (47)

Umbrella is a poem on banyan written by Sally Bayan. She likens the banyan tree to an umbrella and writes that she will never see a poem as lovely as the banyan tree.

"I Think That I Shall Never See
A Poem Lovely as The Banyan Tree....
It stands tall and sturdy
Telling us of unwavering strength
Evidenced by its toughened body.
It speaks with its huge trunk
As it holds itself firmly on the ground.
Its new-grown twigs
Otherwise known as sprigs
And branches, crowded with leaves,
Are shades and shields, replete with stories to weave,
The rings etched inside its trunks are proofs to show
Their age, their truths, and tales from long ago..."
(48)

This discussion on the banyan can be best concluded with a few lines from Lok Sang's poem "The Banyan Tree."

"At the top of the hill is a big banyan tree
It is there for everyone to see.
Its leaves seem forever green.
Its long air roots hang low and lean.
It was under this ancient tree
Those children of many generations had played with glee.
It was under the same tree

That great-grandfather once tumbled and hurt his
knee.
The tree had seen so many variations in seasons;
It had given shade to so many people
Before they could even reason.
It had been there long before the wars.
In it had nested many birds of call.
Generations of people grow up.
Generations of people grow old.
The banyan tree stands silent and still,
Oblivious to joys and sorrows untold." (49).

The eternal banyan – the Akshaya Vata – remains there as the muteness of the strife and struggles, both noble and ignoble, of the human race and the devastation humans are causing to their mother earth.

That is the Great Indian Banyan tree: Alexander the Great was amazed at the Banyan tree; Angkor Wat got its name; Bania entered the Oxford English Dictionary; Bhagavad Gita used it as a simile; Seers of Upanishads used it for boys' experiments; Tamil and Sanskrit literature sang its glory; Shiva and Vishnu sat under/on it; Salman Rushdie, Daniel Defoe and Southey used it in their stories and novels; Guinness Book of Records published it under its Tree Records; Banyan is the *Sthala Vriksham* of many Tamil temples; Spread its branches in the United States; Used as toothpicks and medicines by Indians; Worshipped by Hindu women in *Vata Savithri Vrata*; Served as the meeting point of villagers for thousands of years....The story of the great and glorious BANYAN TREE is never-ending. (50)

Description and uses:

Banyan (*Vata, nygrodha*): *Ficus benghalensis* Linn. (Fig family, Moraceae)

Bar, Bargat (Bengali); *Bargad, Bor* (Hindi); *Aala, Aalandamara* (Kannada); *Peral* (Malayalam); *Aal, Aalamaram, Vada* (Tamil); *Marrichettu, Peddamarri* (Telungu);

Common Names

Assamese: *Bor-goch*; **Bengali**: *Bar, Bargat*; **English**: Banyan, Banyan Tree, East Indian Fig, East Indian Fig Tree. Indian banyan tree, Indian fig tree; **Hindi**: *Bar, Bargad, Barh, Bor*; **Kannada**: *Aalada mara, Alada, Alada mara*; **Malayalam:** *Aal, Peral*; **Manipuri:** *Khongnang Taru*; **Marathi:** *Vada*; **Sanskrit**: *Bahupada, Vat/ Vata, Nygrodha* (vedic name); **Tamil:** *Aalamaram, Ala, Alai, Alamaram*; **Telegu:***Peddimari,* Marri Chettu; **Urdu**: *Bargad.* **Chinese**: *Meng jia la rong*; **French**: *Figuier de Bengal, Banian, Figuierd'Inde, Figuier des pagodes*; **German**: *Banyanbaum, Bengalischer Feigenbaum* (German); **Thai**: *Ni khrot..*

Banyan is a large, fast-growing, evergreen tree, widely introduced across tropical and subtropical areas. It has escaped from cultivation and become naturalized in natural and disturbed areas. The Banyan tree produces an enormous number of seeds, which are dispersed by both native and exotic birds. Banyan tree begins growing on other trees as epiphytes and they grow up, killing the host trees completely. The pollination system of banyan is similar to other fig trees (*Ficus* spp.), and it is one of the most complex within the plant kingdom. In this system, each fig tree species is obligatorily pollinated by one fig wasp species, and each wasp species can only reproduce in one fig species. To date, banyan tree is listed as invasive in the Bahamas, Australia, Singapore, Western Samoa, and the Chagos Islands. (51)

Banyan is medicinal and the properties and uses are similar to those of peepal, both included under the group of drugs known as *vatadivarga,* in classical Ayurvedic texts like Charaka Samhita. It forms one of the *nalpamaras* [*Nalpamaras are:* Peepal (*Ficus religiosa),* Banyan (*Ficus benghalensis*), Cluster fig (*Ficus racemosa*) and Indian laurel (*Ficus microcarpa*)]

Ayurvedic Indications

This extraordinary tree has existed since archaic times and is mentioned in several Ayurvedic scriptures like Charaka Samhita, Raj Nighantu, Susruta Samhita etc. Bhavaprakasha gives the following properties: "Vata is cold in potency, heavy in action, absorbent, cures the diseases of kapha and pitta and heals ulcers. It promotes complexion, astringent in taste and cures herpetic skin lesions, burning sensation and diseases of female external genitalia." Charaka prescribed the decoction of buds mixed with honey and sugar for controlling vomiting and diarrhoea. Decoction in milk is prescribed for curing bleeding piles. Stem bark powdered or in the form of decoction is given in diarrhoea. Latex is used to cure toothache. Stem decoction is used in wound disinfection. Khare gives the following properties and actions:

> "Infusion of bark used in diabetes, dysentery and seminal weakness, leucorrhoea (abnormal mucous discharge from vagina), menorrhagia (excessive or prolonged menstruation) and burning sensation. Milky juice and seeds are applied topically to sores, ulcers, cracked soles of feet and rheumatic inflammation. Aerial root is anti-emetic, topically

applied externally for curing abscesses and wounds. Bark extract has anti-diabetic and lipid reducing activities."

The properties and medicinal uses are like those of the peepal.

Home remedies with banyan

- The milky latex extracted from the bark is applied directly over the wound and swelling to get relief and speed up healing.

- Decoction of the bark is used to treat vaginal infections.

- Tender leaf – decoction is given to strengthen the uterine muscles during pregnancy.

- Latex of the tree is used to deal with premature ejaculation.

- Milky latex of the plant is smeared topically to treat bruises, painful areas, toothache, rheumatic joints, lumbago, and cracked soles.

- Intake of the powdered root mixed with milk is effective in treating and maintaining female fertility.

- Milk juice collected from tree bark is a natural remedy to remove skin moles and enhance skin texture. (52)

The banyan tree contains a wealth of chemical constituents, such as Beta-Sitosterols, glycosides, sterols, leucocyanidin, esters, quercetin, friedelin, several flavonoids and polyphenols, inositol, galactose, rutin and plenty of tannins. It is also abundant in polysaccharides, oxositosterol, ketones, and tiglic acid. The leaves contain triterpenes, oxositosterol, friedelin, and polyphenols; the bark contains bengalinoside, glucosides, and flavonoid glycosides, and is rich in tannins. The main aerial roots of the tree contain several phytosterols and polyphenols; whereas the heartwood contains bengalenoside, tiglic acid, and tatraxasterol and a host of tannins, polyphenols etc. A detailed review of banyan and peepal chemical composition and properties can be found in Murugesu et al. (53). *Vata* is an ingredient in certain ayurvedic formulations such as *Panchavalkala churna, Nyagrodhigana kashaya, Nalapamaradi taaila, Nalapamaradi churna*etc.

Citaions and notes

1. Southey on Banyan, Cited from Swaminathan, S (2013) Indian Wonder – The Banyan Tree; http://www.sisnambalava.org.uk/articles/others/indian-wonder-the-banyan-tree-20130318043049.aspx. 2002

2. Gandhi, M, Brahma's Hair, 1989

3. Desikan, P. (2010) *Nygrodha-Udumbara-Ashvattha*, the three gentle giants. giants/comment-page-1/?sfw= pass1618552500

4. Harshananda, Swami (2008) A Concise Encyclopedia of Hinduism, vol.2, Ramakrishna Math, Bangalore, 2008.

5. Mani, Vettom (1975) *Purana Nighantu,* NBS, Kottayam

6. Anon. (2020) Panchavati, aka: Pañcavaṭī, Paancan-vati; 3 Definition(s), https://www.wisdomlib.org/definition/paancavati

7. Anon. (2021) How This Place Got The Name Panchavati ? http://www.holydham.com/how-this-place-got-the-name-paanchavati/

8. Gandhi (see 2)

9. Gupta SM (2001) Plant myths and traditions of India. Vedam books, Delhi.

10. Sharma S (2015) The Triumph of Love: The Immortal Romance of Savitri and Satyavan. Yogi Impressions, Mumbai.

11. Rodrigues, H. (2016) Savitri and Satyavan, http://www. mahavidya.ca/2017/12/29/savitri-and-satyavan/.

12, 13. Haberman, D.L. People Trees. Oxford Uni. Press, New York, 2013.

14. Chalmers, R. (1895) The Jataka tales; vol.4, Jataka 509: Hatthi-PālaJātaka.

15. Varma, C.B. (2002) The Illustrated Jataka & Other Stories of the Buddha.

(16) Anon. (2020) List of Tirthankaras. https://en.wikipedia. org/wiki/List_of_Tirthankaras

16. Ravindran PN (2020) Sacred and Ritual Plants of India. Notion press, Chennai.

17. Gao, S. (2017) Wishing on a Tree: Where Hongkongers Go for Good Luck. https://theculturetrip.com/asia/ china/hong-kong/articles/wishing-on-a-tree-where-hongkongers-go-for-good-luck/

18. Anon. (2019) Too many wishes? Tai Po wishing tree branch collapses. https://coconuts.co/hongkong/news /too-many-wishes-tai-po-wishing-tree-branch-collapses/

19. Tai, E. (2020) Lam Tsuen 'tradition'; The Wishing Tree. http://varsity.com.cuhk.edu.hk/varsity/0003/culture2. htm.

20. Forbes, J. 1812. A view of Cubbeer Burr, the celebrated Banian Tree, on an island in the Nerbudda, drawn from nature 1772. Oriental Memoirs 3. Plate 85. Accessed 30/06/2010. <http://www.bl.uk/onlinegallery/onlineex/ apac/other/019xzz0000455c9u00085000.html

21. Santos, K. (2019) Bewitching Balete trees around the Philippines. https://www.traveling-up.com/bewitching-balete-trees-around-the-hilippines/#:~:text=The%20Balete.

22. Anon. (2019) The World's Largest Trees? A Catalogue of India's Giant Banyans.https://outreachecology.com/landmark/resources/the-largest-trees-in-the-world/#:~:text=A%20Catalogue%20of%20India's%20Giant,square%20meters%E2%80%93%20almost%20two%20hectares!

23. Anon., (2021a) The World's Largest Trees? A Catalogue of India's Giant Banyans.https://outreachecology.com/landmark/resources/the-largest-trees-in-the-world/#:~:text=A%20Catalogue%20of%20India's%20Giant,square%20meters%E2%80%93%20almost%20two%20hectares!

24. Anon. (2021b) *ThimmammaMarrimanu:* The world's largest banyan tree is followed by a cult of worshipers. Edurudona, India; https://www.atlasobscura.com/places/thimmamma-marrimanu#:~:text=According%20to%20local%20mythology%2C%20Thimmamma,pyre%20of%20her%20dead%20husband.

25. Sayeed, VA (2012) Arboreal wonder. Print edition: June 15, 2012, https://frontline.thehindu.com/the-nation/article30166017.ece.

26. Anon. (2019) India's Superlative Banyan Trees. Asian Geographic No.104 Issue 3/2014, https://www.asiangeo.com/environment/indias-superlative-banyan-trees/#.

27. Forbes, J. 1812. A view of Cubbeer Burr, the celebrated Banian Tree, on an island in the Nerbudda, drawn from

nature 1772. Oriental Memoirs 3. Plate 85. Accessed 30/06/2010. <http://www.bl.uk/onlinegallery/onlineex/apac/other/019xzz0000455c9u00085000.html

28. Kopparapu, A. (2018) 6 Biggest and Oldest Banyan trees in India for the Ultimate Nature lover. https://www.tripoto.com/india/trips/6-biggest-and-oldest-banyan-trees-in-india-   for-the-ultimate-nature-lover-5c23edb6413b5

29. Shukla, N. 2008. UP has its own mammoth banyan. Times of India (Delhi edition). 2 July 2008.

30. Anon. (2014) India's Superlative Banyan Trees. Asian Geographic No.104 Issue 3/2014, https://www.asiangeo.com/environment/indias-superlative-banyan-trees/#

31. Anon., (2021) The World's Largest Trees? A Catalogue of India's Giant Banyans.https://outreachecology.com/landmark/resources/the-largest-trees-in-the-world/#:~:text=A%20Catalogue%20of%20India's%20Giant,square%20meters%E2%80%93%20almost%20two%20hectares!

32. Santos (see 21)

33. Harris, PS. (2020) Banyan Tree. Theosophical Encyclopedia, https://www.theosophy.world/encyclopedia/banyan-tree.

34. Bar-Ness (2023) The World's Largest Trees? Cataloguing India's Giant Banyans www.treeoctopus.net; ydbarness@gmail.com.

35. Anonymous (2021) List of Banyan trees in India. https://en.bharatpedia.org/wiki/List_of_Banyan_trees_in_India

36. Ferguson M (2023) Eternal Banyan Tree – Giant Ancient Tree In Bali.. https://ubudcommunity.com/the-sacred-banyan-tree/

37. Ravindran PN (see 16)

38. Nampoothiri, K.V. (2011) *SagnikamAthirathram,* Kurukshetra Prakashan.

39. Chakravarti, M. (1995) The Concept of Rudra Śiva through Ages, Motilal Banarsidass, New Delhi,

40. Ground I (2017) British Wittgenstein Society Newsletter, No 27, Oct. 2017, www.britishwittgensteinsociety.org.

41. Tagore, R. (1965) Banyan tree, The Crescent Moon, (Reprint)

42. Milton, J. The Paradise Lost 1667. Famous Epic poem in English Language.

43. From *Pancha Tantra* by Vishnu Sharma. Translation.

44. Southey R (2012) quoted from Swaminathan S (2013), Indian wonder-the banyan tree. https://www.sisnambalava.org.uk/articles/others/indian-wonder-the-banyan-tree-20130318043049.aspx.

45. Bond R. (2018) Banyan Tree. In: Banyan Tree and other poems. The Punch magazine, Jan 25, 2018. https://thepunchmagazine.com/the-byword/poetry/banyan-tree-and-other-poems.

46. Chitre D. (1980) Felling of the Banyan Tree. https://www.english-for-students.com/felling-of-the-banyan-tree.html.

47. Spacey A (2023) Analysis of the Poem "The Felling of the Banyan Tree" by Dilip Chitre. https://owlcation.com/humanities/Analysis-of-Poem-The-Felling-of-the-Banyan-Tree-by-Dilip-Chitre.

48. Bayan S (2014) Umbrella, https://hellopoetry.com/poem/858510/umbrella/

49. Sang L (2002) Banyan tree, http://www.ln.edu.hk/cpps/08_highlight/happiness_study/poems.pdf.

50. Anonymous (2023) Indian Wonder: The Banyan Tree. https://tamilandvedas.com/2012/05/26/indian-wonder-the-banyan-tree/.

51. CABI (2015) *Ficus benghalensis* (banyan) CABI Compendium, https://doi.org/10.1079/cabicompendium.24066.

52. Sairam TV (1999) Home Remedies, vol2. Penguin, India.

53. Murugesu S, Selamat J, Perumal V. Phytochemistry, Pharmacological Properties, and Recent Applications of *Ficus benghalensis* and *Ficus religiosa*. Plants (Basel). 10 (12):2749. doi: 10.3390/plants10122749.

04

RUDRAKSHA

Rudra's Tears

Om! Let my limbs and speech, prana, eyes, ears,
vitality
And all the senses grow in strength.
All existence is the Brahman of the Upanishads.
May I never deny Brahman, nor Brahman deny me.
Let there be no denial at all:
Let there be no denial at least from me.
May the virtues that are proclaimed in the
Upanishads be in me,
Who am devoted to the Atman; may they reside
in me.
Om ! Let there be Peace in me!
Let there be Peace in my environment!
Let there be Peace in the forces that act on me!

(Rudraksha – Jabala Upanishad)

"*R*udraksha, or *rudraksh,* is well-known, indeed, it is an inseparable aspect of the sages, *sadhus,* and *sannyasins,* or, for that matter, any godman of India. They all wear *rudraksha* beads strung on a thread as garlands around their neck, head, or hand. Upper-class Hindus wear *rudraksha* chains; for some, they even serve as status symbols. Rich people get the beads strung on gold chains. The word *rudraksha* means tears of Rudra, or Lord Śiva, who was known more popularly as Rudra during Vedic times. This tree is popularly known as *uthram* or *uthrasam* bead tree.

Rudraksha tree: distribution and other details

Rudraksha (Rudraksh) beads are sourced from various species of the genus *Elaeocarpus.* The Rudraksha tree is found in tropical evergreen forests in central, north, and north-eastern India. In north and central India, the beads are sourced from *Elaeocarpus ganitrus* (*syn E.sphearicus*), which was once distributed across evergreen forests from the sea coast to Himalayan foothills up to 2000 m. However, due to extensive habitat destruction, and over-extraction of seeds, the tree is now found only in some patches in northeast India and Nepal. Other species from which the beads are sourced in India are *E. tuberculatus* and *E. serratus.* (1)

Owing to its popularity and over-exploitation, the number of Rudraksha trees in India is dwindling at an alarming rate. Only a few trees are found growing in the wild in the Western Ghats and North East States of India. In the western Himalayas and foothills, only a few individual trees are left in conservation reserves or temples. (2) *Elaeocarpus* had been an associated species in mixed broad-leaved forests of the Himalayas and Himalayan foothills and was found associated with species like Sal (*Shorea robusta*) and Oak (*Quercus* spp.). Extensive deforestation of mixed broad-leaved forests for railways, timber extraction, and large-scale conversion of Oak forests into Pine (*Pinus roxburghii*) in the Himalayas has led to the loss of native species from the region. The extremely low germination rate of *rudraksha* seeds due to their corky, hard seed coat makes an already dire situation worse. Further, due to ethno-religious importance, the seeds are collected in large numbers from the forest floor, causing a depletion of the natural seed bank. The prolonged germination period for the species, along with poor germination rate and commercial collection of seeds, has led to a significant reduction in the number of trees in the wild. Despite its great importance, the renewal of the population has remained unaddressed, as most of the market demands are fulfilled by Nepal and other countries that commercially export the beads (mainly Indonesia.

The genus *Elaeocarpus* is highly threatened, but only a few species have been listed in IUCN red list categories (3). Out of 31 species listed in the IUCN Red List, 5 species (*E. venustus, E. recurvatus, E. munroii, E. gausseniii, E. blascoi*) are from India, particularly from the Western Ghats. The conservation status of other species in India is not known. *E. ganitrus* has been listed as rare in Taiwan. The consequence of ignorance and exploitation has resulted in a severe loss of trees from Indian forests. It has been found that the spread and distribution of this culturally significant tree have shrunk remarkably. Therefore, it is necessary to locate remaining clusters, identify threats, and reverse the declining trend. A recent review can be found in Prasannan et al. (4)

Rudraksha bead is obtained from the seeds of several species of the genus *Elaeocarpus*, with *Elaeocarpus ganitrus* being the principal species. The word *Elaeocarpus* is derived from the Greek words Elaeo = olive and carpus = fruit (referring to olive-like fruits produced by the genus). All the trees in the genus bear white flowers with fringed petals and develop olive-like fruits. The genus *Elaeocarpus* has more than 360 known species worldwide (5). Storrs et. al., in their book 'Trees and Shrubs of Nepal and Himalayas', recorded 26 species of *Elaeocarpus* from the Himalayan region. (6)

Today, the species is threatened and is grown on hill slopes and farms for its commercial (including poverty alleviation) and religious values in Nepal, whereas such plantations or conservation efforts are not known in India. The natural regeneration of Rudraksha is a slow process due to the poor germination rate owing to the extremely hard seed coat. The seeds take up to two years to sprout, depending on the humidity of the soil. The natural germination of *Elaeocrpus* is less than five per cent. The seeds are also prone to fungal rotting. Once planted, the tree starts bearing fruit after 3–4 years and continues until the tree lives. Several factors, including habitat destruction due to changing land use, over-extraction of seeds for commercial use, poor germination, and lack of conservation efforts, have resulted in the tree being either vulnerable (Nepal) or threatened (India). It is time to develop conservation strategies for the conservation of *Elaeocarpus* for both its sacred and ecological values.

The fruits, when dry, exhibit iridescence. Seeds are soaked in water for a few days to remove the outer covering to obtain a hard, woody endocarp, which is known as the Rudraksha bead. The seeds are woody and corky in texture, ranging from yellowish to light brown, reddish brown to dark brown, and black, and covered with the pulp of the berry. The seeds are usually spherical, with a rough surface and a vertical perforation in the centre. running from top to bottom. This perforation is further punctured to form the bead. Each seed has a varying number of vertical lines running down its surface that form 'Mukhs' or faces of the bead. The bead is valued based on these faces, or 'mukhs. The faces in the *rudraksha* bead can vary from 1 to 24, which is equivalent to the number of seeds/seed clefts inside. A large variation in shape and size is observed in *rudraksha*. Very rarely naturally joined *rudraksha* can be found.

Commercially, there are three types of *Rudraksha* available: Nepalese, Indonesian, and Indian. Of these, 75% of *Rudraksha* in the world market is of Indonesian origin, 20% is Indian and from other countries, and 5% is Nepalese. The Nepal Rudraksha is hard, compact, heavy, lustrous, considered more powerful due to the environment they grow in, and hence expensive. Indonesian rudraksha are smaller, *Mukhs* or faces are inconspicuous and are cheaper. The Indian round *Rudraksha* generally lacks lustre and is commonly known as Indian rough beads. These beads are treated with oil and dye to increase their market prices. Rudraksha are differentiated based on variation in the seeds (grooves), and different qualities are attributed to them. Some labs also provide standards or codes of conduct for identifying genuine *Rudraksha* from fake ones. Haridwar and Varanasi are two major centres for Rudraksha trade in India. (7) The major types of rudraksha beads and their trading centres are given below.

The major types of rudraksha traded in India and their details are the following:

1. Elaeocarpus ganitrus

Origin: Nepal.

Bead size: 10-11 mm; No. of mukhs: 1-21

Popularity: The most popular for all the mukhis.

Major trading centres: Varanasi, Haridwar, Mathura, Rameshwaram.

Use: As beads, as rosary, and as mala (garlands)

2. Elaeocarpus (various species).

Origin: Indonesia

Size: 12-35 mm; Mukhs: 1 – 27 mukhs

Popularity: For 5 – Mukhi beads

Major trading centres: Haridwar, Mathura, Varanasi, Mumbai.

Major use: For rosary

3. *Elaeocarpus tuberculatus & E. serratus*

Origin: India

Size: 15-25 mm; Mukhs: Mainly 1,2,3, 5 mukhs.

Popularity: For one Mukhi bead.

Major trading centers: Haridwar, Mathura, Varanasi, Rameswaram, other religious market

Major use: As beads

Beads having 21 – 27 *Mukhi* are extremely rare, and the toughest to find along with the bead constituting only single – *Mukhi* or *'Ek-Mukhi'*. Also, beads of uncommon shapes like *'Gauri-Shankar'* are rarely seen and so are expensive. The trading process from produce to processing to marketing is explained as follows:

- Dharan is the major trading centre in Nepal for *Elaeocarpus* seeds or beads. The seeds are extracted from the fruit, cleaned, and transported from Dharan to Varanasi in the form of beads.
- Varanasi is the oldest and the major trading centre in India. The beads are processed – a) Cleaned, b) Coloured, c) Drilled and are kept in the form of beads and rosaries.
- The wholesalers then supply the processed beads and rosaries in different parts of India. The other major business centre for rudraksha beads is Haridwar and Mathura.

- On the other hand, Indonesia trades beads of small size compiled in the form of a rosary. They are later transformed into a proper rosary by the sellers (both regional and local) depending upon the demand and are always sold in the form of a rosary constituting of *'paanch-mukhi'* bead.
- In a regional domain, the beads and rosaries are usually bought from the wholesalers and are sold in the local market, whereas, the bigger wholesalers have their direct contacts that are kept private.
- There are also different mediators involved who visit the local markets every 2-3 months and sell the beads required. This is about the beads from Nepal.
- A large percentage of fake beads are produced in India. (8)

Supply and Demand

The economic value of the beads is always inversely proportional to the occurrence of the variety (or variety seen). The stakeholders involved in the demand chain of the beads or rosaries from the big wholesalers are *Sadhus*, religious gurus, regional and local sellers, and general people for medicinal and spiritual purposes. Based on the recommendations made by various religious gurus, television has a significant influence on the demand for various types of beads. Cultural significance, as well as medicinal and astrological benefits, influenced the demand for the beads. According to the trade circles, there has always been an equilibrium between the supply and demand of the beads, but the trend of the popularity of Indonesian and Nepali beads relative to each other keeps fluctuating. For the past few years, the supply of beads from Nepal has become constrained due to the increase in demand from other neighbouring countries like China. This has also significantly raised the economic value of the beads from Nepal. The beads from Nepal hold more value in comparison to the beads from Indonesia because of the size and clarity of the faces or *'mukhis'* developed on them. It is reported that the trade in Nepal has suffered because of fake beads available in the Indian market, which is the primary destination for Nepalese beads. (9)

Rudraksha tree
Source:https://upload.wikimedia.org/wikipedia/commons/8/86/
RudrakshaTree.jpg)

Rudraksh tree branch showing ripe iridescent fruits.

Rudraksha: Myths and Legends:

Legends on *rudraksha* are available in *Puranas* like *Śiva Purana, Devi Bhagavata Purana, Padma Purana,* etc. and in the *Rudraksha – Jabala Upanishad.* The following is the most popular legend. Tharakasura, the powerful king of demons, had three sons, Kamalakshan, Tharakakshan, and Vidyutmali. Through penance, they got boons from Lord Brahma, by which they became invincible and their deaths would happen only when all three met once in a thousand years. Mayan, the architect of Asuras, constructed three cities, one for each; hence, they are called *Tripuresvars.* These cities were always in motion in different directions, and their confluence took place only once in thousand years. So, they can be killed only at that precise moment, and that too only with a single arrow. Because of their untold atrocities, all three worlds suffered, and men, women, *rishis,* and *devas* were all in tears and desperation. Finally, Lord Śiva decided to enter the scene.

Siva meditated for a long time, and when he opened his eyes a few tear drops fell on the ground. These drops became the *rudraksha* beads. Śiva was unhappy because the *Tripuresvars* were his devotees and it was painful to kill them. Śiva then sent the beads to earth, where they grew up as the *rudraksha* trees. Śiva had to make elaborate preparations for destroying the three cities and the *asuras* were so powerful that Śiva had to absorb half of the power of other gods also, to gain an upper hand. He located a place on the banks of river Narmada for his operations. He made a bow out of Mount Mandhara, Vasuki the snake king became the bowstring, and Lord Vishnu became the arrow. *Agni* occupied the tip of the arrow, *Vayu* the base, and other *devas* like Indra took seats on various points on the bow. Finally, when the cities met, Śiva shot the arrow and the three cities, along with everything in it, and the demon kings were burnt to ashes. Another version of this legend narrates how Śiva sent his '*thrisul*' (trident) to the three cities and the *thrisul* struck the cities, made them immobile, and then Śiva burst them with the '*Maha Pasupathastra*' (Śiva's arrow which is invincible). Śiva was greatly pained that he killed his own ardent devotees. Tears filled his eyes and a few drops rolled down his cheeks and fell on earth. These tears became the *rudraksha* trees. This legend is given in puranas like *Siva Purana, Skanda Purana, Devi Bhagavatha Purana* etc.

Another legend narrates that Parvathi once asked Śiva about the origin of *Rudraksha*. Śiva replied that he did penance for a thousand celestial years (one celestial year is approximately 225 million earth years), and when he opened his eyes, a few tears drop fell on the ground and from these teardrops were born the *rudraksha* trees. Another legend narrates how Parvathi pestered Śiva for ornaments for adoring her body, which Śiva always ignored. One particularly wonderful spring season, Parvathi, overwhelmed by the desire to adorn herself, insisted on adornments. Śiva opened his hands and *rudraksha* beads fell from heaven into his hands. He gave them to Parvathi and asked her to make necklaces and bangles. Parvathi strung them and wore them as jewellery. Śiva told Parvathi of the greatness of the *rudraksha* bead and then threw a few beads to the earth where they became *rudraksha* trees. (11).

Yet another legend tells that Siva was greatly in anguish after the death of his consort, Sati. He roamed around here and there calling the name of Sati, and crying. His teardrops fell on the earth and the *rudraksha* trees sprang up from these teardrops. (12)

It is well known that Śiva has three eyes, two of them always open, one represents Surya (Sun) and the other Chandra (Moon), and the third eye representing *agni* (Fire) is always closed, but when it opens fire emerges out of it that can engulf anything in its path. It is said that from the eye representing Surya 12 varieties of *rudraksha* beads originated, all dark in colour. From the second eye representing Chandra emerged 16 varieties, all of them white. From the third eye representing *Agni* (fire) 10 dark (black) types of beads originated.

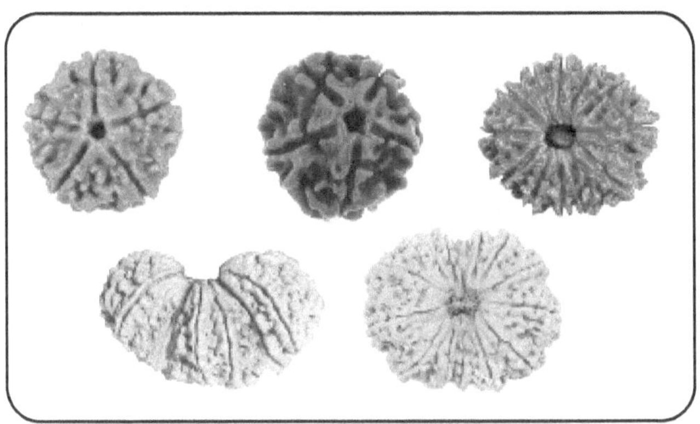

Rudraksha colours. All colours on storage slowly change to brown and then to black. (www.rudralife.com)

Thus, 38 varieties of *rudraksha* beads are mentioned in the ancient texts (13). But only 21 types are important. They include *ækamukhi* (single-faced), *dwimukhi* (two-faced), *thrimukhi* (three-faced), *chaturmukhi* (four-faced), *paanchamukhi* (five-faced) and so on. Usually, the beads are round; the single-faced ones are often cashew nut-shaped. Sometimes double (united) beads also seen, they are called *Gaurishankar rudraksha*. Such beads are believed to have the blessings of Lord Śiva and goddess Parvathi. Very rarely three beads joined naturally also occur, and then it is called *trijuti rudraksha*, which is supposed to have the blessings of the Trinity. Such *rudraksha* beads may have varying numbers of faces. Five-faced *rudraksha* is the most common, 3 7-faced less common, others rare or very rare. One faced and 9 21 faced are extremely rare. Each *rudraksha* type is associated with a deity. The following discussion is mainly adapted from KN Sita's 'The Power of Rudraksha' and Ravindran's Sacred and Ritual Plants of India. (14).

One-faced (ækamukhi) rudraksha: Itis considered the manifest form of Lord Śiva himself. Further, it is mentioned that every year Lord Śiva endows three one-faced (ækamukhi) *rudraksha* seeds; one passes on to his most ardent devotee, the other to a virtuous ruler and the third is kept by the Lord himself. Lakshmi, the goddess of fortune and prosperity, confers her choicest blessings on the persons wearing *ækamukhi-rudraksha* beads. Such beads are usually encased in gold and preserved as heirloom. Some prominent people, who are known to wear such *rudraksha* beads include Yahudi Menuhin, BKS Iyengar, and Ananda Mayee Ma. The ruling planet of *aekamukhi rudraksha* is Sun, and the associated sacred '*mantra*' is *Om namah shivaya* and *Om hrim namaha*.

Two-faced (dvimukhi) rudraksha: This one symbolizes *Ardhanarisvara*. *Ardhanarishvara* is an androgynous deity composed of Śiva and his consort Shakti, representing the synthesis of masculine and feminine energies. Śiva and Shakti are two aspects of the same supreme power. The *Ardhanari* form also illustrates how the female principle of God, Shakti is inseparable from the male principle of God. Wearing this *rudraksha* ensures the fulfilment of desires, it is believed. Its ruling planet is the moon and its associated mantra is *Om shiva shakti namaha*.

The three-faced (*thrimukhi*) rudraksha: It symbolizes *Agni* in its three aspects (or three faces, *dakshināgni, gārhapatya* and *ahavarēya*). The three-faced Agni also symbolises the Trinity. By wearing this, a person will always get the blessings of the Trinity. The way fire consumes everything and still remains pure, the wearer too gets free from all sins or wrongs of his life and becomes pure and blessed. It is believed by wearing this bead even the sins earned in one's past births are burnt as fire burns fuel. The ruling planet is Mars and the associated mantra is *Om klim namah, Om namah Shivaya.*

***Chatur – mukhi* (4-faced) *rudraksha*:** It is said to be the symbol of Brahma and the four faces represent the four *Vedas*. The wearer of this *rudraksha*, it is believed, will gain the four aims of human life, namely, *Dharma* (virtue), *Artha* (wealth), *Kama* (pleasure) and *moksha* (Salvation). The four faces also represent knowledge, action, fate, and freedom. Wearing this *rudraksha*, it is believed, will lead to greater confidence, power, and yogic qualities. The ruling planet is mercury, and the associated *mantra* is *Om hrim namaha.*

Pancha mukhi* (5-faced) *rudraksha: As per *Śiva Purana*, it is symbolic of the five faces of Śiva – *Īśana, Ṭatpuruśa, Āghora, Vamadeva* and *Ṣadjyojata*. This form of Śiva is known as *Kalaagni-Rudra.'* It is also representative of the five elements of nature: earth, water, fire, air, and ether. This type of *rudraksha* is the most commonly available and hence is used by holy men and family men, its use is believed to bestow a long, peaceful life. Such beads are sacred to Anjaneya. The ruling planet is Jupiter, and the related mantra is *Om hrim namaha.*

***Shad mukhi* (Six faced) *rudraksha*:** This type of bead symbolises Karthikeya, the son of Lord Siva and the god of war. This *Rudraksha* bead is believed to be blessed by Devi Parvathi, and it should be worn on the right arm. By wearing this, one can attain wisdom, knowledge, courage, and confidence, and help maintain celibacy. It is said to give control over anger, greediness, and improper thoughts and actions, mental sharpness, and willpower. Its presiding planet is Venus, and the associated mantra is *Om hum namaha.*

Sapta mukhi* (Seven-faced) *Rudraksha: This bead has many associated symbolisms. It symbolizes Mahalakshmi, Kamadeva (the god of love), the seven divine mothers (*sapta mathrukkal*), the seven devas (*sapta devas*, seven gods), and the seven *rishis* (seven great sages). The seven divine mothers are: Brahmani, Vaishnavi, Maheshvari, Indrani, Kaumari, Varahi and, Narasimhi. They are manifestations of the seven gods and are always associated with Parvathi or Durga. The seven devas are: Indra (Śakra), Aditya (Sun), Soma (Moon), Agni (Fire), Vayu (Wind god), Varuna (God of oceans), Yama (God of death). The seven rishis (*sapta rishis*) keep changing in every yuga. The present yuga has Kashyapa, Atri, Vashista, Vishvamitra, Gautama, Jamadagni, and Bharadvaja as the *saptarishs*. (The *Satapatha Brahmana* mentions the following names: Atri, Bharadwaja, Gautama, Jamadagni, Kashyapa, Vasishta, and Viswamithra. According to Krishna Yajurveda the names include: Angiras, Atri, Bhrigu, Gautama, Kashyapa, Kutsa, and Vasishta. The Mahabharatam gives the seven *rishis* as: Marichi, Atri, Pulaha, Pulasthya, Kratu, Vasishta, Kashyapa. Brihat Samhita gives the names as: Marichi, Vasishta, Angiras, Atri, Pulastya, Pulaha, and Kratu). Moreover, this *rudraksha* also symbolizes Goddess Mahalakshmi. According to *Padma Purana* this type of bead also symbolizes the seven great serpents (Vasuki, Takshaka, Karkotaka, Padmaka, Sankhapala, Gulika, Kaliya). The ruling planet of *saptamuhki rudraksha* is Saturn; the associated mantra is *Om Maha Lakshmi namaha, Om hum namaha.*

Ashta-mukhi* (8-faced) *Rudraksha: This type of bead symbolizes Lord Ganesa. Wearing this, it is believed, helps to ward off obstacles in one's life and gives progress in physical, spiritual, and mental spheres. It keeps one away from unpredictable accident, misfortunes, obstacles, and miseries. It is considered to bring peace in home life and deemed well for starting anything in good faith. The ruling planet is Rahu and the associated mantra is *Om Ganeshaya namaha.*

Nava-mukhi **(9-faced)** ***rudraksha:*** Nine-faced *Rudraksha* is the symbol of Durga, who takes the nine forms as Navadurga. It is also considered symbolizing Bhairav and Kapilamuni. This *Rudraksha* is believed to possess nine different powers given by the Nava-Durga. It should be worn with respect on the left arm or hand. By wearing this *rudraksha* a person becomes fearless and self-confident and hence is recommended for those who are suffering from depression and lacking self-confidence. The ruling planet is Ketu and the accompanying mantra is *Om hrim hum Namaha.*

Dasamukhi **(10 – faced)** ***Rudraksha:*** This symbolizes Lord Vishnu, and believed to represent the ten incarnations of Vishnu, occupying the ten faces, and the whole bead then representing Vishnu. Shiva purana recommends this for everyone, irrespective of class, creed, gender, religion or nationality, and everyone will be benefitted. *Devi Bhagavatham* praises the ten *mukhi rudraksha* as it has the power to save the person who is wearing it from worldly sufferings, miseries, misfortunes, evil power, and adverse planetary effects. It has no ruling planet, and the mantra for this *rudraksha* is *Om hrim namaha.*

Ekadasha-mukhi **(11-faced***)*** ***rudraksha***: This *rudraksha* symbolizes Śiva and his eleven manifestations: Mahadeva, Śiva, Maha Rudra, Shankara, Neelalohita, Eshana Rudra, Vijaya Rudra, Bheema Rudra, Devadeva, Bhavodbhava, and Adityatmaka Sri Rudra. The consorts of these eleven forms respectively are: Dhee devi, Dhritti devi, Ushna (Rasala) devi, Uma devi, Neeyut devi, Sarpi devi, Ila devi, Ambika devi, Iervadi devi, Sudha devi, and Deeksha devi – all are forms of Parvathi. Lord Hanuman is considered as a manifestation of Siva and as one of the Rudras. According to scripture the benefits of this *rudraksha* are many. The wearer always attains victory and wealth. When invoked, one is blessed with wisdom, right judgment, powerful vocabulary, adventurous life, and success in all undertakings. Above all, it also protects one from accidental death. One becomes fearless. It also helps concentrate in meditation. It has no ruling planet; the presiding deity is Hanuman. The accompanying mantra is: *Om hrim hum namaha.*

***Dvaadasha-mukhi* (12-faced) *Rudraksha*:** Twelve-faced *rudraksha* symbolizes the twelve *Aditya* (children of Rishi Kashyap and his consort Adithi); they are called *Dwadasa Adityas:* Mitra, Varuna, Aryama, Bhaga, Amshuman, Dhata, Indra, Parjanya, Tvastha, Vishnu, Pushya, Vivasvan. They are the twelve forms of Sun God, and they are believed to reign over the twelve zodiacs. This *rudraksha*, therefore, stands for the twelve qualities of Lord Surya: the light of universal friendship, the light of compelling radiance, the dispeller of darkness or ignorance, the shining principle, the all-pervading light, the light of the mystic fire, the golden-coloured one, healing gold, light obvious and subtle as at dawn and dusk, light of the sage as an aspect of Vishnu, light of enlightenment, light that removes afflictions affecting the light of intelligence. Lord Sun blesses the person wearing this *rudraksha* bead with a life of wealth, fortune, unlimited luxury, and a great personality. Wearing this *rudraksha* enables a human to have an ever-shining appeal. The ruling planet is Sun and the associated *mantra* is *Shree Suryaya namaha.*

Trayodasha-mukhi **(13-faced)** ***rudraksha:*** This *rudraksha* bead is very rare, and it symbolizes Karthikeya (Lord Muruka), Indra, the king of devas and Kamadeva, the god of love. This *Rudraksha* is believed to bestow great accomplishments and qualities to the person wearing it. It bestows charm, worldly comforts, and spiritual upliftment to the wearer, it is held generally. This bead also bestows virtues like love, affection, beauty, and attraction. Because of the three presiding deities 13 – faced *rudraksha* helps the wearer to gain spiritual power, success, physical and mental strength, good luck, power of authority, charismatic personality, honour, wealth, worldly pleasures, high level of social and financial status and glory. Its presiding deities are Indra and Kamadeva, and the ruling planet is Venus. The associated mantra is *Om hrim namaha.*

Chaturdasha-mukhi **(14-faced)** ***rudraksha:*** This *Rudraksha is known as "deva mani"* (the divine bead); it is one of the rarest of the *rudraksha* types. It is believed to have come directly from the eyes of Śiva and he himself wears this bead. Shiva Purana extols the quality of this bead; also tells us how the fourteen *mukhi rudraksha* rules the cosmic world and humans and is regarded it as a favourite possession not just by humans but also by gods and goddesses. It is to be worn on the head to get the full benefits, it is stipulated and when used properly it can bestow the third eye of wisdom and one can even attain the power to see the future. It is said that the wearer attains spiritual freedom. The ruling planet is Saturn, and this *Rudraksha* can nullify the evil effects of Saturn. The presiding mantra is *Om Shivaya namaha.* (15-20)

The rest of the *rudraksha* types are so rare that they may even be impossible to get by anyone. The main qualities associated with them are given below:

Fifteen-faced *rudraksha* is symbolic of Pasupathi (an incarnation of Śiva, as protector of all organisms, the national deity of Nepal). (21)

Sixteen-faced *rudraksha* is symbolic of Lord Sri Ram, and is known as the *Jai* (Victory) *rudraksha.*

Seventeen-faced *rudraksha* represents Vishwakarma, and wearing this is believed to bring wealth.

Eighteen-faced *rudraksha* represents Bhumi Devi, the Goddess of Earth.

Nineteen-faced *rudraksha* symbolizes Lord Vishnu.

Twenty-faced *Rudraksha* is one of the rarest, and it is symbolic of *"OM"*, the *Brahmom* – the ultimate.

Twenty-one *mukhi rudraksha* represents Kubera, the lord of wealth. The wearer of this is believed to become immensely rich (22, 23).

In addition to the types just mentioned there are a few others that are considered very special, and very rare. They include:

Gauri-Shankar rudraksha: Two beads of equal sizes joined firmly, believed to represent Śiva and Shakthi or *purusha* and *prakṛti*. Wearing this bestows blessings of Śiva and Parvathi, it is so believed, that its use leads to family harmony, contentment, happiness, and peace.

Ganesh-Gauri Rudraksha: Two beads, one normal size and another much smaller are jointed, the normal large one is believed to represents Parvathi and the small one Ganesha. Wearing this is said to be good for women who are pregnant. The general belief is that wearing this *rudraksha* helps to maintain the normal health of the womb and the health of the foetus and helps to prevent miscarriages.

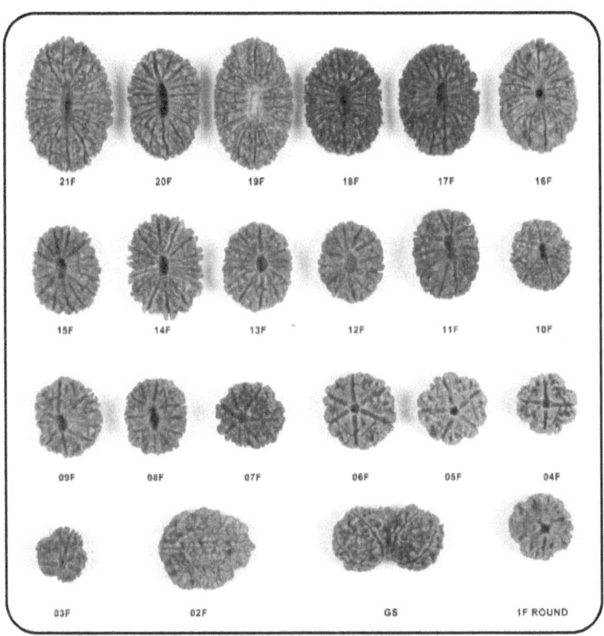

*Rudraksha beads: 21 types, 1-21 faced and the Gowrishanker bead.
(Source: https://www.himalayasshop.com/blogs/blogs/rudraksha-mala)*

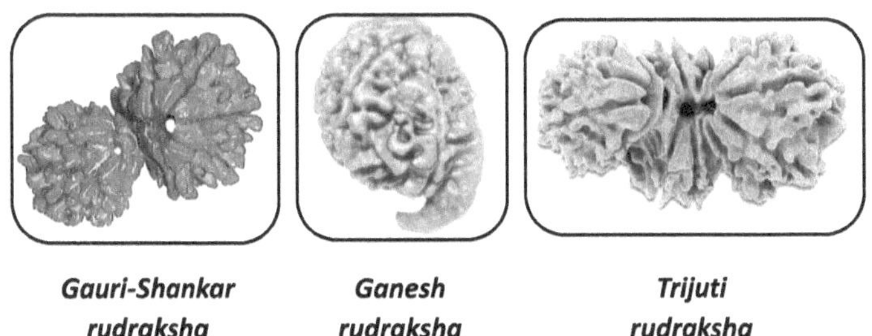

**Gauri-Shankar
rudraksha**

**Ganesh
rudraksha**

**Trijuti
rudraksha**

*(Source: https://www.himalayasshop.com/blogs/blogs/
rudraksha-mala)*

Ganesh rudraksha: A normal *rudrakha* bead of any type but having a tusk – like outgrowth, a thorny protrusion on one side. The associated belief is that this *rudraksha* provides the wearer perfection in every sphere of life and the grace of Lord Ganesha is received by him. His life becomes successful.

There is a related type of Ganesh *rudraksha* that has the impression of the Sanskrit 'Om'.

Ganesh-Gauri-Shankar rudraksha: Two normal – sized beads and a much smaller one in between, joined naturally and this is considered by many as a very auspicious bead. By wearing this, it is believed, that all family members will be blessed by Lord Ganesha, Shiva, and Parvati.

Trijuti rudraksha: Three beads of normal size attached naturally, represent the trinity, Brahma, Vishnu, and Siva. The wearer is blessed by all the three Gods.

Ekamukhigol-dhana Rudraksha: Unlike the usual *aekamukhi* bead that is half-moon or cashew-nut shaped, this one is round like any other *rudraksha* bead with a natural hole. It is extremely rare, and it is generally believed that only a person blessed by Lord Siva in many previous lives will get such a bead.

Ekavimshati rudraksha: Very rare and precious, wearing the 21-faced *rudraksha*, bestows the wearer with blessings and immense prosperity, fulfilment of pleasures, and desires. It gives the wearer immense protection from every kind of evil influence.

Nirakar rudraksha: This is the faceless *rudrakha*, as it does not possess a line, it is round and perfect with a natural hole. The belief is that the wearer of this type of *rudraksha* will feel complete, and that it can remove worries and tensions in life.

***Saptavimshati rudraksha* (27 faced)**: Extremely rare. *Pancha-Parameshvar rudraksha*: Believed to represent the five-headed Lord Shiva (Panchanana).

Gauri Shankar Savar (Nag) rudraksha: This is an extremely rare type, and it represents Siva; possess a cobra-like projection, hence named as *Gauri – Shakar Naag Rudraksha*.

Sivalinga rudraksha: A *rudrakha* with an impression that appears like a *sivalingam*.

Om – rudraksha: This is an ordinary *rudrakha* that carries an *Om*-like impression. (24, 25, 26)

Influence of rudraksha

The yogis and tantric exponents are of the opinion that the type of *rudraksha* influences the body differently. So, the 21 types mentioned influence the human body by affecting different organs or systems of the body. Some information can be given on this aspect in modern terminology. (27, 28).

One-*mukhi:* pineal, pituitary, optic chiasma, hypothalamus

Two-*mukhi:* heart

Three-*mukhi:* throat, celiac plexus

Four-*mukhi:* adrenal, heart

Five-*mukhi:* all major *chakra* points

Six-*mukhi:* prostate and reproductive organs, *mooladhara chakra*

Seven-*mukhi*: optic chiasma, pancreas

Eight-*mukhi:* medulla oblongata

Nine-*mukhi:* pineal and pituitary glands

Ten-*mukhi:* heart power

Eleven – *mukhi:* nerve energy

Twelve-*mukhi:* cerebral hemispheres, hiatus of the stomach, oesophagus

Thirteen – *mukhi*: celiac plexus, prostate

Fourteen – *mukhi:* heart

Fifteen – *mukhi*: ileocecal valve, lymphatic throat area system

Sixteen – *mukhi:* thyroid, thymus, spleen, and pancreas

Seventeen – *mukhi*: small intestine, lungs, bronchial tree

Eighteen – *mukhi*: liver, womb

Nineteen – *mukhi*: lungs, bronchial tubes

Twenty –*mukhi*: adrenal glands

Twenty-one – *mukhi*: reproductive organs.

Type of *rudraksha* for wearing can be selected according to situations or needs, or based on the objectives. There are some guidelines for such selection:

For improving or solving problems related to family relationships, or with the neighbours/ society: Two *mukhi rudraksha* or a *Gaurishankar Rudraksha*

For relief from a life of obstacles: 8-*mukhi*, 11-*mukhi* or 19-*mukhi.*

For countering mental weakness, a wavering mind: 4, 6, 8, 11-*mukhi rudrakshas.*

For a person interested in oratory skills, artistic skills, charm, film stars, HRD persons etc.: 13-mukhi is the best; alternatively, 6-*mukhi* can be substituted.

For anxiety, sleep disorders: 10-*Mukhi*

For securing power, authority, and physical stamina: 12-m*ukhi*

For protection from jealousy, evil eye, black magic-: 10-*mukhi* + 9-*mukhi*, 11-*mukhi*.

For total protection from fear, physical threats, and loneliness-: 9,10 and 11-*mukh* – together.

For marriage and marital happiness: 2-*mukhi*, *Gaurishankar.*

For victory: 16-*mukhi.*

For winning in speculations, business, lottery etc.: 17-*mukhi*, 14 – *mukhi.*

For education (students), concentration, memory improvement, and general health.: 4-and 6-*mukhis.*

For cure from stomach disorders, 12 *mukhi* in combination with 9 and 5-*mukhis.*

For success in new projects, new ventures: 18-*mukhi*

To solve problems related to children: 18-*mukhi* + 12 *mukhi*

For becoming wealthy and powerful-: 15-*mukhi*

For family protection, and success in various professions: 1+ 14 *mukhis.*

For meditation: 1,3,5,9,11-*mukhis.*

For people living abroad, those who need protection: 1+14 *mukhis*

For achieving excellence in any field: 14,17,19,20-*mukhis*

For material and spiritual bliss: Indra mala, which consists of 1-21 *mukhis*and *trijuti.*

For businessmen/ traders: 5-*mukhi, 7-mukhi*

Thinkers, philosophers, researchers: 4-*mukhi*

Lovers: 13-*mukhi* etc.

Usually, the number of beads used in *rudraksha mala* (garlands) is 108 for wearing on the chest, but this varies depending upon the people who use them. *Sadhus* and *yogis* (hermits and ascetics) use such garlands for wearing on waists, shoulders, ears, or on the head and the numbers of beads in such garlands can vary and may even go up to 360, 500, 550, or even 1000. The *japa mala* used by hermits and *yogis* consists of 108 beads, which are said to symbolize the 108 sensory points of the body. This number 108 also stands for 108 Upanishads, 108 synonyms for Vishnu and Śiva as given in *Mahabharata*. *Satapata Brahmana* states that each *samvatsar* (year) has 10800 auspicious moments and 108 *muhurts* (auspicious occasions). *Rig, Yajur* and *Sama Vedas* contain 10800 couplets each and when this number is divided by the human life span (taken as 100 years), we get the number 108. So, 108 is a magical number as far as humans are concerned, and that is why *rishis* and those in meditation chant the *mantras* or the *namajapa* (chanting) 108 times. In Jainism, Buddhism and Sikhism also the *japa mala* (rosary) consists of 108 beads. In Christianity the rosary consists of 58 beads and a cross and each bead has a significance like the cross stands for faith in God and in the memory of Jesus, the first bead adjacent to it is God, the next three beads stand for the Father, Son and the Holy Ghost as well the three forms of energy: energy of will, of knowledge, and action; the fifth bead is in memory of the mission of the Lord, the three triangular beads symbolizes happiness, unhappiness, and bliss; 10x5= 50 beads represent the five secrets of Jesus – Creation, Sustenance, Dissolution, the Covering of great illusion and the Initiation. Rosaries are made from the stem of rose plants as Virgin Mary was very fond of rose flowers, hence the name rosary. The Muslims use a *japa mala* of 33 or 99 beads, as Allah has 99 names. Their *japamala* called *tasabi* is made from marble, ivory, sea shells, camel bones or date seeds, the rich people use *japa malas* of pearls. The Zoroastrians use a *japa mala* that consists of 101 beads, representing the names of the Lord. (29).

Rudraksha beads are also specific for the birth stars and the birth *Rasi leghna s*(zodiacs). Each birth star has a presiding planet, a plant, an animal and a specific *rudraksha* type for wearing.

The type of *rudraksha* prescribed for various stars are given below.

Rudraksha type recommended for various birth stars

Stars	*Presiding planet*	*Rudraksha recommended.*
Aswini	Ketu	9-mukhi
Bharani	Venus	6-mukhi
Krittika	Sun	1, 12, 11 mukhis
Rohini	Moon	2-mukhi
Mrigashirsha	Mars	3-mukhi
Ardra	Rahu	8-mukhi
Punarvasu	Jupiter	5-mukhi
Pushya	Saturn	7-mukh
Ashlesha	Mercury	4-mukhi
Magha	Ketu	9-mukhi
Purvaphalguni	Venus	6-mukhi
Uttaraphalguni	Sun	1,12,or 11 mukhis

Hasta	Moon	2-mukhi
Chitra	Mars	3-mukhi
Swati	Rahu	8-mukhi
Vishakha	Jupiter	5-mukhi
Anuradha	Saturn	7 – mukhi
Jyeshtha	Mercury	4-mukhi
Moola	Ketu	9-mukhi
Purvashadha	Venus	6-mukhis
Uttarashadha	Sun	1,12,or 11-mukhis
Shravana	Moon	2-mukhi
Dhanishtha	Mars	3-mukhis
Shatabhisha	Rahu	8-mukhi
Purvabhadrapada	Jupiter	5-mukhi
Uttarabhadrapada	Saturn	7-mukhi
Revathi	Mercury	4-mukhis

Rasi laghna (zodiac as computed in the Indian astrology based on date and time of birth, is different from the zodiac used in the western world) and the associated auspicious planet and the *rudraksha* type are:

Rudraksha type for different laghnas (Zodiacs)

Rasi laghna	Auspecious planet	Rudraksha type
Mesha (Aries)	Mars, Jupiter	3 & 5-mukhis
Vrishabha (Taurus)	Mercury, Saturn	4 & 7-mukhis
Mithun (Gemini)	Mercury, Venus	4 & 6-mukhis

Karka (Cancer)	Moon, Mars	3 & – 2 – mukhis
Simh (Leo)	Sun, Mars	3 & 12 – mukhis
Kanya (Virgo)	Mercury	4 & 6 – mukhis
Tula (Libra)	Venus, Saturn	6 & 7 – mukhis
Vrischika (Scorpio)	Jupiter, moon	2-mukhi
Dhanu (Sagittarius)	Jupiter, Sun	5 & 12-mukhis
Makar (Capricorn)	Saturn, Venus	6 & 7-mukhis
Kumbha (Aquarius)	Saturn, Venus	6 & 7-mukhis
Meena (Pisces)	Jupiter, Mars	3 &5 mukhis.

Procedure for Use

Rudraksha beads come in four colours — white, red, yellow, and black. In the early days, *Brahmins* wore only white beads, *Kshatriyas* red ones, *Vaisyas* yellow ones, and the *Sudras*, the black ones. Mention has been made earlier about the origin of such beads from the eyes of Shiva. (30, 31)

Brahmins, especially the priests, used to energize *rudraksha* beads before wearing them, for which procedures are given in Vedas This procedure involves washing the beads in water, applying sandal paste, lighting a lamp, applying incense and then chanting the *'panchakshara mantra'* (*Om! Nama Śivaya*) eleven times, keeping the bead at the foot of the idol and then wearing the *rudraksha*. There is also a detailed Vedic procedure to energize *rudraksha*. Here the procedure is very elaborate, which involves immersing the bead in oil, washing in water from river Ganga, applying sandal paste and *ashta gandham* (a mixture of eight types of incenses or fragrant substances), and chanting in sequence *Panchakshara mantra, Sadjojat mantra, Aghora mantra*, then the *rudraksha* bead is smeared with saffron and chanting *Tatpurusha mantra, Eshan mantra*, the specific mantra of the type (*mukhi*) of *rudraksha* and finally *Maha Mrityunjay mantra*. Usually, only *tāntriks* or brahmin ascetics or priests go for such an elaborate energization. Due to the belief that the tree has originated from Lord Śiva's tears, *rudraksha is* not used in any other poojas.

However, the 'æ*kamukhi rudraksha* is worshipped by those who wear it. It is said, that where the one-faced *rudraksha* is worshipped, that place is considered full of prosperity due to the blessings of Lord Rudra and goddess Lakshmi. It is worshipped on the eighth day of the month of 'Chaitra in the *sukhla paksha* (around March 27 annually). That day the one-faced *rudraksha* is worshipped by offering 108 red flowers (usually Ixora flowers). An oil lamp is lit, sandal sticks are burnt, the *rudraksha* is smeared with sandal paste and then flowers are offered with chanting of *mantra*. The worship is again repeated on the *Diwali* day. The one-faced *rudraksha* should be worn by only one person, or it should be kept in a safe box preferably in the *pooja* room. This *Rudraksha* should be worn on a red thread or a gold chain. When it is worn the person should recite the *Rudraksha mantra* every day 108 times; the mantra is given in the *Rudraksha-Jabala Upanishad*:

> *om rudra ek vaktraya*
> *om hreem namaha|*

Rudraksha-Jabala Upanishad

Rudraksha-Jabala Upanishad is assigned to the *Sama Veda,* and consists of 49 sections, set in *anushtip* metre along with prose passages. It is presented as a dialogue between Kälagni Rudra and sages like Bhusunda, Sanatkumara,

Jadabharata, Dattatreya, Katyayana, Vasishta and others. This Upanishad deals with various aspects of *rudraksha*, such as the origin of *rudraksha* trees and beads, results of wearing and doing *japa* with them, varieties of *rudraksha* beads, methods of wearing the beads and the related *mantras*, details of the beads with 1 14 faces and the benefits of wearing them, the dos and don'ts associated with the wearing of the beads, greatness of *rudraksha* and the benefits derived by wearing them. There is a mention that one who wears *rudraksha* should avoid meat, onion, and garlic, and also alcohol. In *Padma Purana*, there is a detailed discussion on *rudraksha* and its greatness and mode of ritual use and worship. In *Śiva Purana*, almost two chapters are devoted to glorification of *rudraksha* and its ritual uses.

Lord Śiva has given a discourse to his consort Parvathi on the greatness of *rudraksha*, this is provided in the 25th chapter of *Śhiva Purana*. Siva explains to Devi the greatness of *rudraksha* beads. The following passages are quoted from *Shiva Purana*.:

> *Panchadevapriyashchaiva sarvadevapriyastatha |*
> *Sarva mantranjapedbhakto Rudraksha*
> *malayapriye ||*

> My love, any God can be worshipped with the Rudraksha which is dear to the five Gods (Panchayatan meaning Ganesha, Surya, Devi, Vishnu, and Shiva) as well as other Gods.

> *Vishnavadideva bhaktashcha dharayeyurna*
> *samshayaha |*
> *Rudrabhaktovisheshena Rudrakshandharayetsada ||*

Devotees of Vishnu and other Gods can also wear Rudraksha, there is no doubt about it. Devotees of Shiva especially have to daily wear Rudraksha.

Rudraksha vividhahaprotasteshambhedanvadam yaham |
Shrinu parvatisadbhaktyabhuktimuktifalapradan ||

Hey Parvati, Rudraksha are of different types. It provides Salvation. I will tell you the secrets of them. You listen carefully.

Ekavaktrah shivah sakshadbhuktimuktifalapradah |
Tasya darshanamatrenabrahmahatyamvyapohati ||

Single faced Rudraksha is Shiva himself, which provides the fruits of Salvation and liberation. Only its glimpse will rectify *brahma-hatya* (sin of killing a Brahmin)

Yatra sampujitastatralaxmirdurtaranahi |
Nashyantyupadravahsarvesarvakamabhavanti hi ||

Wherever Rudraksha is worshipped, Laxmi is never far, peace will overcome tremors and all wishes will be fulfilled.

Dvivaktrodevadeveshahsarvakamafalapradah |
VisheshatahsaRudrakshogovadhamnashayed drutam ||

Two faced Rudraksha fulfills ones wishes. This is the form of Devdeveshwar. It immediately purifies the sin of killing a cow.

Trivaktroyo hi Rudraks hahsakshatsadhanadahsada |
Tatprabhavadbhaveyurvaividhyahsarvahpratis
hthitah ||

Three faced Rudraksha directly delivers the fruits of sadhana. All education are distinguished by its effect.

Charturvaktrahsvayam brahma
narahatyamvyapohati |
Darshanatsparshanatsadyaschaturvargafala
pradah ||

Four faced Rudraksha is the form of Lord Brahma. It eliminates the sin of human killing. Its darshan (glimpse) delivers the fruits of religion, wealth, sex and moksha.

Paanchavaktrahsvayamrudrah kala-agnirnamatah
prabhu |
Sarvamuktipradashchaivasarvakamafalapradah ||

Five faced Rudraksha is the form of Lord Kala-agni Rudra. This Rudraksha delivers all liberation and fulfills all wishes.

Agamyagamanampapamabhakshayasya cha
bhakshanam |
Ityadisarvapapaani paanchavaktrovyapohati ||
Sins arising from adultery and consuming uneatable foods are rinsed by five faced Rudraksha

Shadvaktrahkartikeyastudharanaddakshinebhuje |
Brahmahatyadikai: papairmuchyatenatrasamsh
ayah ||

Six faced Rudraksha is the form of Lord Kartikeya.
This has to be worn on the right hand. There is no
doubt that it rinses the sin of Brahma-hatya.

Saptavaktromaheshanihyanangonamanamatah |
Dharanattasyadeveshidaridropishvarobhawet ||

Hey Parvati, the seven faced Rudraksha is the form
of Ananga. Wearing this makes one God out of
pauper

Rudrakshaschastavaktrashchavasumurtishch
abhairava |
Dharanattasyapurnayurmritobhavatishula
bhrit ||

Eight faced Rudraksha is the form of Asthamurthi
Bhairav. Attiring this Rudraksha delivers complete
life spaan and even after death one attains to the
form of Trishuldhari Shiva

Bhairavonavavaktrashchakapilashchamunihs
mritah |
Durga vatadadhishthatrinavarupamaheshvari ||

Rudraksha with nine faces is said to be the form of
Bhairav and Kapilamuni. Its *Adhisthatri* (presiding)
deity is Goddess Durga, the devi who takes nine
forms.

Tam dharayedwamahasteRudraksham bhaktitatparah |
Sarveshvarobhawenunam mama tulyonasam shayah ||

This nine faced Rudraksha is to be worn with respect on the left hand. There is no doubt the person who wears it will become almighty and of my level.

Dashavaktromaheshanisvayam devo janardanah |
Dharanattasyadeveshisarvankamanavapnuyat ||

Hey Maheshwari, the ten faced Rudraksha is the form of Lord Janardan himself. It completes all works.

EkadashamukhoyastuRudrakshahparmeshvari |
Sa rudrodharanattasyasarvatravijayibhavet ||

Hey Parameshwari, the eleven faced Rudraksha is the form of Rudra. A male attiring it will attain the qualities of Rudra and gain victory on all.

DvadashasyamtuRudrakshamdharayetke shadeshake |
Adityashchivatesarvedvadashaivasthitastatha ||

Twelve faced Rudraksha is equivalent to dwadasa-aditya, the twelve forms of the Sungod Surya. This Rudraksha is to be worn on the hair.

Trayodashamukhovishvedevastaddhar anannarah |
Sarvankamanavapnotisaubhagyammangal
amlabhet ||

Thirteen faced Rudraksha is the form of Vishvedeva. Person who attires this Rudraksha will have all wishes fulfilled and gain good fortune and luck.

Chaturdashamukhoyo hi Rudrakshahpar
amah shivah |
Dharayenmurghina tam bhaktyasarvapapampr
anasyati ||

Fourteen faced Rudraksha is the form of great Shiva. It should respectfully be worn on the head which will cleanse all sins.

Eti Rudrakshabheda hi prokttavaimukh abhedatah |
Tattanmantraanchhrinupritya krama achchhaile
shvaraatmaje ||

Hey Parvati, daughter of Giriraj. I have described the secrets of fourteen Rudraksha. Now you also listen to the *mantras* of the fourteen Rudraksha respectively:

(1) Om hrim namah, (2) Om namah, (3) Om klim
namah, (4) Om hrim namah, (5) Om hrim namah,
(6) Om hrim hum namah, (7) Om hum namah,
(8) Om hum namah, (9) Om hrim hum namah,
(10) Om hrim namah, (11) Om hrim hum namah,

(12) Om kraumkshaumraum namah,
(13) Om hrim namah, (14) Om namah

*Bhaktishraddhayutashchaiva
sarvakamarthasiddhaye |
Rudrakshandharayen mantrair devanalasya
varjitah ||*

Leaving behind sleep and laziness, one – faced to fourteen – faced *Rudraksha* should be attired with the afore mentioned mantras with devotion to fulfill wishes and gain wealth.

*Vina mantrenayodhatte Rudrakshambhuvimanavah |
Sa yati narakamghoramyavadindrashchaturdasha ||*

Any person, who wears the Rudraksha without mantra in this earth, will go to hell for 14 tenures of Indra or one Kalpa.

*Rudrakshamalinamdristvabhootpretpishachakah |
Dakini shakinichaiva ye chanyedhrohak araka ||*

Ghosts, evil spirits, witches etc flees from the person wearing a Rudraksha.

*Kritimanchaivayatkichidabhicharadikanchayat |
Tatsarvamduratoyatidristvashankitavigraham ||*

Such and other artificial thoughts and deeds will also be afraid and stay at bay.

Rudrakshaamalinamdristvashivovish nu: prasidati |
Devi ganapatihsuryahsurashchanyepiparvati | |

Oh Parvati, Lords Siva, Vishnu, Devi, Ganesh, Surya and other Gods also will be pleased to see a person who wears a Rudraksha

AwamgyatvatumahatmyamRudrakshasyam aheshvari |
Samyagdharyahsamantrashchabhaktya dharmavivriddhaye | |

Oh Maheshwari, Knowing the importance of the *rudraksha*, it should be worn methodically with devotion and mantras for the extension of religion *Siva Purana* has these words:

'I wish not for your frightening image
Wearing huge garlands of beads
And *rudrakshas* on your neck
I long for mother Annapurna and her
Honeyed maternal presence and care…'

Description and Uses:

Rudraksha:

Eleocarpus sphaericus* (Gaertn)K.Schum. *(Syn. Elaeocarpus ganitrus* Roxb.), *Eleocarpaceae.

Rudra's tears (English); rudrak, uttram bead (Hindi); rudraksham (Malayalam); rudraksh, rudraka (Marathi); akkam, rudrakai, uttirasham (Tamil); rudrachallu (Telungu).

Rudraksha trees are found at the higher elevations in the North-East India (Arunachal Pradesh, Bengal, Bihar etc.), Nepal and more widely in Indonesian Islands. It is a medium sized evergreen tree with a crown of simple alternate leaves. Flowers white, borne on dense axillary racemes; fruit a drupe, round or obovoid, deep bluish or purple, iridescent when dry, enclosing a hard longitudinally tubercled, normally 5-celled stone (seed).

Rudraksha seed is used in traditional ayurvedic medicine in neurological disorders, brain fags, psychological instability, cardiac depression, restlessness, and insomnia. Externally seed paste is used for alleviating burning sensation, and for treating eruptions of small pox. Khare mentions that the fruit pulp is used in epileptic fits and seed powder in expelling phlegm. Aqueous extract of fruit is sedative, hypotensive, spasmolytic, and anti-convalescent. Seeds contain fatty acids such as palmitic, iso-palmitic, linoleic and myristic acids. Leaves gave alkaloids rudrakine, elaeocarpine, iso-eleocarpione, quercetin, etc. (32)

Citations and notes:

(1) INTACH (2016) RUDRAKSH. Indian National Trust for Art and Cultural Heritage 71, Lodhi Estate, New Delhi.

(2) Ibid

(3) IUCN (2021) The IUCN Red List of Threatened Species™

(4) Prasannan P et al. (2020) A Review on Taxonomy, Phytochemistry, Pharmacology, Threats and Conservation of Elaeocarpus L. (Elaeocarpaceae). Bot. Rev. 86, 298–328.. https://doi.org/10.1007/s12229-020-09229-9.

(5) Coode MJE (2010) Elaeocarpus for Flora Malesiana: new tax and understanding in the Ganitrus group. Kew Bulletin, 65: 355 – 399.

(6) Storrs A (1990) Trees and shrubs of Nepal and the Himalayas Pilgrims Books House, Nepal.

(7-9) INTACH (2016) see (1)

(10) Gupta SM (2001) Plant Myths and Traditions in India, Munshi Manoharla pub., New Delhi.

(11) aas N (2014) Rudraksha: the Seed of Compassion. Mata Amritanandamayi Mission Trust, Amrutapuri, Kollom, Kerala.

(12, 13) Seetha KN (2008), The Power of Rudraksha, Jaico Pub. Bombay.

(14) Ravindran PN (2020) Sacred and Ritual Plants of India. Notion press, India.

(15) Haas (see 11)

(16) Kalanjoor GRN (2006) Rudraksha (Malayalam)

(17) Seetha (see 12)

(18) Ravindran (see 14)

(19) Anonymous (2014a) Rudraksha Beads – The Teardrops of Lord Shiva – http://www.interessantes.at/rudraksha_e.htm.

(20) Anonymous (2014b)) Ekadasa Rudras the eleven forms of Rudra or Lord Shiva.www.astrojyoti.com/11rudras.htm

(21) Seetha (see 12)

(22) Haas (see 11)

(23) Anonymous (2014 – see 19)

(24) Seetha (see 12)

(25) Kalanjoor (see 16)

(26) Ravindran (see 14)

(27) Seetha (see 12)

(28) Kalanjoor (see 16)

(29) Ravindran (see 14)

(30) Seetha (see 12)

(31) Ravindran (see 14)

(32) Khare CP (2008) Illustrated dictionary of Indian Medicinal plants.

05

THULSI (TULASI)

The Icon of Indian Womanhood

Namo namaḥ tulasi kṛṣṇa-preyasi |
rādhā-kṛṣṇa-sevā pāba ei abhilāṣī | |
ye tomāra śaraṇa laya tāra vāñchā pūrṇa haya
kṛpā kari kara tāre vṛndāvana-vāsī
O Tulsi, beloved of Krishna,
I bow before you again and again.
I desire to obtain the service of Sri Sri Radha-Krishna.
Whoever takes shelter of you has his wishes fulfilled.
By bestowing your mercy on him, you make him a
resident of Vrindavan. (1)

Thulsi (also spelled *thulasi, tulsi, tulasi;* all the terms are used indiscriminately), is the most worshipped plant in India, and this worship has an unbroken history of about three thousand years. It is indeed the spiritual icon of Indian women. Its popularity started with the epic period with the spread of *Vishnu Purana,* and *Bhagavatha Purana* and with the beginning of Vishnu and Lakshmi worship. The Hindu women of India were spiritually and emotionally attached to the *thulsi* plant. Womanhood was considered sacred and noble in ancient India, and women were regarded as manifestations of *Śakthi*, the divine female emanating from *Paraśakthi* herself. A verse from *Shaktisangama tantra* (translation) goes like this:

"…Woman is the creator of the Universe
The Universe is her form,
Woman is the foundation of the world.
She is the true form of the body
In woman is the form of all things
Of all that lives and moves in the world.
There is no jewel rarer than a woman,
No condition is superior to that of a woman…" (2)
This belief is portrayed in *Devi Mahatmya* too:
"By you, this Universe is born,
By you, this world is created
O Devi, by you, it is protected"

The Indian women saw *thulsi* as a cultural and spiritual symbol, as the physical embodiment of all virtues. According to the legend, Sri Krishna, and his consort Rukmini daily watered and prayed to the *thulsi* plant in the courtyard of their palace in Dwaraka. So, even God himself worships this plant. Now, mostly the upper cast Hindus worship the thulsi plant, and for the Vaishnavites, there is no plant as sacred as the *Krishna thulsi*. In all traditional Hindu homes, there used to be a special place in front of the house for growing *thulsi*. The lady of the house waters the plant daily, lights a lamp at nightfall, and worships the plant by circumambulating it three times and chanting the *thulsi (thulsi) mantra*.

> *'praseeda Thulsi devi*
> *praseeda Hari vallabhae*
> *kśreeroda madhanodbhuthe*
> *Thulsi thvam namamyaham.'*

Oh! Thulsi devi, bless me, bless me, the consort of Hari (Lord Vishnu), thou had originated from the Ocean of Milk, Thulsi devi, I pray and prostrate before you.

There is also a great saying given in the *Thulsi Mahatmyam,* in which the conservative Hindus believe:

'ġayatrim thulsi gangam
Kamadhenu marundhatim
Pancha mathrusmarenityam
Mahapataka nasanam'

All sins will vanish from a person who, with devotion, thinks of the five great mothers; Gayathri (the sacred mantra for daily chanting), Thulsi, Ganga (the sacred river), Kamadhenu (the wish-fulfilling divine cow, the mother of all cows) and Arundhati (the consort of Rishi Vasiśhta and the embodiment of virtue).

The greatness of this plant is further highlighted in the same text:

'puśkarodyani thirthani
Ġangadya sarithasthitha
vasudevaya deva
Vasanthi thulsidale|'

All the sacred *tirthas* (sacred bathing ghats) like Pushkara, all holy rivers like Ganga, and all gods like Lord Krishna, reside in the thulsi leaf.

The same idea is expressed in the prayer to *thulsi* (*thulsi prarthana*) or hymn on thulsi:

Yanmoole ṣarvatheerthāni|
yan ṁadhye ṣarvaḍevathā||
yadhagre ṣarvaedhāsca|
ṭhulasiṭhvām ṇamāmyaham||

A Malayalam poet Vallathol has written the following lines:

"Devi, thou are great, thou are blessed
Thou are the jewel of Lord Vishnu's chest,

Thou are pure, fragrant, blessed are thou!
Nandini, Vrindavani, Pavani, Dharmaja nandini,
I bow before you Thulsi, I bow before you" (3)

Thulsi is known by the names such as:

Vrindavani: one who first manifested as Vrinda, living in Vrindavan

Vrinda: the goddess of plants, also the name of Vrinda, an ardent devotee of Vishnu and the consort of Jalandhara)

Visvapujitha: worshipped by the whole universe

Pushpasara: the essence of all flowers

Nandini: one who blesses the saints, also the name of the wish-fulfilling divine cow

Krishna-jēvani: The Life of Sri Krishna

Visva-Pavani: one who purifies all the worlds

Thulsi: one who has no comparison.

In *Skanda Purana,* there is a statement that just by touching Thulsi Devi one's body becomes pure. By praying to her practically all diseases get cured. If one waters her or sprinkles water on her, the fear of *Yama raja* (God of death) is removed. Brahmins recite *thulsi gayatri* daily while worshipping the plant. The *thulsi gayatri* is:

Śree thulsiayai vidmahi
Vishnupriyaya dheemahi
Tanno Amrutha prachotayät|

Thulsi is the greatest, purest, and noblest—it has no comparison. That is why it is *thulsi — 'tulām syatethi thulsi,'* she is beyond comparison. The greatness of thulsi is mentioned in epics like *Brahma Purana, Brahma Vaivarta Purana, Vayu Purana, Skanda Purana, Vishnu Purana,* and in *Śree Mahadevi Bhagavatam.* The Mother of Sri Aurobindo ashram in her book 'Flowers and Their Messages' gives the message of basil as:

Sweet basil – Joy of union with the Divine: lavishly scented; it fills the heart with joy

'Sacred basil (*krishna thulsi*) – Devotion: modest and fragrant; it gives itself without seeking anything in return.

Basil (White basil, Sri thulsi) – Discipline: sets the example and hopes to be followed.

Ram thulsi (wild thulsi) – Conquering fervour, an ardour, which fears no obstacles.'

Sweet basil (Garden basil)

For Western people, basil means sweet basil (Garden basil or common basil), which is widely used as an aromatic herb in many cuisines, and its oil is used widely as an aromatic, fragrant oil. There are many myths and legends associated with basil. De Cleene and Lejeune give a collection of such legends and myths in their marvellous two-volume book, 'Compendium of Ritual Plants in Europe.' (4)

The term Basil supposedly derives its name from the terrifying basilisk, a half-lizard, a half-dragon creature with a fatal piercing stare according to Greek mythology. The basil plant was a magical cure against the look, breath, or even the bite of the basilisk when a basil leaf was medicinally applied. Although this story moved into the realm of fable, basil was still considered a medicinal cure for venomous bites. In keeping with its hostile status, later Greeks and Romans believed the most potent basil could only be grown if one sowed the seed while ranting and swearing. This custom is mirrored in French writings where *semer le baslic* (sowing basil) means to rant. In Greece today, basil is readily grown as an ornamental and is used in certain religious rituals as a symbol of fertility. In medieval times, it was thought that scorpions came from basil. Legend says to acquire a scorpion, one should place a few basil leaves under a flowerpot and after a while, the pot would be lifted to expose a scorpion. This legend no doubt ties into the Greek lore of the basilisk. The earlier scientific name of thulsi, *Ocimum basilicum,* was based on the above myth of the Basilisk. (5)

Another legend is associated with the story of St. Helena, the mother of Constantine. Medieval versions of the legend say that Helena was led to the site of the True Cross by following a trail of basil, which had sprung up wherever the blood of Jesus had fallen during his crucifixion. One account even describes basil growing out of the chunk of the Cross itself. But earlier accounts do not mention the basil connection at all, so it's hard to say whether basil got named after the King of Kings (Jesus Christ), or if it was just added to the story later as a kind of herbal-mystical pun – after all, John writes that basil's Greek root, *basileus*, was written on the Cross, as part of the phrase *Iesous o Nazoraios o Basileus ton Ioudaion* (Greek: INBI, Jesus of Nazareth, King of the Jews. (6).

In the folklore of Greece and Italy, basil had double symbolism, as a symbol of mourning and as an erotic symbol. In the southern parts of Italy, it was a custom for girls to wear twigs of basil on their bosom or hang it from their girdle, as a sign of virginity. Married women had worn basil around their necks as a symbol of fidelity and purity. On the island of Crete, Basil was a symbol of mourning. Schwartz has written Basil, herb of mourning:

'...Blossom in front of my little window;
I too will go to sleep full of sorrow
And will fall asleep crying-------' (7)

In the Western language of flowers, basil indicates hate, loathing, and aversion; though it is difficult to trace the origin of this association. Again, poverty was earlier represented by an old woman sitting next to a basil plant. According to a Bulgarian legend, the Devil revealed the secret power of the basil to God himself. God asked Satan how to create a son from his spirit. Satan advised Him to keep a bunch of basil under his pillow and sleep on it thinking of a son being born out of his spirit. The next morning the bunch should be given to the immaculate virgin; when she smells its scent, she will become pregnant. This was done and it was the Angel Gabriel who brought the bunch of basil to the Virgin Mary.

In the Middle Ages and the early centuries of the modern age, basil had the reputation of being an aphrodisiac and a love herb. It was believed that the scent of this herb aroused a feeling of sympathy. When a man wanted a girl to fall in love with him, he would place the herb on her window sill. Earlier, basil leaves were regarded as having magical properties. If basil leaves were slipped under any dish on the table without the diner's knowledge, it would be impossible for any unchaste woman to eat from them. On the island of Crete, basil was considered the 'devil's plant'. It was placed on the window sill of a person for causing harm to him. Seeing a basil plant in a dream was considered a bad omen. (8).

Garden basil: green and purple types

The basil was made immortal by John Keats through his poem, Isabella, or a Pot of Basil (1818). It is a narrative poem adapted from a story in Boccaccio's Decameron. It tells the tale of a young woman whose family wanted her to marry some 'high noble and his olive trees', but who fell in love with Lorenzo, one of her brothers' employees. When the brothers learn of this, they murder Lorenzo and bury his body. His ghost informed Isabella in a dream what happened to him. She exhumed the body and buried the head in a pot of basil which she tended obsessively while pining away. The poet writes:

> "...And she forgot the stars, the moon, and the sun,
> And she forgot the blue above the trees,
> And she forgot the dells where waters run,
> And she forgot the chilly autumn breeze;
> She had no knowledge of when the day was done,
> And the new morn she saw not: but in peace
> Hung over her sweet Basil evermore,
> And moistened it with tears unto the core..." (9)
> It is a poignant, tragic story of love.

Sacred Basil (Holy basil, Krishna thulsi, Sri thulsi; *Ocimum tenuiflorum* syn. *Ocimum sanctum*):

Thulsi in the Vedas and Puranas.

The oldest reference available on thulsi is its ritualistic uses in the *Āsurī-Kalpa* supplement to the *Atharva Veda* (circa 900 BCE) (10). The *Āsurī-Kalpa* deals mainly with practices of witchcraft, with many verses detailing the use of types of plants for rites, and it is concerned with rites invoking the power of goddesses, including Durgā and Lakṣmī. H.W. Magoun (1889) mentions that there is reason to believe the name Āsurī refers to "probably both plant and divinity, in the text, the divinity being Durgā." (11). The name Thulsī, referring to the plant, occurs twice in the text in verse 23, and in the meditation section, second verse. The first mention seems to either mean Thulsī in a *chūrṇa* or powder (made from the plant), or Thulsī the goddess infusing the *chūrṇa* (*chūrṇa-spṛaṣas*) or magical preparation consisting likely of herbs. The second mention, in the meditation section, has to do with a goddess being adorned or decorated with a garland of Thulsī (*thulasī mālāmaṇḍitām*). Interestingly, the earliest reference to the plant is in the context of goddess-centred magic and worship (12). The only other significant mention of Thulsī, in approximate chronological order from the Vedas, occurs in the *Vaiṣhṇava Āgamas,* also known as *Pāñcharātras,* is on the ritual use. *Gauḍīya Vaiṣhṇavites* consider the *Pāñcharātras* as authoritative references on Thulsī and for its worship. Gopal Bhatta, compiled the ritual manual for the Gauḍīya sect titled the *Hari Bhakti Vilas* (HBV), 1570). HBV draws the text and legends from the *Āgastya Saṁhitā, Prahlāda Saṁhitā,* and the *Viṣhṇudharmottara Purana,* as well as several other *Purāṇas,* and created a lengthy section glorifying Thulsī. The *Āgastya Saṁhitā* also states that sins can be removed by the circumambulation of the Thulsī plant.

> *"pradakshinam bhramitva ye namaskurvanti nityasah*
> *Natesamduritam kinchid akshinam avasisyate"* –
> Agastya Saṁhitā (as found in HBV 9.111)
> (If someone daily goes around Tulasi and pays obeisances to her, there is no more sin to be destroyed in him.)

The *Nārada-Pāñcharātra* is a later text, Krishnaite in nature, that mentions the ritual use of Thulsī and was very influential in the *Gauḍīya* School of *Vaishnavism*. According to Chatterji, this text (also known as the *Jñānāmṛtasāra Saṁhitā*), is perhaps as late as the early 16th century (13).

The *Āgastya Samhita* describes Thulsī leaves as pure ritual objects, and as such the best of offerings to Viṣhṇu, and mentions the benefits of rosaries made from the wood of the Thulsi plant. (HBV 9.199).

Brahmavaivarta Purāṇa (BVP) contains one of the longest accounts of the Thulsi plant, including the rules and methods of worshipping thulsi. BVP probably belongs to the 8th century AD, and it is mostly connected with the *Vaiṣṇava pantheon* (mainly Krishna). Chapters 15-22 of this Purana, deal with the story of goddess Thulsī and her husband Śaṅkhachūḍa in detail. This legend is elaborated later in this chapter. In this Purana, we get the full picture of Radha as the primary consort of Krishna. The *Devi Bhagavata Purana* (DBP) also deals with the Thulsi – Shankachuda episode, which is quite like that in the BVP.

The general story of Thulsi-Shankachuda is found in another context too. Here Thulsi is named Vrinda, who is the devoted wife of the fierce asura king Jalandhara (who according to Puranas, was born out of the fire emanated from Siva's third eye that was deposited in the ocean). This story is elaborated in *Padma Purana* (*Jalandharopakhyana* in the *Uttara khanda*), where there is a detailed account of the Thulsi plant and its sacredness. The *Siva Purana* too includes the Vrinda – Jalandhara episode. Shorter versions of the Thulsi / Vrinda story can be found in *Matsya Purana,* as well as in *Vayu Purana*. In *Skanda Purana* (one of the largest of the 18 major Puranas, which contains over 81,000 verses, and is of Shaivite nature), has many verses on thulsi, its sacredness and associated rituals. According to the *Kārttika Māhātmya* of the *Skanda Purāṇa*, Thulsī is born from the teardrops of Dhanvantari, who is considered in the *Purāṇas* as a partial incarnation of Viṣṇu. After the churning of the ocean of milk, Dhanvantari emerges from the Ocean bearing the pot of ambrosia (*amruth*, the nectar of immortality). As he saw the trinity and all other devas, he felt happy and his eyes filled with teardrops, and one drop fell on the pot of ambrosia. The thulsi plant sprang up from this teardrop. Another version states that Vishnu received the *Amrutha kalasa* (pot of ambrosia) from Dhanwanthari when he felt immense joy and that his eyes filled with tears of joy, and a drop fell on the pot from which the thulsi plant sprang up, which was then accepted by Vishnu as his most favourite plant. In the *Padma Purana*, there is also a mention that the thulsi plant sprang up from the sweat of Vrinda. This aspect of the origin of thulsi is further elaborated in the following section. (14, 15)

Thulsi, Sacred (holy) basil plant in flower green (Sri thulsi) and purple (Krishnathulsi)

Origin of Holy Thulsi plant

The basil plant of India is different from the sweet basil mentioned in an earlier part of this chapter. The Indian basil is known as the holy or sacred bail, as thulsi. For the Indians, the sacred basil represents the very spirit of Hinduism, the house of all virtues, and it is the icon of purity and, so the icon of Indian womanhood. To understand the greatness of the sacred basil, one should first learn the legends, and traditions, that bind the basil plant with the life and culture of the Hindus and India. The following discussion is based mainly on the detailed treatment on Tulsi in the Sacred and Ritual Plants of India by Ravindran (2020) (16)

The first legend on the origin of thulsi is from the Ocean of Milk during its churning by the devas and asuras. So *thulsi* is known as the *'Kśheroda madhanotbhave'* — one who originated from the Ocean of Milk. When *thulsi* came out of the ocean, Lord Vishnu, took it for himself, along with Lakshmi Devi, who also merged with Lord Vishnu. This legend is given in many *Puranas* while describing the *Samudra madhana* (churning of the Ocean of Milk) for getting *Amrutha* (ambrosia, the divine nectar of eternity). Such a marvellous effort was necessitated following a curse inflicted on the Devas by the great sage Durvasa, because of which the Devas lost their immortality and they all become aged and their lustre, prosperity and greatness vanished. During this time the goddess of prosperity, wealth and all glories, Sree Lakshmi, disappeared into the depths of the Ocean of Milk, and along with her the wealth, prosperity, and splendour of all three worlds also vanished. While churning the ocean, Lakshmi emerged from the Ocean of Milk standing in a lotus flower, and joined Lord Vishnu. The Ocean of Milk is the mysterious cosmic ocean and many marvellous secrets lie hidden in its depths. As the churning proceeds many gems surfaced from the Ocean of Milk – *Kalpavriksha* (wish-fulfilling tree), *Airavata* (the divine elephant), *Uchaishravas* (the divine horse), *Surabhi* (the divine cow), *Kausthubha* (the most precious of all precious stones), *Parijatha* (the divine tree with magical properties), *Thulsi plant*, Lakshmi (the goddess of prosperity and consort of Vishnu), and finally Dhanvantari (the divine physician) carrying the golden *kalasha* (pot), with *Amrutha* (the elixir of immortality).

This story has a deeper symbolism and meaning. Harsha V Dehejia comments on this meaning:

> "The ocean of milk is a metaphor that stands for the universal mind or consciousness. The cosmic waters, mysterious and full of secrets and treasures, are thus the receptacle of all that makes life precious and contain the pot of nectar that lies in its depths and which assures immortality. This is primal matter from which creation springs. It is the repository of the mind. Therefore, whether it is fortune as epitomized by Lakshmi or valour and energy represented by the horse and the elephant, the fulfilment of wishes by the *Kalpavriksha or* the wish-fulfilling tree, or *Surabhi* the divine cow, all these treasures reside in the Universal Consciousness. It is from here that mankind has to repossess them, and it is on this ocean of Universal consciousness that Vishnu will rest at the dissolution of creation and the start of another cycle of creation." (17)

This Universal Consciousness is akin to the collective unconscious that psychoanalysts like Freud and especially Carl Jung spoke of. (Collective unconscious is a term coined by Carl Jung; the term refers to the unconscious mind and shared mental concepts. According to Jung, the human collective unconscious is populated by instincts, as well as by archetypes: ancient primal symbols such as The Great

Mother, the Wise Old Man, the Shadow, the Tower, Water, and the Tree of Life) (18) A version of the legend found in *Hari Bhakti Vilas* is as follows: Here the golden pot with *Amrutha* (nectar of immortality) came out of the Ocean of Milk last, carried by Lord Dhanwanthari (the presiding deity of Ayurvedic medicine and the lord of health and treatment, an aspect of Lord Vishnu), and this pot was received by Lord Vishnu. At that time Lord Vishnu felt so happy, that a few teardrops of happiness fell on the golden pot. From that teardrop, a plant originated on the pot itself. This plant had such radiance and brightness, it was different from anything that existed then; it was incomparable and hence was called 'Thulsi.' Vishnu took the plant and his divine consort was always present in this plant.

Other Legends on the origin of the Thulsi plant are given in various *Puranas* like *Padma Purana, Devibhagavatha Purana, Bhagavatha Purana, Brahmavaivarta Purana* etc. Such legends on the origin of the Thulsi plant if arranged in a temporal sequence would be as follows:

1.The story of Vrinda and Jalandhara:

The first legend is about Vrinda and the fierce Asura king Jalandhara. This legend is given in *Padma Purana* and *Śiva Purana,* and retold by many like Elwin in his book Myths of Middle India. Even this legend has many versions. In essence, the story is like this. Lord Śiva once got very angry with Indra, the king of devas. Enraged, he opened his third eye. But before the fire engulfs Indra, Brihaspathi, the Deva Guru (preceptor of gods), pleaded with Śiva to pardon Indra, and thus Indra got his life back. The fire emanated from Śiva was laid in the Western Ocean, and from this fire, a child originated after a thousand years. This boy was so powerful, that the whole world trembled when he cried.

The boy grew up as an asura known as Jalandhara (meaning originated in water). He grew up into an all-powerful asura under the tutelage of Sukaracharya, the preceptor of the Asuras, and finally became the leader and Emperor of Asuras. He married Vrinda, the daughter of Kalanemi, a virtuous asura king. Vrinda was an ardent devotee of Lord Vishnu. Lord Vishnu blessed her with a boon that as long as she remained chaste, her husband would be invincible, even to the *Trimurtis* (Trinity). Jalandhara won all three worlds, drove out devas from heaven, and even subdued Lord Vishnu. The famous sage, Narada incited Jalandhara to go to war with Śiva. With a huge army, Jalandhara reached the valley of Mount Kailas, and challenged Lord Siva. A war started between Siva and Jalandhara that goes on for a long time. At one point, Jalandhara disguised as Śiva reached the abode of Parvathi and tried to seduce even the goddess. The story of this 'maya Siva' (false Śiva) is given in *Padma Purana*. In Jalandhara's absence, his commander Sumbhan disguised as Jalandhara had fought with Śiva on the battlefield. Vishnu, knowing the trick played by Jalandhara on Parvathi, decided that it is time to end the life of the asura for which he had to remove the protection offered to him through seducing Vrinda. Knowing the secret of the invincibility of Jalandhara, devas too resorted to the help of Vishnu. In one version of the legend, Parvathi requested Vishnu to take away the protective chasteness of Vrinda, to put an end to the life of Jalandhara. Lord Vishnu disguised as Jalandhara, reached Vrinda's abode. Vrinda thought that her husband returned after winning the battle, and received him with love and affection. The disguised Vishnu embraced and kissed her. At that very moment, Siva discharged his trident and Jalandhara was burned to ashes. While Vrinda and Vishnu were engaged in love play, Thulsi (Thulsi), a purifying nymph, arose from Vrinda's sweat. Thulsi (identified with the sacred plant, holy basil) represented Vrinda's pure erotic desire for Vishnu.

According to another version, Vishnu stayed on with Vrinda fully overcome by her devotion to him. Devas were worried and they sought the help of Lakshmi, Parvathi, and Saraswathi. They gave Devas one seed each and asked them to plant these seeds near Vrinda's palace. These seeds grew up into Thulsi, Amla and Jati plants. They transformed into bewitching celestial damsels, went to Lord Vishnu, and enticed him away from Vrinda. The celestial beauties later returned to plant forms and remained on Earth for the benefit of mankind.

In yet another version, Vrinda flew into a rage when she learned about the trick played by Vishnu. She was about to utter a curse when Lord Vishnu, stood before her in full splendour. He consoled and blessed her saying that she was none other than Lakshmi herself and that he was so pleased with her devotion that she would be reborn as Radha, when he would take the incarnation as Krishna and fulfil all her desires, before returning Vaikunta as Lakshmi. Vrinda then burned herself and from her ashes sprang up the thulsi plant, which Lord Vishnu, accepted as his favourite plant and preferred offering.

According to the version given in *Śiva Purana,* Vrinda cursed Lord Vishnu, that his wife would be abducted by an asura, and would undergo a lot of suffering to regain her. Vrinda then committed Sati. Lord Vishnu, became miserable with grief, that he became the cause of the death of his own most ardent devotee. He threw himself in the ash and wept for a long time. The devas then approached Lakshmi, Parvathi, and Saraswathi and they gave one seed each to be thrown in the ashes of Vrinda. From these seeds sprang up Thulsi, Āmla and Jati. These plants, as mentioned earlier, turned into three divine beauties and enticed Vishnu away. Later they returned to Earth in plant forms. Devas offered these plants to Lord Vishnu and prayed, and he returned to his abode. The reference to the curse by Vrinda mentioned above indicates that the event took place much before the Sri Rama incarnation of Vishnu.).

2. The quarrel among the goddesses

Once there was a quarrel among the three divine consorts, Lakshmi, Saraswathi, and Ganga. In one version of the legend, all three were wives of Vishnu. In another version, Saraswathi and Ganga were visiting Lakshmi. While the three were engaged in conversation Ganga was frequently glancing at Vishnu with love-filled eyes. Lakshmi thought the two were in love and felt sad. Saraswathi, on seeing Lakshmi's mind, felt angry and scolded Ganga. Lakshmi felt unhappy that such a quarrel broke out in her abode. She in turn blamed Saraswathi for creating such a situation. Saraswathi felt angry and cursed Lakshmi to be born as a plant on Earth. On hearing this Ganga became furious and cursed Saraswathi to be a river to wash away the sins of humans. In retaliation, Saraswathi cursed Ganga also to be a river to wash away human sin.

Saraswathi and Ganga then left Lakshmi's abode. Lakshmi felt very sad and unhappy and told Lord Vishnu about what had happened. Lord Hari smiled and said that a cause was needed for anything to happen and that the curse Lakshmi received was such a cause. He then said that Lakshmi would be born as the daughter of the virtuous King Dharmadhwaja and that a renowned *asura* king, Shankhachuda would become her husband. Later, after the death of Shankhachuda at the hands of Śiva, she would become a divine plant, thulsi, capable of purifying the whole world, and he (Lord Vishnu) himself would wear the garland of *thulsi* leaves. Thulsi would be worshipped by mankind as the incarnation of Lakshmi. In due course, she would merge with Lakshmi herself."

3. Story of Thulsi and Shankhachuda

This Thulsi story started with the brothers Dharmadhvaja and Kusadhvaja, born in the lineage of the great emperor Manu Daksha Savarni, who was a partial expansion of Lord Vishnu. They lost their country and everything due to the curse of Lord Surya. To regain the lost glory, they performed penance worshipping Goddess Lakshmi. Pleased by their hard penance Goddess Lakshmi appeared and blessed them. They separately received the boons they desired. With the grace of Goddess Lakshmi, they got back all the lost glory, and their kingdoms. They acquired great spiritual merits, were married, and begotten children. King Dharmadhvaja was married to Madhavi. After some time, she became pregnant with a partial incarnation of Goddess Laksmi. However, the infant remained in Madhavi's womb for one hundred years. Day by day Madhavi's lustre increased. Then, on an auspicious day and moment, when there was a full moon, in the month of Kartika, on a Friday, she gave birth to a girl, who was radiant as the autumnal full moon. Soon after birth, the child grew up into a maiden of great beauty and was named Thulsi (Thulasi, Tulsi). She took an aversion to life in the palace and departed to the Badaryāshram to do penance for getting Lord Vishnu as her husband. Thulsi's severe penance continued for a long time. One day Lord Brahma appeared before her and blessed her, and foretold her marriage with a noble asura youth by the name Shankhachuda.

Yet another event in the above Thulsi story was staged in Vrindavana. In the words of Tulasi as she talked about her previous birth to Brahma: '

"Formally I was a cowherd girl in Goloka Vrindavana, and there I served Radharani, the beloved of Sri Krishna. I am a partial expansion of Radharani and was her favourite companion. But one day in the place where the *rasa* dance took place, Krishna became intimate with me and I fainted from excessive joy. Radharani suddenly appeared and saw me in that condition. She was not at all pleased. Blinded with fury, she first reproached Krishna and then cursed me. She said, `O vile one! Go! And take birth as a human being!'

"Then Krishna said to me, `When you take birth in India if you practice austerities, Lord Brahma will grant you a blessing. He will arrange for you to marry the four-armed Narayana, an expansion of Myself.' Then Krishna disappeared. And out of fear of Radharani, I left Goloka and was born in this world...So please grant me that boon. I want to have that handsome and peaceful Narayana as my husband."

Lord Brahma replied, "O Thulsi, Sudama was a partial expansion of Krishna and was one of Krishna's cowherd boyfriends in Goloka. As a result of a curse by Radharani, he is presently living on Earth among the *Danavas* (Asuras). His name is Shankhachuda (Sankhachuda). He is very energetic and no one can compare with him in strength. While living in Goloka, he was very attracted to you and wanted to marry you. But because he feared Radharani, he did not make any overtures.

"Just as you are a *jatismara* (that is, one who knows her previous births), Shankhachuda too is. Remembering his past desire to be close to you, he has performed severe austerities to obtain you as his wife. I now wish to grant his desire. Therefore, O beautiful one, please agree to wed him. However, later, by the special arrangement of Providence, you will get the beautiful Narayana as your husband. But after that, He will curse you and you will be transformed into the world-purifying Thulsi plant (holy basil). You will be the best of flowers and dearer to Narayana than His own life. No one's worship will be complete without your leaves. You will remain as a tree in Vrindavana and will be widely known as Vrindavani. The cowherd men and women will worship Lord Hari with your leaves. As the presiding deity of the Thulsi plant, you will always enjoy the company of Krishna, the best of cowherd boys."

Shankhachuda was thus the rebirth of Sudama. Dambha, a grandson of Sage Kashyapa, was an ardent devotee of Lord Vishnu. Dambha had no sons, and he did penance for a long time and propitiated Lord Vishnu, who finally appeared and blessed him with the boon of a powerful and illustrious son born to him, who would be a partial expansion of Vishnu himself. Over time, Dambha's wife gave birth to a son, who was named Shnakachuda, He too was an ardent devotee of Vishnu. Eventually, Shankhachuda reached Badaryashram for penance. Shankhachuda and Thulsi met at the Badaryashram, when Lord Brahma appeared there and blessed them, and said to live like Vishnu and Lakshmi, like Śiva and Uma for a long time, and then foretold that Thulsi would return to Lakshmi and Shankachuda to Vishnu. With the blessings of Brahma, they got married.

Shankhachuda became the Lord of the three worlds. For regaining heaven, the devas sought the help of Vishnu and Śiva. Shankhachuda was invincible as long as he has the amulet given by Vishnu and Thulsi remained chaste. A situation was created for a battle between Lord Siva and Shankhachuda. Śiva and Shankhachuda began a war that lasted for many years. Finally, Lord Vishnu came to the help of Devas. Vishnu in the form of a poor Brahmin, reached the abode of Shankhachuda and tricked him to make him donate the amulet given by Lord Vishnu. Vishnu then took the form of Shankhachuda and arrived before Thulsi, who thought her husband had won the war, received him with love and affection. Vishnu embraced Thulsi and at that precise moment, Śiva sent his Trishul to which was attached Vishnu's discus. Shankhachuda was burned to death. Lord Vishnu, appeared there in a golden chariot and received the soul of Shankhachuda. Soon Thulsi realized that she had been tricked. Enraged, she was about to utter a curse when Lord Vishnu, in all His splendour, stood before her. He explained the history of Thulsi and told her that she was none other than Lakshmi herself and that it was time to return to their abode, Vaikunta. Vishnu then blessed Thulsi and said that her mortal remains would be received by Goddess Earth, and from there, a sacred river – Mandakini – would originate and that her hair would turn into *krishna thulsi* (krishna= black, holy basil) plants. These *Krishna thulsi* plants would become the most sacred of all plants, and, would become his favourite, and he would daily wear a thulsi garland, and Vishnu, himself would turn into black stones and would remain in the river; pieces of these stones would become famous as *Salagram* and would be worshipped by his devotees. Thulsi merged with Lord Vishnu and returned to their abode, Vaikunta. Thus, originated *thulsi* plant from Devi Lakshmi.

It is believed that Radha, the heroine of Vrindavana, was the rebirth of Vrinda (of the Vrinda – Jalandhara legend), who first became a thulsi plant, later incarnated as Radha and subsequently reborn as Thulsi when Sudama took birth as Shankhachuda. Vishnu's words to Lakshmi, when she was cursed by Saraswathi, are worth remembering. Everything happened for a definite reason and for the general well-being of the world.

The slaying of the demon king Jalandhara is celebrated in the Virateswar temple in Tiruvirkudi near Tanjavur in Tamil Nadu, where Lord Śiva is enshrined in *Virat* (universal) form, as the destroyer of evil forces. Vrinda is also enshrined here in a temple, and people believe she took the form of a *thulsi* plant after her death. In this temple *thulsi* is the favourite offering to Śiva. The city of Jalandhar in Punjab is believed to be named after Jalandhara. There, in the Kot Kishan Chand locality, there is a temple dedicated to Vrinda, commonly known as *Thulsi Mandir.* This is still a favourite place of worship. There is a tank on one side of the *Thulsi Mandir,* which is believed to be the bathing place of Jalandhara.

The incarnation of Vishnu as Krishna was in the *Dwapara Yuga,* and he spent his early years in Vrindavan. Vrinda of the Jalandhara legend took birth as Radha, and Vishnu incarnated as Krishna. Krishna daily used to loiter in the Vrindavan together with his companion *gopas* and *gopis,* especially with his most devoted companion, Radha.

At that time a thulsi plant grew up on the banks of Kalindi, and this plant was Lakshmi, born as a plant following the curse of Saraswathi. Every day young Krishna plucked a leaf from this plant and kept it on his hair lock. Seeing the young beautiful Krishna daily and hearing his most mesmerizing play on the flute, the thulsi plant worshipped him for his permanent companionship. One day, the *thulsi* plant dried up. Later the same thulsi was born as the daughter of Dharmadhwaja in the Shankachuda-Thulsi legend mentioned earlier. However, there are many contradictions in the various legends, especially about the time element.

4. Story of the Origin of the Thulsi Plant in Krishna's Palace

There is a legend behind the *thulsi* plant in Krishna's courtyard in Dwaraka. This legend is portrayed in many popular folk songs and legends of the Kangra region in the Himalayan foothills, and it is depicted in Kirin Narayan's book: How a girl became a sacred plant. In her article 'The sprouting and uprooting of Saili: the story of sacred Thulsi in Kangra' this legend is reproduced, and it is also quoted by Findley, in her book, Plant Lives (19). The legend goes like this:

Thulsi (Saili is the name in the local language) is the beautiful daughter of an untouchable cobbler. A Brahmin boy brings shoes to her for mending but finds only Thulsi at home. Attracted by her beauty, the boy returns home and tells his parents of his desire to marry her, to the utter dismay not only of them but also of the whole village, who now wants to banish the cobblers from their area. Seeing no difference between the cobblers and the brahmins, however, Thulsi does not understand that her cobbler cast is unhappy and, when the men of the caste declare that they will not marry her themselves, she asks her father what to do. He tells her to go; become a stone and wait for Krishna who will marry her when he takes on human form.

The girl becomes a stone, and when Krishna comes along, she returns to human form and tells him she wants to marry him. Krishna, however, is already married to Řukmini, and Thulsi becomes a milkmaid and sells curd at their house. Krishna urges Řukmini (Rugmini), to buy some curd, which she does. He tells Thulsi to come by every day. Over time, Thulsi becomes a housemaid and helper to Rukmini, who has a heavy workload and with Thulsi's help the two women can finish the domestic chores quickly. One day one hundred and one Brahmins are to be fed and, as Krishna has caused her to forget, Řukmini, sleeps through the preparation of the food, leaving the whole job to Thulsi. Řukmini awakens and is horrified at her forgetfulness, but Thulsi asks her what she would do if she were to find the food already prepared. Řukmini answers, 'I'd give you anything that you asked for' and consents when Thulsi asks to bathe with Krishna for five days.

A crow alerts Řukmini, on the intimacy of Krishna and Thulsi during bathing in the river. However, Řukmini sees that Thulsi has become Krishna's wife, even asking Thulsi not Řukmini, to bring his garments and water pot wherever he is. One day Řukmini hides the garments and water pot, and at Krishna's request, Thulsi searches for them in vain. She is so late in returning, so Krishna calls out to ask her whether she has sprouted and taken roots inside. Since the story took – place in the era of righteousness when speech becomes true, Thulsi becomes a shrub – the Thulsi or holy basil plant.' (20, 21).

This story appears in many versions and it is being transferred from generation to generation through oral traditions. The story is in the form of a folk song and the people of the Kangra region believe in the sacredness of the story as well as that of their Thulsi deity, as exemplified in the lines, quoted from Kirin's article mentioned earlier:

> *'Kanya gave*
> *changa bar pave*
> *suhagan gave*
> *putrakhilave*
> *vidhava gave*
> *vaikunthe jo jave*
> *sunadiyogunadiyo*
> *ganga da nauna*
> *gandebajandeyo*
> *yamuna da nauna'.*
> 'If an unmarried girl sings this,
> she'll get a fine groom.
> If a married woman sings this,
> she'll feed sons.
> If a widow sings this,
> she'll go to heaven.
> To listen to this and hear this
> is to bathe in the Ganga.
> To sing this and play this
> is to bathe in the Yamuna.'

5. The story of Thulsi and Ganesha.

A fascinating legend is given in the *Brahmavaivarta Purana*. Thulsi was an ardent devotee of Lord Vishnu and was practising penance when one day she happened to see Lord Ganesha. He was meditating in a beautiful garden surrounded by fragrant trees. Ganesha was resplendent, wearing a yellow garment and sandal paste smeared all over the body. His sight brought amorous emotions in her and she got excited. She sprinkled some water on his face and tickled him with her forefinger. When Ganesa opened his eyes, she told her that she was the daughter of King Dharmadhwaja, and requested him to marry her. Lord Ganesa said that he was leading the life of a Brahmachari and an ascetic and could not even think of marriage since it would hinder his austere life and he asked her to go to another person who would be willing to satisfy her. Ganesa's words enraged Thulsi and she in a fit of anger cursed him that he would undergo a forced marriage against his will and that his wife would be faithless to him. Ganeśa retaliated with the curse that she would get a demon as her husband and then under a curse become a plant. On hearing the curse, Thulsi grew repentant and she started praising Ganesa. Ganesa, in turn, got pacified and he said: 'Thulsi, when you take birth as a plant, you will be regarded supreme among the plants. All the gods will love you, but you will be especially dear to Krishna. Anyone worshipping the Lord with your leaves as an offering would achieve liberation and will reach heaven. However, you will always remain unacceptable to me. With these words, Ganesa resumed meditation. Thulsi returned to her hermitage and started severe penance. In due course, she became the wife of Shankhachuda.

6. Thulsi and the three goddesses – Story of a quarrel.

There is also another legend about Thulsi given in the same *Brahma Vaivarta Purana*. Let me quote the translation of this story. The story is presented as a dialogue between Sage Narada and Lord Vishnu, as recounted by Suta Pouranika:

> '...Narada said, "Lord, I gather how Thulsi became the favourite of Hari, how she became holy and was adored throughout the world. Now I want to

hear the account relating to her form of worship and her hymn. In olden times, who worshipped her and recited her ode? How did she become adorable in the world? Kindly narrate these matters to me."

Suta said: Narayana smiled at these words and said,

'Hari sported with Thulsi as soon as He got her and made her as blessed and glorious as Rema. Ganga and Lakshmi bore this new acquisition to their society patiently. But it was intolerable to Saraswati. Once the dignified Saraswati in vain quarrelled with Thulsi in Hari's presence and hurt her. Thulsi in shame and disgrace disappeared. That accomplished, wise and adept Thulsi became invisible to Hari out of anger. Hari thereupon took permission of Saraswati and went to the forest of Thulsi plants. There he bathed and with holy basil leaves reverentially adored Thulsi with the mystic formula of ten letters containing seeds of germinating principles of Lakshmi Maya, Kama and Vani.

'O Narada, that mantra prepared by Hari ends thus: 'Swaha to Vrindavani.' After chanting this mantra, which is as effective as a Kalpa tree, whoever will worship Thulsi with the light of the ghee lamp, frankincense, sandal, flowers and sacrificial offerings will attain all perfection. Thulsi, pleased with the worship, emanated from the plant and took refuge in the lotus feet of Hari. Hari blessed her saying, 'You will be adored throughout the world', and said, 'Beloved, I shall hold you on my head and in my heart. All the gods, therefore, will wield you on their heads.' So, saying, Hari took her home.'

Narada said, 'Now tell me about the Dhyana or meditation appropriate to Thulaśi, her ode, and her mode of worship.'

Narayana answered, 'When Thulsi disappeared, the afflicted Hari went to *Thulsi-vana* (the forest of holy Thulśi), worshipped her and adored her with the hymn, which means:

"I adore my beloved Vrinda who in one place grows in the form of plants. I adore the blessed nymph who sprang at first from the forest of Vrindavana and is hence styled *Vrinda vani*.

'I worship that goddess, all adorable in the universe, who is so-called as she is adored by all mankind. Being afflicted by Cupid I adore the all-sanctifying goddess so-called as she is always adored in the three worlds. I want to see the *Pushpa-sāra* – the goddess, the essence of flowers – without whom the gods are not satisfied with the offer of any number of flowers. I crave the favour of that goddess, who is also called Nandini, as the attainment of Thulsi brings faith and joy. I seek the protection of this goddess called Thulsi, as she is incomparable in the world. May she preserve my life, the goddess, also called the life of Krishna.'

Krishna having worshipped her, thus manifested Himself to Thulsi who was lying prostrate at his feet. When he saw that the dignified Thulsi was weeping on account of her being wounded by Saraswati, he clasped her to his chest, took her to Saraswati, and reconciled them both. He blessed her saying, "You will be adored throughout the world and sustained (carried) by everyone on the head. You will be worshipped and honoured by me as well.

When Thulsi was propitiated, Saraswati embraced her and made her sit beside her. Lakshmi and Ganga also embraced her smiling and took her home. Whoever will adore Thulsi by the above eight names, pregnant with meaning, will reap the fruits of a horse sacrifice. The eight names are:

Vrinda (one who has thousands of *sakhis* or friends),

Vrindavani (one who never leaves Vrindavana),

Vishwa-Pavani (sanctifier of the whole world),

Vishwa-pujita (whole world worships her),

Pushpasāra (essence of all the flowers),

Nandini (gives happiness to everyone),

Krishnajivani (the life and soul of Lord Krishna) and

Thulsi (one with an incomparable form).

The benefactress Thulsi was born on the lunar day of the full moon in the month of *Kartika*, hence Hari has prescribed this day for her worship. Whosoever will worship her on this day will be redeemed from all sins and go to Vaikunta (the abode of Vishnu). Whoever offers *thulsi* leaves cut in reverence to Vishnu in the month of *Kartika* will reap the fruits secured by the gift of ten million cows. Nay, the recollection of her hymn gives a son to the sonless, a wife to the wifeless, health to the diseased, liberty to the prisoner, sanctity to the sinner, courage to the frightened, and a friend to the friendless.'

Tales of Thulsi's Greatness

A legend in *Bhagavata Purana* illustrates the greatness of *Thulsi*. Narada, the great sage, played a trick on Satyabhama, Krishna's second favourite wife, and made her donate her husband to Narada. When the other wives of Krishna learned about it, they prayed to the Rishi not to take their husband away and to give him back. Narada then replied that it was a sin to accept gifts from a Brahmin, but they could take him back in exchange for, valuables equal to his weight. The wives were happy. A large scale was brought, on one paan, Krishna sat, and on the other, the wives of Krishna piled their gold and jewellery and all the gold that they could gather from the palace and elsewhere. But the paan on which Krishna sat could not be raised even an inch, and the ladies panicked. At that time, Rukmini, the most favourite consort of Krishna, came to the scene and was told about what had happened. She immediately asked to remove all the gold and jewels from the paan and then placed a leaf of *Thulsi* that she plucked from the plant in her courtyard, which she and Krishna watered daily. Immediately, the scale was balanced. She then told the amazed people about the sacredness of *Thulsi* and said that *Thulsi* had always been his most beloved wife and that a leaf *Thulsi* offered was more valuable than any gold or precious stones. Krishna smiled at Rukmini, got up from the pan, and got relieved from the trick of Narada, who wanted to teach the proud ladies of Dwaraka a lesson.

There is also the story of a very pious woman by the name of Thulsi, who was an ardent devotee of Vishnu. She did penance for getting Vishnu as her husband. The penance went on for a long time. Lakshmi became jealous and she turned Thulsi into a plant. Vishnu, impressed by the devotion of Thulsi, was angry with Lakshmi and turned himself into a *shaligrama,* or black stone, and blessed Thulsi that he would be her consort in this form. This legend is popular among the Vaishnavites of North India and forms the basis for the yearly ceremony of marrying the *thulsi* plant to the stones (*Salagrams*). A variation of this goes like this:

> "Once there lived an old lady who used to perform the *kartik snan* (ritual bath in the month of Karthika) and then water the thulsi plant and offer prayers. She used to worship thulsi without fail and used to perform the *thulsi vivah* ritual. After the ritual, the elderly woman always requests from the thulsi plant that Lord Krishna carry her body to the pyre. *Thulsi* Plant (Thulsi Devi) used to hear her prayer daily, and she could not fulfil the wishes of her devotee to make Lord Krishna carry the dead body of the old lady to the pyre; the task was far beyond her capacity. Saddened due to this reason, *Thulsi* began to wither, and she started shedding her leaves. One day, Lord Krishna visited Thulsi Devi, found her in a withered state, and inquired about the reason. Thulsi narrated the austerities and devotion of the old lady and her daily prayer for Lord Krishna to carry her dead body to the pyre. She could not ask Lord Krishna to do such a thing. As I cannot fulfil her wish I am sad and this is the cause of my sorry state.'

Lord Krishna gave his usual smile and said that the wish of the old woman would be fulfilled. He asked Thulsi Devi to forget about the problem and return to her glorious form.

On the last day of the *Kartik* month, the old woman repeated her usual ritual and prayed to Lord Krishna to carry her dead body to the pyre. After chanting the prayers, the old lady fell and died immediately. Her family members and neighbours arrived on the scene and decided to move the dead body of the old woman. But the body could not be removed. It had become so heavy that even 10 people together could not move it. Thulsi Devi then remembered Lord Krishna. She prayed to the Lord to save her devotee, who was lying at her feet. Many people had gathered at the scene as the news of the death of the old lady spread and the subsequent miracle of the body becoming so heavy. Soon, a young boy appeared and asked what all the commotion was about. An elderly person narrated what had happened. The boy said he would move the body and went to the dead body, chanted some words into the ears of the old woman, and touched the body. The body now became lighter, like a flower. The boy then shouldered the body to the pyre. Everyone gathered there was surprised to see this miracle. The pyre was lit and the young boy slipped out of the crowd." (16)

This news spread all over the country, and from then on, people celebrated the day to symbolize the union of Vrinda and Krishna.

Thulsi and the Radha-Krishna Legend

The thulsi legends will not be complete without a mention of Vrinda (a rebirth of Thulsi) during the Radha-Krishna sojourn in Vrindavana. The Vrindavana Forest is named after Vrinda Devi, who performed penances here for 60,000 years. She was born as the daughter of Emperor Kedera, a very pious king, and his daughter Vrinda Devi, after sanctifying the forest by her penance, also attained *Vishnu loka* (the abode of Vishnu, Salvation). Ever since this forest has been known as Vrindavana. Pleased by Vrinda Devi's austerities Lord Vishnu, granted a boon that she would be reborn as a Gopika girl (a woman in the Yadava community in Vrindavan, commonly known as Gopis, and Gopikas) when he takes the incarnation as Krishna. Later, another devotee of Lord Vishnu by the same name Thulsi Devi, daughter of King Kusadhvaja, performed penances here and attained Salvation. Thulśi's second name is Vrinda. During the time of Krishna and Radha, there was a Gopika, Vrinda. This Gopika was a rebirth of Vrinda Devi, and she played a crucial role in the Vrindvana legend. She was an intimate friend *(sakhi)* of Radha (or Radha Rani as she was commonly called). Her father was Chandrabhanu, her mother Phullara Devi and her husband was Mahipala. She always remained in Vrindavana, immersed in love for Radha and Krishna and yearning to arrange their meetings and taste the nectar of assisting in their transcendental pastimes.

According to the Vaishnavite holy men, Vrinda Devi has a unique and elevated position in Radha and Krishna's pastimes. She is a very close associate of Radha Rani (also known as Radhika), always ready to make arrangements for the secret and intimate meetings of Radha Rani and Krishna. There are twelve enchanting sporting groves in Vrindavana. Under the instructions of *Paurnamasi* (personified Yogamaya) Vrinda Devi, the custodian of Vrinda Vana, takes up the responsibility of arranging the meetings of Krishna and Radha in these enchanting groves.

Vrinda devi is responsible for waking up Radha and Krishna while they rest in the *vanakunjas* (forest groves). She hurries the Divine Couple to their homes before sunrise, before their superiors detect their absence. On Radha's behalf, Vrinda Devi delivers love notes and hand-made gifts, flower earrings and garlands to Sri Krishna. Vrinda arranges all the paraphernalia used in Radha-Krishna's pastime. She provides all the swings, musical instruments, water syringes and colour for squirting, clothing, ornaments and a variety of food and drinks during the night of *rasa* dance (the divine dance of Krishna and Gopis that took place on the banks of the Jamuna River).

Vrinda Devi creates a festive atmosphere for Radha-Krishna to engage in transcendental pastimes with their dear friends. Vrindavana is the land of Vrinda Devi; she is the queen of all the properties and the proprietress of Vrindavana. Earlier, she offered all her kingdom of Vrindavana at the lotus feet of Srimati Radharani. Hence, Radha Rani became known as Vrindavanesvari (the queen of Vrindavana), and Krishna was the actual Lord or King of Vrindavana. Appreciating Vrinda Devi's kindness in making wonderful arrangements for her loving pastimes with Krishna, Radha Rani wanted to reciprocate properly. Radha and her friends fashioned a beautiful throne big enough for two people to sit on. They then made Krishna sit on the throne beside Vrinda Devi. Playing the role of a priest, Lalita (Radha's friend) began chanting the *mantras* for invoking marriage. Radha personally exchanged the flower garlands between Krishna and Vrinda devi, and so this wonderful wedding ceremony was performed... (22)

The *Gautamiya tantra* (also known as the *Brihad Gautamiya Tantra*) is one of the tantra texts belonging to the Vaishnava sect. This deals with the rituals relating to the worship of Lord Krishna (Vishnu,), observation of *Ekadasi* rituals, and various other rituals associated with the day-to-day life of the Vaishnavites. Radharani is described as follows:

devi krisna-mayiprokta
Radhika para-devata
sarva-laksmi-mayisarva
kantihsammohini para

"The transcendental goddess Srimati Radharani is the direct counterpart of Lord Sri Kriśna. She is the central figure for all the goddesses of fortune. She possesses all the attractiveness to attract the all-attractive Personality of Godhead. She is the primaeval internal potency of the Lord."

It was the same Vrinda who appeared in Sri Krishna's palace in later years as Thulsi, as Řukmini's maid, and finally became the holy basil or *Tulsi* plant. It is also believed that the same Vrinda Devi was born as Thulsi in the Thulsi-Shankhachuda legend elaborated earlier.

There are many more myths and legends associated with thulsi all over India. This is the holiest plant for the Vaishnavite Hindus. They believe that goddess Lakshmi, in her aspect as Sri Lakshmi as the bestower of prosperity, lives in the thulsi plant, so the plant itself is regarded as goddess *Thulsi*. Even the *devas* worship *thulsi*. It is believed that all the gods and goddesses stay in *thulsi*. The middle of the leaf is the abode of Vishnu, tip that of Brahma, and the base and stalk that of Śiva. Lakshmi, Saraswathi, Gayathri, Chandika, and other goddesses take the *thulsi* flowers as their abode. Indra, Agni, Varuna, and other such gods stay in the branches. All planets and minor deities *(Vasus, Munis, Devarshis, Vidyadharas, Gandharvas, Sidhas, Apsaras* etc)* take the thulsi grove as their abodes. All sacred *tirthas* and holy rivers (Ganga, Yamuna, Narmada, Saraswathi, Godavari) live in the base of *thulsi*. When one worships *thulsi*, one worships Vishnu, Brahma, Śiva and

Devi in all her three forms as Lakshmi, Parvathi (Durga), and Saraswathi".

Thulsi is the icon of Hinduism. *Skanda Purana,* as well as *Padma Purana,* extols the benefits of *thulsi* worship by elaborating *on thulsi mahatmya* (the greatness of thulsi). Even he who keeps the base of *the thulsi* plant clean goes to *Vishnu Loka* (abode of Vishnu, Salvation), it is believed. Whoever waters *thulsi* or protects the plant gets eternal bliss and all his sins will be removed by Hari (Vishnu). One who sprinkles water on *thulsi* daily will be freed of all sins, and one who sprinkles milk will always be blessed by the goddess with all luck and prosperity; the goddess herself will stay in that house forever. One who applies cow dung to the *thulsi* plant will reach *Brahma Loka* (the abode of Brahma, or *Satyaloka,* indirectly meaning heaven). One who lights a lamp daily before the plant will go to the abode of Vishnu. One who protects the plant from animals and wanton children, in turn, will be protected by Hari. One who looks at the *thulsi* plant daily morning and bows before it with devotion will attain the highest bliss. One who worships *thulsi* will be blessed with all prosperity, luck, and virtuous children. One who chants the name of *thulsi* and the *thulsi mantra* will be relieved of all sins. (The *thulsi mantra* given in the *Brahmavaivarta Purana* is a *dasakshara* (10-syllabled) *mantra:*

> *Om śreem hreem kleem āim vrindavanayai svaha (also transliterated as srēm hrēm klēm āim vrindāvanāyai svāhā).*

Eating a *thulsi* leaf a day will drive out all sins and desires from the body. One will get purified by wearing a garland of *thulsi* beads. Pouring water with *thulsi* leaves on the head is regarded as equivalent to a bath in the holy Ganga. Offerings made to a *thulsi* plant are regarded as equivalent to an offering to Lord Vishnu. Any sacred or religious function without the offering of *thulsi* leaves will make it ineffective and useless, because Lord Vishnu, is not happy. Anyone uprooting *thulsi* and throwing it on the ground will be punished by Hari for the disrespect shown. Hari will take away the wealth and happiness of one who desecrates the plant or the place where the plant stands.

Padma Purana has this to say on the greatness of *thulsi*:

> "*Thulsi* is dearer to the Lord than Laksmi, for, by performing extreme austerities and loving worship of the Lord to have the Lord as her husband. Vishnu surrendered to her wish. There is no better recipient of charity than *vipra* (Brahmin) no better gift than giving of cows, no better *tirtha* (holy ghat) than the ganga, and no better leaf than the *thulsi* leaf. Whatever can be obtained by offering all types of flowers and leaves, may be attained by simply offering one leaf of *thulsi*; offering flowers of gold, jewels and pearls is not equal to offering *thulsi*. By offering *thulsi* one is released from sins accumulated for one *koti* (ten million) of lifetimes. By offering *thulsi* to the head of the Lord all the unmentionable and undetected sins are destroyed. By sprinkling the Lord's house with water using a *thulsi* leaf, one is freed from all great sins. By offering *thulsi,* one destroys enemies, increases wealth, and guarantees liberation from material birth. One is certain to attain *Vaikunta,* the abode of Lord Vishnu. The fragrance of *thulsi* leaves, the flower of the *malati* plant and the milk

from a brown cow are the three items which most quickly satisfy Kesava....If one has *ämalaki* fruits or *thulsi* leaves in one's mouth or on one's head or body when one dies, one is guaranteed not to suffer in hell..."

Skanda Puranam has a dialogue between Lord Śiva and his son Kumara (Karthikeya) that highlights the greatness of *thulsi.*

Karthikeya once asked his father, Lord Śiva, 'My dear father, which tree or plant is capable of giving love of God?'

Lord Śiva replied:

'My dear son, of all trees and plants, Thulsi Devi is the topmost; she is auspicious, the fulfiller of all desires, completely pure, most dear to Lord Krishna, and the topmost devotee. Long ago, Lord Krishna for the welfare of all conditioned souls, brought Vrinda devi in the form of a plant, (*thulsi*) and planted her in the material world. *Thulsi* is the essence of all devotional activities. Without *thulsi* leaves, Lord Krishna does not like to accept flowers, foodstuffs, or sandalwood paste; in fact, anything without *thulsi* leaves is not looked upon by Lord Krishna. One who worships Lord Krishna daily with *thulsi* leaves attains the results of all kinds of austerities, charities and fire sacrifices. He has no other duties to perform, and he has realized the essence of all scriptures. Just as the Ganges River is purifying all who bathe in her, so Thulsi devi is purifying the three worlds. It is impossible to describe the full benefit of offering *thulsi manjari* (flowers) to Lord Krishna, who along with all the other demigods, lives wherever there is Thulsi devi. For this reason, one should plant *thulsi* in one's home and offer worship daily. One who sits near Thulsi devi, and chants or recites prayers will attain the results much faster.

Thulsi Devi is a pure devotee of Krishna and she should be treated with the same respect given to all Krishna's pure devotees. Simply by worshipping her faithfully, a devotee can get freedom from all material miseries. ... It is auspicious in all respects. Simply by seeing, simply by touching, simply by remembering, simply by praying, simply by bowing before, simply by hearing about, or simply by sowing the plant, there is always auspiciousness. Anyone who comes in touch with the *thulsi* plant in the manner mentioned earlier lives eternally in the *Vaikunta* (the abode of Vishnu).

"*Hari Bhaktivilasa* gives a hymn on thulsi; in translation it means:

> "Just by looking at you *(thulsi),* all sins become removed. Just by touching you, one's body becomes pure. By praying to her, all diseases practically become removed. If one waters her or makes her wet, the fear of Yamaraja (death personified) is destroyed".
>
> Just by planting or transplanting, one achieves nearness to the Supreme Personality of Godhead. If someone offers *thulsi* at the lotus feet of Lord Sri Krishna, she awards liberation and devotion to Him, therefore I pay my humble obeisance to such a wonderful Tulasi Devi...
>
> Any person who daily sees *thulsi,* touches *thulsi,* chants *thulsi*'s prayers, meditates on *thulsi,* pays

obeisances to her, hears about her, transplants, and worships her; achieves all auspiciousness.

Any person who does these nine kinds of service goes to the abode of the Supreme Lord Hari and remains there eternally...

What can I say about the wonderful glories of *thulsi?* Her fallen leaves, her rotten leaves, and her water, even if fallen (mixed with her mud?) are purifying. If even a minute quantity of the mud which has emanated from the *thulsi* root has been placed on one's head, all of one's sins are removed.

Although *thulsi* is so glorious (and her leaves are so purifying), but Vaishnavas never eat *thulsi* leaves without first offering them to the Supreme Personality of Godhead, Krishna....'

Quoting from the *Gautamiya-tantra*, the *Hari-bhakti-vilasa* states:

> *"... tulasi-dala-matrena*
> *Jalasya culukenava*
> *Vikrinitesvam atmanam*
> *bhaktebhyo bhakta-vatSalah"* (*Gautamiya tantra*)

Sri Krishna, who is very affectionate toward his devotees, sells Himself to a devotee who offers merely a *thulsi* leaf and a palmful of water.

> *"Thulsi srisakhi subhe*
> *papa harini punyadhe*
> *namasthe naradanuthe*
> *narayana mana priye"*

Oh thulsi, Oh friend of Lakshmi, Oh holy one.
Oh remover of sins, Oh one who blesses with divinity,

Salutations to you who were sung by sage Narada,
Oh darling of the mind of Lord Vishnu (*Thulśi stotra* of Sage Pundareeka)

It is an utterance we find in the *thulsi stotra*. There is no sacred event without the presence of *thulsi*, the darling of Lord Vishnu. No evil spirit can approach a house where there is a *thulsi* plant maintained properly, and being the destroyer of evil, it is called *Bhutagni*. Vaishnavites consider it the holiest offering to Lord Vishnu. They pluck *thulsi* leaves with the chanting of a prayer which means:

"Oh! thulsi, you have originated from *Amrutha* (the divine nectar),
Always the darling of Lord Keshava (Vishnu,),
Is very sacred and the bestower of *moksha,* (Salvation).
All parts of this divine plant are meant only for the worship of Lord Vishnu,
And you are bestowed with the power to purify us.
Oh! thulsi. I may be permitted to pluck your leaves For offering to Lord Vishnu." (23).

Bhagavatha Purana hails the greatness of *thulsi* compared to other flowers like this:

"...*mandara-kunda-kurabotpala-champakarna-
punnaga-naga-bakulambuja-parijatah
gandhercite Tulasi kabharanenatasya
yasmimstapahsumanaso bahu manayanti...*"

Although flowering plants like the *mandāra, kunda, kurabaka, utpala, champaka, arṇa, punnāga, nāgakeśara, bakula,* lily and *pārijāta* are full of transcendental fragrance, they are still conscious of the austerities performed by *thulsi,* for *thulsi* is given special preference by the Lord, who garlands Himself with *thulsi* leaves.

There is a belief, especially among the Vaishnavites, that *thulsi* leaves should not be plucked on Tuesdays, Fridays, and Sundays and on *Amavasya-poornima* and in the evenings. For offering on such days, leaves are collected the previous day itself. Tulasi leaves are plucked using thumb and mid-finger and not by index finger, because the index finger is the 'unholy finger' used by a person to point while uttering a curse or scolding or when using other unholy words. Again, *thulsi* leaves are plucked only after a bath, and by wearing wet or clean clothes. *Vishnu Dharmottara Purana* stipulates that *thulsi* should not be plucked on *dvadasi* (twelfth day after the new moon) and that one who picks *thulsi* without having a bath and without performing worship is an offender, and all his activities become useless. The *Vaishnavites* adhere to this belief.

Planting of *the thulsi* plant is forbidden in the month of *Chaitra* (March April) and *Jyeshta* (May June); other months are good, while planting in *Vaishakha* (April May) brings fame to the planter, according to *Bhavishya Purana*. This *Purana* also gives the details on how to plant *thuls*i. When *thulsi* plants dry up, Brahmins (especially Vaishnavites) cut or uproot the stem and bundle them and keep them. In the Kangra region, even though this act of uprooting was done with ritual practices, it was done only on an auspicious day and only after offering *poojas* (ritual oblations). After death when the dead body is kept in a funeral pyre a few such bundles are added to the pyre. In doing so it is believed that the dead soul will get Salvation. According to belief, even ghosts disappear if water is sprinkled with *thulsi* leaves, together with the chanting of the *thulsi mantra*.

Thulsi Vivah & Thulsi Worship

The account of Thulsi will not be complete without a mention of the *thulsi vivah,* a practice among the Vaishnavite Brahmins of India. During this ceremony, *thulsi* is ceremonially married to Vishnu, annually on the eleventh day of the bright fortnight in the month of *Karthika* (July August) as per the lunar calendar. The festival continues for five days, concluding on the full moon day. This ritual of *thulsi vivah* is the beginning of the marriage season in North India. During the first day the *thulsi* plant and a *Salagram* (when a genuine *Salagram* is not available a black stone of appropriate size and shape is substituted) are given a ceremonial bath, then dressed in red silk cloth, small oil lamps are lit and placed all around the *thulsi* pot and the plant is decorated with garlands. Then the plant and the *Salagram* are joined in wedlock with a garland. Mostly women participate in the function, but often the actual ceremony is performed by a priest.*. When facilities for such an elaborate function are not available the *thulsi vivah* is celebrated between an idol of Thulsi Devi and Lord Krishna, formally. The ceremony is followed by a sumptuous feast. For five days following the *thulsi vivah* (till the full moon), the *thulsi* plant and the *Salagram* are worshipped daily by sprinkling water, lighting lamps, and praying. (*Details of *thulsi-vivah* can be found in many publications and on the www; the basic information is from Puranas such as the *Brahma-Vaivarta Purana* (*Prakriti-Khanda,* Chapters 21 & 22). Also see websites such as: Tulasi Devi: The Sacred Tree http://www.stephen-knapp.com/tulasi_devi_the_sacred_tree.html.)

A thulsi Vivah set up in North India. (Source: Vikas Jindal (2022), https://astroclips.com/festivals/tulsi-vivah-2022/

Thulsi worship

Thulsi worship is extremely prevalent in the Vaishnava community of India. In their houses, a thulsi is always planted on a raised terracotta platform specially made for the purpose. Early in the morning, the women of the house after bath, approach the *thulsi* plant and walk around it three times chanting (often in the local language) the prayer which means:

> "O Thulsi devi, you are the beloved of Vishnu, you fulfil the wishes of the devotees, I will bathe you. You are the mother of the world. Give me the blessings of Vishnu."

The women prostrate before the *thulsi* plant and the lady of the house pours water over the plant from a polished brass pot and sprinkles water on all leaves three times. This is done with absolute devotion, because for the women *thulsi* is the goddess incarnate and the symbol of purity, and prosperity. Then the sprinkling of water is performed by other women too. Camphor is then lit in a special holder, and *arati* is performed (rotating the lighted camphor in front of the plant three times). Incense sticks are then lit and a lady with cupped hands rotates the incense stick and prays:

> "O the divine *thulsi*,
> within your roots are all the sacred places of the world,
> and inside your steam lives all gods and goddesses.
> Your leaves radiate every form of sacred fire.
> Let me take some of your leaves and I may be blessed." (24).

She then carefully plucks a leaf, keeps it between her palms, and prostrates before the plant in total supplication, then she gets up asks for permission to dress the Thulsi Devi, and wraps a piece of red cloth around the plant. She then places a red *japa kusuma* (shoe flower) on the plant and then, decorates the branches with garlands. Finally, the ceremony is over and the lady who performs the pooja devotionally puts the leaf in her mouth. Then all the women walk around the *thulsi* plant chanting:

> "O goddess Thulsi,
> You who are the most precious to Lord Hari,
> Who created the Divine Laws,
> I implore you to protect the lives of my family
> And the spirits of those who have died.
> Hear me O, Devi, bless us all."

Such elaborate worship is only on the first day of the *Kartika* (*kartik*) month (Oct. – Nov.). On other days the worship consists of sprinkling water and lighting a lamp'.

Thulsi puja set up

The Saraswat Brahmins of Karnataka and Goa celebrate a festival known as *'Choodi pooja'*, performed by married women. *Choodies* are tiny bouquets, smeared with vermilion and sandal paste. Around the pedestal of the *thulsi* plant, a *rangoli* design (design made out of rice powder with or without vermillion) is made, the *thulsi* is sprinkled with water, then *kajal* (collyrium, black paste of soot in oil, used by women for beautifying their eyes) and *Kumkum* (vermillion powder which the Hindu married women apply at the parting of their hair and for putting a circular mark on their forehead) (as a symbol of womanhood); fruits and sweets are offered. Finally, the *choodis are* placed before the *thulsi* plant followed by *'arati'* (lighting of incense). Then *choodis* are given to all women and they, in turn, wear them in their hairlocks. The married women then offer the *choodis* to their husbands together with coconut smeared with vermilion and turmeric paste. *Choodi pooja* symbolizes the holistic contentment of a woman in her married life. (25).

Thulsi is again worshipped during the *Uttannna Dwadeshl pooja* or *Damodara pooja*. The Hindus celebrate many festivals, most of which start in the month of *Sravana* (July). These festivals start with *Naga panchami,* then comes *Varamahalakshmi vrata, Upakarma, Raksha Bandhan, Krishna Janmashtami, Ganesh Chaturthi, Ananthapadmanabha vrata, Pithrupaksha, Navarathri, Deewali,* and ends with *Damodara pooja or Thulsi pooja* in October (in the month of *Karthika).* The Vaishnavites in Karnataka, Maharashtra, Gujarat, Rajasthan, U.P etc celebrates the *Uttanna Dwadeshi* (or *Karthika shukla dwadeshi* or *Utthanababodha dwadeshi*), which falls in October November. The *Uttanna dwadeshi* festival symbolizes the waking up of Lord Vishnu on this day and the journey to earth from *Vaikunta.* On this day Lord Vishnu, is believed to have visited Vrindavan. In this festival, *thulsi* is worshipped along with the *Āmla* tree. This festival is also the end of the *Chathurmasya vrata* observed by holy men. (26)

Sage Pundareeka has composed the *Thulsi Stotra,* which is very sacred to *Vaishnvites* and they chant it daily. The opening verse of this *stotra* is:

> *Jagaddhathri namasthubhyam*
> *Vishnu ca priyavallabhe*
> *Yathro brahmadayo deva*
> *Sruśtisthithyantha karina |*
> Salutations to mother of the universe,
> Who is the darling wife of Lord Vishnu,
> And due to you only, Brahma and others,
> Are engaged in creation, upkeep and destruction.
> (27).

There is also a famous *Thulsi kavacha.* This great prayer is given in *Brahmanda Purana.* While fighting with Tharakasura, Lord Subrahmanya becomes tired and prays to Lord Śiva. Lord Śiva appears before him and teaches him this great prayer. Later by the power gained by reciting the *Thulsi Kavacha*, Lord Subrahmanya kills Tharaka. It is mentioned in this *stotra*, that it fulfils all wishes of those who are chanting it. In another place, it is generally held that if a childless lady or a lady prone to stillbirth is caressed by a *darbha* (*kusa* grass) over which this *Kavacha* is chanted, then, she will give birth to a great baby. The opening verse of this *kavacha* is:

> *Ö thulsiñrimaha devi*
> *nama pankaja dharini*
> *ñiro may thulsipathu*
> *halam pathuyaçasvini*
> *drusov may admanayane*
> *ñriñakhi sravane mama*
> *úranam pathuñuganda may*
> *mukham ca ñumukhi mama*

'My Salutations to Goddess Thulsi who holds the lotus.
Let my head be protected by Thulsi,
Let my forehead be protected by she who is famous,
Let my eyes be protected by the lotus-eyed one,
Let the friend of Lakshmi protect my ears,
Let the sweet-scented one protect my nose,
And let the pretty-faced one protect my face.' (28).

"The *Thulsi ashtaka* is equally famous, in which thulsi is personified as Thulsi Devi. This has been translated into English and is available in public domains. (29).

Thulsi is offered during most sacred rituals and *poojas*. The most important among such rituals and poojas include: *Sidhi Vinayaka vrata pooja, Sankasthi Chathurthi vrata pooja, Satyanarayana patra pooja, Sri Varamahalakshmi vrata pooja, Marga Shirsha Sri Mahalakshmi vrata pooja, Sri Anantapadmanabha vrata pooja, Ananta Padmanabha patra pooja, Swarna Gauri vrata patra pooja, Shanipradosha vrata pooja, Dhana Lakshmi pooja, Sri Krishna pooja, Sri Venketeswara pooja, Anjaneya pooja and Rishi pooja. (30)*

To sum up, *thulsi* is the spiritual symbol or icon of Hinduism, Hindu culture, and Indian womanhood. When grown in houses its surroundings should be kept clean, watering (i.e. sprinkling water even in monsoon time) regularly and as far as possible lighting a small oil lamp in the evening. Some ladies pluck the leaves and flowers and keep them in their hairlocks. This should not be practised. The *thulsi* leaves should first be offered to Lord Krishna, i.e. kept at his feet, and only after it should be worn. The age-old belief that *thulsi* bestow prosperity and glory runs still deep in Indian society; and perhaps this is the plant that one can describe as the embodiment of Indian womanhood."

Descriptions and Uses:

Thulsi (Thulsi): Ocimum tenuiflorum Linn. (syn. O. sanctum Linn.) Lamiaceae

Holy basil, sacred basil (English.); thulsi, varada (Hindi.); krishnathulsi (Bengali); krishnathulsi, srithulsi, vishnuthulsi (Kannada); thulsi, krishnathulsi, karimthulsi (Malayalam); thulasa (Marati); karimthulsi, nalla thulsi (Tamil); brinda, krishna thulsi, thulsi (Telungu).

Thulsi (Thulsi) is commonly known as sacred basil and holy basil; in Sanskrit there are many synonyms. This is also known as Thai holy basil and used widely in cooking there. Two varieties (morphotypes) exist green and purple, the former is called *Sri thulsi* or *Lakshmi thulsi* and the latter *Krishna thulsi*. (There is another *thualsi, Rama (Ram) thulsi,* which is equated with *Ocimum gratissimum,*). *Thulsi* is native of the Old-World tropics and it is widely cultivated, especially in India, while in many places it is considered as a weed. It is cultivated for religious importance, for its medicinal purposes, and for its essential oil. It is widely used as a herbal tea, mixed with other herbs-including *Ram thulsi* and *vanathulsi* (*Ocimum canum*) – as well as in combination with tea powder.

The genus *Ocimum* consists of sections and sub-sections. *O. tenuiflorum* is included in Sect. Hierocymum, which consists of 11 species including *O. tenuiflorum*. *Thulsi* is an aromatic shrub, growing to about 60 75 cm, stems and leaves hairy; leaves are petiolate, opposite, green or light purple; young stem green or purple. Inflorescence is typical of the genus, a thyrsus composed of opposite, 1-3 flowered cymes that are arranged around a central axis. Under hot tropical conditions the plants die out after flowering and fruiting. (31)

Thulsi is highly medicinal and is widely used in Ayurveda, Siddha, and Unani medicines as well as in home remedies. According to the classical Ayurvedic text Bhava Prakasa *thulsi* is pungent, cordial, hot in potency, and reduces burning sensation and *pitta dosha.* It is an appetizer, cures skin diseases, dysuria, diseases of *rakta*, pain in the flanks and vitiated *kapha* and *vata.* Charaka Samhitha asserts that 'Thulsi cures hiccups, coughs, toxemia, laboured breathing, and pain in the flanks. It promotes secretion of bile and destroys *vata, kapha* and bad breath. Khare in his Dictionary gives the following qualities: "Leaf is carminative, stomachic, antispasmodic (alleviating spasms or convulsions), anti-asthmatic, anti-rheumatic, expectorant, stimulant, hepatoprotective (protective of liver), antipyretic (reducing fever), and diaphoretic (inducing perspiration)". It is recommended for the treatment of rhinitis, influenza, cold, fever and bronchial congestion. Seed is indicated in psychological disorders such as fear psychosis and obsessions. Leaves and seeds have anti-stress and anti-fatigue properties. Widely used in herbal remedies as well as in traditional medicines. (32)

It is a wonderful home medicine in the grandmas' medicine chest, and is still being used widely in South Asia for treating common cold, indigestion, fever, cough, and congestion to skin diseases and even as a beautifier. There are hundreds of time-tested home remedies in which *thulsi* finds a place. Yash Rai has compiled this information of the home remedies; almost a hundred pages are devoted for describing its medicinal properties. Sairam also provides a long list of home remedies based on *thulsi.* (33).

A traditional *vaidya* (Ayurvedic practitioner) extolled *thulsi's* benefits in these lines:

> "...With sharp taste and bitter aftertaste
> Hot, light, and dry in effect
> It cures ailments originating in *kapha* and *vayu*
> It stimulates hunger and improves digestion
> It sharpens the intellect and grants spiritual ennoblement
> It improves vision and benefits the heart
> It imparts flavour and disseminates fragrance." (34)

In traditional and folk medicines, *thulsi* is used in the treatment of fevers caused by *kapha* and *vayu*, colds, coughs, laboured breathing, pains, lack of appetite, slack digestion, vomiting, hiccups, migraine, poisoning, headaches, sore throat, suppuration (pus formation) of ears, skin diseases, flatulence, toothache, tetanus, dyspepsia, excessive thirst, urticaria, halitosis, cholera, small pox, worms, chest pains, night blindness, liver disorders etc

Thulsi contains large number of chemical components. The composition of aromatic oil from leaves and flowers differs depending upon the varieties and populations. The general components include eugenol, carvacrol, nerol, ocimene, eugenomethyl ether; ursolic acid, glycosides of apigenin, luteolin, orientin, molludistin etc. The various scientific aspects on thulsi (Basil in general) are presented in the monograph, Basil: the genus *Ocimum* edited by Raimo Hiltunen and Yvonne Holm. (35).

Annexure 1

Prayers and Mantras for Tulasi

When bowing down (*pancanga pranam*) upon seeing Thulsi Devi

> *vṛndāyai tulasī-devyai priyāyai keśavasya ca*
> *viṣṇu-bhakti-prade devī satya vatyai namo namaḥ*

"I offer my repeated obeisance to Vrinda, Srimati Tulasi Devi, who is very dear to Lord Keshava (Krishna). O goddess, you bestow devotional service to Lord Krishna and possess the highest truth."

When collecting leaves

> *oṁ tulasy amṛta-janmāsī*
> *sadā tvaṁ keśava-priyā*
> *keśavārthaṁ cinomi tvāṁ*
> *varadā bhava-śobhane*

> "O Thulsi, you were born from nectar. You are always very dear to Lord Keshava. Now to worship Lord Keshava, I am collecting your leaves and *manjaris*. Please bestow your benediction on me."

Srila Prabhupada explained:

> "The collecting of leaves should be done once in the morning for worshiping and for putting on the

plates of foodstuff to be offered to the Deities. On each bowl or plate there should be at least one leaf. So, you follow and practice Thulsi affairs and you try to distribute your experience to all other centres, that will be a new chapter in the history of the Krishna Consciousness Movement." (36)

Sung while offering ārati

namo namaha tulasi! krishna-preyasi
radha-krishna-seva pabo ei abhilashi

je tomara sharana loy, tara vanchha purna hoy
kripa kori' koro tare brindavana-basi

mor ei abhilash, bilas kunje dio vas
nayane heribo sada jugala-rupa-rashi

ei nivedana dharo, sakhir anugata koro
seva-adhikara diye koro nija dasi

dina krishna-dase koy, ei jena mora hoy
sri-radha-govinda-preme sada jena bhasi

"O Thulsi, beloved of Krishna, I bow before you again and again. My desire is to obtain the service of Sri Sri Radha-Krishna.

"Whoever takes shelter of you has his wishes fulfilled. Bestowing your mercy on him, you make him a resident of Vrindavana.

"My desire is that you also grant me a residence in the pleasure groves of Sri Vrindavana-dhama. Thus, within my vision I will always behold the beautiful pastimes of Radha and Krishna.

"I beg you to make me a follower of the cowherd damsels of Vraja. Please give me the privilege of devotional service and make me your own maidservant.

"This very fallen and lowly servant of Krishna prays 'May I always swim in the love of Sri Radha and Govinda."

"O Thulsi, beloved of Krishna, I bow before you again and again. The only desire left in me is to serve Radha and Krishna. O dweller of Vrindavana, the wishes of all those are fulfilled who seek your favour. Bestow your kindness upon me. I wish you to live in my small garden and you remain green forever, O storehouse of beauty. I am your follower and shakti, pray that by making me your maidservant of Krishna and this body is His—not mine. Bless me that in this body dwells only love for Radha and Krishna." – (37)

While circumambulating thulsi

yani kani cha papani
brahma-hatyadikani cha
tani tani pranashyanti
pradakshinaha pade pade

"By the circumambulation of Srimati Tulasi Devi all the sins one may have committed are destroyed at every step, even the sin of killing a brahmana."

Sri Thulsi ārati

namo namah tulasi krishna-preyasi namo namah
radha-krishna-seva pabo ei abilashi
ye tomara sarana loy, tara vancha purna hoy
kripa kori' koro tare vrindavana-vasi
mora ei abhilasha, vilasa kunje dio vasa

nayana heribo sada yugala-rupa-rasi
ei nivedana dhara, sakhira anugata koro
seva-adhikara diye koro nija dasi
dina krishna-dase koy, ei yena mora hoy
sri-radha-govinda-preme sada yena bhasi

O Tulasi, beloved of Krishna, I bow before you again and again. My desire is to obtain the service of Sri Sri Radha and Krishna.

Whoever takes shelter of you has his wishes fulfilled. Bestowing your mercy on him, you make him a resident of Vrindavana.

My desire is that you will also give me a residence in the pleasure groves of Sri Vrindavana-dhama. Thus within my vision I will always behold the beautiful pastimes of Radha and Krishna.

I beg you to make me a follower of the cowherd damsels of Vraja. Please give me the privilege of devotional service and make me your own maidservant.

This very fallen and lowly servant of Krsna prays, "May I always swim in the love of Sri Radha and Govinda. (38)

Vrinda devi *Ashtakam*

(This great prayer is addressed to Vrunda devi who later became the Thulsi plant. There is a story that she was doing penance to marry Lord Vishnu and once when Ravana tried to molest her, she jumped in to the fire and became ash. This was written by Sri Harivallabhadasa.) (Translated by P.R.Ramachander) (39)

1.Gangeya champeya tadith vinindi-
Rocih pravaha snapitatma vrinde
Bandhuka bandhu dyuthi divya vaso
Vrinde namaste charanaravindam

My Salutations to your lotus-like feet, Oh Vrinda devi,

Who is surrounded by the glow like Bandhuka flowers*,

Whose splendour puts to shame gold, Champaka** flower and lightning,

And by the flow of that same splendour you continuously anoint your devotees.

*Red Ixora flowers. ** *Michelia champaka*

> *2. Bimbadharo udithvara manda hasya-*
> *Nasagra mukta dyuti dipitaysye*
> *Vichitra rathnabharana sriya adhye*
> *Vrinde namaste charanaravindam*

My Salutations to your lotus-like feet, Oh Vrinda devi,

Who has a very pretty, rising smile beaking,

Out of her reddish lips resembling Bimba fruits,

Whose pearl nose ring illuminates the tip of her nose,

And who wears several amazing gem studded ornaments.

> *3.Samasta vaikunta – siromanau sri*
> *Krishnasya vrindavana dhanya dhamni*
> *Datta adhikare vrsuhaabhanu-putrya*
> *Vrinde namaste charanaravindam*

My Salutations to your lotus-like feet, Oh Vrinda devi,

Who is the crown jewel of the entire land of Vaikunta,

And who has been given the power to rule the blessed Vrindavana,

By Radha who was the daughter of Vrusha Banu.

> *4,Thvad aajnaya pallava pushpa bhrnga,*
> *Mrugadibhir Madhava keli kunja*

Madhvadibhir bhanti vibhushyamana
Vrinde namaste charanaravindam

My Salutations to your lotus-like feet, Oh Vrinda devi,

By whose order the garden of Lord Krishna,

Is decorated with blossoming flowers, bees,

Deer and other things, for enjoying his playful pastimes.

5. Thvadiya dhothyena nikunja-yunor
Athi yutkayoh keli vilasa siddhih
Thvat saubhagyam kena niruchyatam thad
Vrinde namaste charanaravindam

My Salutations to your lotus-like feet, Oh Vrinda devi,

Due to the service rendered by you, the divine couple,

Were able to enjoy perfect playful acts in the grove,

And who can ever describe your very great luck?

6. Rasabhilasho vasatis cha vrunda-
Vane thvadeesa anghri Saroja seva
Labhya cha pumsam krupaya thavaiva
Vrinde namaste charanaravindam

My Salutations to your lotus-like feet, Oh Vrinda devi,

Indeed, due to your great mercy the people of Brindavana,

Were able to do service to the lotus feet of Lord Krishna,

In fulfilling his desire to perform the Rasa Leela.

Thvam kirthyase satvata tantra vidhibhir
Leela abhidhana kila Krishna sakthih
Thavaiva murthis tulasi nru loke
Vrinde namaste charanaravindam

My Salutations to your lotus-like feet, Oh Vrinda devi,

The saints well versed in the science of pure strength,

Have praised you as the power of the sports of Lord Krishna,

And that the Thulsi plant is your form in the human world.

> *8. Bhakthyaa viheena aparadha lakshaih*
> *Ksiptha scha kamaadhi taranga madhye*
> *Krupamayi thvam saranam prapanna*
> *Vrinde namaste charanaravindam.*

My Salutations to your lotus-like feet, Oh Vrinda devi,

Being devoid of devotion and having committed millions of sins,

And having been thrown deep in the middle of the waves of passion,

Oh merciful one, I have completely surrendered to you.

> *9. Vrundashtakam yah srunuyat padeth va*
> *Vrndavana adhisa padhabja bhrungah*
> *Sa prapya vrundavana nitya vasam*
> *That prema sevam labhate krutarthah*

If this octet addressed to Vrunda devi is heard or read,

By one who is like the bee visiting the lotus like feet of the Lords of Brindavan,

He would reach and stay forever in Brindavan,

And get loving service there and would be blessed.

Citations and notes

(Refer the list at the end of the book for general and common references)

1. Krishna Dasa, Namo Namah Tulasi Krsna Preyasi (Thulsi kirtana), http://kksongs.org/songs/n/ namonamah tulasikrsna.html.

2. *Shaktisangama tantra*. One of the tantric texts dealing with Shakti worship. The basic message of this tantric text is the greatness of woman who is in the form of Śakthi (Devi, known by names such as Durga, Parvathi, Śakthi, Kali and so on). The basic concept of this tantra is given in these lines.

3. Vallathol Narayana Menon. Quoted from the poem on thulsi. (Malayalam).

4, 5. De Cleene M. and Lejeune M C., Compendium of Symbolic and Ritual Plants of Europe, 2 Vols. 2002/ 2003.

6. Folkard R (1884) Plant Lore, Legends, and Lyrics Embracing the Myths, Traditions, Superstitions, and Folk-Lore of the Plant Kingdom (Reprint 2014). [E-Book #44638] https://www.gutenberg.org/.

7. De Cleene M. and Lejeune (see 4)

8. Ibid

9. Keats J (1818) Isabella, or the Pot of Basil. https://genius.com/John-keats-isabella-or-the-pot-of-basil-annotated.

10. Carbone JC (2008) Vaishnava goddess as plant: tulsi in text and context Thesis submitted to the Florida state university, Florida State University Libraries, https://docslib.org/doc/2589682/vaisnava-goddess-as-plant-tulasi-in-text-and-context-john-carbone.

11. Magoun H. W. "The Asuri-Kalpa; A Witchcraft Practice of the Atharva-Veda". The American Journal of Philology, Vol. 10, No. 2. (1889), pp. 165-197 (Cited from Carbone 2008).

12. Miller R. (2003) Tulsī Queen of Herbs: India's Holy Basil. B.C. Canada: The Green Isle Enterprise (Cited from Carbone 2008).

13. Carbone (see 10)

14. Ibid

15, 16. Ravindran PN (2020) Sacred and Ritual Plants of India. Notion press, Chennai.

17. Dehejia, H. V. Ocean of Creativity, http://www.speakingtree.in/spiritual-articles/faith-and-rituals/Ocean-Of-Creativity.

18. Anonymous (2024) Collective unconscious. https://en.wikipedia.org/wiki/Collective_unconscious.

19. Findley, E. B. (2008) Plant Lives. Motilal Banarsidass Pub., Delhi.

20. Narayan, K. (1995) How a girl became a sacred plant. This paper appeared in a book edited by Donald Lopez titled 'Readings in Indian Religion (1995).

21. Narayan, K. (1997) The sprouting and uprooting of Saili: The story of sacred Thulśi in Kangra.

22. Ravindran PN (2020) Sacred and Ritual Plants of India. Notion press, Chennai.

23. Anonymous (2004) About Srimati Vrinda-devi. https://vrinda-kunda.com/vrinda-devi.html.

24. Knapp S (2024) The Tulasi-devi Handbook: Guidelines and Instructions on the Importance, Care and Worship of the Tulasi Tree. (e-book).

The basic information on the ritual worship of thulsi and the use of thulsi in rituals come from texts such as *Gautamiya tantra* (also known as *Brihad –Gautamiya tantra*), one of the tantra texts belonging to the Vaishnava sect. This deals with the rituals relating to the worship of Lord Krishna (Vishnu,), observation of *ekadasi* rituals, and various other rituals associated with the day-to-day life of the Vaishnavites.

25. Anonymous 2020. Krishna and *tulsi vivah* (marriage) story (as per Hindu texts). https://bhagavanbhakthi.com/2020/10/krishna-tulasi-vivaha-story/. Details of *thulśi-vivah* is available in many publications and in the www; the basic information is from puranas such as the *BrahmaVaivarta Purana* (Prakriti-Khanda, Chapters 21)

26. Puranik S (2016) *Chudi pooja* and its significance. https://kkaj.in/2016/08/15/chudi-poojan-and-its-significance/.

27. Ravindran PN See 22.

28. Ramachander PR (2019) *Thulśistotra* by sage Pundareeka, translated by P. R. Ramachander. https://www.shastras.com/devi-stotras/thulsi-stotram/

29. Ramachander PR (2018) *Thulśi Kavacha* (The armour of thulśi), Translated by P. R. Ramachander. https://www.celextel.org/other-stotras/thulsi-kavacham/.

30. Ramachander PR (2018) *Sri Vrunda devi ashtaka* by Sri Harivallabhadasa, Translated by P. R. Ramachanderhttp://stotrarathna.blogspot.com/2011/01/vrinda-devi-ashtakam.html.

31-33. Ravindran see 22

34. Sairam, T. V. (1998) Home Remedies, vol. 1. Penguin India, New Delhi

35. Rai. Y (2005) Holy Basil: Thulśi. Navneet Publications (India) Ltd., Mumbai

36. Hiltunen, R and Holm, Y. (1999) Basil, The genus Ocimum. CRC Press, USA.1999.

37. ISKCON (2024) Srila Prabhupada on Srimati Tulasi Devi. ISKCON Desire Tree, https://iskcondesiretree.com/page/srila-prabhupada-on-srimati.

38. ISKCON (see above)

39. *Vrunda Devi Ashtaka*, Translated by P. R. Ramachander, Vedanta Spiritual library, https://www.celextel.org/other-stotras/vrunda-devi-ashtaka/.

06

VILVA (BAEL)

The Tree of Lord Śiva

*Tridalam trigunākäram trinethram cha
triyāyusham
trijanma papa samharameka vilvam
Śivārppaanam|
I offer one leaf of vilva to Lord Śiva,
Which has three leaves,
Which causes three qualities,
Which are like the three eyes of Śiva,
Which is like the triad of weapons,
And which destroys sins of three births
lakśmyāsca sthanautpaannam
mahādevasadāpriyam
bilvavrikśam prayacchāmi eka bilvam
ṣivārpaanam|
ḍarśanam bilvavrikśasy asparśanam
pāpaanāśnam
āghora pāpasamhāram eka bilvam
ṣivarpaanam|.(1)*

'Born from the breast of Goddess Lakshmi, the *vilva* tree is ever dear to Mahadeva. So, I ask this tree a *vilva* leaf to offer Lord Śiva. To have darshan of the *vilva* tree, and to touch it, frees one from sin. The most terrible *karma* is destroyed when a *vilva* leaf is offered to Lord Śiva' (Trans. P.R. Ramachander)

*V*ilva (*vilwa, bilva, vilvom, bilvam*) known popularly as *bel, bael;* common name being Bengal quince, is one of the holiest plants in India. It is Lord Śiva's tree and is so worshipped, by all Hindus, especially the *Saivites* (followers of Lord Śiva). It is also sacred to the *Vaishnavites,* because they believe that the goddess Lakshmi resides in this tree, and Vishnu resides in the trunk of this tree. From the stanza in *Vilvashtakom,* quoted above, we learn the legend about its origin from the breast of goddess Lakshmi. The earliest evidence of this plant being seen as a sacred tree in Hinduism was found in the *Shri Suktam* of *Rig Veda*, where it has been described as one of the abodes of Goddess Lakshmi. (*Sri Suktam* is one of the *Khila Suktas, Khila* means "the space that gives room to a newly emerging reality. It consists of sixteen mantras. The first fifteen mantras invoke the sacred fire and request that it bring the presiding forces of health, wealth, peace, and prosperity to us. The sixteenth mantra proclaims that the first fifteen mantras awaken the infallible power of the divine force that rules over the conditions resulting in inner and outer prosperity. The practice of Sri Sukta is grounded in a philosophy that sees this world as a manifestation of divine will.).

Bael tree, and fruits.

The following discussion of the various aspects of the *vilva* tree is primarily based on the sacred and ritual plants of India by Ravindran. (1)

Origin of Vilva tree

In the *Taittariya Samhita* of *Krishna Yajurveda* (11.1–8.1-2), there is a reference to the origin of *the Vilva* tree. According to this, there was a time when the Sun God stopped shining. To make the sun shine again, the devas carried out a *yaga* and propitiated Lord Surya, and he started shining again. The *Vilva* tree came into existence at this time. In *Satapatha Brahmana* (XII.4.4.8–9), there is a mention that the *vilva* tree is formed from the marrow of Prajapati. According to the tantric scripture, *Banihi Purana,* once Lakshmi came down to earth in the form of a cow, and from the dung of this divine cow arose the *vilva* tree, hence it is sacred. According to another legend from the same source, both Lakshmi and Sarasvathi were wives of Lord Vishnu, Vishnu loved Sarasvathi more, and

Lakshmi was unhappy about it. She started meditating, Śiva. Even after a very long time, Śiva did not appear, and Lakshmi got transformed into a *vilva* tree, and Śiva resides in the tree. According to the folkloric *Bhubaneswari Tantra,* Goddess Lakshmi holds a *vilva* fruit in her lower left hand, signifying her as the deliverer of the fruits of one's action. [Bhuvaneshvari, according to Hindu belief, is fourth among the ten Mahavidya goddesses in Shaktism, and one of the highest aspects of Mahadevi (Devi Parvati or Durga). (She is identified as Adi Parashakti in the Devi Bhagavatam.)]

The *Vilvashtakom* quoted at the beginning alludes to the incident that led to the origin of the *Vilva* tree. The legend based on the *Brihad-Dharma Purana* goes like this: Goddess Lakshmi used to worship Lord Śiva daily with one thousand lotus buds. Śiva wanted to test her devotion. One day, while worshipping, he made two buds vanish; so, Lakshmi found that the lotus buds are short by two. She felt miserable, as the pooja remained incomplete. Lakshmi then, recalled that her consort Lord Vishnu had always compared her breasts to lotus buds, and she decided to substitute her breasts for the missing lotus buds. She cut off her left breast, and even before making the offering, Lord Śiva, satisfied with her devotion and worship, appeared, and blessed her. With Siva's blessing, Lakshmi regained her original physique. Further, he said her breast that was cut off would grow into a tree, and that tree would be the most beloved to him and that Laksmi too would reside in it.

Yet another legend on the origin of the *vilva* tree is related to Parvathi. (2). Parvathi, determined to win the love of Lord Śiva, searched the whole of the Himalayas for an appropriate leaf or flower for daily offering to the

Śivalingam, worshipped by her. She could not find any, and her father Himavan offered to help her. With his help, Parvathi created a new plant, with leaves resembling the shape of Śhiva's eyes. Parvathi made garlands with the leaves of this plant and offered them to the *Śivalingam* and eventually won the love of Śiva. This new plant is the *vilva* tree, and Śiva ever since has resided in it. This plant is very dear to Parvathi too.

In *Skanda Purana,* there is a mention that the *vilva tree* grew from Parvati's sweat, which fell to the ground while she performed penance. The following is a quote from *Skanda Purana* (Translation GV Tagore (3).

> *"Vāṇī said*:
>
> 1. It is impossible to describe the glory and greatness of *Bilva* leaves adequately. O Mahendra, I shall tell you accurately. Listen to it.
>
> 2. The splendid Daughter of the Mountain; the goddess, became tired due to her sports. Drops of sweat appeared on her forehead.
>
> 3. They were wiped off by Bhavānī and a drop fell on the ground. It became a great tree on the excellent mountain Mandara.
>
> 4. Once again, the daughter of the Mountain came to that place during her sojourn in the forest. On seeing a tree in the forest, she was surprised. It was evident from her eyes that beamed.
>
> 5. She asked her female companions Jayā and Vijayā: "What is this great divine tree shining in the centre of the forest? It appears very beautiful. Indeed, it gives great delight."

Jayā said:

6. O goddess, this tree has originated from your own body, from a drop of your sweat. Do name this tree soon. If it is worshipped, it destroys sins.

Pārvatī said:

7-12. Since this excellent great tree pierced through the ground and rose near me, let it be named *Bilva*.

If anyone approaches this tree devoutly and collects the leaves, he shall certainly become a king of the earth. If anyone with perfect faith worships me with its leaves, he will realize whatever desire he may cherish. If a person, after seeing the leaves of *Bilva*, at least maintains faith in the rite of adoration, I shall undoubtedly be the bestower of wealth on him. If one decides to eat the tip of the leaves, thousands of his sins perish automatically. If a man places the tip of the leaf on his head, no torture of Yama will give him pain.

13. After saying this, the delighted Goddess Pārvatī went to her abode accompanied by her companions and Gaṇas (security guards).

Vāṇī said:

14. This *Bilva* tree is excellent, sacred, and destructive of sins. There is no doubt about this that Goddess Girijā resides at its root.

15. It is remembered that Dākṣhāyaṇī is present on its stem Maheśvarī on its branches, Goddess Pārvatī on its leaves and Kātyāyanī on its fruit.

16. Gaurī has been mentioned as present on its bark, Aparṇā at the middle of the bark, Durgā in the flower and Umā in the branches and twigs.

17. At the behest of Girijā, nine crores of Śaktis have stationed themselves on all its thorns for the sake of protecting living beings.

18. They worship her using the excellent leaves. They adore the eternal goddess. Whatever there is a cherished desire, it will certainly be realized.

19. Maheśvarī, the daughter of the Mountain, is a great goddess. She is pure in form and she bestows Salvation on people. On Seeing Hara resorting to *Palāśa* she created the physical form of *Bilva* playfully."

Skanda Purana thus ascertains that the various incarnations of Parvati reside in each part of the tree, as indicated in the above passage. [Dakshayani (Sati – 'daughter of Daksha'; Maheswari – aspect of Maha Devi as the consort of Maheswara (Siva); Katyayani – an aspect of Mahadevi, incarnated to kill Mahishasura, the sixth among the *Navadurga*; Gauri-: one of the names of goddess Parvati; Aparna – another name of Parvati (Parna means leaf and Aparna means not even leaf. Parvati got the name when she forsook even eating leaves during her intense austerity to get Shiva as her husband. Thus, Parvathi was named Aparna, or the one who did not eat even leaves. This is an aspect worshipped by those who undertake fasting); Durga – principal aspect of the mother goddess Mahadevi (Parvathi) associated with protection, strength, motherhood, destruction, and wars; Uma – another form of Parvati, this feminine goddess represents light and wisdom; she is also known as "The Peace of Night" and "The Bright One." She manifests the loving, nurturing spirit of the mother and reminds us of the immense beauty of womanhood and love].

Vilva is called *Sri Vriksha* because it is the abode of Devi Lakshmi. According to *Bhavishya Purana*, Lakshmi after emergence from the Ocean of Milk, rested at the V*ilva* tree, when Lord Vishnu in Mohini form had gone to recapture the pot of *amrutha*, the divine nectar, from the *asuras.* This event, according to belief, happened on the ninth of the bright half of *Bhadrapada* (August-September). So, on this day, the tree is worshipped. *Vilva* leaves are offered to Lakshmi, Saraswathi, Savithri, and Chandika. (4)

According to a tribal belief in Orissa, *the vilva* tree sprang up from the testes of a pig, and for them, it is not a sacred tree. Such beliefs are examples of the wide gap in beliefs among the orthodox Hindus and the tribal people.

Vilva Tree Worship & Rituals

Śivaratri (*Shivaratri*, The Night of Siva) was the day when Śiva manifested in the form of *Shivalinga*. On this day, which falls between the months of *Magha* and *Phalguna*; the devout Hindus spent the day worshipping Lord *Śiva* with *vilva* leaves. On this day, the *Śivalingam* is bathed in water, rose water and milk, decorated with *vilva* leaves and flowers, and worshipped by offering *vilva* leaves, while chanting the *Panchakshara mantra* (*Nama Śivaya*). In Kerala, the offering of *vilva* leaf garland is an essential item of Śiva worship, and maidens of marriageable age offer *vilva* leaf garlands for getting suitable husbands. *Śiva Purana* asserts that *the vilva* tree originated from Śiva, that it is his manifest form, and that he stays in its roots. So, the reading of *Śiva Purana* under a *vilva* or in a *vilva* grove is recommended as a sublime offering to the Lord.

The Vilva tree plays an important socio-religious role. In rural Bengal, during the *Durgapooja* festival; *Durga is* invoked on a *vilva* tree twig. Bansilal Malla, in his study, mentions that in this festival, the goddess *Durga* is worshipped in the *Navapatra pooja* or *Nava patrika*, the worship of nine leaves as symbols of nine forms of the goddess. This worship (*Navapatra pooja*) needs some explanation. (5)

In India, there are several festivals associated with plants and many are observed by women for removing barrenness, for getting male progeny, or for a long-married life with husbands and children. Some such ceremonies are simple and consist only of praying, lighting a lamp, or tying a thread; some can be very elaborate and last for a few days. Perhaps the most elaborate one is the *nava patra pooja* (worship of nine leaves/plants), prevalent in many parts of India, most noticeably in Bengal. *Navapatra pooja* (*Nabapatra pooja*, *Nabapatrika*, *Navapatrika*) forms part of Durga pooja ceremony. Here, nine aspects of Durga, symbolized by nine plants, are worshipped. The nine aspects are:

Brahmani: A benevolent aspect of Shakthi, the female counterpart of Brahma, represented by a plantain (banana plant) with stem and leaves.

Kali {Kalika}: A terrible form that Shakthi had taken while fighting with Mahishasura. There are several episodes about her origin and worship. She is represented by the Kachu (colocasia) plant.

Durga: Durga (the most-worshipped aspect of *Shakti* (Devi Parvathi) is symbolized by the *haridra* (turmeric) plant, and so this is the third plant.

Kritika: Durga took this form (also known as Karttiki) while fighting Sumbha and Nisumbha and she is represented by *jayanthi* (*Sesbania sesban*)

Raktadantika: Shakthi took this form and fought against the demon Raktabija. The fifth plant, *dadima* (pomegranate), is representative of her.

Sokarahita: It is believed that Parashakti when incarnated as Parvathi, worshipped Lord Siva with flowers of *asoka*, and Siva made it as his abode, and that Devi made it her abode too in the aspect *Sokarahitha*, the remover of sorrow. So *asoka* becomes the sixth plant.

Chamunda: A fierce aspect of Durga emanated from the forehead of Kartyayani (an incarnation of Durga who killed the invincible demon Mahishasura) for killing the fearsome demons Chanda and Munda. The arum plant, which makes up the seventh plant, represents her.

Annappoorna /Devi Lakshmi: *Parashakthi* in the aspect of nourisher of humanity is present in the rice plant as Annapoorna (goddess of food and nourishment, an aspect of Parvathi), and as Devi Sri Laksmi. So, the rice plant forms the eighth plant.

Lord Shiva/ Devi Laksmi/ Devi Parvathi: Vilva leaves represent Lord Shiva, Devi Laksmi, and Devi Parvathi and this forms the ninth leaf. Here a branch bearing a pair of fruits (representing Siva – and Shakthi) is used. (6, 7)

All nine plants are tied into a bundle with a *girikarnika* vine (*Clitoria ternatea, shankapushpi*), which also symbolizes Durga. This bundle is ceremoniously given a bath, then dressed in red silk, vermillion is applied, decorated, and placed on the altar by the side of the idol of Durga and worshipped as Devi Durga for nine days. Each day, an aspect of the Devi is invoked separately and pooja is offered. Here each plant or leaf is collected ceremoniously, and many formalities exist in bundling them, in giving ceremonious baths and in dressing and decorating the goddess. Once it is decorated and placed on the altar the bundle of leaves is treated just like an idol of Durga and all offerings and poojas are offered to it. The whole festival is an elaborate one in which all people in the neighbourhood participate. Here is an example of an evolution of simple plant worship to a complex and elaborate one with a lot of symbolism attached.). On each *Navarathri* day, the deities presiding over each plant are individually invoked by the chanting of sacred hymns. While the *Navapatrika* ritual has found its way into the mainstream contemporary Durga Puja festival, originally it was a popular agricultural ritual performed by the peasant folks for a prosperous harvest. In Bengal, it was during the autumn (*Sharat*), the time for reaping crops (the Aman paddy) that the peasants worshipped the *Navapatrika* deity for a good harvest. (8, 9)

The branch of the *vilva* tree needed for making the bundle of nine plants mentioned above is cut with the chanting of a hymn, which means:

> "O *Sriphala* tree, you are born in the
> Mountain Mandāra, Meru, Kailasa,
> And at the top of Himavat. You are
> Always a favourite of Ämbika |
> Born on the top of the Seri hill
> *Sriphala*, you are the resting place
> Of prosperity.

I take you away to worship
You as *Durga* herself
O, *vilva* tree, the most prosperous,
Always the favourite of Sankara|
I worship the *Devi* having
Taken away your branch.
O Lord, you must not mind
The pain generated by the
Separation of your branch.
I bow to the *vilva* tree, born on
Himalaya Mountain, favourite
Of Parvathi and embraced by Siva,
You are auspicious in action and
A favourite of *Bhagavata*
For the sake of Bhavani's words
Give me all success."

Bael tree does not have much of iconographic significance, except in a few cases. According to *Vishnu Dharmottara Purana* goddess Lakshmi holds a *Sriphala* (*vilva* fruit) in one of her hands. In *Shilparatna,* goddess Lakshmi is represented with two hands, one holding a *vilva* fruit. (10) Goddess Lakshmi is associated with vegetation, agriculture, as well as prosperity, and the *vilva tree* is especially related to her. According to *Sri Tatvanidhi* the image of Karthikeya is depicted as holding a *vilva* fruit on his head (11), Gopinath Rao, in his book on Hindu Iconography, mentions that Bala Ganapathi is represented as carrying a *vilva* fruit in his trunk. Similarly, the image of Taruna Ganapathi holds a *vilva* fruit in one of his hands. (12)

Legends on the greatness of Vilva tree

There are many legends associated with *vilva* and Śiva worship. *Garuda Purana* mentions the story of how a hunter got the vision of God. He was pursuing a deer and found himself on the bank of a river. Suddenly he heard the roar of a tiger. Frightened, he climbed a nearby tree and the tiger came on and sat under the tree. The hunter had to stay on the tree overnight and to keep himself awake, he plucked one leaf after another from the tree and threw it down. Under the tree, there was a *Śiva lingam*, and the tree happened to be a *vilva.* Without realizing what he was doing, the hunter offered *vilva* leaves to Lord Śiva the whole night, which happened to be a *Sivarathri*. In the morning, the hunter looked down and found the tiger gone. In its place, Lord Śiva was standing. The hunter climbed down, prostrated at the feet of the Lord who blessed him, and the hunter attained *Śivaloka* (Salvation).

This legend has another version, given in *Siva Purana* and retold by many. The story is as follows:

"Once there was a cruel-hearted hunter, Gurudruh, who lived in the lonely forest. On the auspicious day of *Maha Sivaratri*, he went hunting because his family had nothing to eat. *Maha Shivaratri* (the great night of Shiva) is the most sacred time for fasts, prayers and offerings, when even the most involuntary acts, if pleasing to Lord Shiva, are made holy. By the sun set Gurudruh had not been successful in the hunt. Coming to a lake, he climbed a tree and waited for some unsuspecting animal to come and drink. He did not notice that the tree he had climbed was the Bilva tree. Neither did he notice the *Shivalingam* beneath it, nor the water pot hanging in the branch just above it. After some time, a gentle deer came to quench her thirst, and Gurudruh prepared to shoot. As he drew his bow, he accidentally knocked the water pot hanging in the tree and some water fell on the *Shivalingam* beneath, along with a few Bilva leaves. Thus, unknowingly, and unwittingly,

Gurudruh had worshipped Shiva in the first quarter of the night. As a result, his heart was a little purified by this act performed on such an auspicious night. Meanwhile, the deer, startled by the movement in the tree, looked up and saw the hunter about to release his arrow. "Please do not kill me just yet," pleaded the deer. "I must first take care of my children, and then I will return to be food for your family." The hunter, whose heart had been softened a little by the accidental worship, on noticing the beauty of the deer, let her go on condition that she would return on the morrow to give her body as food for his family. Later that same night, the sister of the deer came looking for her. Once more the hunter aimed, and once more, unaware, the water and the Bilva leaves fell upon the *Shivalingam*. Again, unknowingly, the hunter had worshipped Shiva in the second quarter of the night. The effect of this was that Gurudruh's heart was further purified. His *pranas* softened a little more, and he allowed this animal to go and tend to its young, provided it returned the next day to provide him and his family with food. In the third quarter of the night, the mate of the first deer came in search of her, and again the strange worship took place as the hunter aimed for the third time. But the hunter's heart was beginning to melt due to the worship, and he let the deer's mate go, also for the same reason and under the same conditions. Later when the three deers met, they discussed who should go and offer themselves for the hunter's food. Even the children offered to give their lives. Finally, the whole family decided to surrender to the hunter together, for none of them could bear to live without the others. Thus, they set off towards the lake with heavy hearts. When they arrived at the Bilva tree, Gurudruh was very pleased and relieved to see them, and he immediately prepared for the kill. He took aim for the fourth time, but in the same accidental manner as before, worship in the fourth quarter of the night too took place, unknown to him. This final action of Gurudruh brought about a complete change of heart and, as he was about to release the first arrow, his heart overflowed with pity for the innocent deer. Tears filled his eyes at the thought of all the animals he had killed in the past, and slowly he lowered his bow. Greatly moved by the selfless action of these animals, he felt ashamed and allowed the whole family of deer to leave unharmed. Such is the purity and spiritual power of the Bilva tree that, even without his knowledge or conscious effort, the cruel-hearted hunter had been transformed into a man of compassion and understanding, and he was delivered from his past bad karma by the grace of Shiva and the Bilva tree. The hunter, now completely transformed, hurriedly climbed down, but slipped and fell, and died. Just before dying, he had the darshan of Lord Shiva, and he attained Siva Loka (Salvation)." (13, 14)

Another legend on the greatness of the *vilva* tree is given in *Garuda Purana*. In this, the hero is one Sundersen, the vicious king of Arunda. Once while hunting in the forest, he rested under a *vilva* tree and his servants went to bring water from a nearby river. While waiting there for water, he casually plucked the leaves and threw them down, and they fell on the Sivalingam installed under the tree. When water was brought, he happened to sprinkle some water around, possibly to create some humidity around him or to settle the dust, but the water also got sprinkled on the *Shiva lingam*. While leaving, he bent down to take his bow, quiver, and arrows from the ground. Without realizing it, his head touched the *Sivalingam*. Thus, unknowingly, he fulfilled all the three conditions stipulated for the worship of *Śivalingam;* offered *vilva* leaves, sprinkled water, and prostrated before the *Śivalingam*. That was a *Sivarathri* day, and the King's action brought him the vision of Shiva, and he received Salvation. There is also the legend of the king of Pataliputra, Vikramatunga who made *Agni deva* (God of fire) appear before him carrying a golden *vilva* fruit, with a single offering of a *vilva* fruit, which he did for the sake of a Brahmin. This story is found in *Katha-Sarithsagaram.* (15)

There is a folk tale in which bel (*vilva*) trees have important roles. The tale relates how a Prince when looking for a Princess, encountered a fakir. The latter told him that the Princess would be found in a garden grove, on a *vilva* tree bearing one solitary golden fruit, concealing the Princess. The fakir told him to pluck the fruit, not allowing it to fall, and not to look back. Unfortunately, when leaving after being successful, he did look back, the sorcerers overtook him, changed him and his horse into stones, and replaced the fruit on the tree. (16)

The *Vilva,* being the manifest form of *Śiva* himself, all the great 'thirthas' (sacred or holy bathing ghats) are believed to reside at its base. *Śiva Purana* mentions that one who worships *Śivalingam* while sitting under *a vilva* tree attains the world of Śiva or Salvation. Rubbing *vilva* leaves on the head is equivalent to bathing in all the sacred *Thirthas*. *Śiva Purana* claims that a person who does *vilva pooja* with flowers and incense attains Śiva's abode, the abode of pure consciousness and will achieve all happiness and prosperity. The lighting of a lamp before the tree alone is enough for one to reach the *Shiva Loka,* the abode of Lord Śhiva, it is claimed. *Śiva Purana* also declares that if a devotee worshipping *a vilva* tree with its leaves would be freed from all vices; the one who feeds a devotee under the *vilva* will grow in virtue. In the month of *Bhadrapada*

(August – September), *Agni Purana* recommends the worship of Śiva under the *vilva* tree together with eating only its leaves in night. *Śivalingam* installed under a *vilva* tree is called *Bilveswara.* (17). *Vilva* was also worshipped for victory in battles. In Ramayana, we get the reference that before the start of the Rama and Ravana war, Lord Brahma appeared before Rama and took him to a nearby *Vilva* tree to invoke the blessings of *Devi*. Rama's prayers were answered by *Devi's* voice from heaven that he would be victorious.

The Bilva tree is important for certain tribal communities, and there are many instances of the relationship between *the Vilva* tree and the tribal communities. The *Vilval* clan of *Bhils* holds *vilva* as a plant totem. The *Gauria* snake charmers of Madhya Pradesh believe that an appeal to the *vilva* tree and Dhanwantari, the presiding deity of Ayurveda, cures snake bites. There are also many other socio-religious beliefs associated with *vilva*. On the *Maha Shivaratri* day, Lord Śiva is worshipped by all *Śaivites* with 108 *vilva* leaves. During the *Durga pooja* festival, goddess Durga is invoked to descend to earth through a newly grown *vilva* sapling amidst the chanting of hymns. Then all the participating devotees pray:

> 'I shall get hold of the *vilva* tree and worship thee as goddess Durga/.
> Thou art *Sriphala*, thou art great in virtue and always dear to Śankara.
> I welcome thee to invoke Chandika.' (18)

Sriphala (vilva fruit), according to belief, is the manifest form of Lord Shiva himself. In Shiva Purana, Sage Romaharshana expounds to the sages of Naimishaaranya:

> "Bilva fruit is an embodiment and manifest form of Lord Shiva himself. It is believed that all the places of pilgrimage dwell at the base of *"Bilwa vriksha"* The sacred tree can only be known to a limited extent. Adored by all the Gods, its importance is difficult for anyone to comprehend. If a devotee removes a new leaf from the branches and worships the tree with it, then he would be free from all forms of vices."

Because of this belief, women folk in rural Bengal, Bihar and adjacent regions embrace the trunk of the tree and pray for the fulfilment of their wishes. Orthodox Hindus believe that if one dies under a *vilva* tree, he attains Salvation. Incidentally, *vilva* is also considered the abode of the ghosts of Brahmins (*Brahmadaityas*). *Śaivites* believe that the trifoliate leaves of *vilva* symbolize creation, preservation and destruction, the attributes of Brahma, Vishnu, and Śiva. The leaves symbolise the three *gunas* or attributes *satva, rajas* and *tamas*. They also stand for Siva himself, the three leaflets representing his three eyes. The leaf is also said to be symbolizing the three states of mind – *jagrat, sushupti* and *swapna*, and the three lives, past, present, and future. There is a belief that since *Saivites'* pluck *vilva* leaves every day to worship Śiva, Goddess Lakshmi, who dwells in the tree, feels unhappy, and does not favour the brahmins with luck and prosperity and therefore they remain poor forever. In rural North India, the *Vaishnava* Brahmin community, both men and women, wear neck strings called *kanthi* made of *thulsi* stem or *vilva* fruit shell. At the time of marriage, there is a ritual exchange of these strings between the bride and the groom. This forms part of a marriage ceremony known as *kanthi badal,* and thus plays a role in the socio-religious life of the *Vaishnava* community. *Vilva,* a symbol of the goddess of wealth and its fruits are believed to have been produced from her milk. In *Sri Venkateshwara Ashtottara Satanamavali,* there is a mention that Lord Venkateswara is referred to as *"Bilvapatra archana priyaya nama:"* At Tirumala temple, there is a tradition to worship Lord Venkateswara with *Bilva patra* during the month Dhanu (Dec. – Jan.), and on Fridays. (19)

In South India, especially in Kerala, there is a belief that *vilva* leaves should not be plucked on certain days – on *ashtami* (the eighth day after the new moon), new moon day, full moon day, the first day of the month (Malayalam era), *Somvar* (Monday) and *Chathurthi* – fourth day after the new moon). On such cases, the leaves are collected on the previous day itself. In Kerala, *vilva* is grown mostly in temple premises only; the fruit is not eaten because it is held sacred and believed to symbolize the head of Lord Śiva. Planting *vilva* in house compounds is considered inauspicious in Kerala because for ordinary people it is difficult to maintain the plant in such sacredness and purity. The *Vilva* tree is important to Jains too. The 23rd Thirthankara, Bhagawan Prasnathji, attained *nirvana* under a *vilva* tree. Vilva is the *Sthalavriksha* of most Siva temples. (20)

Of all the Śiva *poojas, vilva patra pooja* is the most sacred. There is a *vrata* known as *Sri Sanipradosha vrata,* performed on a Saturday, hence the name *Sanipradosha vrata.* It is performed in the month of *Shravan (July August)* or *Karthika (Oct. Nov.)* when a combination of Saturday and 13th come together. During this *pooja, vilva* leaf is offered to Lord Siva in twelve steps, accompanied by invocation of the Lord. *Vilva* leaf offered during *Siddhi Vinayaka pooja, Sankastha chathurthi vrata patra pooja and Pushpa pooja, Satyanarayana pooja, Vara Mahalakshmi vrata pooja,*

Margashirsha Mahalakshmi pooja, Sri Swarna Gauri vrata pooja, Harathalika Gauri vrata pooja, Nityasomavara vrata pooja, Sanipradosha vrata patra pooja, Üma – Mahesvara pooja, Sri Venkateswara pooja, Sri Krishna pooja and *Sri Suryanarayana pooja.* (21)

According to *Siva Purana*, the worship of *Vilva* can bestow on the devotee many benefits.: *Vilva* tree is the manifest form of Shiva and hence considered at par with Him. All the holy *tirthas* (holy bathing places) of Hindus reside below the tree and its roots, it is believed. If one worships *Shiva linga* under the *vilva* tree, he will gain Shiva's blessings and eventually reach *Sivaloka* (the world of bliss). One who protects, and maintains the tree and waters it regularly will benefit from the blessings of Shiva. A person who worships the *Vilva* tree with incense and flowers is sure to reach *Shiva-loka,* after death. One, who lights an earthen lamp at the base of the tree daily is dear to Shiva and will attain *Shiva loka.* One, who holds a young blooming branch of the *Vilva* tree and worships it will get absolved of all past sins. One, who devotedly feeds food to a Siva devotee under the *vilva* tree is sure to reap the benefits equivalent to feeding a crore of people. One, who gives food to Siva devotees prepared from milk and ghee under a *vilva* tree, will always remain prosperous.

Of all the offerings to Siva, *vilva* leaf offering is regarded as the most auspicious and beneficial. By offering a lakh (100,000) *vilva leaves* to Śiva, all the desires of devotees will be fulfilled. Installing *Shivalinga* beneath a *vilva* tree is considered a very holy and virtuous deed. He who does so, and offers prayers and regularly visits there can get rid of even the worst sin including *Brahmahatyā* (killing a brahmin). Offering even one leaf is considered highly virtuous. One who offers just a blade of *vilva* to

Śiva attains the virtue of *Somayajña*. He also attains spiritual bliss, which is possibly equal to the offering of a *Śaligrāma* stone to a Brāhmaṇa. Offering *vilva* leaf to Śiva is regarded as above all other virtuous deeds. Giving millions of elephants in charity, performing hundreds of *Vājapeya* sacrifice, or giving away millions of daughters in marriage is equal to the offering of one *vilva* leaf to Śiva. (*Vajapeya* is the highest form of *Soma Yajna*, involving the pressing of "Soma" juice and performed in the autumn season. It is called an *'AtiYajna'* as it is ranked as great as *Rajasuya,* or *Aswamedha Yajna*, which demanded immense manpower and resources). *Vamana Purana* asserts that the one who offers prayers to Lord Viṣhṇu with one lakh *vilva* leaves is bound to achieve the supreme goal of life (*mokṣha* or Salvation). For the worship of Lord Vishnu, *vilva* and *tulsi* leaves are the best. (22)

Social customs related to Vilva

Among the upper-class Newars of Katmandu Valley in Nepal, there is a time-honoured custom known as *Ihi (Ihin, Ehee).* It occupies an important place in the life of a Newari girl. Girls from Nepal's Newar community are married thrice. They are first made to marry a a small golden idol of Vishnu in presence of a vilva fruit, then the Sun, and finally a man, when she attains the marriageable age. The custom involves all the formalities of a real marriage ceremony. It is mostly celebrated collectively by all the families in a community living in a locality. The ceremony is conducted with much pomp and show and ritualistic formalities in the presence of family members, and invitees as in a real marriage. This ritual (*Ihi samskara*) must be done before the onset of menstruation and is conducted at any time between, approximately, five and eleven years of age. At the core of the *Ihi* is akin to a traditional Hindu marriage ceremony, but the spouse is Vishnu/Narayana. The premenstrual virgin girl is given in marriage to the deity as a gift or offering in the traditional Hindu marriage act called *kanya dan*, "the giving of a virgin daughter." Because of this prior gift in the Newar mock marriage, the *kanya dana* segment of the marriage ceremony is, in contrast to traditional South Asian practice, omitted in Newars' true marriage ceremony. Newar traditions ensure that even in the unfortunate event of the death of the girl's husband in life later, because of her prior marriages, the girl will not be deemed a widow, which was looked upon with great disdain and intolerance by older societies. These traditions may therefore have been designed by the Newars to save their little girls from scornful treatment by the community. (24)

The legend behind the *Ihi* ceremony is as follows: Parvati was the daughter of Himavan, the deity of the Himalayas. When she was to be married to Siva, Himavan gave Nepal (that is, the present Kathmandu Valley) to her as the dowry. One day, as Parvati was walking through the Valley, she heard an old woman crying. Parvati asked her why she was crying. "My husband is dead. A husband is necessary for a woman; without a husband a woman's life is terrible." Parvati pitied her and asked Siva for a boon. "Can you do something for the women of my natal home so that they will not become widows?" Siva answered, "Narayana and I will arrange it so that there will no longer be any widows in Nepal." Thus, the Newars were given the *Ihi* ceremony. Here, Narayana is the groom, and Siva is the witness. (25). Due to this ceremony, there are no widows in the community. When the legal husband of a woman dies, she is not considered a widow because she is married to Vishnu, and so already has a husband that is believed to be still alive. This was done basically to dodge the tradition of the inhuman 'Sati' ritual, where after the husband dies, the widow sacrifices herself in the burning fire. This custom was prevalent in the Upper caste Hindus until it was banned by the British Government.

On the day of the Ihi ceremony, girls are given ceremonial baths and are dressed in new clothes (mostly in red or red and yellow silk) and adorned with jewellery. Each girl is given a bael fruit (representing Siva, the witness) and a gold image of Lord Vishnu (Suvarnakumaran, symbolizing the bridegroom). A priest performs the marriage ceremony in a decorated arena where the presiding deities are invoked. For the marriage, unblemished bel fruits are selected. The parents perform the *kanya daan* ceremony; then married women apply vermillion at the parting of the girl bride's hair. All formalities of a real marriage are observed in marriage too. The *vilva* fruit and the gold image of Vishnu used in the marriage are preserved in the girls' home; the *bael* fruit is sometimes immersed in a temple water tank. (26, 27).

Worshipping Bilva tree

To worship the *Vilva* tree, early morning (*Brahma muhurta*) is considered the ideal time. One should get up early, and take bath before sunrise. One should wear white clothes while worshipping a *Bilwa* tree. Clean the base of the *Vilva* tree, sprinkle water on the ground and the tree trunk and spread a new white cloth below the tree close to the trunk, which forms an altar for the pooja. Light a lamp, then offer sacred items such as sandalwood paste, incense, flowers, fruits, sesame seeds, grains etc to the tree. Sandal paste and Vibhuti (holy ash) are applied to the tree trunk. Following the offering, the following prayer is chanted, ideally 108 times. The prayer is:

> *"Shrinivas Namatestu Shrivriksha, Shivavallabhe Mamaabhilakshitam Kritva Sarvavighraharo Bhava"*

Devotees use a *Rudraksha japamala* for counting the prayers. Subsequently, incense sticks are lighted and *aarati* is conducted while circumambulating the tree three times. The devotee then recites the *bilvashtakom.* Once recitation is over, the devotee prostrates before the tree and reverently touches the tree with his / her forehead. After that the devotee takes a bit of the sweet item offered and eats it. That completes the pooja. The devotee collects all items, returns home and distributes the prasad to the family members.

Vilvashtakom

Vilvasatakom is a composition of Aadi Jagadguru Sri Shankaracharya. It is considered a powerful mantra that eulogizes the power and glory of *vilva* leaf. This is to be recited while offering *vilva* leaves to Sivalingam. The *vilva* leaves are to be offered in a group of three. The *vilvashtakom* is given below together with the English translation.

> *tridalaṃ triguṇākāraṃ trinĕtraṃ ca triyāyudham.*
> *trijanma pāpasaṃhāram ĕkabilvaṃ śivārpaṇam..1..*

I offer one leaf of *vilva* to Lord Śiva,

Which has three leaves,

Which causes three qualities,

Which are like the three eyes of Śiva,

Which is like the triad of weapons,

And which destroys sins of three births.

triśākhaiḥ bilvapatraiśca hyacchidraiḥ komalaiḥ śubhaiḥ.
śivapūjāṃ kariṣyāmi hyekabilvaṃ śivārpaṇam.. 2..

I offer one leaf of *vilva* to Lord Śiva,

Which has three shoots,

Which do not have holes,

Which are good and pretty,

And worship Lord Śiva.

akhaṇḍa bilvapatreṇa pūjite nandikeśvare.
śuddhyanti sarvapāpebhyo hyekabilvaṃ śivārpaṇam..3..

I offer one leaf of *vilva* to Lord Śiva,

For if an uncut leaf offered,

To his steed the god Nandi,

We get cleaned of all our sins.

śāligrāma śilāmekāṃ viprāṇāṃ jātu cārpayet.
somayajña mahāpuṇyam ekabilvaṃ śivārpaṇam.. 4..

I offer one leaf of *vilva* to Lord Śiva,

For it is equal to, offering a *Saligrama* to a brahmin,

Or the great blessing got out of performing *soma yaga*.

dantikoṭi sahasrāṇī vājapeya śatāni ca.
koṭikanyā mahādānaṃ ekabilvaṃ śivārpaṇam..5..

I offer one leaf of *vilva* to Lord Śiva,

For it is equal to gifting a thousand elephants,

Or the performing of hundred fire sacrifices,

Or giving away billions of girls in marriage.

lakṣmyāstanuta utpannaṃ mahādevasya ca priyam.
bilvavṛkṣaṃ prayacchāmi hyekabilvaṃ śivārpaṇam..6.

I offer one leaf of *vilva* to Lord Śiva,

For it is equal to giving a tree of *vilva*,

Which was born from the breast of Lakshmi

And which is very dear to the Lord Śiva.

darśanaṃ bilvavṛkṣasya sparśanaṃ pāpanāśanam.
aghora pāpasaṃhāraṃ ekabilvaṃ śivarpaṇam.. 7.

I offer one leaf of *vilva* to Lord Śiva,

As seeing and touching of a tree of *vilva*

Washes away ones sins and also very great sins.

mūlato brahmarūpāya madhyato viṣṇurūpiṇe.
agrataḥ śivarūpāya hyekabilvaṃ śivārpaṇam.. 8..

I offer one leaf of *vilva* to Lord Śiva,

As Brahma resides at its bottom,

Lord Vishnu lives in its middle,

And Lord *Śiva* lives in its tip.

bilvāṣṭakamidam puṇyaṃ yaḥ paṭhet śivasannidhau.
sarvapāpa vinirmuktaḥ śivalokamavāpnuyāt..

Reading this holy octet of *vilva*,

In the presence of Lord Śiva,

Would save one from all sins,

And in the end, take him to the world of Śiva.

"Composed by Sri Adi Shankaracharya, the famous *Bilvashtakam* extols the virtues of the *Vilva* leaf (also spelt *Bilva, Bilwa*) and Lord Shiva's love for it. *Shri Shiva Bilvashtakam* is a very powerful chant that describes the power and glory of offering *vilva* leaves to Lord Shiva. They are to be offered in a group of three leaves and are said to have features that identify them with Lord Shiva himself. The *Vilva* leaf is trifoliate which signifies the holy Trinity: Brahma, Vishnu and Maheshwara. It also signifies the three eyes of Shiva. it is difficult to understand its greatness. Blessed are the ones who offer the *vilva*. One Bilva is equal to a thousand lotus, says the Siva Purana. According to the Skanda Purana, the *vilwa* (Bel) tree grew from the sweat droplets of Parvati which fell on the Mandrachal mountain. From there the *vilva* tree emerged. Hence, it is believed that the Goddess resides in this tree in all Her forms. She resides as Girija in the roots of the tree, as Maheshwari in its trunk, as Dakshayani in its branches, Parvati in its leaves, Katyayani in its fruit and as Gauri in its flowers. Therefore, as Parvati resides in Her various forms in this tree, Shiva is extremely fond of its leaves." (28)

A report that appeared in a Tamil newspaper on January 15, 2010, says: (translation):

At the Siva Temple in Thepperumanallur, large numbers of devotees witnessed a miracle of a cobra doing *archana* (a ritual offering) with *vilva* leaves on Siva lingam. In the Thanjavur district of Tamil Nadu, near Thirunageswaram, there is a Siva Temple at Thepperumanallur. Here, the main deities are Vedhanthanayagi (Sakthi) and Viswanathaswamy

(Siva). In this temple, it has been customary to do *archana* with *Rudraksha* only.

> "Yesterday morning, just before the solar eclipse, at about 10:30 AM, the temple priest, Sivachariar Satish, noticed a cobra lying on top of the Siva lingam. The snake slowly descended from there and went towards the *vilva* tree, the *sthala vruksham* (holy tree of the temple). The snake climbed the tree, picked a leaf, returned, and entered the *sannadhi* (sanctum sanctorum). It hissed at any devotee trying to get near it. It climbed onto the Sivalingam, opened its hood, and dropped the *vilvam* leaf. All of the devotees present there witnessed the miraculous sight in awe. The cobra repeated this activity three times. As the news spread, hundreds of villagers rushed to the temple to see this event of a cobra worshipping Siva. The event has been photo-documented." (29)

Description and Uses:

Vilva (Bilva, vilvam, bilvam) Aegle marmelos (Linn.) Corr.

Bael tree (Bel tree), Wood apple. (Citrus family-Rutaceae)

Bael fruit tree, stone apple, Indian quince (English); bael, sriphal (Hindi, Bengali); bilva, bilvaphal (Gujarathi); bilvapathre (Kannada); bael (Marati); koovalam, vilvam (Malayalam): villuvam, vilvamaram (amil); bilvachettu, maraedu (Telungu).

Bael trees occur throughout the Indian subcontinent; medium to fairly large trees, branches armed with axillary spines, leaves alternate trifoliate, gland – dotted, lateral leaflets sessile, terminal long-stalked. Flowers greenish –

white in short axillary panicles; fruit globose, rind woody; seeds numerous, pulp sweet and cooling, white to light orange.

Vilva is medicinally very important; it is a member of the *dasamoola* group of drugs. *Bhavaprakasa* gives the following properties:

'*Vilva* is astringent, bitter in taste, absorbent, drying, appetizer, increases *pitta*, reduces *vata* and *kapha*. It is strength-giving, light in action, hot in potency, and digestant. Immature fruit is absorbent and controls *kapha*, *vata,* malabsorption and colic. Ripe fruit vitiates all three *doshas*, difficult to digest, irritant, constipative, sweet in taste, and suppresses the digestive capacity.'

Dhanwantharinighantu mentions that *vilva* root is sweet, pacifies all the three *doshas* and are useful in vomiting. Charaka prescribed tender fruits paste in buttermilk to check diarrhoea. Susrutha recommends tender fruit paste mixed with jaggery, honey and oil for checking diarrhoea with blood. Susrutha also recommends the internal use of tender fruits in cases of migraine, internal ulcers and for reducing obesity. Ripe fruit is indicated as an appetizer and laxative and leaves for toning up digestive system. *Ayurvedic Pharmacopoeia* recommends *vilva* root in dysuria and stem bark in diabetes and lipid disorders.

Several chemical compounds were isolated from various parts of *vilva* tree. They include:

- coumarins (like marmin, aurapetin, xanthotoxol, alloimperatorin methyl ester);
- flavonoids (such as rutin, marmesin);
- alkaloids (skimmianine, fragarine or aegelenine, dietamineetc),; triterpenoids (lupeol, betulinic acid, protolimonoids, tannins, condensed tannins and

- aromatic acids such as cinnamic acid and methoxy benzoic acid).

Vilva root is an ingredient of the famous *dasamoola* group, a standard remedy used for many centuries for treating loss of vitality, appetite, and inflammations. Currently, leaf is used as an anti-diabetic drug. It is useful in treating hyperthyroidism, as its extract is found to reduce serum levels of the thyroid hormone, triiodothyronine. In Ayurveda, it is an ingredient of many formulations such as *vilvataila, vilvarasayanasava, vilvaditaila, bilvadi leha, dasamularishta, jeeraka – vilvaadi – lehya, vilvadi-vati* etc. (30).

Citations and notes

(General references listed at the end of the book)

1. *Vilvashtakom*, Translation by PR Ramachander

2. Ravindran PN (2020) Sacred and Ritual Plants Of India. Notion press, Chennai.

3. Tagore GV (2021) The *Skanda-Purana*, Chapter 250, https://www.wisdomlib.org/hinduism/book/the-skanda-purana/d/doc502229.html.

4. Ravindran (see 2)

5. Malla BL (2000) Trees in Indian Art, Mythology, and Folklore. Aryan Books International, Delhi.

6. Sengupta, S. (2013) *Navapatrika:* Worship of nature's creative force, http://www.prabashipost.com/n-61kolabou.aspx#. V4Ocgrh97nE., 2013.

7. Ravindran (see 2)

8. Sengupta (see 6)

9, Ravindran (see 2)

10. *Shilparatna:* Quoted from Malla, see (5)

11. *Sri Tatvanidhi.* It is a voluminous compilation made in the early nineteenth century from hundreds of old texts under the direction of Krishnaraja Wodeyar III (1780-1865), then King of Mysore. It is divided into nine sections (called "treasures," nidhis), describing traditional poetry, arts, music, as well as contemporary games and entertainment.

12. Gopinatha Rao, T.A. Elements of Hindu Iconography, 2 vols,. 1914. Quoted from Malla, see (5).

13. Debroy B (2022) A Hunter's Penance: Divine intervention graces forgiveness. https://openthemagazine.com/columns/a-hunters-penance/

14, Advaitadas (2007) Beltalāy – under the Bilva tree. https://madangopal.blogspot.com/2007/05/beltalay-under-bilva-tree.html.

15 - 18. Ravindran (see2)

19. Anonymous (2024) *Bilva. Samskaram*, https://samskaaram.com/nature_spirituality/bilva... A5%8D%E0%A4%B5/.

20 - 22. Ravindran (see 2)

23. Singh M (2018) Nepal's Newari community: Where girl marry a fruit and the sun. http://timesofindia.indiatimes.com/articleshow/64643311.cms?utm_source=contentofinterest&utm_medium=text&utm_campaign=cppst.

24. Shakya U (2010) Newar Traditions: A Ceremony Called Life.https://ecs.com.np/features/newar-traditions-a-ceremony-called-life.

25. Levy RI (1991) Mesocosm: Hinduism and the Organization of a Traditional Newar City in Nepal. University Of California Press, Berkely, USA.

26. Majupuria, T.C. and Majupuria, I. (1978) Sacred and Useful plants and Trees of Nepal. Sahayogi Prakashan, Kathmandu.

27. Sharma, D.D. (2000) Peculiar Customs And Rites of The Himalayan People. Mittal publications, New Delhi.

28. Ravindran (see2)

29. Anon. (2024) Bilwashtakom. https://shlokam.org/bilvashtakam/.

30. Ravindran (see 2)

07

LOTUS

The Cosmic Flower

(Note: This chapter is adapted from the author's book: Lotus, the Cosmic Flower, 2017).

The Lotus flower is the symbol of Oriental mystics. In India, the lotus symbolises spiritual purity, indicating the soul that rises from the muddy water of *samsara* (ego-consciousness that binds a person to worldly life and pleasures), unfolding its petals of enlightenment. Perhaps there is no symbolism in Indian poetry, sculpture, and painting more extensive than that of the lotus. No symbol is more sacred in ancient and modern mysticism than the divine lotus or Indian Lotus (also known as the Chinese or Asian lotus). It is called Padma and Kamala, among many other names. It is an ancient and favourite epithet, metaphor, and simile; even the cosmos is believed to have evolved from a divine golden lotus, according to the Hindu cosmogony.

The lotus is the cosmic flower, as the famous theosophist Madame Blavatsky called it; no flower is so much associated with religion, philosophy, art, and sculpture. It is the cosmic flower, and the whole world or even the universe can be visualised as a lotus. Lotus symbolism was intimately linked with Gokul and Vrindavan, the places associated with Lord Krishna. Lotus had a pervasive influence on Buddhism; for Buddhists, it was and still is the most revered object, along with the Bodhi tree. For the Hindus, lotus represents Vishnu, Lakshmi, and Saraswathi. It is thus intimately related to sustenance, wealth, power, progress, purity, knowledge, and learning. The lotus, with its deep association with religion and philosophy, has the power to enlighten and inspire those who contemplate its significance.

The lotus's journey began in the murky distant past of the Lower Cretaceous Period, around 125 million years ago. It has traversed the long geological path, captivated millions and earning their love and respect. From the perspective of the devout Hindu, its journey began aeons ago when the first, the primaeval lotus of a thousand golden petals and the radiance of a thousand suns, emerged from the navel of Lord Vishnu during his yogic meditation, cradling the creator, Lord Brahma. This event occurred in an unimaginably distant past. From that remote past, the lotus journeyed through all the vagaries of nature, geographic upheavals, climatic changes, and so on, to the lotus lakes, ponds, and gardens of China, Japan, Korea, Vietnam, India, Nepal, Tibet, Sri Lanka, Thailand, the Far East, and to the lotus gardens of America. It has traversed many cultures and religions, adorning the gods, goddesses, temples, and art objects, proclaiming its vivacity, greatness, holiness, and highest excellence; unparalleled in beauty and influence, and with universal appeal.

The Lotus flower

Lotus concept in ancient India

The first references to lotus are found in the Rig Veda, in which the lotus flower is mentioned in eight places, mostly used as a metaphor (RV. V.78.7, X.184.2, X107.10, VI 16.13, VII 33.11, VI.61.2, VIII.1,33, X.142.8). Two lotus types are mentioned in the Rig Veda, white and blue (*pundarika*–white lotus and *pushkara* possibly the blue water lily). In the first of the three references cited above, there is mention of the womb, and the foetus (RV. V.78.7, X.184.2, X107.10). Lotus is associated with waters bringing health and offspring, and waters are associated with the Aśvins (divine physicians), who in their turn are associated with the pregnant or delivering woman, which is evident from a later marriage hymn, where there is a prayer addressing Asvins to help a woman (obviously to get pregnant). In stanza 16.13 the lotus is associated with the birth of Agni (O Agni, the Atharvan brought you forth, by churning, from the lotus; from the head, the bearer of all things. Atharvan –

Lord Brahma). (*For details refer to Lotus-the Cosmic Flower by PN Ravindran, 2017*).

Lotus figures very prominently in ancient Sanskrit literature, appreciated mostly for its aesthetic beauty and therefore mentioned very frequently when describing the beauty of a woman. Equally significant is the comparison between lotus, and the divine beings, especially goddesses. In the subsequent centuries, lotus has also influenced the art, sculpture, and architecture of India, mainly from the period of Emperor Asoka, when innumerable pillars depicting lotus motifs were built across the length and breadth of his empire. Lotus has ignited the imagination of painters in China, Japan, and India; they created many paintings of the flower, depicting its moods and fabulous beauty. Lotus has played a unique role in the life of Sri Buddha, from the very time of his birth till his *nirvana*, and subsequently, this flower became the most important symbol of Gautama Buddha and the doctrine that he propagated; thus Buddhism too has intimately embraced the lotus flower. Lotus is also basic in the mythology and traditions of Tibetans, Nepalese, Chinese, Japanese, Thais, Sri Lankans, and other countries where Buddhism survives. In all these countries, legends and myths about lotus are woven into the history and culture of the land and built into the ethos of the people.

Lotus is considered fundamental to the spiritual awakening of an individual. It is emblematical to the *padmasana* (the lotus posture of sitting) and the practice of Yoga. The word lotus is used to express the concept of *chakra*, energy vortices, or the spinning wheels of spiritual energy, located above the spinal axis. The lotus stands for the thousand-petalled golden lotus of the *siro chakra,* the ultimate bliss in yogic and tantric practices.

History of Lotus in India

Lotus concept, from its initial reference in the Rig Veda, has evolved in the subsequent Puranic periods and was further embellished with symbolism and philosophical dimensions. During this period, Buddhists adopted the lotus as an important symbol for explaining some of their difficult philosophical ideas. There are three phases in the development of the lotus concept in the Indian context (3-5)

1. The first phase was the Vedic stage when we got the first references to a lotus (*Pundarika* and *Pushkara*). Here, we come across the first glimpse of the philosophical and symbolic dimensions of the lotus leaf and flower. In the Vedas, lotus was mentioned in connection with Agni, Heaven, Sun, Asvins, Vasishta, cosmic wheel, womb, immortality, and righteousness.

2. In the second phase these concepts were developed further in the Brahmana, Aranyaka and Samhita periods, when lotus leaf and flower were woven into a mythological story and creation myths came into existence. During this time the Agni verse of the Rig Veda branched out into various myths such as the Agni myth, creation myth (cosmogony, lotus, and Prajapathi), the relation of womb and lotus, lotus and heaven and sun, and explanation of the *Pushkara srajau,* and about Asvins in *Satapatha Brahmana.* Further, we have Satapatha Brahmana's interpretation of lotus ponds in heaven and immortality and identification of the river Saraswathi with *vach* (speech – and in this process, Saraswathi comes to be associated with lotus), myths about the origin of lotus and its relation with Lakshmi. This period witnessed further elaboration of the concepts presented in the Rig and Atharva Vedas.

3. The third phase witnessed the development of the concepts of metaphysics and symbolism associated with the lotus and it became the exalted seat of Lord Brahma. The relation of water and lotus, that water does not cling to the lotus leaf, has been first expressed in this period, symbolizing non-attachment and indifference towards the material world. The example of a negative relation between water and lotus emerges at this phase, wherein the lotus leaf is the body and a drop of water on it is the undying soul. Lotus (Padma was the most widely used name in Sanskrit) became a favourite of most gods and goddesses; and as a result, the word Padma became the prefix or epithet to denote many gods and goddesses:

Padmakara – Vishnu, Sun (Surya)
Padmagarbha – Brahma, Surya, Śiva
Padmaguna – Lakśhmi
Padmagruha – Lakśhmi
Padmajatha – Brahma, Lakśhmi
Padmanabha – Vishnu
Padmanivasa – Lakśhmi, Saraswathi
Padmapaani – Brahma, Vishnu, Surya, Buddha
Padmabandhu – Surya
Padmotbhava – Brahma
Padmabhasa – Śiva
Padmabhu – Brahma
Padmamalini – Lakśhmi
Padmayoni – Brahma
Padma lochana (female) – Lotus-eyed lady, Lakshmi.
Padma lochanan (male) – Lotus – eyed man, Vishnu
Padmavasa – Lakśhmi
Padmasnusha – Lakśmi, Ganga, Durga
Padmahasa – Vishnu
Padma – Vishnu

Padmaksha – Vishnu, Surya

Padmalaya – Lakśhmi

Padmavathi – Lakśmi, Manasadevi

Padmasana – Brahma, Śiva, Surya

Padminikantha – Surya, consort of lotus (Padma)

Padmi – Lakśhmi, Vishnu

Padmasaya – Lakśhmi

Padmodbhava – Brahma.

4. The fourth phase is the entry of lotus into Buddhist beliefs and practices. This aspect will be discussed later.

Birth of lotus and cosmos

Lotus plays a prominent role in the Hindu mythology. Puranas (epics) like *Vishnu Purana, Matsya Purana* and *Vayu Purana* give brief accounts of the origin of the Universe. According to such descriptions, the universe existed as a cosmic egg, the *Brhmanda.* The Paraśakthi (The Ultimate Creative Force visualized in the feminine form, the Absolute, the term defies definition) manifested itself and the cosmic egg expanded. In the beginning, only water existed. From the Parāśakthi, Vishnu is the sustaining force of the Universe, manifested. Vishnu spent millions of years in *'yoganidra'* (yogic meditation), and then from his navel grew a golden lotus of a thousand petals with dazzling radiance. In this lotus flower, Brahma manifested. So, according to Hindu mythology, the lotus is the most primaeval object that came into existence; it is indeed the lotus of eternity on which Brahma sits or stands, indicating his birth. This legend of the golden lotus that grew up from the navel of Vishnu holding Brahma, is widely popular, about which Jones wrote:

> "A form Cerulean fluttered o'er the deep;
> Brightest of beings, greatest of the great,

Who, not as mortals steep
Their eyes in dewy sleep,
But heavenly pensive on the lotus lay,
That blossomed at his touch, and shed a golden ray.
Hail, primal blossom! Hail, empyreal gem,
Kamel or Padma or whatever high-name
Delight thee, say. What four-faced godhead came,
Forth from thy verdant stem,
With graceful stole and beamy diadem." (6).

Shantilal Nagar writes in his book, Botanical and Medicinal Plants as Depicted in Ancient Texts, Art & Archaeology from Dawn of Civilization to the Modern Age:

> "...The birth of the lotus has been described in the *Matsya Purana*, according to which Hari, the creator of all the worlds, plays for some time and brings forth out of his navel a wonderful lotus of a thousand petals, shining like a sun. That beautiful lotus, looking like the hair of that high soul, was brilliant like fire and bright like the autumnal sun. That lotus of extravagant beauty began to shine. Thereafter, Vishnu, out of the golden lotus begot Brahma, the creator. This lotus was many yojanas wide, endowed with the qualities of the earth, full of *Gunas* and all *Tejas* and golden colour ..." (7) (yojana = unit of distance in ancient India, defined variously, the consensus is that it is approximately 13km; *gunas*= innate qualities; *tejas* = radiance, shining spiritual powers).

The cosmic egg contained everything – sun, moon and stars, all living, non-living, movable, and immovable matter. The lotus represented the universe. Everything inside the Universe revolves around an axis as the shining stem (axis) represents the axial support by Lord Vishnu (Purusha), similar to the dormant state of life inside an egg.

Other legends on the origin of the primary gods of Hinduism (the Trinity, Tri-murtis) are available in Puranas. *Naradeeya Purana* mentions how the three primary representations of the *Guna-avatar* (qualitative incarnations of the Ultimate – the *Tri-Murthis,* or Trinity) originated from the *Adi Parāśakthi*. In the beginning, Brahma (the creator) originated from the right side of *Parāśakthi*, Vishnu, the preserver from the left side and finally, Śiva, the destroyer from the middle.

Lalithopakhyana and *Devibhagavatha* tell us that the entire universe originated from the *Parāśakthi*. *Parāśhakthi* or *Ādi Parāśakthi* is the Eternally Limitless Power, considered in the feminine form. She is the active energy that both creates and dissolves the entire universe. Everything in the universe was condensed into the cosmic egg (*Brahmandum*), which existed in the *Parāśakthi*. At the time of the new cycle of creation, *Parāśakthi* extended 'Itself' (or Herself) in both male and female forms, and the creation was initiated. From the left eye, which was of the nature of Soma (moon) emanated the creator Brahma and Lakshmi Devi, the goddess of life-sustaining forces like wealth, prosperity, and good fortune. From the right eye, which was of the nature of Surya (sun), came out Vishnu and Pārvathi. From the third eye, which was of the nature of Agni (fire), came Rudra (Śiva) and Saraswathi. As soon as they came into being the complementary pairs joined together; Lakshmi joined Vishnu, Pārvathi joined Śiva, and Saraswathi joined Brahma. Brahma became the creator, Vishnu the preserver and Śiva the destroyer. Parāśakthi herself took up the creation of sun, moon, stars, planets, mountains, Vedas, Vedangas, and divine goddesses and gods such as Bālaadevi,

Shyamala Devi, Varāhi devi, Vighneswara, Sampatkare devi, Gayathri, Nakuleshari devi, various devas and so on. Brahma was entrusted with the rest of the creation. The *Devi sukta* (hymn on Devi) of Rig Veda (10.125.8) tells us:

> "I (Devi) have created all worlds at my will, without being urged by any higher being, and I dwell within them. I permeate the earth and heaven, all created entities are with my greatness, and I dwell in them as eternal and infinite consciousness".

The legend of the creation also appears in the famous *Agama Pancharatra* text, *Lakshmi Tantra.*

Lotus leaf too has played an important role in the creation myth according to the narrative found in the *Krishna Yajurveda*. In *Taittiriya Samhita*, we find that Lord Brahma in the form of wind swayed on a lotus leaf alone in the causal waters. On the lotus leaf, he piled up a fire, thereby turning the leaf into a stable earth. *Taittiriya Samhita* says that:

> "Waters were the world at first, the moving ocean; Prajāpati, becoming wind, rocked about on a lotus leaf; he could find no support; he saw that nest of the waters, on it he piled the fire, that became this earth; then indeed he found a support."

Satapatha Brahmana (SB) has also reiterated the concept that Prajāpati puts it down on the lotus-leaf; the lotus-leaf is a womb: in the womb, he thus places him (Agni). According to the *SB*, the Prajāpati (Brahma), transformed into a wild boar dived into the eternal causal waters to discover the origin of the lotus leaf. He reached the bottom, however, could not find the origin of the lotus. He brought above a ball of matter from the ocean bed ('soil') and spread it out on the lotus leaf thereby creating the earth. In *SB*, it is said that in the beginning there was nothing except the expanse of the primordial waters, and in it was Brahma Prajāpati. He beholds a huge and vast lotus leaf. Brahma in the form of a boar seized her. She, becoming Viswakarma, extended and became the earth, and hence came to be known as *Prithvi* (earth), literally meaning the extended one. (For further details see the book Lotus-The Cosmic Flower.)

Lotus – pink and white – showing the central torus and stamens.

Myths about the origin of Lotus

Lotus is the most captivating flower in the aquatic environment and this fact has led to the origin of many myths associated with it. Generally, lotus is associated with strength and power, which according to the ancient lore, is obtained from heavenly bodies. A myth about the origin of lotus alludes to the fight between Indra and Vritra, the invincible demon. In Vedic mythology, the dark side of nature, particularly drought and darkness is personified as the demon Vritra. Indra finally killed the asura with the weapon, vajra (thunderbolt). In *Maitrayani Samhitha* of *Krishna Yajur Veda*, we get the reference:

> "Indra slew Vritra. These two (earth and heaven) obtained his forms; she (earth) obtained the variegated forms and he (heaven) the heavenly bodies. Through the down-shining of celestial bodies, the lotus (*Pundarika*) sprang up. It is a form of power."

Panchavimsa Brahmana gives the same story:

> "Indra slew Vritra when earth obtained his variegated forms (and) heaven his appearances. Through the down shining of heavenly bodies the lotus (*Pundarika*) is born. In that, he (the sacrificer) fastens a lotus garland (*puskasrajam*) on himself to avail the appearance of Vritra's power."

In *Satapatha Brahmana*, the same idea is repeated:

> "Lotuses are appearances of heaven, appearances of heavenly bodies". In short, the above references affirm that the lotus was born out of the light of the heavenly bodies, thereby alluding to the power associated with these flowers. In *Taittariya samhita*, there is the reference: 'Growing mighty

like the lotus flower, do thou extend in width as the heaven?'

Lotus is also connected to the creative energy of Varuna, the god of oceans and rishi Angiras to emphasize the supernatural strength of this highly esteemed flower. In the *Panchavimsa Brahmana,* there is a passage: The lustre of Varuna departed as he was consecrated. It fell into three parts. One-third became Bhrugu (the seer), one-third *srayantiya* (saman, which refers to the Sāma Veda and its mantras), and a third part entered the water and became the lotus. He, who puts on a lotus garland, achieves that virility.

Varuna, during Vedic times, was regarded as the universal monarch. He was also associated with water, and lotus was the symbol of water, hence became the symbol of the lustre of Varuna. During Vedic rituals like *Rajasuya*, the king put on a lotus garland to obtain the lustre of Varuna, the universal monarch. There is also another legend provided in *Taittariya Samhita* that Angiras (mind-born son of Brahma), while doing intense penance (*tapas*) became so radiant that the heat and light from him served the purpose of an Agni (fire), and knowing this Agni (the God) withdrew from earth and hid in a forest. When Angiras came to know about it, he went to Agni and promised that he would reduce the brilliance. He also managed to get a boon that he would be the first son of Agni. The brilliance from Angiras entered the water and became the lotus.

None of the legends mentioned above is famous or popular among the people, only the lotus that sprang up from the navel of Vishnu is popular. The lotus, since it had originated from Vishnu, is held sacred by all Hindus. This flower came to be associated with the Buddha and Bodhisattvas and became sacred to Buddhists.

In the ancient texts, the lotus leaf is referred to as a symbol of non-attachment; for a character and attitude uncorrupted. *Chandogya Upanishad* gives an example of the relation between a lotus leaf and water to explain the mental condition of one who has attained the knowledge of *Brahman*, which is the ultimate knowledge. Such a person's mind never clings to anything material or evil thoughts, just as water does not get attached to the lotus leaf.

The Teacher said:

> "My friend, they (friends of the disciple) have taught you about the worlds, but I shall tell you this; as water does not cling to a lotus leaf, no evil deed clings to one who knows it."

The same idea has been mentioned in the Gita as well: He, who performs selfless actions, offering them to Brahman and abandoning attachment, is not tainted by sin as a lotus leaf by water. Lotus leaf thus became the best image to use for explaining non-attachment and has remained prominent in Buddhist literature as well.

Association with Hindu Gods and Goddesses.

Brahma

The Lotus has been referred to on several occasions in the *Puranas* as this flower is associated with many legends, gods, and goddesses. Brahma is associated with lotus in more than one way. He was born inside a lotus (the lotus of eternity) that emanated from the navel of Vishnu. He is seated on a lotus (the lotus of eternity). He stays in *Pushkara Thirtha* (lake of lotuses, the lake of eternity). As mentioned earlier, the legend of the first lotus flower originating from the navel of Lord Vishnu holding Lord Brahma in it is so well known and can be found in most of the *Puranas* with minor variations. While Vishnu was immersed in yogic meditation in the eternal waters, a lotus flower grew from his navel. On that lotus, the four-headed Brahma manifested as sitting in *padmasana* (lotus posture). He did not see anything except that lotus flower and wanted to know about his own identity. So, he entered the hollow tubular stalk of the lotus flower and started his search; however, he could not find the source of the origin of the lotus. He, therefore, returned to the same place and sat in the lotus. Suddenly a voice resounded that directed him to do penance.

Brahma stands for the spiritual evolving or developing energy-consciousness of a solar system, called the Egg of Brahma (*Brahmanda*). Brahma is called the creator or Logos (a Western philosophical term, originally used for a principle of order and knowledge). Burnouf, the great Oriental scientist, expressed the idea perfectly when he wrote about Brahma:

> "Having evolved himself from the soul of the world, once separated from the first cause, he evaporates with, and emanates all nature out of himself. He does not stand above it, but is mixed up with it; Brahma and the universe form one Being, each particle of which is in its essence Brahma himself, who proceeded out of himself" (8)

The word 'Brahman' is both masculine and neuter, and therefore has two meanings. According to Blavatsky:

> "In the masculine (Brahma), it is the evolving energy of the cosmic egg, as distinguished from the neuter (Brahman). Brahma is the vehicle or sheath of Brahman. The *Vishnu-Purana* says that Brahma in its totality has essentially the aspect of *Prakriti*, both evolved and unevolved (*mūlaprakriti*), and the aspects of spirit and of time. Brahma, as 'the

germ of unknown Darkness,' is the material from which all evolves and develops 'as the web from the spider, as foam from the water,' etc. Brahma the 'Creator' is, as a term, derived from the root *brih*, meaning to increase or expand. "Brahma 'expands' and becomes the Universe woven out of his own substance." (9)

In an iconographical manner, Brahma is represented with four hands and faces (pointing to the four cardinal directions and representing the four Vedas) and with a white beard on each of the faces, a symbol of his long period of existence since the beginning of time. His four hands hold *akshamala* (rosary, representative of time), *kamandalu* (water pot with water; representative of creation, life, and all creations that emanated from him), a *sruva* (ladle, associated with the pouring of holy ghee in sacrificial fire, which signifies that he is the lord of all sacrifices) and one hand holding the sacred book (Veda). The hand with the rosary is held in *Varada mudra*. Brahma is represented either as sitting or standing in a pink lotus. His dress is the black hide of an antelope; in paintings, he is shown as wearing white, red, or pink. His vehicle is a swan, which is a symbol of intelligence and discretion. (10, 11)

Vishnu

Lotus is Vishnu's favourite flower; it is held as sacred as thulsi (holy basil). Vishnu holds a fully opened lotus flower in one of his hands and the other three, he carries *chakra* (bladed discus by the name Sudarśanam), *gada* (mace by the name Kaumodaki) and *shankh* (conch by the name *Paanchajanyam*). Vishnu's lotus symbolizes his power and that he is the source of the unfolding of life and soul and represents absolute truth, *dharma* righteousness), and *jnana*(knowledge). In his incarnation as Varaha, he holds a lotus flower in one of his hands. Lakshmi's image is on the left of Vishnu and she holds a lotus in her hand.

The lotus in Vishnu's lower right hand symbolizes:

a) Spiritual liberation, divine perfection, purity, and the unfolding of spiritual consciousness within the individual; the lotus opening its petals in the light of the Sun is indicative of the expansion and awakening of our long dormant, spiritual consciousness in the light of god;

b) Indicates that he is the power and source from which the universe and the individual soul emerge;

c) It also represents Divine Truth, the originator of the rules of conduct or righteousness and Divine Vedic knowledge.

d) The lotus symbolizes Vishnu as the synonym of spiritual perfection and purity and the wellspring of these qualities and the individual soul must seek to awaken these intrinsic Divine qualities from Vishnu by surrendering to and linking with Him. (12).

Vishnu is also known by lotus epithets, such as:
Padma, Padmi – having the complexion of lotus, lotus-like
Padmalochana – having eyes like lotus petals
Padmahasa – having a lotus-like smile
Padmaksha – having eyes like lotus petals
Padmanabha – having lotus on his navel
Padmakara – having lotus in hand.

Lakshmi

Goddess Lakshmi, known commonly as Maha Lakshmi, Sri Lakshmi or Sri, is inseparable from the lotus flower. From the mythical Ocean of Milk, standing on a pink lotus, the goddess of beauty, the peerless Sri, arose out of the waves:

'Queen of the gods, she leapt to land,
A lotus in her perfect hand;
And fondly, of the lotus sprung,
To lotus-bearing, Vishnu clung,
Her, gods above and men below,
As beauty's queen and fortune know."(13)

Lakshmi is the goddess of love, prosperity, beauty, and all complementary qualities essential for sustenance; she is eternal, has imperishable qualities and is inseparable from Vishnu, the all-prevailing productive power. Lakshmi is portrayed as enchantingly beautiful, standing or sitting in a pink lotus and holding lotuses in each of her two hands. She is also adorned with a lotus garland. Laksmi's idols are depicted with four hands holding *Padma* (lotus), *Sankha* (conch), *Amruta kalasa* (pot of ambrosia), and *Bilva* fruit. When depicted with eight hands, bow, arrow, mace and discus are added; that is the form usually known as Mahā Lakshmi (or Adi Lakshmi), which is a representation as she emanated from the Parasakthi. If Lakshmi is pictured as dark in complexion, she is represented as the consort of Vishnu. In Golden yellow, she is the source of all wealth (Dhana Lakshmi); in the white form, she is symbolic of the purest form of *'Prakriti'* (Mother Nature), in the pinkish form she is the goddess of compassion as she is the mother of all. Her four hands signify her power to grant the four *purushardhas* (*dharma* – righteousness, *artha*-wealth, *kama* – the pleasure of the body and *moksha* – beatitude). She holds lotuses in different stages of blooming that represent the world and its beings at various stages of evolution.

Lakshmi has mainly eight forms, known as *Ashta Lakshmi*, eight manifestations of the Goddess, though she has many other manifestations apart from these. All the forms are associated with the lotus. Ashta Lakshmi (eight forms of Lakshmi) is associated with eight forces or energies. They are *Sri* – Wealth, *Bhu* – Earth, *Sarasvati* – learning, *Priti* – love, *Kirti* – fame, *Shanti* – peace, *Tushti*–pleasure, and *Pushti* –strength. In their manifestations as Ashta Laksmi, she is the bestower of all the above boons. The eight forms include Ādi Laksmi (or Mahā Lakshmi, the primaeval Lakshmi as originated from the *Parashakthi)*, Dhana Lakshmi (showers continuing wealth), Dhānya Lakshmi (giver of abundant crops and prosperity), Gajalakshmi (giver of cattle wealth and royalty); Santāna Lakshmi (blesses with children and continuing progeny); Vijaya Lakshmi (bestows victory in all the efforts), Vidyā Lakshmi (the bestower of knowledge). According to some sources, other forms of Lakshmi are indicated: Aishwarya Lakshmi (bestower of prosperity), Soubhāgya Lakshmi (giver of continued prosperity in all fields), Rajya Lakshmi (bestower of blessings to the rulers and nations), Vara Lakshmi (bestower of boons; a form widely worshipped especially by women). Iconographically all the forms are depicted as sitting or standing in lotuses. Lakshmi's vehicle is shown as Uluka (owl, by the name Peechaka) and there is a whole lot of symbolic significance attached to this bird being kept as her vehicle (14-16).

The attributes of the main forms of *Ashtalakshmi* are:

- Ādi Lakshmi (Mahā Lakshmi): Eight or four-armed in red garments. When four-armed, each arm carries a lotus and a white flag; two arms show *abhaya* and *varada mudras*. In the eight-armed form, bow, arrow, mace, and discus are added to the attributes.
- Aishwarya Lakshmi (Soubhagya Lakshmi): Four-armed, in white garments, carries two lotuses,

and the other two arms are in *abhaya mudra* and *varada mudra.*

- Dhana Lakshmi: Six-armed, in red garments; carries *chakra* (discus), *shankh* (conch), *kalasha* (water pitcher with mango leaves), *amrita kumbha* (pot of ambrosia), bow and arrow, a lotus, and an arm in *abhaya mudra* with gold coins falling from it.
- Dhānya Lakshmi: Eight-armed, in green garments, carries two lotuses, gada (mace), paddy crop, sugarcane, *kadali* (banana) and the other two hands are in *abhaya mudra* and *varada mudra.*
- Gaja Lakshmi: Four-armed, in red garments, carries two lotuses, other two arms in *abhaya mudra* and *varada mudra*, surrounded by two elephants showering water on her with pitchers in their trunks.
- Santāna Lakshmi: Six-armed, in the red or golden yellow garment, carries two *kalashas* (pitchers with water and mango leaves), a sword, shield, a child on her lap, a hand in *abhaya mudra* and the other holding the child. The child holds a lotus.
- Veera Lakshmi: Eight-armed, in red garments, carries *chakra, shankh,* bow, arrow, *trishul* (or sword), a bundle of palm leaf scriptures, and two hands in *abhaya mudra* and *varada mudra.*
- Vijaya Lakshmi / Vara Lakshmi): Eight-armed, in red garments, carries *chakra, shankh,* sword, shield, lotus, *pasha*, other two hands in *abhaya mudra* and *varada mudra.*

Lakshmi in Padmavathi (lotus goddess) form has four hands, two upper hands carrying lotuses and the lower hands in *abhaya mudra* and *varada mudra.* She imparts freedom from fear, from worldly bonds, and bestows blissfulness (17).

Due to the inseparable association with lotus, Lakshmi is often qualified using the epithets meaning lotus such as:

Padma: Lotus dweller
Padmalaya: One whose house is a lotus
Kamala: Lotus dweller.
Padmapriya: One who likes lotuses
Padmamaladhara: One who wears a garland of lotuses
Padmamukhi: One whose face is as beautiful as a lotus
Padmakshi: One whose eyes are as beautiful as a lotus
Padmahasta: One who holds a lotus
Padmasundari: One who is as beautiful as a lotus
Padmavathi: One who possesses lotuses

Lakshmi is also known by names such as Manushri, Chakrika, Kamalika, Aishwarya, Lalima, Kalyani, Nandika, Rujula, Vaishnavi, Samruddhi, Narayani, Bhargavi, Sridevi, Chanchala, Jalaja, Madhavi, Sujata, and Shreya. She is also held as the *Jagatmātha* ("Mother of the Universe") in *Shri Maha Lakshmi Ashtakam*. Rema and Indira are popular synonyms of Lakshmi.

Saraswathi

Goddess Saraswathi is the Shakti behind Brahma; hence, she is the procreator, the mother of the entire creation. Saraswathi means the 'flowing one'. In the Rig Vedic times, she was depicted as the River Saraswathi; hence, she was associated with fertility and purification. She is *Mahavidya* (knowledge supreme), *Vageswari* (goddess of speech), and *Sarada* (giver of essence). Saraswathi is the personification of all knowledge—arts, sciences, crafts, and skills. Knowledge, being the antithesis of darkness, Saraswathi is depicted as pure white, and being the goddess of all arts, she is supremely beautiful. She is also associated with the lotus flower; her seat is the white lotus flower; hence, she is *Svetapadmasini*, the epitome of purity. White clothes and white lotus also depict the inclusion of all colours, which is symbolic of all-encompassing knowledge. She is the mother of the Vedas and wisdom. Saraswathi is shown with four arms that stand for the four aspects of human personality in learning: mind, intellect, alertness, and ego. Alternatively, these four arms also represent the four Vedas (*Rig, Sama, Yajur,* and *Adharva*), the primary sacred books of the Hindus. She holds a book (Veda) in one hand depicting knowledge, learning, and holy scriptures; a garland in the second hand to symbolise the power of meditation and spirituality; a pot of sacred water in the third hand, which is symbolic of her creative and purifying powers; and in the fourth hand, she holds a *veena* that is emblematic of music, art, and love. Saraswathi is often portrayed as playing the veena with two hands, the other two hands holding the book and the garland. Her vehicle is the swan, and it stays at her feet. The swan is also a symbol of wisdom and discrimination (the belief is that the swan can drink milk alone from a milk-water mixture, indicating its power of discrimination of the truth from the rest of things) and hence stands for vidya (knowledge) (18). In the worship of Saraswathi, the white lotus flower is essential and is also used in many tantric worship rites. Details of such tantric rites are given in books like Lakshmana Desikedran's *Sāradātilakom*, which deals with the tantric worship rites related to Saraswathi. (Readers may also refer to the book Lotus the Cosmic Flower).

Parvathy

Pārvathi (Pārvathy) is the *'shakti'* (power) and consort of Lord Śiva, and she is also regarded as the incarnation of Parāśakthi or *Ādi Parāśakthi* herself. Most Hindu goddesses are variations or emanations of Parvathi. Many names are given to her, and some manifestations, like Durga and Kali, are widely worshipped and related to the tantric forms of worship. Pārvathi, when represented as the consort of Śiva in *Ardhanareeswara* (androgynous form—half man, half woman), is shown with two hands, one holding a lotus (specifically a blue lotus) and the other hanging loosely by the side. She has four hands when portrayed independently; two hold lotuses, and the other two are in the *varada mudra* and *abhaya mudra.*

Pārvathi has expressed herself in many forms, some very well-known. Nine manifestations of Durga, known as *Nava Durga*, are worshipped during the *Navaratri* (festival of nine nights); each day, a particular manifestation of Durga is worshipped. The nine Durga forms are Sailaputri, Brahmacharini, Chandraghanta, Kushmānda, Skanda Māta, Kātyayani, Kālarātri, Mahā Gowri, and Siddhidāyini. The characters of the nine forms are indicated below.

- Shailaputrii is considered the first manifestation of Durga. She carries the *trishul* (trident) and a lotus in her hands. Her vehicle is the Bull, Nandi. Her worship is on the first day of Navaratri.
- Brahmachārini is two-armed, clad in white, carrying a *rudraksha mala* (garland of rudraksha beads) and sacred *kamandalu* (holy water pot carried by sages). She is in a highly pious and peaceful state or is meditating. She is worshipped on the second day.
- Chandraghanta, or Chandra-khanda form of Durga, is 10-armed and rides a tiger. She is a terrible facet of Durga roaring in anger and is worshipped on the third day of *Navratri.* Being a terrible form, she does not carry a lotus.

- Kushmānda is the fourth manifestation, worshipped on the fourth day of Navaratri. She is represented by eight arms, one of which carries a lotus. She dwells in the realm of the sun, and her divine refulgence illuminates all ten-quarters of the universe.
- Skanda-māta is worshipped on the fifth day. She is four-armed; two of the arms carry lotus flowers. She is represented with Lord Karthikeya in infant form, sitting on her lap.
- Katyāyani (Karthyāyani) is the sixth form of Durga, worshipped on the sixth day of *Navaratri*. She is four-armed, one of the arms carries a lotus.
- Kalarātri, also known as Kāli and Bhadra Kāli, is the most violent and ferocious form of Durga, and she is worshipped on the seventh day. Kali is black, wears a garland of skulls, and is sometimes represented as standing or dancing over Śiva. She is the force which governs and stops time (kala). Everything comes from Kali, and she devours everything. Kali is the embodiment of the force of destruction, the divine wisdom which puts an end to all illusions. As she has a fierce form, she does not carry a lotus.
- Mahāgauri (Mahā Gowri) form of Durga has four arms in which she carries a *trishul* and a *damaru*. Two hands are in blessing postures. She is pure and is believed to have been in the form of Devi Parvathi when she did penance to get Śiva as her husband. She is worshipped on the eighth day.
- On the ninth day, Durga is worshipped as Siddhidāyini or Siddhidātri. In this form, Durga is four-armed and seated in a lotus. She holds a lotus, mace, discus, and book. She is the bestower

of all siddhĩs (Ashta siddhis, eight great qualities or occult powers) and victory in all noble pursuits. She rides a lion, which is the symbol of strength and protection. This form of Durga is venerated by Gods, demigods, sages, and holy men (19–21).

- [The eight great occult powers or Divine Siddhis or Brahma Siddhis, are: *Anima* (reducing one's physical self to the size of an atom), *Mahima* (growing one's physical self to an incredibly large size), *Garima* (making one's physical self so heavy as immovable by others), *Laghima* (becoming almost weightless), *Prapt*i: (being able to go/travel wherever one wants), *Prakamya* (being able to obtain whatever one wants), *Istva* (possessing lordship, *Vastva* (being able to control the minds of others. There are other *Ashta Siddhis* mentioned in Ayurveda)].

Krishna and Radha

Lotus played a romantic role in the Radha-Krishna love dalliance at the Vrindavan. Radha's beauty is often compared to a freshly bloomed pink lotus, and Krishna is compared to a blue lotus. Srila Goswami writes (Translation by Sriman Kusakratha Dasa)

> "...yad etad bimbatvallasatimukhamasyahkamalato drisordvandvamcancat-kuvalaya-mriganamivacayat udancan-nasa-srihsuka-nava-yuva-troti-valanal lasad-bandhukebhyo 'pi ca ruci-ghata-rajyad-adharah..."

The reflection of Radha's face is more beautiful than a host of lotus flowers. Her eyes are more gorgeous than moving lotuses or a restless deer. The beauty of her raised nose is greater than that of the beak of a young parrot.

Her glistening lips are more beautiful than the splendid *bandhuka* flowers. (22). (*Bandhuka* flower is the midday flower; also known as scarlet mallow and copper cups, botanically *Pentapetes phoenicea*, shoe flower family).

The feet of Krishna and Radha are compared to lotus flowers, and there is a belief that their feet bear the sign of lotus (one of the 19 opulence of their feet). The significance of the lotus marks on the feet of Krishna and Radha is indicated as follows:

> "The lotus mark increases greed for nectar in the minds of the bee-like devotees who meditate on the lotus feet. The lotus also signifies that just as a lotus grows out of the water, those whose eyes swell with tears upon holding the Divine lotus feet to their heart receive the highest benefit. This mark also shows that the goddess of fortune, Sri Laksmi Devi, always resides at His feet, rendering humble service. It signifies that His feet are so soft that they can only be compared to lotus petals; indeed, upon first glancing at the lotus feet, you would think you were directly seeing fresh lotus blossoms. It also reveals that just as a lotus bloom by day and contracts by night, those who remain steeped in meditation on lotus feet always feel the blossoming and unfolding of brilliant *sattvika* (noble) ecstasies that dispel the darkness of ignorance. Indeed, the bee of the devotee's mind cannot fly beyond the bondage of dry *jnana* (knowledge) and *vairagya* (renunciation) without the temptation offered by the superior nectar of the lotus feet." (23, 24).

Radha's feet are compared to lotuses, and we get references like:

"...Her lotus feet are more beautiful than a forest of blossoming land-growing lotuses....." and "... The lotuses and other flowers here are as splendid as the face and limbs of Sri Radha...."

Krishna's lotus feet arouse rapturous feelings in devotees. They eulogise and sing in praise of his lotus feet. One devotee sing:

"nikhila-bhuvana-lakshmi-nitya-lilaspadabhyam,
kamala-vipina-vithi-garva-sarvamkashabhyam|
pranamad-abhaya-dana-praudhi-gadhadritabhyam,
kimapivahatucetahkrishna-padambujabhyam"

"Those lotus feet of Lord Krishna are the refuge (splendour) of Lakshmi of fourteen worlds. In splendour and beauty, they defeat lotus clusters who take pride in their beauty and are honoured (must be worshipped) as they are capable of giving shelter to humble devotees. May the lotus feet of such a Krishna make the inexpressible joy of *madhurya* or sweetness constantly gush forth in my mind, or in other words, may my mind continue forever to relish the unutterable ecstasy of religious rapture." (25)

The devotee is describing the majestic grandeur of Krishna's feet and wishes that these lotus feet stay in his heart forever. May the rush of *madhurya rasa* (the sentiment of sweet love) always drench his heart, making it soft. The pair of Lord Krishna's lotus feet is the refuge of Lakshmi, who resides in the fourteen worlds and is the site of her splendour. They are the abode of divine majesty (*aishwarya*) and this world's ineffable beauty (*saundarya*). Goddess Lakshmi is also forever steeped in the devotion of these holy feet and they are the site of her playful dalliance.

These feet uproot the arrogance of the lotus forests with their coolness, tenderness, heart-stealing charm, beauty, and fragrance. These lotus feet are worthy of great respect because they assure protection to hordes of bhaktas (devotees) who seek refuge in them. They are famed for making those who bow their heads before them their very own.

Bhakta Meera sang on the lotus feet:

> *man! re paras harikecharan |*
> *subtagsheetalkamal-komal, trividhjvalaharann|* (26)

How lovingly tender, comforting and granter of boons and auspicious are these lotus feet; the innate virtue of a lotus is to distribute coolness; therefore, these lotus feet instantly relieve the threefold suffering. These blue-hued lotus feet douse the searing pain of *daihik* (physical) *daivik* (spiritual), *bhautik* (material), and all other kinds of sorrows. (27)

Srila Goswami has gone rapturous while praying on the lotus feet of Krishna:

> "The faces of Krishna and the Gopis were naturally fragrant like lotus flowers, beautiful like lotus flowers, and sweet like lotus flowers. Why would Krishna and the Gopis not have been bewildered when, in their water pastimes, they hid among the lotus flowers?
>
> Seeing a smiling blossoming blue lotus, and in her heart seeing Krishna's face and relishing its nectar, a frightened Gopi hid amongst her Gopi friends who were splendid like her.
>
> His lotus eyes, surrounded by curly locks of hair, Krishna gazed at Radha as a black bee gazes at

a lotus flower. Frightened, Radha backed away. Then Krishna entered amongst the gopis, which was Radha's army. He defeated them........

The Gopis' words were like the swans' warbling. Their garments were like the nearby waters. Their faces were like lotus flowers. Their restless eyes were like those of black bees. Their graceful limbs were like that of lotus stems..." (28)

In *Sri Krishna Karnamrutham,* we get the mellifluous devotional lines:

"...mukulaya-mana-nayanambujamvibhor
murali-ninada-makaranda-nirbharam
mukurayamana-mridu-ganda-mandalam
mukha-paankajammanasi me vijrimbhitam..."

"May the lotus of my Lord's face blossom within (the lake of) my mind. The eyes of that face resemble the half-closed lotus buds, and the delicate mirrors-like orbs of its cheeks are puffed with the honey of the flute sound." (29).

In *Bhagavatha Purana*, we find many instances of lotus deftly employed as comparisons, epithets, or similes. Look at these lines from the chapters (29 33) that describe the love dalliance between Krishna and Gopis.

"...your lotus-like feet that remove the sins of the embodied souls surrendered to you, which follow the cows grazing grass, that are the abode of the goddess and that stood on the hoods of the serpent, please put them on our breasts and dispel the lust in our hearts..."

"...Oh, You with Your lotus eyes, because of your sweet, charming voice and words that are so attractive to the intelligent ones, these maidservants, oh Hero, are getting bewildered. Please restore us to life with the nectar of your lips..."

"...Your lotus feet grant the highest satisfaction in fulfilling the desires of those who bow down to them and worshipping the one born on the lotus [Brahmâ]. They are the ornament of the earth and the proper object to meditate upon in times of distress. Therefore, please, Oh Lover, Oh Remover of the anxiety, place your feet upon our breasts..."

The Gita Govind and the poems of Vidyapathi contain many mellifluous lines picturing Krishna's lotus feet and eyes.

Other Gods and Goddesses

According to *Matsya Purana*, Vighneswara is portrayed as holding a broken tusk in his right hand and a lotus in his left. Indra is depicted with the thunderbolt in one hand and a lotus in another, while on his left is Indrani, who holds a lotus flower in her hand. A legend in the Mahabharata associates Indra and the lotus; the former lay hidden in a lotus stalk to absolve himself from the sin of killing a Brahmin. Bhairava, the wrathful aspect of Śiva, holds a lotus flower in one hand and represents the purifying nature of the lotus.

The Sun god (Aditya, Surya) is the life-giving deity in Hinduism, and Brahmins worship him daily with the chanting of the Gayatri hymn. According to mythology, Surya is the son of sage Kashyapa and Vinita, and he combines in him aspects of the trinity: Brahma, Vishnu, and Siva; Brahma until midday, Shiva in the afternoon and Vishnu in the evening. His consort is Padmini (Lotus), and he holds a lotus in one of his hands. Sometimes, two lotuses and blue lotuses are shown on his shoulders. Often Surya is depicted riding a chariot, harnessed by seven horses or one horse with seven heads, representing the seven colours of the rainbow or the seven chakras. He is the most important of the *navagrahas* (nine planets). Planet Kuja (Mars, Angaraka, Mangala) holds a lotus in one of its hands, so do Jupiter (Brihaspati) and Venus (Sukra). Chandra (Soma), the Moon God, is depicted as sitting on a lotus and holding a lotus in one of his hands.

Ancillary divinities like Varuni, Vayavi, Rakshovidarini, Sahaja, Mayavati, Vyapini etc, are associated with Śaivism; they are two-handed, red in complexion, carry lotus in one hand and skull in the other. Vaishnavite ancillary deities like Riddhi, Samruddhi, Suddhi, Sakthi, Buddhi, Smruthi, Kshama, Rema, Uma, Kledini, Para, Parayana, Sandhya, Prabha, Nisa, Vidytha, Keerthi, Medha, Saharsha, Sraddha, Lajjha, Jaya, Sathya, Vaani, and Vilasini are golden complexioned, two-handed, and they carry lotus in one hand and the other hand is held in '*abhayamudra*' or in blessing pose. (30)

The lotus is held in high esteem in Thailand due to the prevalence of Buddhism there. According to legend, the Thai Elephant god Erawan (same as Airavath, the white elephant of Indra, the king of gods) has as many as 79,233 lotus flowers blooming on its thirty-three elegant heads and in each of the seven petals of each flower reside seven goddesses, each attended by seven heavenly maidens (31). The Thai people always use lotus blooms, along with joss sticks (incense sticks) and candles, in paying homage to their deities, including the Buddha and the Brahmanical gods such as Phra Phrom (equated to the Hindu God Brahma) enshrined in the famous Erawan shrine in Bangkok.

In Jain mandirs, a *Siddha chakra*, a five-petal lotus symbol, is sculpted on the walls and ceilings. According to Gupta, it represents the concept of the *Pancha paramesthins*, or the five supreme ones in Jainism, namely, *Arhat (Thirthankārā), Siddhā, Achārayās, Upādyaya,* and *Sādhus.*

Lotus and the Buddhist and Jain deities

Buddhism places great importance on the lotus flower. According to Buddhist cosmogony, it was the very first creation of nature. Five holy lotuses appeared at the time of prophesying the enlightenment of five Buddhas in the human world. Four of these were enlightened, and the fifth was yet to come. The four Buddhas were represented in Buddhist iconography by four lotus flowers, the fifth by a lotus bud. Yet another relationship between Buddha and the lotus is related to the belief that the Buddha is a part of the Hindu pantheon as the ninth incarnation of Vishnu. So, his throne with a lotus base, backdrop or canopy parallels the iconography of Lord Vishnu. Such an iconographic feature is seen in the case of Bodhisatva Avalokiteśvara, Padmapani, the Lord with the Lotus in his hand.

As Buddhism spread from India to other South Asian and South East Asian countries (Myanmar, China, Thailand, Korea, Cambodia, Laos, Vietnam, and Japan) in the early centuries AD, the saga of the lotus flower too travelled to these regions. As a result, lotus flowers became popular in these countries and were increasingly used to represent the Buddha. In the architecture of Buddhist pagodas, lotus flowers are frequently depicted with petals turned both up and down. In Buddhist iconography, the Buddha is often pictured as sitting cross-legged in a lotus seat or, occasionally, standing on a lotus pedestal.

Lotus as an emblem of Amitabha, Avalokiteśvara, and Manjusri

The lotus is primarily the emblem of Amitabha, the celestial Buddha described in the scriptures of Mahayāna Buddhism. He is also known as the Buddha of infinite light, as indicated by his name. He is regarded as the Lord of the Padma or Lotus family of Buddhas and Bodhisattvas, whose qualities of discernment represent the transmutation of passion into discriminating awareness or wisdom. Worshipped by millions, Amitabha Buddha has attained a monotheistic status in Buddhism. Amitabha means immeasurable light, also known as Amitayus or immeasurable life span. He is not mentioned in the *Theravada* canon and belongs exclusively to the *Mahayāna* tradition (32).

Amitabha presides over the western part of the universe, the pure land. The sutras such as the Innumerable Life Spaan Sutra and the Sutra on Visualizing Amitayus, originated in India and were translated from Sanskrit to Chinese. According to these sutras, the 'Pure Land' is a world where splendid lotus flowers, as large as cartwheels, radiating blue, yellow, and red lights bloom in water. When a person devoted to Amitabha dies, the Buddha places that person on a lotus leaf, upon which the person will be transported to the Pure Land of Amitabha. There, the person will be reborn from the bud of a lotus and achieve Buddhahood. Amitabha is also known as Padmakumara, by which name he is famous in Korea and Vietnam.

Amitabha's presiding Bodhisattva is Padmapani Avalokiteshvara, the 'Holder of the Lotus', the Bodhisattva of great compassion, and the patron deity of Tibet. Padmapani, meaning 'lotus-handed' bears the attribute of the eight-petalled white lotus as a symbol of his immaculate purity, love, and compassion. As emanations of Avalokiteśvara, the fourteen successive incarnations of the Dalai Lama are each commonly portrayed with his white lotus of compassion in their right hands. Padmapani is also known as the Jewel of the Lotus.

Avalokiteśvara is also known as the 'lotus king'. According to the Lotus Sutra, Avalokiteśvara transforms himself into thirty-three forms to save all the beings in the world. These forms are depicted in various ways; the most famous representation is as an icon with eleven heads and one thousand arms, with an eye on each hand. The Avalokiteśvara pantheon, consisting of his various manifestations and related ones, constitute the Padma (lotus family) in Buddhist iconography. This family represents reality, compared to the Vajra family, which represents wisdom and the Buddha family, which encompasses reality and wisdom. The members of the Lotus family always hold lotus buds a closed lotus; a closed lotus is a flower not yet unfurled and represents the Bodhisattva's vow to awaken all beings. The temple of Rengeo-in (The temple of the Lotus King), in Kyoto, Japan, houses one thousand gilded statues of the thousand-armed standing images of Avalokiteśvara (known in Japanese by the name Kannon), along with fierce-looking images of guardian deities. Such figures were installed with the belief that each arm of the Bodhisattva saves beings in the twenty-five realms, including the six paths of transmigration the world of celestial beings, humans, animals, hungry spirits, fighting demons, and hell. Each statue stands on a lotus pedestal. (33) Avalokiteśvara, known by the name Chenrezig in Tibet, is the guardian deity of Tibet; it is believed that he was the founder of the first Tibetan dynasty, Songtsen Gampo, in the seventh century.

The *Pundarika*, or white lotus, is a specific symbol of the Buddha Shikhin, who attained enlightenment in a previous era while seated before this delicate flower. The *pundarika* is a symbol of rarity and transience, as this flower seldom blossoms, and its delicate petals fall easily when touched.

Manjusri, one of the most worshipped Bodhisattvas, is a devotional deity considered an enlightened Buddha in esoteric Buddhism. He is visualized as meditating in the centre of a lotus, one of his hands holding a lotus and another hand holding a scripture (*Prajñāpāramitā sūtras*), representing his attainment of ultimate realization from the blossoming of wisdom. He is attended by eight 'youths' (representations of the eight wisdoms). (34). (*Prajnaparamita Sutras* are the sutras on 'perfect wisdom'. The *Prajnaparamita Sutras* are among the oldest Mahayana Sutras and are the foundation of Mahayana Buddhist philosophy. These venerable texts are found in the Chinese Canon and Tibetan Canon of Buddhist scriptures.)

Significance of lotus leaf in Buddhism

As mentioned earlier, the lotus leaf also holds much significance in Buddhism and is often used as a symbol for non-attachment in various Buddhist literatures. The Pali Canons have referred to this idea in innumerable instances, and it has become a standard example to illustrate the mental condition of a truly spiritual person. Buddhist disciples must undergo rigorous training to discipline their mind and bodies. Guarding the senses from sensual thoughts is one of the most essential Items in disciplining the mind. We get references on many occasions such as the one given in *Majjhima Nikaya,* the Tathagatha told his disciples:

"…. Just as drops of water roll off a gently sloping lotus leaf and do not remain there, that is how quickly, how rapidly, how easily, no matter what it refers to, the arisen agreeable thing… disagreeable thing… agreeable and disagreeable thing ceases, and equanimity takes its stance…"

In *Majjhima Nikaya*, we get this reference to the lotus leaf:

"… Like water that does not stay on the lotus leaf, the mustard seed that slips from the tip of the row, when not soiled in sensuality, I call him a Brahmin."

[The *Majjhima Nikaya*, or "Middle-length Discourses" of the Buddha, is the second of the five *nikayas* (collections) of the *Sutta Pitaka* (the second of the three divisions of the *Tripiṭaka*, the definitive canonical collection of scripture of Theravada Buddhism. This *nikaya* consists of 152 discourses by the Buddha and his chief disciples, and it is a comprehensive body of teaching concerning all aspects of the Buddha's teachings].

Such references to the negative relationship between water and lotus leaf are prevalent in Buddhist texts.

Lotus leaves

In Buddhist teachings, various stages of spiritual progress have been compared to the different stages of the growth of the lotus till it blooms and to the plant's relationship with water to make the idea clear to the laity.

> ".... Just as a water lily or a blue or a white lotus, born in water, growing in water, having arisen above the water stands unwetted by the water. Similarly, *bhikkhus*, the Tathagata, brought up in the world and conquering the world, lives unsullied by the world....".

In *Samyutta Nikaya,* we get this example of a lotus flower used to drive in a point: (*Samyutta Nikaya* means group – discussions. It is the Sutta Pitaka's third division, containing 2,889 *suttas* grouped into five sections (*vaggas*).

> "It's just like the scent of a blue, red, or white lotus: If someone were to call it the scent of a petal, the scent of the colour, or the scent of a filament, would he be speaking correctly?"
>
> "No, friend"
>
> "Then how would he describe it if he were to describe it correctly?"
>
> "As the scent of the flower: That's how he would describe it if he were describing it correctly."

The holy discourses in Buddhist scriptures are expounded with parables, similies, and metaphors derived from the sacred lotus.

Lotus and Buddhist Ancillary deities

Tāra

Buddhists also believe in a female version of Buddha, Tara, the goddess of universal compassion. She represents virtuous and enlightened action. Tara is supposed to have been born out of the tears of compassion of a bodhisattva (a Buddha-to-be). He wept as he looked upon the world of suffering beings, and his tears formed a lake in which a lotus sprang up, which, on opening, revealed the goddess, Tara. Like Avalokitesvara, she is a compassionate, succouring deity who helps men "cross to the other shore of samsara." She is the protector and leads one to spiritual bliss.

The widely known forms of Tāra are:

- Green Tāra Known as the Buddha of enlightened activity
- White Tāra Known for compassion, long life healing and serenity; also known as The 'Wish-fulfilling Wheel', or Chinta chakra.
- Red Tāra Of fierce aspect associated with the magnetizing of all good things
- Black Tāra Associated with power
- Yellow Tāra: Associated with wealth and prosperity
- Blue Tāra Associated with the transmutation of anger
- Cittamani Tāra, A form of Tārā widely adopted at the level of the highest yoga tantra in the Gelug School of Tibetan Buddhism, is portrayed as green and often conflated with the Green Tāra.
- Khadiravani Tāra appeared to Nagarjuna in the *Khadiravani* forest of South India and is sometimes called the 22nd Tāra.

There is also recognition in some schools of Buddhism of twenty-one Tārās. (35, 36).

However, only two primary forms are commonly represented: white and green. The Green Tāra, with her half-open lotus flower, represents night, and the White Tāra, with her lotus in full bloom, symbolizes day. Together, the two Tārās symbolize the unending compassion of a goddess who labours day and night to relieve suffering. Tāra's attribute of a sixteen-petalled white lotus represents the perfection of all her qualities and likeness to a sixteen-year-old maiden.

The blue lotus (*utpala*) is an attribute of Green Tara and many other Vajrayana* deities. It is also known by the Sanskrit terms *nīlabja, nīlotpala, pushkara*, and *nīlanalina*. Green Tara is usually associated with protection from fear and the following eight obscurations (hidden traits leading to unexplained fear and character states): Lions (pride), wild elephants (delusion/ignorance), fires (hatred and anger), snakes (jealousy), bandits and thieves (wrong views, including fanatical views), bondage (avarice and miserliness), floods (desire and attachment), evil spirits, and demons (deluded doubts). (**Vajrayana* is an esoteric tantric form of Buddhism practised mainly in Tibet. It is one of the three routes to enlightenment, the others being Hinayana, Theravada, and Mahayana). White Tara is a deity associated with long life. She counteracts illness and thereby helps to prolong life. She embodies compassion and is considered white and radiant, like the full moon.

Tara is a succouring and protecting deity and is essential, as she vows to protect the women folk and to remain in female form until all living beings attain enlightenment:

> "There are many who desire enlightenment in a man's body, but none who work for the benefit of sentient beings in a woman's body. Therefore, until *samsara* is empty, I shall work for the benefit of sentient beings in a woman's body!" (37)

The male and female Bodhisattvas commonly bear their emblems on handheld lotuses, with these attributes resting upon the domed pericarp or central dome-shaped torus of these lotuses. The handheld objects differentiate the eight great Bodhisattvas. Among them, Avalokiteśvara is most intimately associated with the lotus. The goddess, White Prajnaparamita, bears the attributes of two texts on the 'Perfection of Wisdom' (Sanskrit: *Prajnaparamita-sutra*), which rest upon white and red lotuses that sprout from the palms of her right and left palms, respectively.

Lotus in Jainism

One Jain deity intimately associated with the lotus is Padmavathi. Padmavathi is adopted from the Sarasvathi of Hinduism. However, in Jainism, she is a Yakshi. She is a subordinate deity to the twenty-third Tirthankara, Parsvanatha. Digambara texts describe the iconographic details of Padmavathi. She is conceived in with two, four, six, twelve and twenty-four arms. She sits in a lotus, like the Hindu goddess Saraswathi. The two-armed form holds a long-stalked lotus in one hand and the other hand held in *Varada mudra*. The earliest representation of the four-armed Padmavathi is found at the Deogarh archaeological sites. The image is labelled as Padmavati. She holds a spiral lotus, a shield, and a water pot in three hands, and the fourth hand is held in *Varada-mudra*. The six-armed form does not hold a lotus. The 12-armed form found in Deogarh carries a lotus in one of the arms. The 24-armed form, too, holds a lotus in one of the hands. (38-39)

In Jainism, there are 16 Vidyadevi's (or Mahavidya's). They are important semi-goddesses in Jainism. Of the 16 *Vidyadevi's,* the following are associated with lotuses:

Prajnapti: She rides a peacock and holds a lotus in one hand and a *sakti* (a weapon like a spear) in the other. Her name suggests 'intellect,' and she is also referred to as Sarasvathi.

Maanavi: She sits in a lotus, and her hands hold a rosary and the bough of a tree in one hand, and the other in *Varada mudra.*

Vairotya: She rides a snake and has 16 arms, one of which holds a lotus flower.

Mahamanasi: She holds a long-stalked lotus in one hand and a fruit in the other hand.

Gauri: She holds a long-stalked lotus in one hand, mace and fruit in two other hands, and one hand held in *Varada mudra.* (40)

Thus, in the three great Indian religions—Hinduism, Buddhism, and Jainism—and throughout the length and breadth of the Indian subcontinent, the lotus forms a pervasive symbol and metaphor, most intimately associated with the deities and religious practices. No wonder the region's people likened it to the human heart, and it became the cosmic flower for the Indians.

Lotus: Philosophy and Symbolism

Madame Helena Blavatsky (often known as Madam B), a Sanskrit scholar and Asian philosopher (and co-founder of the Theosophical Society), writes in her occult philosophical treatise 'Secret Doctrine', published in 1888: (41)

> "There are no ancient symbols without a deep and philosophical meaning attached to them; their importance and significance increase with their antiquity. Such is the Lotus. It is the flower sacred to nature and her gods. It represents the abstract and concrete universes, standing as the emblem of the productive powers of both spiritual and physical nature. It was held sacred from the remotest antiquity by the Aryan Hindus, the

Egyptians, and the Buddhists after them; revered in China and Japan, and adopted as a Christian emblem by the Greek and Latin Churches, who made it a messenger as the Christians do now, and replaced it with the water lily. It had, and still has, its mystic meaning, identical to every nation on earth.

With the Hindus, the lotus is the emblem of the productive power of nature through the agency of fire and water (spirit and matter). "Eternal!" says a verse in the Bhagavad Gita, "I see Brahma the creator enthroned in thee above the lotus!" Sir W. Jones shows, as noted in the Stanzas, that the lotus seeds contain, even before they germinate, perfectly-formed leaves, the miniature shapes of what one day they will become. The lotus, in India, is the symbol of the prolific earth and Mount Meru. The four angels, or genii, of heaven's four quarters stand on a lotus. The lotus is the two-fold type of the divine and human hermaphrodite, being of dual sex, so to say."

Blavatsky further comments:

"The underlying idea in this symbol is wonderful and shows its identical parentage in all the religious systems. Whether in the lotus or water-lily shape, it signifies the same philosophical idea, namely, the emanation of the objective from the subjective, divine ideation passing from the abstract into the concrete or visible form. As soon as darkness, or rather that which is "darkness" for ignorance, has disappeared in its realm of eternal light, leaving behind itself only its divine manifested ideation, the creative logos* have their understanding opened. They see in the ideal world (hitherto concealed in the divine thought) the archetypal forms of all, and proceed to copy, build or fashion upon these models forms evanescent and transcendent." (42)

(*Logos: a philosophical term with many meanings—roughly means the eternal creative principle; in the esoteric philosophy, equated to the demiurge or creator).

The Book of the Dead, the most ancient sacred text of the ancient Egyptians, talks about God's transformation into the lotus; '…. a head emerging from this flower, the god exclaims: I am the pure lotus, emerging from the luminous one. I carry the messages of Horus. I am the pure lotus which comes from the Solar Fields.'

The lotus has been the favourite flower symbol of oriental mystics. In India, it symbolises spiritual purity and a soul that rises from the mud and water of *samsāra* (ego-consciousness that binds a person to worldly life and pleasures) to unfold the petals of enlightenment. No symbol is more sacred in New Age mysticism than the divine lotus of India. Madame Blavatsky, in her Secret Doctrine, states:

> "One of the symbolical figures for the dual creative power in nature (matter and force on the material plane) is PADMA, the water lily of India. The Lotus is the product of heat (fire) and water (vapour or Ether); fire stands in every philosophical and religious system as a representation of the Spirit of the Deity, the active, male, generative principle; and Ether, or the soul of matter, is the light of the fire, the passive female principle from which everything in this universe emanates. Hence,

Ether, or water, is the mother, and fire is the father... The hour had not yet struck, the ray had not yet flashed into the germ; the Matru-Padma (mother lotus) had not yet swollen." (43)

Here, the mother lotus symbolises the creative force from which manifested things emerged. Madame Blavatsky dwells at length on the occult philosophy embedded in these words. The lotus, or Padma, is a very ancient and favourite symbol for the Cosmos and man. The following are the popular reasons given for this:

- Firstly, the fact that the lotus seed contains a perfect miniature of the future plant itself typifies that the spiritual prototypes of all things existed in the immaterial world before they materialised on Earth.
- Secondly, the lotus plant has its root in the mud, grows through the dirty water, and spreads its flower in the air, untouched by the dirt below. The Lotus thus typifies the life of a man and the Cosmos, for the Secret Doctrine teaches that both elements are the same and develop in the same direction. The root of the lotus that is sunk in the mud represents material life, the stalk passing up through the water typifies existence in the astral world, and the flower floating on the water and opening to the sky symbolises spiritual awakening.
- The blossom unfolds petal by petal, and by morning, with the touch of the first rays of the sun, it opens fully. This relationship is interpreted as a symbol of love.

The lotus thus represents the evolution of a person's consciousness (in other words, life itself) from the instinctive, inborn impulses of a child through various stages of higher consciousness (and self-realisation) to the level of the highest enlightenment or liberation from everything, which is the final stage of the blossoming of the lotus. (44)

As the first creation, the lotus has the androgynous nature built into it. In the lotus flower, above the mud and water and untainted by them, the whole cycle of vegetation of life is accomplished. Within the seed, it holds the continuity from bud to flower and fruit and again to the new young plant, the beginning and the end, and the new beginning once again. Within this resides the centre of productivity and the cycle of generations; the mud and water below are but an intermediate medium for the achievement of the final aim of the flower; the flower is then the centre of immortality, of the continuance of generations, of the cycle of beginning and end, of birth and death. As Blavatsky states:

> "It is the womb of the universe, the seat of generation and regeneration; it is a symbol of fecundity. It signifies prosperity and youth. It invokes images of purity and beauty. It suggests detachment and wisdom."

The lotus is a magical plant that evokes rich poetic and spiritual metaphors. Though it grows and blooms on earth, in water, and amidst light, it enacts the transmutation from earth to light, from mud to scent, through the water to gleaming colour in the regularity of its shape and its movements, opening and closing with the measure of time, of days and nights. In Indian sacred art, the most profound and widespread meaning is that of spiritually enlightened beings such as Sri Buddha and Sri Mahavira. Like the lotus, they have arisen from the mire of earthly temptations and have blossomed fully, untainted by the chaotic existence of lower levels.

> "Just as, Brethren, a lotus, born in water,
> Full-grown in water rises to the
> Surface and is not wetted by the
> Water, even so, Brethren, the
> Tathagatha, born in the world,
> Full-grown in the world,
> Surpasses the world and is
> Unaffected by the world" (45)
> (Tathagatha Sri Buddha)

As a newborn child, the Buddha took seven steps to announce his spiritual sovereignty over the earth; in each step, a lotus sprouted from the Earth to receive his foot. In works of art, seven lotuses represent his seven steps. Later, after his awakening under the Bodhi tree, the Buddha is said to have been moved to infinite compassion for his fellow beings. He saw them like stems and buds of a lotus in the lake; some immersed in the mud, others just coming out of it or appearing above the water, and others beginning to blossom. Seeing this, he was determined to bring them all to full bloom and the bearing of fruit. (This idea is mentioned earlier also.)

The self-fertilising power of the lotus makes it a symbol of the androgynous creative god that gives life to matter; thus, it is also symbolic of Goddess Earth, the Bhudevi. As the birthplace of Lakshmi and of the Creator-God Brahma himself, the lotus becomes the metaphoric womb of creation and the womb of the universe (46). Additionally, Lakshmi's depiction in Indian art as Gaja-Lakshmi, bathed by elephants, represents the sky, which pours rain, fertilising the earth, which the goddess herself represents, and the lotus in which she stands. This act is a kind of conception and is like that of Mayadevi, mother of the Buddha, who dreamt that the future emancipator had entered her womb as a white elephant, holding a lotus.

Shantilal Nagar writes in his book (Botanical and Medicinal Plants as Depicted in Ancient Texts, Art, and Philosophy from the Dawn of Civilization to the Modern Age):

> "The lotus has been extolled as the prime symbol of creation, the seat, and substratum of universal creative force, which springs from the navel or centre of the primaeval creator. Simplified to concise Sutra of art, it is expressed as Brahma, the genius of creation, seated in a full-blown lotus with a long stalk springing from the navel of Vishnu. As the lotus floats above the water, the created cosmos emerges to the surface of the primaeval deep or chaos, which originally was the confused mass out of which the order of the universe evolved." (47)

When the divine life substance is about to put forth the Universe, the cosmic waters grow a lotus of pure gold with a thousand petals, radiant as the sun. Zimmer writes in his scholarly treatise Myths and Symbols in Indian Art and Civilisation:

> "This is the door or gate, the opening or mouth of the womb of Universe. It is the first product of the creative principle, gold, as a token of incorruptible nature. It opens to give birth first to the demiurge (creator), Brahma. From its pericarp, then issue the hosts of the created world".

According to the Hindu conception, the waters are female; they represent the maternal, procreative aspect of the Absolute, and the Cosmic Lotus is their generative organ. The Cosmic Lotus is called the 'highest form of or aspect of the earth, 'the Goddess Moisture', 'the Goddess Earth.' It is personified as the Mother Goddess, through whom the Absolute moves into creation (48). Maury, in his scholarly book On the Folk Origins of Indian Art, writes:

> "Though itself of ancient inception, the lotus emblem appears to have been an elaboration of a pre-existent, simpler design; a floral configuration of the circle, always and everywhere the elementary ideograph of the female organs, known in India by the term yoni. This role as the fundamental allegory of female sexuality has endowed the flower with its aura of sacred mystery imparted to its diagrammatic, abstract form, and the lotus has come to present the ultimate equation of female being and female magic; its petals enclose the magic of generation and regeneration; its centre is the omphalos of the universe, the source, and substance of life itself." (49)

Stella Kramrisch writes in her study:

> "India's foremost sacred plant is the lotus.... With its root in the mud, its stalk traversing the entire depth of the waters on which it rests its leaves, its flower open to the light of heaven, the lotus belongs to this world and those below and above, to light, earth, and water... This wondrous plant, having its being in the earth, water, and light, enacts its transmutation from earth to light, from mud to scent, through the water to gleaming colour in the regularity of its shape, not only ordered as it is in all the directions of space but

also in the regularity of its movement, opening, and closing with the measure of time, of days and nights." (50)

The lotus blooms daily with the rising sun and closes its petals in the evenings. Thus, it symbolises the endless cycle of life and death and the cosmic cycle of birth and dissolution of the universe. The lotus is, therefore, an approximate iconographic symbol of Surya. Surya holds two lotuses in his hands, symbolising the upper, *paraa*, and lower, *aparaa* waters, "representing the possibilities of existence 'above' or 'below' in this world and this world, Heaven and Earth.

From the Vedic cosmogony in which the lotus leaf forms an integral part, we also understand that the lotus symbolises the firmament or middle space (*antariksha*), which is why the gods are frequently placed on lotuses. This idea was later adapted when the creator god, Brahma, was shown seated in a lotus springing from the navel of Vishnu or Narayana. Vishnu's navel is the universe's centre, forming the firmament for the Prajapathi. This idea also led the ancient sculptors to place their gods and goddesses in lotuses and to give them a lotus halo and a lotus footrest. From the Gupta period onwards, the Buddhas and the Jain Tirthankaras were also given a lotus halo behind their heads, as well as a lotus support below their feet; in both cases, the halo symbolises the heaven and the earth beneath their 'feet'.

Sehdev Kumar, in his study on the Jain Temples of Rajasthan, has mentioned that the lotus represents earth and water. Thus, it is an appropriate attribute of Sri Lakshmi, the earth's mother, personifying all possibilities of existence and abundance. She is described as Padmavati, a dweller in the lotus, and *Pushti Da*, a provider of nourishment. A frequently used Sanskrit word for lotus is Pushkara, with the same root as *pusht,* meaning nourishment. As stated earlier, Sri Lakshmi is shown in early Indian art as Gaja Lakshmi. The goddess herself and the lotus on which she stands are both representations of the earth. The elephants serve as a metaphor for the sky, which showers rain, fertilising it. This is interpreted as a conception. (51)

The symbolism of the lotus changes depending on who is holding it.

- The lotus emerging from the navel of Vishnu symbolises the earth, while the stalk represents the cosmic mountain Meru, the axis of the universe. When held in the hand of Vishnu, the lotus symbolises water as well as holistic perfection.
- When Sri-Lakshmi holds the lotus, it stands for wealth.
- When held in the goddess Parvati's hand, the lotus symbolises detachment;
- In the hand of Indra, it signifies prosperity and power.

The flower also represents the idea of divine play. The universe and all its manifestations are often characterised as nothing but reflections of the playfulness of the Supreme Being. Pal argues that Buddhists were the first to adopt the lotus as both a divine seat and an emblem held by a deity. By the 2nd century AD, the lotus was adopted as a seat of the Buddha himself, and represented so in the remains found in Sanchi, Gandhara, Mathura, and in the Buddhist remains of Andhra Pradesh. The flower was given to the Bodhisattva long before it became an emblem of Vishnu. Pal thinks that in early Buddhist literature, the lotus is used as a metaphor for essence (*pudgala-pushkala, pundarika*), and one of the early Mahayāna texts is called Lotus of the True Religion or Padma Sutra (Lotus Sutra). (52).

Thus, in the Buddhist context, the lotus symbolises the faith itself and would be an appropriate attribute for Avalokiteswara. Later, in Buddhist iconography, the lotus was often used to support other emblems such as the thunderbolt or book. The most widely uttered incantation associated with Avalokitesvara is *Om mani Padme Hum* (the jewel in the lotus).

From very early times, the lotus has remained the metaphor without parallel for the devotee's heart (*hrid-padma, hrid-kamala, hrid-pushkara*), the primary abode of the deity. The lotus heart is further likened to space (*akasa*): its eight petals represent the compass's four directions and four intermediate points. The eight-petalled lotus is basic to the drawings called *mandalas*, which later came to play an essential role in all three religions. One of the earliest uses of lotus with this symbolic meaning is represented in the ceilings of the Buddhist cave temples at Ajanta (Gupta period). Significantly, tantric spiritual practice requires the practitioner to pass through several stages or processes of cosmogenesis, to the final plane located at the summit of the skull being known as the lotus head (*Ushṇīsha Kamala*), to the Buddhists and the thousand-petalled lotus (*sahasrapadma, sahasra kamala, siro chakra*) to the Hindus. A very early representation of this idea occurs in a mid-sixth century Narasimha, where a lotus grows from the god's head. In the tantric philosophy, the thousand-petalled lotus is related to the crown chakra, which is believed to be identical to the seat of Brahma.

Lotus and Chakras

Lotus has a close relationship with *chakras*. The *chakras* are wheels of energy or energy vortices in tantra or yoga and are related to the concept of *kundalini*, awakened at seven energy levels. Such an unfolding of the *kundalini* is compared to the blooming of the lotus. Invoking the *kundalini* is perhaps the highest level of meditation in the Tantric system. The *chakras* are associated with the five elements plus the mind and enlightenment. In tantric philosophy, *kundalini* is the 'corporeal energy', defined as the unconscious, instinctive, or libidinal force that lies coiled like a serpent at the base of the spine. Through the rigorous practice of yoga and meditation, it is possible to awaken the kundalini, which finally leads to the seventh level of awakening, the *sirochakra,* associated with the thousand-petalled golden lotus.

Seven *chakra* levels are associated with seven types of lotuses. They are listed below (53-55).

- *Mūlādhāra chakra* (root chakra): It is located at the base of the spine and associated with the earth. On activation, the 4-petalled crimson (orange-red) lotus blooms.
- *Svādhisthāna chakra (adhisthana chakra):* Located near the genital area, associated with water, when activated, the 6-petalled vermilion (bluish-red) lotus blooms.
- *Manipura chakra (Manipuraka chakra)* is located in the lower abdomen. It is associated with fire and yellow; the 10-petalled blue-black lotus blooms on activation.
- *Suddha chakra (or anahata chakra):* This chakra is also known as *padma-sundar chakra* and, more commonly as, the heart chakra. It is located near

the heart and associated with air. On activation, a 12-petalled red lotus (green petals according to some Yogic schools) blooms.

- *Visuddha chakra:* This chakra is located at the base of the throat and is associated with the sky and the 16-petalled turquoise-coloured lotus.
- *Ājna chakra or the third eye chakra:* The "third eye" between the brows is associated with consciousness, truth, healing, and single eyed-divine vision; it is associated with the 2-petalled white lotus and with the colours violet, indigo, or deep blue, though it is traditionally described as white.
- *Sirochakra*: Also known as *Sahasrara*, the crown lotus or chakra is at the top of the head. The 1,008-petalled rainbow (multi-coloured) lotus, like a canopy or a fountain, is associated with wisdom and enlightenment.

Some of the minor chakras are also associated with lotuses:

- *Manas chakra*: A chakra known as *manas* (mind) is located between the navel and the heart, close to *the Sudha*, or above *the Ajna* on the forehead. The version on the forehead has six petals connected to the five sense objects plus the mind. In Tibetan Buddhism, the chakra on the forehead is called the 'wind wheel' and has six spokes.
- *Brahmarandra /Nirvana chakra*: In some systems, *Sahasrara* is the chakra on the head's crown. However, other systems, such as that expounded by Shri Aurobindo, state that the real *Sahasrara* is located some way above the top of the head and that the crown chakra is, in fact, *brahmarandra*, a sort of secondary *Sahasrara* with 100 white petals.

- *Shri /Guru chakra*: This is a minor chakra located slightly above the top of the head. It is an upward-facing 12-petalled lotus associated with the Guru (preceptor), the higher force that guides us through our spiritual journey.

The associated *shakthis* of the *chakras* (from the *Mooladhara chakra* upwards) are Dakini, Rakni, Lakini, Kakini, Shakini, Hakini, and Nirvanashakti; all of them are manifestations of the Shakthi (Durga). In the *Hathayoga* systems of yoga, these shakti control the manifestation of their respective presiding chakras, and these representations are symbolic.

The lotus is said to represent sexuality, too. Sexuality is simply the most intimate and best-known manifestation of the cosmic principle of polarity. Everything in the universe comes into being due to the interaction of the opposites, the duality of *samsara*. The lotus thus represents creativity, life and death, birth and rebirth, and the promise of renewal and continuation. Most famously, the lotus represents our life in the four human worlds: the physical, the emotional, the mental, and the spiritual. The lotus symbolises holy wholeness, the yogic union that combines all aspects of our being in harmonious oneness. Lotus blossoms are pink, blue, or white. Pink and blue lotuses represent the sun and the moon, respectively, complementary polarities. But just as white light combines and unifies all colours, the white lotus symbolises the ultimate unified wholeness of all life. The white lotus symbolises the holiness or wholeness that is the aim of human evolution. Like the lotus flower, we are rooted in physicality, often in a very murky, grubby condition. Like that flower, we need to extend ourselves upwards, with the help of a firm stalk through emotional waters to blossom in the pure intellectual air of understanding. We cannot yet reach the blazing sun of spirituality, but we can open ourselves to its warmth and absorb its energy. (56).

Lotus as a Symbol of Immortality

As the seat of Brahma, Lakshmi, Saraswathi, and Agni, Lotus is considered immortal. In Atharva Veda, we get the following reference:

"*Viṣṭārin** is the best carrier of sacrifices. Having cooked the *viṣṭārin*, the one who offered has entered heaven. The bulb-bearing lotus spreads all over the pond, as do the lotus stalk, the root, and the lotus fibre. Let all these streams come to thee, and the complete lotus pond, swelling with honey, let approach thee in the heavenly world." (**Viṣṭārin* is a cooked rice dish used in ritual offerings).

"Let complete lotus ponds swelling with honey approach thee" is an expression of blessing for immortality or blessing for immeasurable and infinite bliss.

In *Satapatha Brahmana,* the lotus is referred to as immortal, and the immortal element is the flame glowing, which is the lotus leaf.

> "Having laid down that which is lotus leaf, he (one who offers) piles up the fire (constructs a fire altar). On that, he prepares an immortal existence for himself, consisting of *ṛk*, *yajas* and *sāman*. He becomes immortal."

This idea led to the spreading of lotus leaves on the ground, on which only the priests built the fire altar of *a yajna (yajna-vedi).* The fire lit on this altar is kept indefinitely in the chief priest's house, thereby making that fire immortal and the lotus immortal. *Jaiminīya Upanishad Brahmana* qualifies the lotus as the flower of immortality. For the Buddhists, it indicates the time or the three states of time – past, present, and future. A partly decayed or worm-eaten leaf represents the past; the present by a handsome open leaf, often called the 'mirror leaf', on account of its resemblance in shape to that of a mirror, and the future by a curled leaf, not fully open.

Lotus as a symbol of non-attachment:

This aspect is discussed in the next section on Lotus and Buddhism.

Lotus, Zen and Zen Koans (Zen canons)

Zen is the Japanese transliteration of Chinese Chan, an abbreviation for *channa,* which arose from the Sanskrit root *dhyana,* meaning meditation or absorption. A semi-mythical South Indian (Kanchipuram) monk Bodhidharman, established the Chan school in the 6th Century in China (Chan School of China). Later, the school was established in Japan and came to be famous as the Zen school of Buddhism. Zen teaching and practice involve highly formalised systems to make a person 'totally aware' of himself and his surroundings. The Zen teaching does not follow any formal system of verbal classes or sermons. Zen masters often speak in enigmatic words, and the training in Zen also involves questions and answers that appear enigmatic and even border on nonsense. The capability of a Zen practitioner depends on the ability to understand such enigmas. In Zen practice, lotus plays an important role, especially in the questions and answers. Buddha once gave a flower sermon to his disciples, and the origin of Zen thinking is said to have been with that sermon.

The Flower Sermon is considered a symbolic origin story in Zen Buddhism, and the founder of Japanese Sōtō Zen Buddhism, Great Master Dōgen, writing in the 13th Century, quotes it frequently in his great work, the

Shobogenzo. Dōgen's retelling of the flower sermon (Face Face-to-Face Transmission, chapter 57 in the translation of the Shobogenzo by Tanahashi et al.) is as follows. (71) (*There is some controversy over the flower that Buddha held up, lotus, not *udumbara* according to most Indian/South-East Asian writings.).

Buddha was addressing a congregation of disciples at Vulture Peak (Vulture Peak Mountain, by tradition, was one of the several sites frequented by the Buddha and his community of disciples for both training and retreat. It is in Rajgir, Bihar, India). When Tathagata (the Buddha) was at the Vulture Peak preaching the dharma, various devas presented him with flowers. The World Honoured One took a white lotus flower, held it to the assembly and winked. Everyone sat there confused as Mahakasyapa (Mahākāśyapa)* smiled. The World Honoured One announced to the assembly:

> "I possess the treasury of the true dharma eye, the wondrous mind of nirvana. I entrust it to Mahakasyapa to spread it in the future, not allowing it to be cut off."

Buddha passed on his entire teaching in an instant, without words. Mahakasyapa had his eyes opened and signalled his understanding without words with a simple smile. This story is an icon of the Zen tradition; Buddha's dharma was and is still passed from Master to disciple wordlessly, mind to mind. (72) From that day, Mahakashyapa became Buddha's successor.

[*Mahakasyapa (Mahākāśyapa, Sanskrit) Mahākassapa (Pali) was the principal disciple of Gautama Buddha. He is regarded in Buddhism as an enlightened disciple, being foremost in ascetic practice. He assumed leadership of the

Buddhist community following the *parinirvāṇa* (death) of the Buddha.]

Another scene:

Buddha was nearing the end of his life span. One day, he led the disciples to a pond where lotuses grew. He stood silently with his back to the pool for a long time. He did not open his mouth; only silence prevailed. Then Buddha turned, reached into the pond, pulled out a single lotus flower and held it up for all the disciples to see. He then took the flower to each of the disciples. All of them were confused and stood there transfixed, not knowing what to do or what the Master meant to convey. Finally, he reached Mahakashyapa (Pali: Mahākassapa).,, who suddenly laughed. Buddha then announced to his disciples: "What can be said I have said to you; what cannot be said I have given to Mahakashyapa". From that day onwards, Mahakashyapa became the successor of Buddha.

Welter has carried out a very critical study of the flower sermon and the Mahakasyapa's smile and concluded that this story was probably fabricated in the later years, as no reference to such an event could be found in the early Chan (Zen) literature. Welter called it the silent transmission of knowledge, and the most receptive minds could only receive it (73). The point Tathagata was making may have been that an enlightened (ego-less) mind (lotus bloom) springs from our egoistic minds (mud). Another interpretation is that Buddha was trying to make a point that all things come and go and that all things are transient, even the most beautiful of flowers, the lotus. Perhaps Buddha's explanation that he silently gave "all that cannot be said" makes it clear that he was not giving his students knowledge but a method to attain the knowledge. As a teacher, Buddha 'gave his disciples an encrypted book and the cypher's key, and asked them to figure out the rest by themselves. (74)

Zen masters treat the lotus flower as an unadorned pointer for awakening. The founder of the Rinzai Zen School, Hakuin (Hakuin Ekaku), was an outstanding teacher and Master. He introduced the concept of the sound of one hand clapping, which was created for the students to break the habit of dualistic thinking. He introduced the idea of lotus land in his famous poem, 'In Praise of Zazen'. This poem starts with the lines:

> "All beings by nature are Buddha,
> As ice by nature is water.
> Apart from water, there is no ice;
> Apart from beings, no Buddha."
> And ends with the famous lines:
> "Boundless and free is the sky of Samádhi!
> Bright the full moon of wisdom!
> Truly, is anything missing now?
> Nirvana is right here, before our eyes,
> This very place is the Lotus Land,
> This very body, the Buddha" (75)

This poem is still recited daily in the Rinzai monasteries. The last lines point to the century-old Zen tradition focused on an authentic experience of "here and now", "moment by moment".

Lotus and Sexuality

As mentioned earlier, both the sacred and Egyptian lotus (blue water lily) are associated with sexual symbolism. In Sanskrit, Padma (lotus) is quite often used as a secret code for *yoni* (literally a vagina, womb, or sacred place in Sanskrit). Furthermore, the lotus symbolises different aspects of female sexuality depending on its parts and age. "The sacred lotus is like the fruitful womb; its pistil, the foetus. As a bud, it represented the genitals of a virgin, when in bloom, the yawning labia of a productive woman," says Barbara Walker. Lotus is "Asia's primary symbol of the *yoni* (vulva, vagina), often personified as the Goddess Padma, 'Lotus' also known as Lakshmi or Shakti" (76). This symbolism is prevalent in Tibetan Buddhism as well. Padma and Kamala are synonymous with the 'lotus of the female', or vagina, which is soft, pink, and open. Likewise, the *vajra* is synonymous with the male penis, which is hard and penetrating. "The union of *vajra* and *padma* is a sexual symbol for the union of form and emptiness, or skilful means to wisdom. On an inner level, this union symbolises the penetration of, and an ascent of the psychic winds into the subtle body's central channel, which pierces and opens the lotuses of the channel-wheels or chakras." (77)

The lotus flower has sex symbolism built into its floral architecture. The lotus flower resembles a chalice or cup. The lotus chalice has soft curves and creates inner spaces. These chalices are turned upward, thereby creating a container. In ancient and medieval symbolism, the chalice was an emblem of the female sex organ. This idea is presented vividly by Dan Brown in his book, The Da Vinci Code.) The conical torus stands in for the masculine aspect, and together they represent the ideal fusion of the male and female polarities. In Indian philosophical thought, this is the perfect harmonious union of *prakrti* and *purush* (Shakti and Siva, from the Shivite viewpoint). No other flower represents such a harmonious union of the male-female aspect so beautifully. This flower is, therefore, unique in that it represents nature in a microcosm in a harmonious, holistic manner. This may be why it has been considered the seat of many gods and goddesses. (78)

Lotus and Buddhist philosophy

The Buddhist thinkers held that the transformation of the world into paradise can happen through the lotus, which expounds fully, the oneness of all life. According to Buddhist tradition, the fully opened lotus blossom is strongly associated with the sun; the petals are compared to the sun's rays, which stand for enlightenment. Because of this, the Buddhists give great importance to meditation on the lotus. Such meditation brings harmony into all aspects of one's being—external, internal, and spiritual; the lotus is the spiritual elixir; it calms the mind and improves concentration. The lotus also symbolises faithfulness. A golden lotus is mentioned in Chinese Buddhist texts, which simultaneously stands for the achievement of enlightenment; it is a natural flower of such exquisite beauty and hence is beyond the capacities of ordinary perception. Lotus also symbolises 'divine birth'. According to the Buddhist text, *Lalita Vistara*, 'the spirit of the best of men is spotless, like the new lotus in the muddy water, which does not adhere to it'.

For Japanese Buddhists, an unopened lotus bud symbolises the human heart. When the virtues attain full development, the lotus blossoms; hence, the blossoming of the lotus means reaching the highest virtues. When one is boundless in virtue, one achieves the lotus seat. That is why the Buddha sits on a lotus. In Chinese tantric practices, the closed lotus stands for the human heart, and the open lotus, or fully bloomed one (like the full moon), represents the heart of the Buddha. The closed lotus stands for the heart of an ordinary person, as it is known in Taoism and among the Khmers. (Lotus opens in the wise man). In tantric traditions, the lotus is a symbol of the feminine principle, and the various stages of the lotus flower, from the emerging bud to the one in full blossom, are compared with the different stages of a woman's life. (79)

In the *Vimala Kirti sutra*, a famous Buddhist text, the Bodhisattva Manjushri addressing the Buddha, says:

> "Noble sir, one who stays in the fixed determination of the vision of the uncreated is not capable of conceiving the spirit of unexcelled, perfect enlightenment. However, one who lives among created things, in the mines of passions, without seeing any truth, can conceive the spirit of unexcelled, perfect enlightenment.
>
> Noble sir, flowers like the blue lotus, the red lotus, the white lotus, the water lily, and the moon lily do not grow on the dry ground in the wilderness, but they do grow in the swamps and mud banks.
>
> Just so, the Buddha-like qualities do not grow in living beings, certainly destined for the uncreated, but do grow in those living beings, who are like swamps and mud banks of passions. Likewise, as seeds do not grow in the sky but in the earth, the Buddha-like qualities do not grow in those determined for the Absolute but in those who conceive the spirit of enlightenment after having produced a Sumeru-like Mountain of egoistic views.
>
> Noble sir, through these considerations, one can understand that all passions constitute the family of the Tathagatas. For example, Noble sir, going out into the great ocean is necessary to find precious, priceless pearls. Likewise, without going into the ocean of passions, it is impossible to obtain the Mind of Omniscience."

Manjushri presents the view that being born into *Samsāra* is vital for the birth and growth of the Bodhisattva aspiration. Also, the experience of existence is essential for realising the Buddha-like nature, and this is superior to the way of a saint or yogi who always strives to dwell in *samadhi* (meditative bliss). (80)

Tibetan Buddhism (Vajrayana Buddhism)

In Tibetan Buddhism, too, the lotus is an important symbol, and it is commonly associated with the process of evolving into a Buddha. In Tibetan Buddhist iconography, Buddhas are often seated on lotus thrones, indicating their transcendent state. Like a lotus that arises only from the mud, the compassion and wisdom of Buddhas arise from the muck of the ordinary world, which is characterised by fighting hatred, distrust, anxiety, and other negative emotions. Such emotions tend to cause people to become self-centred, leading them to suffer and take harmful actions. But just as the world is the locus of destructive emotions, it is also the place in which one can become a Buddha, a perfect being who is awakened from the sleep of ignorance and who perceives reality as it is, with absolute clarity and with profound compassion for suffering living beings. Just as the lotus rises from the bottom of a swamp, Buddhas were former humans, immersed in the negative thoughts and actions in which all ordinary beings engage: the strife, wars, petty jealousies, and hatreds to which all humans, animals, and other creatures are subjected. Through their meditative training, however, Buddhas have transcended such things and, like lotuses, have risen above their murky origins and look up, unsullied by the mud and mire below.

The symbolism may be extended still further because Buddhas do not simply escape the world and look down on others with pity or detached amusement; instead, like the lotus, which has roots that still connect it to the bottom of the swamp, Buddhas continue to act in the world for the benefit of others, continually manifesting in various forms to help them, to make them aware of the reality of their situations, and to indicate the path to the awakening of Buddhahood, which can free them from all suffering.

(Note: This idea of the lotus emerging from the mud and blooming in the free and open air has appeared repeatedly in many Buddhist writings and discourses. The idea is mentioned earlier in this chapter).

Lotus symbolism in Tibetan, Tantric and Chinese Buddhism

In Tibetan Buddhism, the lotus flowers have symbolism similar to that given earlier, with minor variations. The most sacred utterance for Tibetan Buddhists is the prayer *Om Mani Padme Hum*. They believe that saying this prayer aloud or even silently to oneself invokes the powerful attention and blessings of Chenrezig (Avalokitesvara), the embodiment of compassion. The central phrase of Tibetan Buddhism and Buddhist Tantrism is the *'mantra' Om Mani Padme Hum.* It is the six-syllabled *mantra* of Avalokiteśvara, the Bodhisattva of compassion (Tibetan Chenrezig, Chinese Guanyin). The *mantra* is mainly associated with the four-armed Shadakshari form of Avalokiteśvara. The mantra is believed to have been revealed to a great Indian master, Padmasambhava, who brought Buddhism to Tibet in the 8th century. Padmasambhava (also called Guru Rimpoche) is revered as the "Second Buddha" and is credited with spreading the teachings of the Buddha in the Himalayan region. (81)

The meaning of each syllable of the *mantra' OM Mani Padme Hum'* is as follows:

- *Om*: The syllable "Om" is the primordial sound, representing the univerSal consciousness and the essence of all existence. It symbolises the beginning and end of everything, encapsulating the entirety of the universe.

- *Mani:* The syllable "Mani" translates to "jewel" or "gem." It signifies the qualities of compassion, love, and wisdom. It is believed that reciting this syllable invokes the power of these qualities within oneself.
- *Padme*: The syllable "Padme" means "lotus." The lotus flower is a powerful symbol in Buddhism, representing purity, enlightenment, and spiritual growth. It signifies the journey from ignorance to enlightenment, just as the lotus rises from the muddy waters to blossom in full beauty.
- *Hum*: The syllable "Hum" represents all things' indivisible and inseparable nature. It symbolises unity, harmony, and the interconnectedness of all beings. It reminds us of our interdependence and the importance of compassion towards all living beings.

Tibetan Buddhists believe that the six syllables prevent rebirth into the six realms of cyclic existence. *OM* prevents rebirth in the God – realm; *MA* prevents rebirth in the Asura (Titan) realm; *NI* prevents rebirth in the human – realm; PAD prevents rebirth in the animal realm; ME prevents rebirth in the hungry ghost realm, and HUM prevents rebirth in the hell realm, (82, 83)

This mantra, Jewel in the Lotus, means Jewel (male) in the lotus (female), with interlocking connotations, the penis In the vagina, the foetus in the womb, the corpse in the earth, the God in the Goddess, and representing all of these. Additionally, there is phallic symbolism, which has to do with the resurrection and the forces of reproduction in nature that the lotus represents. In its phallic aspect, the jewel in the lotus thus represents the union of the masculine and feminine principles, the jewel indicating the masculine and the lotus the feminine, and the bursting seed pods symbolise fecundity. (84)

The Dalai Lama's followers continue to revere *Om Mani Padme Hum,* despite modern Buddhists denying the phrase's implied sexuality. This phrase has become a popular Buddhist meditation mantra.

As stated in earlier chapters, the lotus was also the emblem of Nirvana among the Buddhists. Its mysterious growth, rising from stagnant water and blossoming into a perfect, glorious, and unsullied flower, typified the future possibilities of the soul, just as its expanded flower resting upon the surface of the calm waters typified the ultimate repose of the soul after all desire has fled.

Lotus sutra

The Lotus Sutra is a famous primary philosophical document of Mahāyāna Buddhism. The Lotus Sutra serves as the primary, authoritative text of the Mahayana Buddhist tradition and represents the teachings of Buddha. According to the Mahāyāna tradition, the Lotus sutra was stored for five hundred years in the dragons (Nagas) realm and then presented to the human realm at the time of the fourth Buddhist Council in Kashmir. The authoritative translation accepted now is that of Kumarajiva in 406 A.D to Chinese and from Chinese to Japanese and English. The Lotus Sutra is also known as the Sutra on the White Lotus of the Sublime Dharma, and in Sanskrit, it is known as the *"Sadharma Pundarika Sutra"* (*Pundarika* is white lotus). Here, the lotus stands for the essence of Buddhism. Recitation of *Om Nam-myoho-renge-kyo*, the mantra associated with the Lotus

Sutra, is considered a complete form of Buddhist practice by followers of Nichiren (a 13th-century Japanese teacher) (*Om Nam-myoho-renge-kyo* means 'devote oneself to the mystic law of the Lotus Sutra').

The Lotus Sutra is considered by many as the finest gem of Buddhist philosophy. This text is one of the most famous scriptures of Mahāyāna Buddhism. Lotus sutra is the second of three sutras. The entire work is called The Threefold Lotus Sutra. The titles are The Sutra of Innumerable Meanings, The Sutra of the Lotus Flower of the Wonderful Law, and The Sutra of Meditation on the Bodhisattva Universal Virtue. The defining doctrine of Mahāyāna Buddhism is the belief that all people can reach an enlightened state. This idea is quite unlike the Theravada belief that enlightenment is reserved for a select few scholars and monks. Since Mahāyāna Buddhism is dedicated to believing that all beings someday achieve Buddhahood, it is called The Greater Vehicle." (85) Johnson writes in his commentary on the Lotus Sutra:

> "The Lotus blossom symbolises the causality of the spiritual life. Rising from the mud of the swamp (the physical world, the body), growing up through its murky waters (the world of sensory desire and emotions), penetrating the air (the mental world of thoughts and ideas), and aspiring towards the light of the sun (the spiritual illumination, the Dharma). It blossoms into a pure white flower (*Pundarika*). It thus represents the Four Virtues of Nirvana personified by the four Bodhisattvas leading the countless Bodhisattvas that spring up from the earth. The Lotus Blossom symbolises the inseparability of cause and effect, provision

and reality, and the source and manifestation of enlightenment." (86).

(A detailed discussion is beyond the scope of this chapter; readers may refer to the book *Lotus the Cosmic Flower* by PN Ravindran).

Lotus in Architecture, poetry, and art

Lotus is the favourite flower of the artists and poets of the Orient. This flower has gone so deep into the cultural ethos of the people that the temples and monasteries are often replete with lotus motifs. Seldom, if at all, do we find a temple not associated with lotus in some way or another, especially in India, Sri Lanka, and Tibet. Lotus is depicted in many ways: as full bloom, as bud, as fruit, as petals, as decorative designs, and so on. Deities are depicted sitting on the lotus, standing on the lotus, holding the lotus flower, sitting in lotus posture, and so on. An entire plant with flowers, buds, and fruits is sometimes depicted. Likewise, the lotus is the preferred subject for many romantic poets; they sang on it and used it as an object of comparison as a simile or epithet for feminine beauty, purity, and enlightenment. Painters were equally in love with lotus. The beauty and shifting moods of lotus flowers have inspired hundreds of paintings and photographs by artists. (For details, see the book Lotus the Cosmic Flower).

Lotus in Temple Architecture and Sculpture

Most Hindu and Buddhist deities are sculpted as seated on lotus seats or pedestals. However, certain deities like Brahma and goddesses like Lakshmi and Saraswathi, and the Buddhist goddess Tara are inseparably associated with lotus. Hence, their paintings and sculptures, including their idols, are either in a sitting or standing pose in a lotus, and when seated, their foot is placed on a lotus footrest, and they carry lotus flowers in one of their hands. Often, an eight-petal lotus is depicted. The eight-petal lotus symbolises the eight directions, and holding such a lotus symbolises suzerainty over the eight directions of space. However, such a lotus is only symbolic as no lotus has eight petals. Iconographically, many deities are represented as holding lotus flowers. For example, Surya, the sun god, is depicted with four hands, two hands holding fully opened lotus flowers and a garland of lotus flowers in one of his backhands.

Lotus is most closely associated with Lakshmi, the goddess of prosperity, beauty, and fertility, and she is known by many names that denote lotus (See earlier section under Lakshmi). She is represented either as sitting or standing in a lotus. Zimmer (87) concludes from his studies on Rig Vedic literature that the Lotus Goddess is Shri (Sri) or Lakshmi (Shri Lakshmi or Sri Laksmi), and her symbol is the lotus. All the various forms of Lakshmi, like the Ādi Lakshmi and the other forms of the Ashta Lakshmi icons, are represented as holding lotus flowers. However, sometimes, she is represented not in a form but by her symbol alone, the lotus flower. In tantric cults, there are nude female images where the head is replaced with a lotus flower. Such images are called Kamalamukhi Devi (lotus-faced goddess), and such deities are linked to fertility. Banerjee states:

> "The immaculate lotus arising from the depths of vassal waters of creation is associated with the notion of purity and with a cohesive tendency (*sattva*)and represents not only the unfolding of creation but the lotus symbolically represents the seed of endless millions of universes." (88)

The creator (Brahma) appears in a golden lotus with a thousand petals (*Sahasradala kamalam*). The lotus is his home, and this manifestation of Brahma is a personification of the Goddess Padma, who is none other than the *Parashakthi.*

Nagar compiled the following list of lotus medallions: Lotus designs, lotus stylised with birds, lotus serving as the throne, lotus leaves, lotus supporting Buddha, lotus medallions with the human head, lotus as a tree of life, lotus supporting Brahma, lotus with Nandipada, lotus as an emblem of immaculate birth, lotus supporting Maya Devi, lotus grasped by an elephant, lotus springing from *Bhadra-ghata*, lotus springing from a tortoise, lotus supporting elephant, and lotus as an attribute of Avalokiteśvara. (89)

Nagar further elaborated that the lotus is the most widespread image carved on stones, marble, and wood in most temples across the length and breadth of India; this is true from ancient times to modern times. The earliest and the finest expression of lotus motifs in architecture is in the Buddhist sculptures of Barhut, Amaravathi, and Sanchi, which are the living monuments for the pervasiveness of lotus symbolism. Many medallions have been located by those who researched the sculptures of the above places, some of them possessing interesting lotus symbolism. Griffiths felt ecstatic about the Sanchi *stupa* (pillar), and he writes:

> "In Sanchi's great pillar (stupa) – of all these swarming details, none is as profuse or ecstatic as the lotus. On the inner face of the north Torana, the plant becomes the main theme as well as the leitmotif. On the columns, within two squares, each over a meter square, lotuses soar from the neck of an elaborate vase, with seven and nine blooms on each panel respectively, each held on sinuous stems and illustrating a stage of the

lotus life cycle. There are fully ripened fruiting receptacles, tightly closed buds, and open flowers. Still more intriguing are the pollinated flowers pictured sideways, their fading petals reflexed, their developing receptacles held uppermost and pitted with nascent seeds." (90)

There are so many that one may lose count of the lotus depictions. However, some are striking, have marvellous details, and are highly symbolic. Three identical lotus flowers are depicted in one such medallion: one blooming below water, one remaining on the surface and the third rising above the water. The symbolism associated with this medallion comes from a famous utterance of Buddha that is found in the Pali text *Majjhima Nikaya* and *Vinaya – Mahavagga*:

> "Just as among the *upalas* or the *padumas* or *pundarikas*, some are born in the water, grow in the water and remain submerged in water, being reared under the water; some, though born in the water, remain on a par with the water; and some, though born in the water remain untouched by the water, rising above the water. Even so, Oh! Bhikhhus, when I surveyed the world, with the all-seeing eye of a Buddha, I saw among the beings some with little defilement, and some with much, some possessed of astute faculty; and some moderate, some well-formed and some deformed; some intelligent and some unintelligent, and some of them acting with a clear perception of the fear of life hereafter and of sin." (91)

In Sanchi gateways, a tree of life is drawn on the top and bottom of the architraves in the front of the southern gateway on the former in its simple form, with birds resting among its foliage and Mayadevi in association with it. In the carvings of the eastern gateway, there is a full-blown lotus sculpted on the Eastern pillar of the older gateway, there is a serpentine lotus on the opposite side of the same gateway. The Western Gateway depicts the finest sculpture; here, the stem of the lotus is straight and thick; flowers and leaves are arranged in five successive groups, and, between them, pairs of animals and riders. Here the 'lotus tree' is conceived as rooted in Buddha, represented by his footprints. In the Northern Gateway, a carving shows lotus plants and flowers arising out of a *Bhadra-ghata* (jar of fortune), where there are also carved *Yakshas* and *Yakshinis*. On another pillar two lotus plants arising from a fish (*makaras*) are carved together with male and female figures. Similar 'lotus trees of life' are depicted on the pillars and balustrade of the north side. Such lotus carvings are found in Amaravathi, Gaya, Mathura, and Barhut temples. These carvings of the trees of life depicting birth and immortality prove that the lotus symbolised life, birth, and immortality; it also became the symbol of the blessed one and the religion that he promulgated.

The temples that dotted the land of the Indian sub-continent were built in the post-Buddhist era, especially during the Renaissance period of Hinduism ignited by Shankaracharya in the 8th century AD. In all the temples, ceilings are often decorated with lotus motifs; there are also representations of the mythical thousand-petal golden lotus that sprang up from the primaeval waters (from the navel of Vishnu). The description of the thousand-petal lotus symbolically represents infinity. When stagnant waters like pools and lakes abounded in India and the adjoining regions in ancient times, lotus might have been growing profusely in these water bodies. The lotus appeared to the ancient people as a flower of exceptional beauty and magnificence in the aquatic environment, unsoiled and unstained by the surroundings, and gradually, the flower acquired a divine penumbra. Then, the flower was introduced into the iconography of gods and goddesses. Sometimes, the lotus alone was depicted as a symbol representing a deity. Zimmer writes about the female deities (goddesses) adorned with lotuses:

> "The ubiquitous lotus was a sign of her presence even where her human features do not appear. Not uncommonly, the masculine divinities even copy her traditional poses. A characteristic attitude of the goddess that is known as 'lotus in hand' (Padma hasta, Padmapani) is taken over in the iconography of Mahayāna Buddhism by the universal saviour Padmapani (lotus in hand), the greatest among the Bodhisattvas, or immortal helpers of the Buddha." (92)

Some of the finest representations of lotus in temple architecture are available at the Jain temples at Dilwara in Mount Abu. These temples are the epitome of the art and architecture of Jains, known for their marvellous marble carvings and sculptures. Located close to Mount Abu, they were constructed during the 11th to the 13th century AD by the kings of the Chalukya dynasty that ruled the region. Connoisseurs think these temples' architectural beauty and fineness are irresistible and unparalleled. In these Jain temples of Dilwara and Ranakpur near Mount Abu in Rajasthan, lotuses have been carved on the ceilings, and on the marble domes of the *ranga mandapa*, or in the porches and the corridors in myriad ways, and with mesmerising magnificence and subtlety. Hundreds of *yakshas, Vidyadharans, vidya devis, apsaras, jinas,* dancers and musicians adore the ceilings, domes and columns of these temples meditating, dancing, celebrating, amid lotus flowers, on lotus petals, reflecting, seems, on the nature of the lotus itself. (93)

The Dilwara temple complex includes Vimala Vasahi Temple, Luni Vasahi Temple, Pittalhar Temple, Parshvanath Temple, and Mahavir swami temple; the first two (Vimala Vasahi and Luni Vasahi) are the most important. We get the finest representation of the lotus motifs in these temples. Many people have written on these temples eloquently, the latest one being Sahadev Kumar. For a detailed description, one may refer to the beautifully illustrated book Jain Temples in Rajasthan by Kumar. (94)

Aamir and Malik, in their review, discussed the impact of lotus on Muslim architecture and art. Islam does not attach any cultural or divine significance to the lotus, nevertheless, it served as an ornamental motif in their architecture and textile designs. (95) In the contemporary architecture the lotus found its finest expression in the Baha'i House of Worship in New Delhi, known as the Lotus Temple. The Lotus temple is an effort to bring together the two aspects of Baha'i life — worship and service. The House of Worship consists of a central prayer hall, with nine entrances, symbolizing the oneness of religion and the idea that the teachings of the Messengers or Avatars of God are all ultimately doors to one reality. The temple itself is surrounded by gardens which serve to prepare the visitor spiritually for their devotions. The lotus temple is constructed in the shape of a lotus flower.

*The Bahai temple of worship, known as
the Lotus temple. (New Delhi)*

Lotus in Poetry

Behold the lotus, out of the mud whose mighty
leaves unfurl
Catching dewdrops like pools of glittering jewels
with her embrace
Out of the mud, I rise with buds and leave tightly
wound
To burst forth with colour and form of delicate
strength (96)

Many poets have written poems inspired by the lotus
flowers as they come out of the dirty water, in dazzling
glory, keeping their freshness, purity, and beauty intact.
Chinese poets often use the lotus as a role model to inspire
people to keep on doing what they must do and to give their
best part to the world outside, just like the lotus flower,
no matter how poor and bad the circumstances may be.

Chinese poets were the most influenced by the lotus, and from ancient times onwards, they wrote and sang about the lotus, showering their love and praise on this flower. A few selections from the old, modern and contemporary poems on lotus are quoted below.

There is a story associated with the legendary poet Kalidasa (ca. 370 450 AD), who went to see his friend, Kumara Deva, who lived in the *Simhaladwipa*. A beautiful courtesan with whom he spends a night told him that the king had announced a massive reward for a person who would solve a riddle. The riddle was:

"Kamale kamalotpatti shruyaate na drishyate"

The riddle means: 'One lovely lotus grows two lotuses, but nobody has seen that?'

Kalidasa, holding the beautiful face of the courtesan in his two hands, said: "O lovely girl, has not anybody seen two beautiful blue lotus-like eyes growing on your charming lotus-like face?"

kamale kamalotpattiḥ śrūyate na ca dṛśyate |
bāle tava mukhāmbhoje dṛṣṭa mindīvaradvayam (97)

According to legends, the courtesan killed Kalidasa to grab the prize all for herself. Kumara Dasa was so grief-stricken that he burned himself on the pyre.

Kalidasa used the lotus flower as a metaphor and a simile in many contexts in his works.

Perhaps the earliest poem on the lotus, 'On loving the lotus', was written by Zhou Dun Yi of the Northern Song dynasty of Northern China, who lived between 1017 1073. In 1071, he dug a pond and planted lotus. The lotus filled the pond, and there was a profusion of blooms. On seeing this, he wrote this poem, translated as 'on loving the lotus or 'on the love of the lotus'. It was translated into English by Feng Xin-ming in 2009. The poem goes like this:

> "Among the flowers of water, land, herb, and wood, many are loveable.
> During Jin times, Tao Yuan-Ming loved only the chrysanthemum,
> And since the Tang times, people have greatly loved the peony.
> I love only the lotus for rising from the mud but is not stained,
> Bathed by clear waves but is not seductive.
> Inside, it is open; outside, it is straight.
> It neither crawls nor forks.
> The farther away one is, the purer is the fragrance.
> Upright and elegant, it establishes itself cleanly.
> It can be viewed from far away but cannot be toyed with.
> I say: the chrysanthemum is the recluse among flowers,
> The peony is the wealthy among flowers,
> And the lotus is the gentleman among flowers
> Aye, the love for the chrysanthemum is seldom heard of after Tao
> As for the love for the lotus, is there anyone like me?
> Ah, the love for the peony is right for most people."
> (98)

On the surface, this poem is the poet's heartfelt ode to the flourishing blossoms in his garden, evoking the serene presence of flowering chrysanthemums, peonies, and lotuses, each with its distinctive aura and beautiful form. Yet, the poem hints at subtle depths of meaning, pointing to the poet's anthroposophic* vision. For the poet, the lotus exemplifies the cosmic /spiritual harmony everyone should seek. Thus, he says, "Inside, it is open; outside, it is straight (Zhi)" – a line recalling the time-honoured Chinese ideal. The poet contrasts the lotus with the chrysanthemum, a "recluse" among the flowers, and the peony, which, according to the poet, is "wealthy," or showy, and appealing to the masses. The lotus, on the other hand, is the "gentleman among flowers". The term "gentleman" (*junzi*), of course, has been the ideal human being since the time of Confucius. This Chinese poem teaches a typical story depicting how ancient Chinese people expressed themselves indirectly. As the poet writes, "I love only the lotus, for rising from the mud yet remaining unstained; bathed by pure currents and yet not seductive." "On the Love of the Lotus" pulses with subtle yet powerful symbolism, evoking a deep, tranquil mood while encouraging a dynamic and attentive state of awareness. It thus gives a glimpse of the sage mind itself (99). (*Anthroposophy is a spiritual movement which was founded in the early 20th century by the esotericist, Rudolf Steiner, and which postulates the existence of an objective, intellectually comprehensible spiritual world, accessible to human experience. Followers of anthroposophy aim to engage in spiritual discovery through a mode of thought independent of sensory experience.)

The lotus flower, born inside her mother's womb, slumbers in her mother's deep, warm muck, waiting for her eternal lover's first kiss to break open. She feels the water's weight above and the fish's movements below. Gentle waves caress her, stars wink at her, and the moon shines over her. As daybreak approaches, she wakes up and rises above the water, shivering in the early morning cold as the dew falls on her; she waits for the first touch of her lover. As the lover imprints on her the first kiss, as his golden rays fall on her, she flutters, her petals break apart, she opens up slowly to receive that first kiss, and she stands there embraced in the golden rays of her lover, with serenity, dignity, and beauty unparalleled. Looking at her, the poet writes:

> "Spiritual flower your beauty,
> Your mystery inspires me
> Taking root in muddy, murky water,
> In the darkest of places,
> You rise above to bloom beautiful,
> Powerful on the surface;
> I want to be like the lotus!
> Whatever trouble I face,
> How dark my waters may get,
> I will rise above and let
> The beautiful flower in me blooms." (100)

The lotus rises through the murky waters of ponds and lakes, yet when it blooms, it grows and stands above the murky surface, its petals shining and untainted by the mud from which it has emerged, as an epitome of glory and beauty. In the scriptural language and sacred poetry of Hinduism and Buddhism, the lotus perfectly embodies the soul, rising through the murkiness of worldly experience until it reaches the surface of the spiritual realm and blooms, vibrant and pure, free from all taint and attachment.

Many poets have been so eloquent while writing about lotus; many haikus have been written, and many songs have been composed to extol the virtue and beauty of lotus. Akiko Yosano writes:

> *"Emerging from the water*
> *a white lotus opens*
> *over the faint*
> *red surface*

of the world."
"In a lake of lotus plants
waves rise
under the floating
lotus leaf.
My heart is moved
To touch you"

Looking at a white lotus, the German poet Heinrich Heine wrote:

"The lotus flower is troubled
At the sun's resplendent light;
With sunken head and sadly
She dreamily waits for the night.
The moon appears as her wooer,
She wakes at his fond embrace;
For him she kindly uncovers
Her sweetly flowering face
She blooms and glows and glistens,
And mutely gazes above;
She weeps and exhales and trembles
With love and the sorrows of love" (9)

Ryokan, the celebrated Japanese Zen poet, wrote a small poem on white lotus:

"First blooming in the Western Paradise
The lotus delighted us for ages
Its white petals are covered with dew,
Its jade green leaves spread out over the pond;
And its pure fragrance perfumes the wind.
Cool and majestic; it rises from the murky water,
The sun sets behind the mountains.
But I remain in the darkness, too captivated to leave" (13).

A fascinating haiku:

> *"I am a lotus flower,*
> *delicate, fragile, yet strong,*
> *floating, unfolding and blossoming*
> *into the life where I belong"* (14)

A haiku, from Emily Romano:

> *"Lotus to lotus*
> *a dragonfly's shadow*
> *lighter than air"* (15)

A Chinese poem by Hsiung Hung:

> *"Time is engraved on the pale green faces*
> *Of the floating lotus leaves*
> *Our hearts are a sea, a lake,*
> *Finally, a little pond, where*
> *Spider webs interlock over the round leaves,*
> *And below them our longing*
> *Is only a single drop of dew"* (16)

An old Chinese lotus poem often found engraved on traditional teapots:

> *"The leaves break the bondage of the green stem*
> *Stretch them and form a green pool with untidy edge*
> *Now the flower comes from out of the vast surface*
> *of water*
> *Just like a very beautiful woman coming gracefully*
> *from her bath"* (17)

A Chinese poet writes about the lotus leaves as they float on the water:

> *"One next to another,*
> *the lotus leaves to face the morning sun,*
> *Their roots lying in the spring water,*

Their flatness interrupts the floating weeds;
Their frequent wiggling speaks of fish" (18)

Water is life. The lotus grows in water but springs from the mud, its signature of exquisite beauty from the muck of the primordial earth. That signature is earthbound, reaching spiritually skyward, and embodies the four elements:

—   Progression from earth /mud through water /life,
—   within its cycles, the fire of transformation/
—   leaves and flowers unfurl,

-always reaching upwards towards the sky and the sun into the air /ether of the spiritual kingdom.

The influence of the lotus is best seen in the Chinese and Chinese poetry, art, and crafts. For them, the lotus is not just a flower, it is the embodiment of many attributes and qualities. Such attributes include the following: (101)

Lotus as beauty: As early as in the Book of Poetry (Shijing or Shih-ching, translated variously as Book of Poetry, Book of Songs and Book of Odes, is the oldest existing collection of Chinese poetry, comprising 305 works dating from the 11th to 7th centuries BC). There have been writings associating lotuses with beauty. In Guofeng, part of the Book of Poetry whose contents mainly concern the ordinary senses of nature and everyday life, the skills of production and the principles of adoration and sacrifice, one man compares the beauty of the love he had felt for a long time to a lotus on the other side of the river. He was overwhelmed with grief over their long separation.

Lotus as the symbol of love: Though the lotus stem (leaf stalk) breaks, the two parts remain linked through fibres inside the stalk. The connection is usually used to describe the reconciliation or constancy of love between couples.

Lotus as a symbol of harmony: In Chinese, the word for lotus is pronounced "HE," the same as the word for harmony. So, in folk paintings, images of two fairies holding a lotus and a box in their hands symbolise auspiciousness and harmony.

For the people of China, the lotus is a symbol of integrity and honesty. The word for a light blue lotus is pronounced similarly to the word for rectitude. The lotus is used to illustrate an official's righteousness and incorruptibility.

Artists of the Orient have always been enamoured of the lotus flower. Many artists have painted pictures representing the lotus flower in all its splendour and glory, painting its changing moods from the sunrise to the sunset, from season to season, by day and by night in full moon and new moon; for the artist, this journey from one lotus to another is a pilgrimage as in the case of the famous Chinese lotus painters. Nowhere lotus paintings have acquired more symbolic meaning than in China due to the association of lotus with practices such as Feng shui. In Feng shui, the lotus flower is associated with love and marriage is often used to represent love, relationships, and bedroom Feng Shui. In Feng Shui, the lotus symbolises health, harmony, and luck in the home. In Feng shui practice, the lotus flower is believed to induce people with more noble, upright, and honest characteristics, 'replace negative energy with positive, clearing the mind and causing clarity to achieve enlightenment.' (102). [Feng Shui is a Chinese philosophical system that harmonises everyone with the surrounding environment. The term feng shui is translated as "wind-water". Feng shui is one of the Five Arts of Chinese Metaphysics. The feng shui practice discusses architecture in metaphoric terms of "invisible forces" that bind the universe, earth, and humanity together, known as *qi* (which is roughly equated with the life force or vital energy].

The lotus has many exclusive associations with Buddhism. The poets in China, who grew up imbibing the cultural associations and significances, tried to capture the various moods of the lotus. Looking at the lotus growing in a lake, a poet writes:

> *"Lovely is the Southern River where lotus flowers grow,*
> *How densely the leaves huddle one to another,*
> *And there are fishes playing in the water under.*
> *Fishes playing to the east of the leaves,*
> *Fishes playing to the west;*
> *Fishes playing to the south of the leaves,*
> *Fishes playing to the north too"* (20)

As the poet watched on, he found the withered petals of old lotus flowers falling in the water and drifting away like a boat, and he wrote:

> *"A fallen petal becomes a boat*
> *Gusted to the handle of a lotus parasol.*
> *It stops, floats, floats, and stops.*
> *Its reflection traverses the sky".*
> *"Now it comes, mid-June on West Lake,*
> *Four seasons, the vista ever unique.*
> *Lotus leaves to the horizon, boundless green,*
> *Sunglow on lotus buds, peerless red"* (21)

Collections of lotus flowers and seeds are mainly girls' jobs in China, and girls collecting flowers have inspired many poets. Wang Changling (696 756 AD) of Tang Dynasty wrote a whole set of poems known as the '*Song of Picking Lotus Seeds*'. A sample is given here:

"Lotus leaves to match the flower pickers' skirts.
Blossoms open around girls' faces,
Scattered in the pond, none are visible,
Singing announces their presence." (23)

The poet pictures bright green lotus leaves and girls' skirts as the same colour and pink flowers reflecting on the girls' faces, making them red; the poem alludes to peaceful flowers, the sound of water as the girls move around, the activity of lotus seed picking, and the girls' song, all of which merge into a verbal picture.

Lotus seed-picking girl is explicitly rendered in Li Bai's (Li Po) poem *"Song of a Yue Girl."*

"She is gathering lotus in the river of Ye.
She spies a passer-by, and turns round,
Singing her boat song.
She laughs, and hides away among lilies;
And seeming shy, she will not show her face again."
(24)

Wang Wei (701-761) of the Tang Dynasty writes about the lotus seed-picking girls in his poem' lotus basin':

"They go with the sun to harvest lotus seeds
On the long shoal and come home at nightfall.
Putting your pole gentle,
Or the splash will wet the pink lotus skirt." (25)

Picking lotus seedpods is often used as a metaphor for love-making or an act to show the readiness to be in love. To get wet is like the metaphor of the broken pitcher used by the Western poets (elaborately portrayed by the famous artist Jean-Baptiste Greuze in many paintings).

"The boat stirs the trembling autumn lake,
A young man skilfully steers past a maiden.

She throws lotus seeds toward him with abandon.
Discovered by another, she hides in embarrassment
for hours." (26)

A 16th-century Chinese poem captures the lotus like this:

"Time is engraved on the pale green faces
Of the floating lotus leaves
Our hearts are a sea, a lake,
Finally a little pond, where
Spider webs interlock over the round leaves,
And below them our longing
Is only a single drop of dew" (27)

Toru Dutt (1856-1877), the gifted Indian poet who died at a very young age, wrote the beautiful poem on lotus:

"Love came to Flora asking for a flower
That would of flowers be undisputed queen,
The lily and the rose, long, long, had been
Rivals for that high honour; Bards of power
Had sung their claims; "The rose can never tower
Like the pale lily with her Juno mien"—
"But is the lily lovelier?" Thus between
Flower factions rang the strife in Psyche's bower.
"Give me a flower as delicious as the rose
And stately as the lily in her pride"—
"But of what colour?"—"Rose-red', love first chose,
Then prayed, "No, lily-white, —or, both provide;"
And Flora gave the lotus, "rose-red" dyed,
And "lily-white"—the queenliest flower that blows."
(28)

In this poem, Toru Dutt presents the idea that the sacred lotus is the most beautiful of all flowers. For a long time, Lily and Rose had been vying for the title 'Queen of Flowers.' Each flower, with its support from poets, claimed the title.

At this time, the God of Love (Cupid) came to Goddess Flora asking for a flower, which would be the unchallenged queen of flowers. She wanted a flower that was as stately as the lily and delicious as the rose. Goddess Flora gave God of Love the lotus flower and resolved the long-standing quarrel between Lily and Rose. Great poets supported the flowers according to their wishes, and some poets even raised doubt that the lily was more beautiful than the rose. Lotus combines the redness of the rose with the paleness of the lily. Goddess Flora created Lotus, which was rose red and lily white (29).

A contemporary poet, Persad uses lotus deftly in a poem to depict the beauty of love that is unaware of the harshness of real life:

"Secluded and fearful, I waited
With bated breath until one day
I bloomed with eternal joy
With a pinkish hue lightening my way.
I looked around and looked ahead
Serene ripples, shimmering waves
The sun shone beautifully at each drop
Jewel-like beauty, of which he raves.
I glided along, each petal smiling
Timid and fresh, bound in self-care
Surrounded by you, and your pearl drops
Charisma blossomed with a sensual bare.
It was love, that's all I knew
You kept me alive, kept me strong
I never knew the world without you
A single lotus away from the throng
Until I banked on a shallow shore
Weary and dropping I reached for you
You seemed to move away from me
To sustain the ones that freshly grew

I knew then my love was forsaken
You looked away when I most needed
With each falling petal, I bade adieu
To your womb, I benignly seeded." (30)

This poem is about the purity of love that is unaware of the world's harshness. A lotus that swims away with the flow of the water on which it breathes feels that the water is everything to it, and it comes to love the water with every move. It moves along with the tide merrily, all consumed in its love for the water, until the day comes when it is time for the lotus to say goodbye to the world. The lotus dies, realising that it made no difference to the water, but is determined to leave a mark of its love; it ensures its seeds are dropped into the water that may help a new lotus to come up and bloom someday.

The Lotus achieved a very high place in Buddhism, one of its divine symbols. Many Buddhist monks have written short poems and haikus on the lotus.

"Flowers in the sky.
Flowers on Earth.
Lotuses bloom as Buddha's eyelids.
Lotuses bloom in man's heart.
Holding gracefully a lotus in his hand,
the bodhisattva brings forth a universe of art.
In the meadows of the sky, stars have sprung up.
The smiling, fresh moon is already up.
The jade-colored trunk of a coconut tree
Reaches across the late-night sky
My mind, travelling in utmost emptiness,
Catches lushness on its way home" (32)

In a highly erotic Chinese poem, *'To the tune of soaring clouds'* Huang O (1498-1569) makes the lotus a wonderful symbol:

"You held my lotus blossom
In your lips and played with the
Pistil. We took one piece of
Magic rhinoceros horn
And could not sleep all night long.
All night the cock's gorgeous crest
Stood erect. All night the bee
Clung trembling to the flower
Stamens. Oh, my sweet perfumed
Jewel! I will allow only
My lord to possess my sacred
Lotus pond, and every night
You can make blossom in me
Flowers of fire" (33).

Hung Tsun-Hsien (1848-1905) the 19th-century poet wrote on a more earthly plane:

"I cook the lotus soup,
Slice fine the lotus roots
I await my husband's return
To relieve the hunger
If he should cover
Pairs of chopsticks elsewhere
Just so he forgets not
The key in his heart" (34)

On a more spiritual Buddhist note, Kokusai (1816-1874) writes:

"Whoever in this world overcomes his selfish cravings?
His sorrows fall away from him,
Like drops of water from a lotus flower." (35)

From the Dhammapada (Early Buddhist teachings):

"When you contemplate the waters
At daybreak, you can hear
The lotus blossom" (36)

The blooming lotus fills the poet's mind with hope and he writes:

"When I see the pond
Where the lotus is blooming
I harbor faith in
A dewdrop on the petal
Even in this muddy world." (37)

The poet gazing at the marvel of lotus longs to be a part of it; even the transient life of a dew drop becomes valuable when it is on a lotus leaf:

"A dewdrop
on the lotus
in paradise
I would hope for my soul
to be that jewel." (38)
"I see now
that this dew drop's life
is not regrettable
as it's destined to be
a pearl on the lotus leaf." (39)

In ancient Indian poetry, the lotus played a role, though not as popular as in the Chinese. For the romantic poet, lotus was a beautiful simile, metaphor, and epithet. Vidyapati, who is known as the Maithili Kavi Kokil (the poet cuckoo of Maithili), catches the mood of the approaching spring season:

"Blue lotuses
Flower everywhere
And black kokilas sing

King of the Seasons
Spring has come…
And wild with longing" (41)

Vidyapati combined eroticism, love, devotion and bliss when he wrote the mellifluous lines depicting Radha and Krishna:

"Her feet showered lotuses.
The glitter of her body
Brought waves of lightning
The enchanting beauty
Has entered my heart
Her eyes opened
Like lotuses in flower
Her widening smile
Cast nectar-spells on all
Her sidelong glances
Issued darts of love
I saw her beauty
Only in a flash
But thinking of it
Fills three different worlds" (42)

Whether in longing or rejoicing, Vidyapati captures the beauty of the romantic moment for Radha (of the Radha – Krishna episode of Bhagavatha Purana):

"The moon spits fire
Lotuses droop
And loaded with fragrance
Mingle in sad love
Kokila bird of spring
Why do you torture?
Why do you sing?" (43)

A devotional poet, Kannappanar, of Tamil Nadu (India), uses lotus imagery in a devotional poem eulogising Meenakshi, the guardian goddess of the city of Madhura:

"Goddess Saraswathi sits in her house
A lotus in bloom
Its golden stamens gush honey,
While bees joyously make sweet music
In response, the long lotus petals
Shaped like silver serving trays." (44)

Saraswathi, the goddess of learning and fine arts, sits on a white lotus, her home. The white lotuses in the pond in front of the temple of Meenakshi put out the golden stamens, honey flowing, bees humming over the flower singing, in response to which the lotus petals, shaped like silver spoons, open out,

"Open……
Again
The two goddesses on their lotuses
Approach the eternal golden pond
And share a lotus there."

Here, the poet alludes to the two goddesses – Saraswathi and Lakshmi, who are sometimes rivals, but in the golden tank of Meenakshi temple, because of her greatness, they share the lotus. (45).

Lotus will continue to inspire the poets, and they sure will use the lotus imagery to express humankind's myriad feelings and emotions. See Mary Bone's small poem, Lotus flower:

"Oh, Lotus flower with beauty kissed by dew,
Waits upon the water for its spring debut
No other flower anywhere,

Has such beauty to compare.
Lotus flower, I love you.
This love song is just for you" (52)

The lotus blossom in muddy water lives on in the exalted minds of many from the distant past to the present and will do so to the distant future-

"Beyond yesterday, beyond today
White lotus
Blooming" (53)
"Here in this world, today,
Life and death are of grave importance
The blossoming of the great lotus
Is complete" (54)

The lotus flower is featured quite frequently in the Baul songs of Bengal, where it forms a symbol and is used deftly on many occasions by many singers. The Baul songs form a part of the cultural history of Bengal. Bauls are the gypsy-like wandering Vaishnavite singers, and they move from location to location, singing and dancing mainly to the *bhajans* (devotional songs) in praise of Lord Krishna. Baul songs are mostly philosophical and allegorical. The Baul sect is heterogeneous; music is what holds them together tightly. One of the Baul songs goes like this:

"You and I are bound together
In the six-petal lotus of heart
There is honey in this flower, the nectar of the moon
As sweet as Kama's dart.
Through the garden of emotion
Raging river flows
On its banks, we're bound together
In the six-petal lotus of the heart" (55)

These lines symbolically indicate the union of the two people; they are bound together in the six-petalled lotus of the *Svādhisthāna chakra* (or *adhisthana chakra*), located at the genital area; they experience the Kama's dart (Cupid's arrow), the raging river of passion, and finally the union at the 6-petalled lotus. Above the six-petal lotus is the ten-petal *manipura (manipuraka) chakra*, the 'jewel city'. In the physical body, this *chakra* coincides with the place of digestion. In the metabolic breakdown of food, the good and useful ones are assimilated, and the undesirable and unwanted ones are eliminated. In spiritual terms, *Manipura chakra* is where the fire within the microcosm burns away the undesirable impurities so that only Truth remains. Only those *yogis* who have transcended the realm of the senses are pure enough to withstand this 'ordeal of fire'.

> *"The Man is playing*
> *In the spiralling tube,*
> *The five elements*
> *Surrounding the ten-petal lotus*
> *Are tough indeed" (56)*

Bhattacharyya writes in his book *The Path of the Mystic Lover*:

> "As the *kundalini* energy rises, layers of consciousness unfold, and the lotuses turn inward. *Rasa*, restless sexual passion, is transformed into *rati*, the calm, restful experience of transcendent love. The Bauls also visualise the six-petal lotus as floating on the causal waters; in the depths below is a "hundred-petal lotus". Like a pearl – diver, the aspirant remains his breath (a reference to yogic practice), dives deep into the "ocean of *rasa*" and retrieves the jewel that rests deep within. Above

the causal waters, where raging fire burns, is a ten-petal lotus; above that is a two-petal one. The thousand petal lotus rests in a place beyond time and space..." (57).

Another beautiful song titled 'Be like a Woman' has these lines:

> *"......Take the dweller of the six-petal lotus*
> *Up the "inverse path"*
> *Light will burst forth*
> *When it reaches the eye between the eyes*
> *Take the dweller of the root lotus*
> *To the thousand-petalled one*
> *United with her, you will cross*
> *To the shores of freedom..." (58)*

Bhattacharyya writes:

"The song alludes to Radha, the symbol of passion, the "youthful, sensual, ecstatic maiden," who seduces Krishna, the Supreme Being. She dwells at the six-petalled lotus that floats on the "causal waters", the sexual centre of the body. This passion is aroused by awakening the dormant psychic force, *kundalini*, which rests in the root lotus. The sexual energy moves up through the various psychic centres within the body until it reaches the Third Eye, the two-petalled lotus, where the transformed sexual energy comes to rest....." (59).

Again:

> *"...Having reached the two-petal lotus,*
> *Everything becomes known;*
> *No obstacles remain..."*
> *"Between the hundred –petal lotus*

And the thousand – petal one,
Rasa and Rati move to and fro..."
'At the six-petal lotus
Their play evokes a new life"
"The Six Truths manifest
At the six-petal lotus
From the ten-petal lotus,
The river Ganges gently flows"
"...The stem of that lotus is open
Filled with nectar,
It sways by itself..." (60)

The six 'Truths' mentioned in the song are the six delusions: lust, pride, anger, envy, greed, and avarice. Those who can overcome these delusions while in a passionate state can go through the fire of the ten-petal lotus above the six-petal lotus. Having gone through it, the yogi baths in the cool waters of the Ganges.

Lotus in Paintings

Artists of the Orient have always been enamoured of the lotus flower. Many artists have painted pictures representing the lotus flower in all its splendour and glory, painting its changing moods from the sunrise to the sunset, from season to season, by day and by night in full moon and new moon; for the artist, this journey from one lotus to another is a pilgrimage as in the case of the famous Chinese lotus painters. Nowhere lotus paintings have acquired more symbolic meaning than in China due to the association of lotus with practices such as Feng shui. In *Feng shui*, the meaning of the lotus flower is associated with love and marriage, and it is often used to represent love, relationship, and bedroom *Feng Shui*. The Lotus is used to attract health, harmony and luck to the home. In *Feng shui* practice, the lotus flower is believed to induce people with more noble, upright, and honest characteristics, 'replace negative energy with positive, clearing the mind and causing clarity to achieve enlightenment.' (62). [*Feng Shui* is a Chinese philosophical system that harmonises everyone

with the surrounding environment. The term *feng shui* translates to "wind-water". Feng shui is one of the Five Arts of Chinese Metaphysics. The *feng shui* practice discusses architecture in metaphoric terms of "invisible forces" that bind the universe, earth, and humanity together and are known as *qi* (which is roughly equated with the life force or vital energy].

As a result, Chinese lotus paintings are set in specific environments, and their symbolic meaning and significance differ accordingly. People consider hanging a lotus painting in the house auspicious and believe it will bring harmonious relationships and lovely babies. The important types of lotus paintings are the following:

- ***Chinese fish and lotus Feng shui painting***: Fish flirt with lotuses. This combination means "living in affluence" and "every year, may you always get more than you wish for." In ancient China, the lotus represented the female and the fish the male, so this combination also implied the male-female connection.
- ***Chinese Mandarin duck and lotus painting: a pair of Mandarin ducks, lotus flower, and seeds.*** Mandarin ducks often appear in pairs, so they have symbolised the perfect couple since ancient times and are regarded as an auspicious symbol of love and marriage. The lotus seed symbolises "having lovely babies." This combination implies a perfect

couple living in harmony and mutual respect and growing old together.

- ***Chinese egret /and reed and lotus painting***: Egret, reed, and lotus are interconnected; the reed is often found growing together with the lotus in groups. So this combination in a painting symbolises "success in the imperial examinations again and again" "and "having a successful official career."

- ***Chinese lotus and sweet osmanthus (Osmanthus fragrans) painting***: The lotus flower and seeds grow together, and sweet osmanthus is a symbol of nobility, so this combination symbolises the perfect marriage and the prosperous family.

- ***A child holding a carp and a lotus painting***: Fish is homonymous with surplus in Chinese, while lotus with harmony, so this combination symbolises "living in affluence and harmony" and "living in a wealthy family." It expresses ancient Chinese people's good wishes for affluence and abundance year after year.

To the Chinese, the lotus is one of the most essential cultivated flowers, grown for its beauty and usefulness. The Lotus flower and associated symbolism play a significant role in their lives, which is also reflected in the Chinese lotus paintings. The most famous are the Chinese brush paintings of lotuses. In this painting style, the object is presented with minimum details, just enough to identify it. It is more of an artist's projection of his idea or vision on the subject that is translated into the painting surface.

Thangka painting of Tibet is an age-old traditional art form in which lotus pictures are widely used. These paintings are valued for their aesthetic beauty, but more than that, they aid meditational practices. Practitioners use *thangkas* to develop a clear visualisation of a particular deity, strengthening their concentration and forging a link between themselves and the deity. The sacred art of *thangka* painting dates back to the 7th century. Originating in Nepal, it has evolved into several schools of painting. Most *thangkas* are scroll paintings usually framed in rich, colourful silk brocade and have a thin silk veil covering the front surface. They are distinctively Tibetan, highly religious, and possess a unique art style. Tibetans have always considered the thangka a treasure of tremendous value. In most paintings, lotus images are represented as a seat of the deity, as offerings, and as decorative items (63, 64).

Lotus in Ornaments, Textile, Porcelain Wares

In India, the lotus motif is the most frequently and widely used ornamental design – whether in gold, silver or diamond. Stylised lotus images, lotus with a rosette of five, six, seven, or eight petals, lotus buds, lotus with many petals, etc., are seen widely in gold and silver jewels. Such lotus figures are used either on the central chain portion of the pendant or both. Rosettes are prevalent in art, architecture, and jewellery designs as it is the most artistic and balanced picture representation and is also aesthetically appealing.

Lotus motifs are popular as textile designs throughout the Orient, especially in countries where Buddhism is prevalent. Lotus motifs and floral prints are used in sheets, pillowcases, sarees, shawls, and other dress materials. Hand-painted lotus pictures are used on coffee and teapots, mugs, cups, and plates. Even an online search is sufficient to show the popularity of the lotus designs and motifs in textile and ornamental designs prevalent in both the East and the West. One comes across innumerable variants of such designs. The lotus tattoo designs are equally popular and widespread, perhaps the most used.

Lotus in Other Ancient Cultures

Herodotus and Theophrastus both wrote about the sacred Egyptian lotus, but such a lotus is no longer found in Egypt. What the Egyptians called blue lotus was a variety of water lily, known as the lily of the Nile and the blue water lily. Though water lilies of other colours were also growing in the Nile, the Egyptians were most attracted to the blue water lily, which became famous as the Egyptian blue lotus (Nymphaea nouchali)

The Egyptian blue lotus (lily of the Nile) (source: https://www.ancient-origins.net/ancient-places-africa/blue-lotus-0017940)

In the Egyptian cult, the circular leaf is considered a seat of gods. A sacred lotus leaf was the cradle of Harpocrates, the Egyptian god of stillness and silence.

The Egyptian hero Osiris also floated on a lotus leaf. Isis was represented as a lotus bud sticking out of the water. Aum, the primordial god, was depicted rising from the lotus flower floating on the sea. Lotus was also associated with the sun. The Egyptian god Horus was reborn daily from a lotus flower (the blue lotus).

In Greek and Roman mythology, the lotus is mentioned only rarely. There are some lotus-related myths. Heracles (Hercules) seduced a nymph and then abandoned her. The nymph threw herself into a lake and drowned. The other gods felt sorry for her and changed her into a lotus. In another myth, Dryope was pursued by Appollo, and she was later transformed into a lotus flower together with her son Amphissus (According to Greek mythology, Amphissus was Dryope's son following her rape by Appollo). In another legend, there is the incident of Heracles borrowing a golden lotus-shaped bowl from the sun. Ovid mentions a myth in which Priapus, the Greek god of fertility and protector of livestock, fruit plants and gardens, once pursued a nymph, Lotis. To escape from the assault of Priapus, the gods changed Lotis into a lotus plant. (This myth is perhaps better applied to the lotus (lotos) plant of the 'lotos eaters' made famous through Homer's Odyssey and Tennyson's poem Lotos-eaters; the lotos plant is *Ziziphus lotus*, the lotos or lotus tree that is closely related to the jujube tree.).

Ancient Sumerians and Assyrians were also familiar with the lotus flower. Griffiths gives a detailed outline of the representation of the lotus in these ancient civilizations. The people of Uruk, raised a ziggurat. On its summit was a temple dedicated to the patron deity, Inanna. This great fertility goddess would become the model for later mothers of earth and queens of heaven in the Near East, including the Akkadian Ishtar and the Phoenician Astarte. Inanna was also the lotus goddess. Plaques, pendants, and seals dating from the fifth to the third millennium BC reveal the proliferation of her cult and the plant's role in it. They are the initial evidence of the presence of lotus in early Mesopotamia and the reverence Sumerians accorded to it. The representations of lotus were often abstract, a seed pod-like carving or a more detailed carving in which:

> "She is shown holding two receptacles face on to present their seed-poked discs. At other times, just one disc is shown, floating in space and haloed with petals like the sun. These solar lotuses are often reduced to an astral form, the star or rosette of Ishtar as it would become known. Their points or petals are almost always eight, predominating, in both ancient and modern lotus iconography of the Middle East and the Far East." (103)

Griffith discussed this aspect in his scholarly book, The Lotus Quest.

In the Chinese Feng Shui, the Lotus Flower's meaning is associated with love and marriage and is often used for love-relationship and bedroom Feng Shui. (See the previous section.).

In Christianity, the lotus is called the 'Flower of Light' and 'Flower of Life,' 'Flower de luce' and 'fleur de Lys' and "as an emblem of the Trinity": it is one of the few survivors still retained in Christian ecclesiology. The "Fleur de Lys," a symbol of life, represents this light shining in the darkness as Christ, the Light of the World.

Worship of Lotus

Kamala Pooja

Lotus is worshipped on the *Kamala Saptami* and *Kamala Shahthi*—on the seventh and eighth days of the bright fortnight in Bhādra (August–September). The procedure as given in Matsya Purana is like this:

On the 7th day of a bright fortnight of *Bhadrapada*, the devotee should bathe in water mixed with white mustard, make a golden lotus, and lace it in a golden vessel full of sesame. The lotus should be covered with clothes, and the Sun god should be worshipped with incense, flowers, etc. The following mantras (ritual chanting) should be recited at the time of worship:

> *Kamalahastāya namaha*
> *Visvadhārine namaha*
> *Divākarāya namaha*
> *Prabhākarāya namaha.*

The devotee should then give away the golden lotus in the evening, together with the pitcher of water, ornaments, clothes, and garlands adorning it, and then give it to a brāhmana.

Kamala is also worshipped as it is the abode of gods and goddesses and the abode of *Yaksha ganas* during the rainy months. It is believed that during the rainy season (the month of *Ashāda*), all the gods take rest; it is the time when Lord Vishnu sleeps. During this time, all gods and goddesses also take rest, and they enter into various plants for this purpose; the demigods, *Yaksha ganas*, rest on the fourteenth day of the Hindu month of *Ashādh Shukla Paksha* in lotus flowers. (108)

Recently, Lotus festivals have been held annually in countries such as China, Japan, the Netherlands, America, and Korea. In these festivals, lotus flowers of diverse varieties are showcased; these festivals are, in a sense, the saga of lotus that continues to the present. The annual lotus lantern festival in South Korea is the most elaborate function to celebrate Buddha's birthday. There is a story associated with the Lotus Lantern Festival. At the time of the Buddha, a poor woman named Nanda wished to make a lantern offering in honour of the highest and noblest person in the world. Thus, she begged for money all day and took the two coins she earned to a street corner where the Buddha was to pass. There she lit a lantern and prayed with her whole heart:

> "Lord Buddha, I am so poor that I am not able to make any offering. Although this is not very much, I have lit a lantern, and if this may bring even a little merit upon me, I will be able to attain Buddhism in future life."

The night grew deeper, and a strong wind started blowing. The embellished lanterns of the king and the aristocrats died out. Only Nanda's lantern shone brightly. Buddha's assistant and one of the ten disciples, Ananda, attempted to extinguish the lantern with the end of his robe but failed. Then Buddha spoke to Ananda thus:

> "Ananda, do not waste your energy. Since a poor woman lit the lantern with great devotion and sincerity won't go out. Due to the pious lighting of the lantern, this lady will most surely attain enlightenment after 30 aeons (i.e. a very long time). Her name at that time will be SumidungwangYorae" (the Lantern Light Tathagata of Mt. Meru). (109)

A lantern offering is lighting a lantern before the Buddha, praising his benevolence with a bright, clear, and untainted heart, pledging to take refuge in his great mercy and compassion on the road to one's enlightenment. Thousands of people light every year over a lakh lotus lanterns, gathered from all over the world.

Use in Vrata poojas

In Hinduism, the term *vrata* has been widely known since the Rig Vedic Period, a tradition that continues vibrantly. Vrata denotes a religious vow and signifies a set of rules and disciplines stemming from the verbal root *'vrn,'* which means 'to choose'. These vows are said to be imperative ritualistic obligations serving the sacrificer for several reasons. Vratas, throughout the Hindu tradition, are contemplated as part of dharma (righteousness) for everyone, placing each of the gods at their highest level. Pearson defines *vrata* as a rite performed regularly to achieve objectives, following rules transmitted from generation to generation. In the lives of Indian Hindus, *vratas* and *vrata poojas* are essential components of their religious life, observed chiefly by the higher caste people and mainly by women.

In Northern India, *vratas* are closely associated with *bhakti* (devotional rituals) and comprise a crucial element of many devotional practices. Wadley explains that most *vratas* are also performed to gain *moksha* (liberation from the cycle of life and death), recuperate life, alleviate past *karmas*, and, most prominently and commonly, appease the gods and goddesses. The observers of vrata believe such practices can better their lives and bring them closer to attaining their wishes and prayers.

This betterment, nevertheless, requires the abolition of previous sins that have led to current difficulties. Moreover, through observing vratas, one could also expect to gain *bhukti* (objects of enjoyment), *mukti* (liberation from life and birth), and the destruction of sins. More often, the primary aim of a *vrata* is to influence some deity to come to one's support as one traverse the ocean of existence.

The Lotus flower is essential in many *vrata poojas*. However, due to the non-availability of lotus and many other flowers mentioned in the procedures, they are substituted with readily available ones. Conventionally, lotus flower is used in the following *vrata poojas*:

> *Sankastha Chathurthi vrata pooja, Satyanarayana vrata pushpa pooja and patra pooja, Vara Maha Lakshmi vrata pooja, Margashirsha Sri Maha Lakshmi pooja, Dhana Lakshmi vrata pooja, Swarna Gauri vrata pushpa pooja, Vaikunta chathurdasi vrata pooja, Narasimha Jayanthi vrata pooja, Shanipradosha vrata pooja, Umamaheswara pooja, Nirashanarka vrata pooja, Sri Krishna pooja, Saptarshi pooja, Sri Venketeswara pooja,* and *Sri Suryanarayana pooja*. (110)

Use of Lotus in Tantric Rites

Offering lotus in the tantric performances is an essential item. Some such tantric rites are mentioned below, mainly from the famous tantric text, *Saradathilakom*. (111)

Offering lotus dipped in ghee to Maha Lakshmi for the attainment of one's aspirations.

> *ütpalairjuhuyat tatdvamahalakçi prajayate*
> *palāsha kusumairhutva valsarena kavirbhavet*

Goddess Lakshmi will stay permanently in the person's house who offers the blue lotus *(utpalam* is indicated as blue lotus by the interpreter) 10,000 times in *homa; homa* with *palaash* flower for one year would make him a poet.

raktholpala hutanmantri dhanam aptotivanchitam
medhakamane hotavyam palasa kusumai navai

Offering red lotus in homa makes one rich, and homa with palaash flower makes a person highly intelligent.

raktolpalais trimadhuraktai sahasram juhuyannavai
nityam masatbhavshtam valsaradvanadhayavan

Red lotus dipped in *thrimadhuram* (three sweet things – sugar, honey, jaggery/ sugar, honey, raisins if offered in *homa (a fire ritual)*, makes one achieve all his wishes and become rich in one year.

rakthaisthrimadhuropethai
padmaibhanusahasrakam
jhuyanmahatim Lakshmim ayurvasya mavapnuyat
utpalairjuhuyattatvin Mahalakshmi prajayate
palasakusumair huta vatsaranekavirbhavet...

Offering red lotus dipped in *thrimadhuram* 12000 times to Devi Lakshmi can achieve prosperity, wealth, and influence worldwide. Reciting the Saraswathi mantra and offering white lotus dipped in milk one lakh (100000) times in sacred fire are methods to get the blessings of Devi Saraswathi.

Maha Lakshmi is visualized as sitting under a *parijatha* tree on a diamond throne on a divine island in a lake filled with lotuses and water lilies.

For worshipping Devi Saraswathi, one needs white lotus flowers, along with others like *durva*, barley, yellow cassia flowers, the flower of *bhoo-champaa* (*Kaempferia rotunda*), etc. The lotus occupies the first position among these. A pink lotus is essential for worshipping Devi Lakshmi, and an offering of 12000 pink lotus flowers dipped in honey or milk is prescribed to receive the blessing of the goddess of prosperity.

Offering a red lotus dipped in honey 100,000 times to Devi Lakshmi, together with the recitation of the *Devi Dhyana Manthram* (hymn on Devi Lakshmi), will result in Devi staying permanently in the devotee's house and bestowing all prosperity and luck. By offering red lotus dipped in *thri – madhuram* (mixture of honey, sugar, and ghee) 10000 times and reciting the required mantra to Bhuvaneswari devi (one of the Mahavidyas, an emanation of Devi Parvathi), one can subjugate all three worlds. According to tantric texts, there are many such offerings through which one can fulfil one's wishes. In Buddhist countries (Sri Lanka, China, Japan, Thailand, and Vietnam), lotus flowers are the most valuable offerings made before the altars of Buddhist temples.

Lotus seed garland *(Kamala mala)* is used as a rosary to pray to Mahalakshmi, the goddess of wealth and fortune. Usually, 108 lotus seeds are used in such garlands. Garlands are also offered to deities, especially to Mahalakshmi. The seeds used in such garlands are processed with oil and other materials to keep the beads long-lasting and insect-free.

Lotus plays an essential role in the religious life of Hindus and Buddhists. New uses are being discovered. Lotus garland is now preferred as wedding garlands. Flowers are used as a sacred cum ornamental display flower in wedding festivals. They are used daily in many ritual practices in hundreds of temples in India and Buddhist shrines all over the world. The old traditions continue to be alive and vibrant in the Hindu society of India.

Uses in Indian medicine

Lotus is an essential medicinal plant in the traditional Indian system of medicine (Ayurveda). In Ayurveda, lotus is known by names such as *kumuda, padma*, and *utpala*. Both white and pink floral types are used, but the white flowered one is preferred. Charaka, the father of the Ayurvedic system, and Vagbhata, another great exponent of the system, included lotus in the group *Mutravirajaniya* (diuretics); Susurtha, the second of the triumvirate in Ayurveda, included it in *Utpaladi gana.* The whole plant with its flower, fruit, leaves, and rhizome is called *Padmini* in ancient Ayurveda texts. Fresh leaves are known as *samvartika*, the fruit capsule as *karnika*, the stamens as *kinjalka*, the sweet honey inside the flower is *makaranda*, and the fruit stem as *mrinala* and *bias* (112 – 115).

According to Ayurveda, lotus has the following properties:

> *Rasa: madhura-kasaya-tikta,*
> *Vīrya: sīta*
> *Guna: laghu, snigdha, picchila*
> *Vipaka: madhura*
> *Karma: tridoshahara, mutra virajenīya, medhya, grāhi.*
> Indications: *raktapitta, tranha, daha, premeha, jvara, atisara.*

Bhavaprakasa, one of the primary classical texts in Ayurveda, gives the following properties:

Kamala is cold in potency, enhances complexion, is sweet, suppresses aggravated kapha and pitta, and cures thirst, burning sensation, diseases of the blood, pustular skin eruptions, poisons, and herpetic skin lesions. The whole plant (Padmini) is cooling, heavy in action, sweet and salty, reduces pitta, *rakhta*, and *kapha;* drying and restricts the free flow of flatus. Fresh leaf (*samvartika*) is cold in potency, bitter and astringent in taste; reduces burning sensation and thirst, and diminishes dysuria, haemorrhoids, and haemorrhages. Fruit capsule (*karnika*) is bitter, astringent, cold in potency, clears the oral cavity of its mucous, is light in action and suppresses thirst and diseases of *rakta, kapha*, and *pitta*. Kinjalka (stamens) are aphrodisiac, astringent, and cold in nature. They also absorb and help with *kapha* and *pitta* diseases, burning sensations, bleeding piles, poisons, and swelling. Lotus stem (stalk and rhizome, *mrinala* and *bias*) is cold in potency, aphrodisiac, controls excess *pitta* and *raktha* (blood), burning sensation, heavy in action, digests with difficulty, promotes breast milk, vata, and kapha, acts as an absorbent, sweet in taste, and drying. (v*ata, pitta,* and *kapha* constitute the *tridoshas*, a fundamental concept in Ayurveda. These three elemental humours (body fluids), together with *raktha* (blood) control the body's function).

Bhavaprakasa also gives the following recommendations:

In high fevers, infusion of the flower is prescribed with sugar to reduce debility; hot infusion prevents threatened abortion;

The rhizome is powdered and given in piles.

Dosage: Rhizome 10 gm; infusion 100 ml.

Khare provides the following properties for lotus:

Filaments: Astringent and hemostatic—prescribed for bleeding piles and menorrhagia.

Flowers: Decoction is given for cholera, fever, strangury, and heart palpitation.

Rhizome: Given in piles, chronic dyspepsia and dysentery; applied externally to cutaneous eruptions, scabies, and ringworm. Rhizome starch is used as a substitute for arrowroot and is given to children with diarrhoea and dysentery.

Root: Astringent and diuretic, antiemetic, cooling. It is used in dysentery, dyspepsia, piles, and skin afflictions and for its anti-coagulant properties (116, 117).

The Ayurvedic Pharmacopoeia of India recommends dried rhizomes with roots attached in syncope and vertigo.

Folkloric Medicine (118):

- Roots, rhizomes, and flowers are used as astringent.
- The leaves and seeds are used in poultices.
- Flowers, filaments, and juice of flower stalks are used in diarrhoea, cholera, liver complaints, and fevers.
- Syrup made from the flowers used in coughs, to check hemorrhages in bleeding piles, menorrhagia, and dysentery.
- Stamens are used for bleeding piles and parturition.
- Nodes of the rhizome used to stop bleeding.
- Astringent petals used for syphilis.
- Seeds used in leprosy and skin diseases for spermatorrhea and erotic dreams.
- Roots and young leaves used for piles.
- The milky juice of leaves and flower stalks used in diarrhoea.
- Leaves are used as a deterrent for skin maladies.
- A decoction of seeds used in dysentery and as a diuretic.
- Pounded leaves are applied to the body for high fevers, mucous membranes, skin irritation, and over the forehead for headaches.
- Embryo used in China and Malay for fevers, cholera, hemoptysis, and spermatorrhea.
- Rhizome root is used as a rejuvenating tonic.

- Receptacle or flower stalk used in Chinese medicine to stop menorrhagia, parturient haemorrhage, and internal bleeding brought on by gastric ulcers.
- Joints of rootstock used as haemostatic for haemoptysis, postpartum haemorrhages, hematuria, and bloody stools.
- A decoction of flowers used for premature ejaculation.
- A decoction of floral receptacles used for abdominal cramps and bloody discharges.
- Flower stalk used for bleeding gastric ulcers, excessive menses, and postpartum haemorrhages.
- A paste of root starch used for ringworm and other skin ailments.
- There is folkloric use in the treatment of cancer.
- In Chhattisgarh, India, the oil prepared from the roots is applied to the genitals to increase retention time.

The information presented above shows that lotus is as essential in the traditional healthcare system as it is in religious practices.

Nutritional quality

Rhizomes consist of 1.7% protein, 0.1% fat, 9.7% carbohydrate and 1.1% ash and exhibit mild flavour and are extensively used in Chinese recipes, while stem on cooking tastes like beet. Ogle et al. reported that the lotus stem consists of 6, 2.4, and 0.2 mg/100 g calcium, iron and zinc,, respectively. Seeds of lotus comprised of 10.5% moisture, 10.615.9% protein, 1.932.8% crude fat, 7072.17% carbohydrate, 2.7% crude fibre, 3.94.5% ash and energy 348.45 cal/100 g. Minerals of lotus seeds consist of chromium (0.0042%), sodium (1%), potassium (28.5%), calcium (22.1%), magnesium (9.2%), copper (0.0463%), zinc (0.084%), manganese (0.356%), and iron (0.199%).

Culinary Uses

Lotus rhizome, leaf stalk, and flower are edible and used widely in certain countries, especially in South East Asia, China, Japan and to some extent in India, Bangladesh, Pakistan, Nepal, and Sri Lanka. The primary reason for the renewed interest in lotus is its rhizome (sometimes called roots) and seeds. The whole plant is harvested in late summer when the seeds reach maturity. Lotus rhizomes are widely used as food, sold whole or in cut pieces, fresh, frozen or canned. They are consumed as a vegetable, usually fried or cooked with other vegetables, soaked in syrup or pickled in vinegar. Young leaves are used raw or cooked.

Japan is one of the largest users of lotus rhizomes, representing about one per cent of all the vegetables consumed there. Lotus seeds are a major product of southern China, where they are cooked with other vegetables, soaked in syrup, or pickled in vinegar. Young leaves, cooked or raw, are used as vegetables (119-121).

Lotus leaves are used as flavouring and wrappers for rice preparations and in making *dim sum* (a style of Cantonese food prepared as small bite-sized or individual portions traditionally served in small steamer baskets). In China, they wrap food and merchandise from markets and grocery stores. Lotus stems are used in preparing salads, and the dried flowers are used in cooked dishes, such as Mandarin duck and lotus flowers; the fresh flowers are a typical decoration. The bitter lotus embryo within the seeds and the lotus stamens are primarily used as medicines rather than food. Lotus flower is widely used in making tea (lotus-flavoured tea). Lotus seeds are roasted or candied for eating directly; made into a paste for producing sauces and cake fillings (in mid-Autumn it is customary to serve "moon cakes" which have a filling made of lotus seeds and walnuts); and cooked in soups, usually with chicken or beans. An example of the latter is a soup presented at banquets for newlyweds, made with red beans and lotus seeds (122). Red lotus seeds (*hongdou*) represent strength, while white lotus seeds (*lianzi)* symbolize the newlyweds being blessed with a child each year. The soup is also presented at the New Year's festival. Seeds are roasted to make puffed *makhanas*, a popcorn-like snack. Combined with sugar, lotus seed paste is a common ingredient in pastries such as moon cakes, *daifuku* (Grains used as food either unpolished or more often polished), rice (fine powdery foodstuff obtained by grinding and sifting the meal of cereal grain) flour (any of various soft sweet desserts thickened usually with flour and baked or boiled or steamed) pudding. (123).

Petals of lotus are floated in soups or used as a garnish, while the stamens are used in flavouring the tea. Lotus roots (rhizomes) are highly starchy and are eaten raw, roasted, pickles, dried slices, fried as chips, or used as vegetables, and sometimes mixed in the flour to make delicious lotus bread. In some places, the whole plant is used, as in Cambodia. In China, a refined white starch, similar in properties to that of arrowroot, is obtained by pulping the clean-washed rhizomes and pressing the resultant pulp in a wooden press. The milky extract is collected and mixed with an equal quantity of pure, clean water, and the starch is left to settle out. It is filtered and then dried in the sun. In Thailand, red and white wines are made with red and white lotus flowers. (124)

Jacqueline Newman has provided much first-hand information on the lotus plant's culinary greatness and varied uses. It has a unique role in food for the ill and the elderly. For them and young children, lotus rhizomes and their various parts balance food choices that contribute to healthy living. The people of Hangzhou in China, use lotus in a special sweet called Lotus Jelly. This candy, made from a fresh plant, is famous around the New Year as it symbolizes hope for a sweet year. Other times, the same candy is made from lotus rhizome flour. (125).

Lotus is a staple at many banquets, where one can invariably see sausage–shaped lotus rhizomes with holes stuffed with meats or preserved fruits. Meat pieces and fish are coated with lotus rhizome flour and then fried or steamed. Ancient lotus recipes such as kang (a type of stew in which lotus rhizome, vegetables or meat are used) are still popular. Present-day lotus casseroles are the rage for those who want to ensure their or their guests' longevity. Some of the ancient recipes (such as fresh sturgeon, Salted fish and lotus, lotus with carp, rice, Salt and spices, lotus with celery, and dog meat) are less popular in modern restaurants but are found in the villages. There is also a practice of steaming the seeds and serving them at weddings to wish the couple many sons. During the Moon Festival, lotus seeds are used to fill moon cakes. At holidays, the New Year included, both seed and root are cooked in honey as a wish for a sweet year.

In China today, restaurants serve many lotus dishes such as lotus-leaf-wrapped duck, steamed stuffed lotus root–filled with rice, minced black mushrooms, and other ingredients, duck stuffed with lotus and ginkgo nuts, melon seeds, chestnut pieces, barley, mushrooms, bamboo shoots, and rice, and sweet lotus soup and so on. Those that serve dim sum (traditional Chinese cuisine in which a variety of foods, including several kinds of steamed or fried dumplings, are served successively in small portions), prepare lotus leaves filled with rice and meat or poultry and steam the packet. The diner needs to unwrap and enjoy the contents; they are flavoured from the lotus leaves. Lotus petals are enjoyed fresh or fried, as are chrysanthemum petals; both are popular snacks and garnishes. Slices of lotus can be used in any recipe that calls for bamboo shoots. They are eaten fresh, dried, steamed, stuffed, or left plain, and the rhizomes and stems are sliced, deep-fried, and served as chips. Lotus flour is used as a batter component or plain coating on foods before steaming or frying. Imperial Congee, a recipe used before the Qing Dynasty (1644 – 1911 CE), and lotus leaf and rice porridge are typical recipes for older people. In addition to culinary uses, young and older women use the petals and flowers as both an astringent and cosmetic (126). Tarla Dalal provides culinary tips for using lotus seeds and rhizomes. (127 – 129).

Other Uses

Lotus fibre clothing

Lotus textile history gives the credit for discovering lotus stem fibres and the art of weaving these fibres to a Burmese (Myanmar) lady by the name of Daw Sa U. She cut a few lotus flower stems for offering to the Buddhist temple, and she noticed very fine fibres oozing out of the stem. Out of a sudden inspiration, she slowly pulled out the fibres and found that the fibres were smooth and silky. She collected more of such fibres and wove the first lotus robe, which she offered to a venerable Buddhist monk. This lady continued to create lotus robes throughout her life, including small robes for Buddha statue. (130)

Over time, lotus textile weaving has spread to other places and countries, and lotus clothes were first made in Thailand, Cambodia, and China. Conventionally, every process of textile making is infused with spiritual significance. The Guardian Spirit of the Lotus is given ritual offerings before the stems are plucked. The handloom is consecrated as a sacred space. The women weaving the robes follow the five precepts of Buddhism. The robes are offered to the monks during Buddhist Lent, which coincides with the rainy season when the lotus flowering is at its peak. And, when worn, the Burmese believe the lotus robes can calm the mind and aid in meditation. Hall has given the following details:

> "Ideally, the lotus flower should fully bloom when the stems are picked, and the deep pink flowers contain the best lotus fibres. Once a stem is picked, its fibres are extracted within three days while still fresh. On a small wooden table, a handful of about five stems are simultaneously cut, and their spongy fibres are pulled out, twisted and hand-rolled together with water. Then, the fibres are spun, washed and woven in the traditional looms. Raw lotus threads are neutral and creamy, and natural dyes are often used to colour the fabric. The whole process is extremely labour-intensive, making lotus cloth one of the most expensive textiles in the world. A small neck scarf requires about 4,000 lotus stems, a large scarf requires about 40,000 stems, and a full set of monk's robes (30 meters) requires about 220,000 lotus stems and 60 weavers to complete over ten days. Cool in summer and warm in winter, lotus fabric is breathable and wearable year-round. With a

texture similar to raw silk and linen, lotus fabric is soft, lightweight and naturally waterproof. Besides its supposed calming powers, the Burmese claim that it helps relieve headaches, neck aches, and health issues related to the throat, lungs and heart." (131)

Cambodian lotus fabric weaving is concentrated in the north of Cambodia; Fraser-Lu and Ma Thanegi have written about the legend and the history of lotus textiles in Cambodia. This activity began hundreds of years ago when one Daw Sa Oo (meaning Madame Sparrow's Egg), in the interest of gaining merit, set out to produce a set of robes for the highly revered abbot of a nearby monastery from the fibres of the local *padonma-kya*lotus plant, which grew wild in the shallows of the lake. With the help of her friends, she experimented with various filament extraction and preparation processes, eventually weaving a set of robes to her liking. The delighted abbot changed the weaver's name to Daw Kya Oo (meaning Madame Lotus Egg) in honour of her pious achievement. Daw Kya Oo and her friends continued to weave with lotus yarn for meritorious rather than commercial purposes, producing one or two sets of robes a year for eminent local abbots. None of Daw Kya Oo's progeny are currently involved in weaving, but the descendants of her friends have continued the tradition. (132)

A mythical legend associated with lotus fabric tells how Manu, the mythical progenitor of the human race, fetched the thread for weaving from the heart of the lotus stems that grew out of the navel of Vishnu. Stone reliefs depicting this creation myth uncovered from the fifth – to ninth-century Burma archaeological sites attest that early inhabitants there were familiar with the famous Hindu mythology. There is also a reference to the weaving of lotus robes for a future Buddha in a neighbouring central Thai version of the Hindu Ramayana epic, where the hero Rama slays a mighty giant whose daughter was betrothed to Maitreya, the Buddha of the future. While awaiting his arrival, she kept herself busy by weaving him a robe made from the filaments of lotus stalks. It has been noted that some legendary beauties of Burmese literature owed their physical charms to the fact that they had woven lotus thread in previous existences. (133)

Fraser-Lu and Ma Thanegi say that the Burmese like to trace the weaving of sacred robes from lotus fibres to a popular local nineteenth-century Buddhist text, the *Jinattha-pakasani*, which states that when the Buddha-to-be severed his hair to symbolize the renunciation of his former princely existence, he was offered a set of monks' robes by the Brahma Ghatikara who found them in a lotus blossom. While this text may be at variance with orthodox accounts, there is no doubt that lotus robes refer to a set of garments of great purity and significance. (134)

Traveler writers like Fraser-Lu, Ma Thanegi, and Julie Hall provided details on lotus stem harvesting, fibre extraction, and weaving.

> "About a week before harvesting, popped rice is scattered on the water, and offerings are made to appease the spirits of the locality, seeking their permission and ensuring a good harvest. On the day of harvesting, the gatherers propitiate their patroness. Prayers are also offered to the Buddha for a bountiful harvest. Bamboo talismans and small banana plants are tied on the looms to protect the loom and its products. In addition,

throughout the process, all involved must strictly observe the Buddhist precepts. Younger women gather the lotus leaf stems in the morning. After removing the prickets with a coconut husk, the stems are placed beside the young woman seated at a low table. A shallow knife cut is made around 5-6 stems, quickly snapped off and twisted to reveal some 20 – to 30 fine white filaments drawn and rolled into a single thread coiled onto a plate. It takes approximately 15 women making thread to keep one weaver busy. The yarns are prepared for weaving by placing the skeins on a bamboo spinning frame and transferring the thread onto winders in readiness for warping, taking care to avoid tangling. The 100-yard-long threads are lifted from warping posts and coiled into huge plastic bags, while yarn for the weft is wound onto small bamboo bobbins." (135)

Lotus fabric is woven on a traditional Cambodian frame loom. Weaving components include:

- A cloth beam.
- A large warp spacer-beater.
- A pair of heddles supported by a transverse bar resting above the frame.

A pair of wooden foot treadles in the shape of discs are connected to the heddles by rope. A Cambodian loom does not have a warp beam. The excess warp is stored behind the weaver and released as the weaving progresses, limiting the width of cloth woven to around 24 inches (6075 cm). The use of a temple keeps the selvedges straight while water is used to moisten the threads during weaving. Given the aquatic origin of the fabric, weavers feel that lotus fibres need to "remain cool." The lotus fabric is woven in 100-yard (90 m) batches, which take about a month and a half to complete. The weavers have estimated that fibres from around 120,000 lotus stems are needed to weave a set of monk's robes. The Cambodian lotus fabric is then dyed either with chemical or natural dyes to a reddish-brown shade before being cut into patches of different sizes and machine-sewn together in rows to resemble the mosaic-like appearance of community-owned rice fields prevalent at the time of the Buddha. Every bit of this precious lotus fabric is well-spent. Remnants are made into sequin-stitched mini-robes for Buddha images. Leftover scraps of yarn are twisted into wicks for pagoda lamps. Aquatic in origin, lotus wicks are thought to cool the flames of worries and bestow on the donor a calm heart. (136, 137)

Use in Aromatherapy

Lotus yields an essential oil; the yield is meagre, and the extraction process is arduous. About 75,000 100,000 pink blossoms are needed to make one kilo of lotus flower absolute. That is a significant number of flowers handpicked from ponds on the third day after blossoms open. There is a rapidly closing window of harvest time where waiting even a day will render a weaker fragrance. After picking and separating flowers from the stem, they are loaded into extracting units. Several washings are required to remove the waxes, pigment and oil from the flower petals. This process renders concrete that must be separated to extract the absolute oil contained within. Before the absolute is obtained, a delicate, painstaking process of chilling, filtering, and vacuum distilling separates the hexane-free solvent from the absolute. Pure lotus flower oil (absolute) has a strong, exotic floral, and fruity aroma with a slightly herbaceous back note. The oil blends with all floral (flower essential oils) and many spice oils, including neroli, cinnamon, rose otto, rose Moroco, rosewood, sandalwood, Siam wood, ylang ylang etc. (138)

Pure Lotus oil was used by ancient Greeks and Romans to cure health problems like asthma and rheumatism. It has been used for spiritual enlightenment for hundreds of years, particularly in Asia and SE Asia. Pink lotus enhances love, relationship and spiritual growth. It has an exotic, strong aquatic floral aroma that is popular and sought after for designer perfume. Lotus Absolute can be used in aromatherapy to benefit conditions of asthma, rheumatism, and epilepsy. Pink lotus oil promotes heightened spiritual growth, often used during meditation to soothe, calm, and promote kindness, understanding, and forgiveness.

Pink lotus absolute has a slightly viscous consistency at ambient room temperature. It is easier to work with in a more liquefied state. To liquefy, the bottle is placed in a warm water bath; its melting point is 35 degrees Celsius (95 degrees Fahrenheit). Pink lotus absolute, properly diluted, can be used in designer candle making, luxury soaps, home fragrances, anointing blends, lotions, massage oils, diffusers, potpourri, air fresheners, body fragrances, perfume oils, aromatherapy products, bath oils, towel scenting, in spas, incense, light rings, laundry, facial steams, and hair treatments. Aromatherapy uses of the oil are for asthma, rheumatism, and epilepsy; the oil evokes emotional calm, soothing, balancing, meditation, and yoga. (139, 140)

Brief scientific notes:

Lotus – *Nelumbo nucifera* Gaertner Nelumbonaceae.

Lotus, sacred lotus, Indian sacred lotus (English); Kamal, Amber, *Lalkamal* Red Lotus);

Kamal, Padma (Bengali); Kanwal (Punjabi); Kamal (Marathi); Thaamara, Aravindam, Kamalam, Padmam (Malayalam); Tamaraichenthamari (Tamil); Kamalamu, Padmamu (Telungu). Nelumbo, Lotus Indien (French); Pactige Nelumbo, Lotus Sacre, Indischelotosblume (German); Taamara (Maly); Nilufer (Persian, Arabic); Nelum (Sinhalese); Hasu (Japaanese); Iilian (Chinese); Lotosagrado (Spanish).

Lotus belongs to the genus Nelumbo, which has only two species, Nelumbo lutea, the American yellow lotus and Nelumbo nucifera, the Indian sacred lotus.

Lotus is widely distributed in the world. It grows in all continents Asia, Oceania, North and South America and Australia. However, most of the lotus in the world is grown in China, Japan, India, the Philippines, and Indonesia. The centre of commercial cultivation of this flower is China. In Western countries, lotus is grown as an ornamental and forms the essential component of a water garden.

Lotus plants are aquatic herbs, laticiferous, rhizomatous, hydrophytic and rooted. Leaves are heterophyllous – regular leaves and scale leaves are present. Typical leaves are simple and peltate and have long petioles. The stem of the lotus is the underground type (root or rhizome-like stem). It branches out in the soil. It resembles a whip or a stolon in the early stages of development. Flowers are solitary, bisexual, bracteate (bract is the upper scale leaf), large, regular and acyclic. Perianth has distinct calyx and corolla, sequentially intergrading from sepals to petals, and is about 20–30 in numbers and free. Calyx lobes 2–8; polysepalous, not persistent, imbricate. Corolla consists of 18–28 petals, polypetalous, imbricate, coloured white, red, and various shades of pink. The Lotus flower has a very prominent torus (also known as receptacle and thalamus; it lacks in many improved varieties developed through breeding). Stamens are about 200–400, maturing centripetally, free, spiralled, filamentous, fertile. The flower is about 12–40 carpelled, apocarpous, superior, sunken in the fleshy torus cup or found free (in many cultivars developed through breeding). Carpels are single or rarely 2-ovulated. The plant is hermaphrodite, pollination entomophilous; beetles are the primary pollinating agents. The fruit is an aggregate of indehiscent nutlets. Ripe nutlets are ovoid or roundish or oblongata, about 1.0 cm long and 1.5 cm broad, seed coat smooth, brown or black.(140)

The lotus' unusual genetic features give it some unique survival skills. Ichiro Oga of Japan (a famous Japanese expert on lotus) germinated a seed carbon dated 2000 years old. From this, a line of lotis was established; this is the famous 'Oga lotus', and it became famous as the oldest lotus in the world that awoke out of its 2000-year-long slumber. A group of 70 scientists led by Ray Ming of the University of Illinois, Shen-Miller of California at Los Angeles and Shaohua Li of the Wuhan Botanical Garden at the Chinese Academy of Sciences jointly sequenced the lotus genome.

Pharmacologically active constituents have been isolated from the seed, leaf, flower, and rhizome. The chemical constituents include alkaloids, steroids, triterpenoids, flavonoids, glycosides, polyphenols, and various minerals.

The seeds are rich in protein, amino acids, unsaturated fatty acids, minerals, starch, and tannins. Numerous alkaloids are the major secondary metabolites in the seeds. N-nor nuciferine, O-nor-nuciferine, nuciferine, and romaine are the four main aporphine alkaloids responsible for the pharmacological properties of the plant. Numerous chemical analyses document several alkaloids in the leaves., Several flavonoids are located in the leaves and stamens; the stamens contain kaempferol and seven of its glycosides. Higenamine, linesnine, taurine, isoliensinine, and nuciferine are found in the green embryo of lotus seeds and exhibit high bioactivity. The starch in the rhizomes is comparable with maize and potato starch, with a fresh rhizome containing 31.2% of starch. Vitamin content includes the following:

- Thiamine 0.22 mg per 100 g
- Riboflavin 0.6 mg per 100 g
- Niacin 2.1 mg per 100 g
- Ascorbic acid 1.5 mg per 100 g

An asparagine-like amino acid (2%) has also been isolated in the rhizomes. (For details, see the research papers and reviews available in the public domain.) (141)

Citations and notes

(General references are listed at the end of the book)

1. Ravindran PN (2017) Lotus the Cosmic flower. Blue rose pub., Delhi.

2. Ravindran PN (2020) Sacred and ritual plants of India. Notion press, Chennai.

3. Basu S (2002) The Lotus Symbol in Indian Literature and Art. Originals, New Delhi.

4-5. Ravindran PN (see 1)

6. Siwek S (2013) The sacred lotus; a plant study. http://www.flowersociety.org/lotus-plant-study.htm. retrieved on 16-10-2013.

7. Nagar S (2000) Botanical and Medicinal Plants: As depicted in ancient texts, art &archeology from dawn of civilization to the modern age. Vol1. BR Pub. Corporation, Delhi.

8-9. Blavatsky HP (1888) The Secret Doctrine, Vol.1, Book I – part ii, The evolution of symbolism in its approximate order, chapter 8, The Lotus as a UniverSal Symbol, P.379 (See 1.2). http://www. theosociety.org/pasadena/sd/sd1-2-08.htm.

10. Mani V (1989) Puranic Encyclopedia, Current Books, Kottayam.

11. Harshananda, Swami (2011) Hindu Gods and Goddesses. Sri Ramakrishna Math, Madras.

12. Anon (2011) Iconography of Lord Vishnu. https://sites.google.com/a/sapasagroup.com/ sapasagroup1-com/home/religion/iconography-of-lord-vishnu.

13. Jones, Sir William (1889) A Hindu poem. Quoted from Thiselton-Dyer T F, The Folk-lore of Plants, 1889.

14. Ananda Saraswathi, Yogi. (2013) Ashta Lakshmi, http://vedicgoddess.weebly.com/3/post/   2013/01/ashta-lakshmi-by-yogi-ananda-saraswathi.html.

15. Agrawal P (2013) Faith and rituals – Ashta Laxmi. http://www.speakingtree.in/spiritual-blogs/seekers/faith-and-rituals/b2-ashta-laxmi.

16. Anon (2013) Ashta Lakshmi. Wikipedia. org/wiki/Ashta_Lakshmi

17. Anon (2012) Devi Lakshmi as Padmavathi (lotus goddess). http://www.exoticindiaart.com/product/   sculptures/devi-lakshmi-as-padmavati-lotus-goddess-RL17

18. Saboo S (2012) Goddess Saraswati – Goddess of Learning. http://www.speakingtree.in/spiritual-blogs/seekers/philosophy/goddess-saraswati-daughter-of-goddess-durga.

19. Goswami, M et al. (2005) Saptamatrikas in Indian art and their significance In Indian sculpture and ethos: a

critical study. Anistoriton, 9 (March), section A051, 1 8. http://www.anistor.co.hol.gr/index.htm.

20. Rampuri, Baba. (2012) Navadurgas – The Nine forms of Durga. http://rampuri.com/navdurga-navratri/, retrieved on 23-04-2013), also see Swami

21. Harshananda and Jansen, E.R. (1993) The Book of Hindu Imagery, Binkey Kok pub., Holland.

22. Goswami SRD (2013) The Splendid Flower Pastimes of Sri Sri Radha-Krishna, Translation by Sriman Kusakrathadasa. http://www.harekrsna.com/sun/features/06-07/features688.htm.

23. Kakkar G (2010) Lotus Feet of Srimati Radharani and Lord. http://www.iskcondesiretree.net/profiles/blogs/lotus-feet-of-srimati-1.

24. Goswami (see 22).

25. Thakura SB (2013) Sri Krishna Karnamrutham. http://www.bvml.org/VS/SBT_skk.html

26. Bhakta Meera The beauty of Krishna's Lotus Feet. http://www.iskcondesiretree.net/ profiles/blogs/the-beauty-of-krishna-s-lotus-feet.

27-28. Srila Jiva Goswami, http://www.harekrsna.com/sun/editorials/05-13/editorials10131.htm.

29. Thakura (see 25)

30. Ravindran (see1, 2)

31. Anon (2013) The Elephant God – Erawan. According to Aryan legends, the god Erawan (same as Airavath the vehicle of Lord Indra in Indian Mythology) is huge, white, and has 33 heads. Each head bears seven tusks. For each tusk there are seven lotus ponds. Each pond has seven lotus pads, each pad has seven lotus

blossoms and each blossom has seven petals. On each petal dance seven angels. Each angel has seven ladies-in-waiting. So altogether the god Erawan has 33 heads, 231 tusks, 1,617 ponds, 11,319 lotus pads, 79,233 lotus blossoms, 554,631 lotus petals, 3,882,417 angels, and 27,176,919 ladies-in-waiting ! http://www. erawanbangkok.com/myth.php.

32. Anon. (2013) The Lotus Flower, hand held emblem and ritual attribute, http://www dharmasculpture.com/lotus-flower-hand-emblem-ritual-attribute.html

33. Tanahashi K. (2006) Lotus. Wisdom publications, Somervelle, USA.

34. Lu S-Y, Grand Master (1984) Highest Yoga Tantra and Mahamudra, chapter 22, The Levels of Mahamudra. (Trans. Chung, CY). http://www.tbsn.org/ENGLISH2/articlelist.php

35. Anon (2014) Tara-Tibetan Goddess of Compassion. http://www.goddess.ws/tara.html

36. Willson M (1986) In Praise of Tara. Wisdom Pub., London. 1986,

37. The Golden Rosary of Tara, by Lama Taranatha, translated by Vajranatha. http://www.chinabuddhismencyclopedia. com/ ...the_Golden_Rosary_of_Tara, This is the great vow or *mahapranidhana* of the bodhisattva Tara. She vows to always appear as a woman until all beings are liberated from samsara.

38. Kalpasutra, translated from the Prakrit by Hermann Jacobi, 1884.Sacred Books of the East, vol. 22; http://www. hinduwebsite.com/... jainscripts/kalpa_sutra.asp.

39. Anon (2012) The iconography of Padmavati, Deogarh. http://www.indianetzone.com/61/iconography_padmavati.htm,

40. Anon. (2012) The iconography of Jain Mahavidyas. http://www.indianetzone.com/61/iconography_jain_ mahavidyas.htm.

41-44. Blavitsky HP (1888) Blavatsky H P(1888) The Secret Doctrine, Vol.1, Book I – part ii, The evolution of symbolism in its approximate order, chapter 8, The Lotus as a Universal Symbol, P.379 (See 1.2). http:// www. theosociety.org/pasadena/sd/sd1-2-08.htm.

45. Anon (2009) Prophecy of Dipankara Buddha. http:// www.jatakaonline.com/jataka-tales/0011-the-first-prophecy,

46. Park C (2013) The Illustrated Life of the Buddha (Based on Gethin, R., The Foundations of Buddhism, Oxford University Press, 1998, http://orias. berkeley.edu/ visuals/ buddha/ Life.html #1. The Conception of the Buddha.

47. Nagar S (2000) see 7.

48. Park C (2013) The Illustrated Life of the Buddha (Based on Gethin, R., The Foundations of Buddhism. Oxford University Press, 1998, http://orias. berkeley.edu/ visuals/ buddha/ Life.html #1. The Conception of the Buddha

49. Maury C (1969) Folk Origins of Indian Art. Columbia University Press, Quoted from Kumar, 2001.

50. Kramrisch S (1983) An image of Aditi-Uttanapad. In Miller, B. S. (ed.), Exploring India's Sacred Art, Philadelphia, University of Philadelphia Press, 149 158.

51. Kumar S (2001) A Thousand Petalled Lotus: Jain Temples of Rajasthan, Indira Gandhi National Centre for the Arts, New Delhi.

52. Pal P (1986) Indian Sculpture Vol.I, Univ. California Press, Los Angeles.

53. Mercier P (2007) The Chakra Bible, Octopus Pub., US.

54. Anon (2011) All about Chakras. www.scribd.com.

55. Richadson C (2012) The Chakra's presented in Goddess form. http://mgck59.webs.com/ kundaliniawakening.htm

56-58. Ravindran (see 1)

59. Kochetkova M (2023) The Art of Mandala – An Artistic Road Towards Enlightenment. https://www.dailyartmagazine.com/art-mandala/.

60. Baillie A. and Suzanne, O.S. (1999) The Lotus, Tricycle Magazine, http://www.tricycle.com/feature/the-lotus.

61. Bhaktivedanta Swami Prabhupāda, Śrī Brahma-saṁhitā 5.4, Bhaktivedanta Veda Base, http://vedabase.awardspace.com/ bs/5/4.htm.

62. Gupta S M (2001) Plant Myths and Traditions in India, Munshirm Manoharlal, Delhi.

63. Holdrege BA (2015) Bhakti and Embodiment: Divine Bodies and Devotional Bodies in Krishna Bhakt iF. Routledge Pub., Abingdon, UK.

64. Vrindavana Mahatmya of Padma Purana, quoted from Holdrege (2015)

65. Jung CG, Quoted from Schweig (2007).

66. Schweig GM (2007) Dance of Divine Love. Motilal Banrsidass, New Delhi.

67. Basu S (2002) see 3

68-69. Takahashi, K. (2006) Lotus. Wisdom Pub., Somerville, USA.

70. Kukai, cited from Takahashi (see 68)

71. Anonymous (2023) Flower sermon Turning Wheel Buddhist Temple (Zen Buddhism in the East Midlands). https://www.turningwheel.org.uk/buddhist_stories/the-flower-sermon/

72. Jones JJ (2009) The significance of the flower sermon to Zen Buddhism. http://www.spiritualliving360.com/index.php/the-significance-of-the-flower-sermon-to-zen-buddhism-18490/

(73-74) Welter A (2006) Mahakasyapa' s smile. In: Heine, S. and Wright, D.S. (eds) The Koan: Texts and Contexts in Zen Buddhism. Oxford Univ. press, NY, USA., pp.. 75 109.

75. Hakuin's Song of Zazen, trans. Waddell, http:// www. thezensite.com/ZenTeachings/Translations/Song_of_Zazen.htm.

76. Walker BG (1983) The Woman's Encyclopedia Of Myths And Secrets. Harper & Row, San Francisco, USA (Digitised edn.2007), http://archive.org/stream/womansencycloped00walkrich/womansencycloped00walkrich_djvu.txt.

77. Banerjee R (1988-1989) *Lalitavistara*, Chinese Buddhist Encyclopedia, http://www.chinabuddhismencyclopedia.com/ en/index.php/Lalitavistara.

78-80. Ravindran (see 1,2)

81. Anon. (2024) Padmasambhava. https://en.wikipedia.org/wiki/Padmasambhava.

82. Studholme A (2002) The Origins of Om Manipadme Hum. Albany NY: State University of New York Press.

83. Anonymous (2024) Om mani padme hum. Wickipedia https://en.wikipedia.org/wiki/Om_mani_padme_hum.

84. Beer, R. (2003) The Handbook of Tibetan Buddhist Symbols. Serindia publications, Chicago, Illinois, USA

85. Kern H (1884) The Sutra of the Lotus Flower of the Wonderful Law Translated by H. Kern (1884) http://reluctant-messenger.com/lotus_sutra.htm. (The entire text is available online. Introduction byRichard St. Clair, http://www.mit.edu/~stclair/lotus.html; retrieved on 15th Nov. 2009. Also see http://en.wikipedia.org/wiki/Lotus_Sutra, for a brief note on Lotus sutra.)

86. Johnson P (2001) The Lotus Blossom. (Kuang-Ting's Kuang-Ting's introduction of the 'Hidden Meaning of the Lotus Sutra' (C. Fa-Hua Hsuan-I, J.Hokke Gengi), (http://www. tientai.net/teachings/pundarika/renge.htm.

87. Zimmer H (1972) Myths and Symbols of Indian Art and Civilization. Princeton University Press, USA.

88. Banerjee, cited from Gupta, Gupta, S. (1996) Plants in Indian Temple Art. BR Pub. Corporation, Delhi.

89. Nagar S (2000) see 7.

90. Grifiths M (2010) The Lotus Quest: In Search of the Sacred Flower. St Martin's Press, UK.

91. Majjhima Nikaya: Editing and interpretation by Bhikkhu T (1998 – 2013) 152 PTS: M iii 298. (Cited from Ravindran, see 1).

92. Zimmer (see 87)

93 – 94. Kumar S (2001) A Thousand Petalled Lotus: Jain Temples of Rajasthan, Indira Gandhi National Centre for the Arts, New Delhi.

95. Aamir N and Malik A (2017) From divinity to decoration: the journey of lotus symbol in the art of subcontinent. Pakistan Social Sciences Review 1(2)>201 – 225.

96. Siwek, S. (2013) The sacred lotus; a plant study. http:// www.flowersociety.org/lotus-plant-study.htm.

97. Paande, V. (2005) Kalidasa. In: History of Indian Theatre. Abhinav pub., New Delhi.

98. Yi, Z. D. (2009) Translation by Feng Xin-ming, "On Loving the Lotus" – by the Northern Song Dynasty; http:// www. hudong.com/wiki.

99. Thompson, J. (2016) Zhou Dunyi (Chou Tun-i, 1017-1073). Internet Encyclopedia of Philosophy, http:// www.iep.utm.edu/ zhou-dun.

100. By an unknown poet, The Lotus, http:// lotusonapond. tumblr.com.

101. Ran, Q. (2016) The symbolic meaning of lotus flowers in chinese culture. China Culture.Org., http:// www. chinaculture.org / chineseway/2010-07/23/ content_386723_4.htm.

102. Watanabe, S. (2013) Chinese Lotus Painting http:// www. inkdancechinesepaintings.com/chinese-lotus-paintings.html.

103. Griffith (see 90)

104. Cited from Ravindran (see 1).

105. Iles, L. (2013) Isis, the Lady of the Lotus. Mirror of Isis, Official Fellowship of Isis publication, http:// mirrorofisis. freeyellow.hcom/ id206.html.

106. Blavitsky HP (1888) The Secret Doctrine, (Chapter 13.12, called Transformation into the Lotus). See 41.

107. Blavitsky HP (1890) Legend of The Blue Lotus. https:// blavatsky.net/legend-of-the-blue-lotus/.

108. Ananda Saraswathi,Yogi. (2013) Ashta Lakshmi. http://vedicgoddess.weebly.com/3/ post/2013/01/ashta-lakshmi-by-yogi-ananda-saraswathi.html.

109. Retold by Narrenaditya Komaragiri (2022) under the title: A Poor Devotee Of Buddha Who Lighted An Eternal Lamp. The author of this legend is unknown. https://www.tirumalesa.com/a-poor-devotee-of-buddha-who-lighted-an-eternal-lamp/.

110. Ravindran (2017, 2020 – see 1&2).

111. Desikendran, L. *Saradathilakom*, Commentary, Nair, K.K. 2006, Samrat Pub., Trichur, Kerala, India. A tantric text from 8th century AD, gives details about the rituals associated with the worship of Devi, in the aspects of Lakshmi, Durga and Saraswathi.

112. Kamat SD (ed.) (2002) *Dhanvantari Nighantu*, Chaukhamba Sanskrit Prasthan, New Delhi.

113. Sriram B (ed.) (2006) *Bhavaprakasha* of Bhavamisra, Vol. 1, 2006.

114. Sharma PV (2004) Classical uses Medicinal Plants, ChaukhambaVisvabharati, Varanasi.

115. Sastry JLN (2008) *DravyagunaVijnana,* Chaukhamba Orientalia, Varanasi

116. Khare CP (2004) Indian Herbal Remedies, Springer Verlag, Berlin.

117 Nadkarni AK (1982) *K.M. Nadkarni's Materia Medica*, Vol.1 Popular Prakashan, Bombay.

(118) Sairam TV (2002) Home Remedies, vol.4, Penguin Books, New Delhi.

(119) Dharmananda S (2002) Lotus seed: food and medicine, http://www.itmonline.org/arts/lotus.htm.

120. Facciola S (1998) Cornucopia II – A Source Book of Edible Plants, Kampong pub., Vista, California.

121. Anon. (2012) *Nelumbo nucifera* Gaertn., PFAF,, http://www.pfaf.org/user/Plant.aspx?LatinName=Nelumbo+nucifera.

122-123. Newman JM (2001) Lotus: A Plant with many purposes. Vegetables and Vegetarian Foods, 8(4): 11-12, 31.

124. Orozco-Obando W et al. (2009) Is Lotus an ornamental plant or a vegetable? Yes! Water Garden International (Online), 4(2), http://www.watergardenersinternational.org/journal/4-2/warner/page1.html,

125 – 126. Newman, see 122.

127. Anlan L (2021) Beautiful and delicious lotus: culinary splendor of lotus plant. https://www.shine.cn/feature/taste/2107152068/.

128. Anon. (2013) Lotus in Thai Cuisine and Culture. https://shesimmers.com/2013/01/lotus-in-thai-cooking-culture.html.

129. Chou C (2024) Lotus root (ultimate guide from a pro chef + 10 ways to use it). https://thesoundofcooking.com/lotus-root/.

130. Ravindran (see 1).

131. Hall, J (2013) Lotus weaving, http://handeyemagazine.com/content/lotus-weaving.

132-135. Fraser-Lu, S. and Thanegi, M. (2014) History of lotus fabric, Buddhism, and indigenous folk beliefs. http://www. samatoa.com/ PrestaShop/content/9-lotus-flower-fabric-handmade.

136. Hall J (see 131)

137. Fraser-Lu, S. and Thanegi, M (see 132)

138. Lawless, J. (1995) The Illustrated Encyclopedia of Essential Oils: The Complete Guide to the Use of Oils in Aromatherapy & Herbalism. Shaftesbury, Dorset, England.

139. Anonymous (2024) Benefits of Lotus Oil in Aromatherapy. https://www.aromatherapyandmassage.com/benefits-of-lotus-oil.html#:-extracted%20from%20[th]e%20fresh%20flowers%20of%20[th]e%20plant.

140,141. Ravindran see1.

08

NIMBA (NEEM)

The Tree of Goddess Durga

My lovely Neem,
That intercepts the sun's scorching beam,
Yet bears the heat all-day
Without the rain's refreshing spray,
Thou charm'st the wanderer's woe away
With soothing shade.
How strong you are, how unafraid,
How green the leaves in spite of all
The mid-day flames that burn fall
Upon thy unprotected head....
Could man be as bold as thou and rise
Above the earth, with the sheltering arm
To save the suffering ones from harm,
From sorrows, poverty and vice
Through sacrifice.
Could man be steadfast, and like thee
Face every fate, would it not be
Fulfilment of life's loftiest dream
My lovely Neem! '
(The Neem tree by Elza Kazi) (1)

Neem (*Nimba,* Margosa tree) is a magnificent tree. In Sanskrit, the Neem is known as *Arishtha (Arishta),* meaning the reliever of sickness, and it is a great gift from Mother Nature. It is commonly known as neem and

Margosa trees and as *Nimba* in traditional medicines, which still plays a significant role in serving humanity. According to the World Health Organization, around 80% of people from developing countries depend on ethnomedicines for primary health care, and half of the world's population still relies on ethnomedicines obtained from plants' active ingredients. Neem (Margosa tree) is one of the most important medicinal plants ever found in the history of humankind. Neem is the first medicinal plant used in India's most ancient medical system, the Siddha system of medicine, whose history goes back to about 10,000 years. Since then, neem has been used to treat many infectious diseases (such as smallpox) and other health ailments. Its uninterrupted use was recorded as a regular medicinal plant from 4500 years onwards; its use possibly started from the time of Indus Valley civilization. In 1922, during Harappan excavations under the leadership of British archaeologists, the investigators discovered the remains of several herbs, including neem leaves. Researchers found evidence of using neem on a skull that underwent cranial surgery. These discoveries suggest neem use in surgical and medicinal areas in those times, and the legacy is still vibrant. At the beginning of the 20th century, neem trees spread to several countries and were carried by Indian emigrants. The neem tree can now be found in almost 72 countries in Asia, Africa, and Central and South America. (2,3)

The Neem tree is interwoven with the socio-cultural life of the Indian diaspora from ancient times. Neem is derived from the Sanskrit *Nimba*, meaning 'bestower of good health.' It has also been known as *sambha*, which has sun-ray-like effects (in providing health). The Neem tree has been revered through the ages in the Indian countryside, and the rural masses had implicit faith in its miraculous healing powers. Often, they lived in close association with the neem, even in the shade, and drank infusions of various parts (Leaf, bark, etc) as advised by the herbal tradition. They used young twigs as toothbrushes and ate tender leaves as salad or cooked leaves with vegetables as food. Gum from the tree found its use as lozenges for dryness of the throat and to alleviate thirst. In summer, villagers used to eat ripe fruit for their sweetish pulp. (4). All this together probably strengthened their immune system to meet any challenges they faced in the complex circumstances in which they had to exist.

Myths and Legends on Neem

According to Indian mythology, the origin of the neem tree is related to the story of the churning of the Ocean of Milk (*Ksheera Sagara* or *Palazhi*) by the Asuras and Devas, a legend presented in many Puranas. During this churning, a variety of things emerged from the ocean, and finally, Lord Dhanwantari appeared carrying the pot of nectar of immortality (*amrutha*). Indra, the king of Devas, tactfully took the pot away to *deva loka* (the abode of Gods, heaven). This legend also relates to Lord Vishnu's avatar as Mohini, the divine damsel. On the way to heaven (*deva loka*), a drop of *amrutha* spilt and fell on earth. The legend is that the neem tree originated from this drop of nectar. (It is a common legend for a few other plants as well).

A young neem tree (above) and neem flowers and fruits (below)

According to legends, Neem is a legendary tree in the celestial garden, *Nandanavana*. It is believed that Neem once sheltered the sun god, Surya, from demons and that this tree is very dear to the sun god. This legend is given in *Brahma Purana* and *Padma Purana*. Hindus in rural India believe that the neem tree is the abode of six goddesses: Durga (Kali), Bhavani, Sitala, Mariamma, Yellamma, and Manasa. These goddesses control diseases (such as smallpox and chickenpox) and the well-being of the people. These deities are believed to unleash diseases on humans to punish them for their misdeeds. In certain parts of India, the tree is regarded as a deity, *Neemari Devi*. The neem tree is held as a symbol of truth and righteousness, and the rural people believe that anyone who utters falsehood or foul things beneath a neem will fall ill. (5)

Neem is the abode of Bhavani, an aspect of the goddess Durga or Kali. Incidentally, Prince Śivaji – who came to be known as Chatrapathi Śivaji, certainly one of the most heroic personalities of Modern India, was an ardent devotee of goddess Bhavani. Mariamman and Yellamma are well-known tribal goddesses of South India and are believed to reside in Neem. Idols of Mariamman hold a neem leaf sword in one hand and a cobra in the other. So, this deity is also related to the snake worship. Tamil women who worship the goddess Kali (Bhadra Kali) dress in red, carry branches of the neem tree, and even dance in public, waving neem twigs to purify the surroundings and protect the place. Neem trees are invariably grown in all Kali or Durga temples, and the temples of Mariamman and Yellamma are always built in association with neem trees. Neem leaves are offered to Kali.

In Karnataka, worshipping Yellamma (also known as Holiyamma, Jogamma, and Renuka Devi) is restricted primarily among the tribal people. In such worship, a young neem tree sometimes became the icon, representing the deity. In a few Yellamma temples during the annual festival, girls in large numbers are offered as *dasis* or slaves of Yellamma. They clad themselves in neem tree branches, smear their forehead and head with *kumkum* (vermilion powder), and dance in front of the temple. Castrated priests also dress up like women and decorate themselves in neem leaves (6).

Yellamma is believed to be the incarnation of Renuka Devi, another name for Yellamma, who was the wife of Rishi Jamadagni, and himself was an aspect of Lord Śiva. The legends of Jamadagni, Renuka, and Parasuram (Rama, Parasurama) are well known and are available in Puranas like *Mahabharata, Brahmanda Purana*, etc. 'Renuka or Yellamma is worshipped as the goddess (devi) of the fallen in the Hindu pantheon. Yellamma is a patron goddess of many oppressed people, such as the Dalits, scheduled castes, scheduled tribes, and backward castes. Her devotees have revered her as the "Mother of the Universe" or *Jagadamba*. Legends say that Yellamma was the incarnation of Kali, who, on the one hand, symbolizes the death of ego and, on the other hand, is the mother who is compassionate about her children. (7)

The story of Renuka and Parasuram is given in detail in *Brahmanda Purana*. Renuka was the wife of the great Rishi Jamadagni, an aspect of Lord Shiva. They had five sons; the youngest one was Ram. Renuka was known for her virtue and devotion to her husband. Such was her faith that she could fetch water from the river in a pot of unbaked clay made by her on the spot, with the pot held together only by the strength of her devotion. One day, while at the river, a group of Gandharvas in a chariot passed by in the sky above. On seeing the exquisitely handsome Gandharva youths, Renuka wavered momentarily, her mind filled with desire. The feeling lasted only for a moment as she controlled her thoughts and started to make the pot. Though she tried many times, Renuka could not make one, as they all dissolved in the water. She became sad and frightened, and tears rolled down her cheeks. Meanwhile, Jamadagni noticed that his wife had not returned. Through his yogic powers, he divined all that had happened, and he became mad with anger. Meanwhile Renuka reached the hermitage, without the usual pot of water. Jamadagni summoned his eldest son, handed him an axe, and asked the boy to kill his mother. Horrified, the boy refused, and an angry Jamadagni turned him to stone. He then asked each of his sons, and as they refused, he turned them all into rocks one by one. Finally, only his youngest son, Ram, was left. Ever obedient, the boy beheaded his mother. Pleased, Jamadagni then offered two boons to Ram. The boy asked that his mother be brought back to life and his brothers be returned from stone to flesh. Impressed by the affection and devotion of his son, Jamadagni granted his request. (8)

In later years, Renuka became a goddess for the fallen and the downtrodden. She was the forerunner of a continuous lineage of women who all received cruel punishments for simple and even silly mistakes and faults, which were only too natural for humans. Renuka became a deity for women, especially for the fallen women. Renuka became famous as the deity of the socially backward classes in the Southern states of India, with a mass following. This deity became known as Yellamma, Mariamma, Bhavani, and many other names. She is the suckering deity of the oppressed and backward classes.

Temples were built for Yellamma over time. Such Yellamma temples were managed by women known as *"devadasis"* (the servants of gods), who dwelt in the temples and were trained as courtesans or artists. To this day, girls are being dedicated as devadasis to Yellamma, even though the practice is now illegal. Such women lead a miserable life as sex workers to earn their living, and they were all shunned by the rest of the public. In his book Nine Lives, William Dalrymple beautifully sketches the life of one such devadasi, as well as the agonies and tragedies of such people.

In Bengal, as well as in some north Indian regions, neem is regarded as the abode of Sitala Devi, the 'pox-mother' who can cause or cure pox diseases. People worship Sitala under the neem tree and give offerings to appease her. From this belief arose the customary treatment of rubbing the bodies of smallpox and chickenpox victims with neem leaves to cure them. Bengalese observe the *Pat Gosain* festival, which focuses mainly on the worship of neem.

Neem is also the abode of Manasa (Mansa) Devi, the goddess of serpents, who protects people from snake bites, and she is offered neem leaves at her altar. There is a belief that if a person lives on food cooked on a neem wood fire, he becomes immune to snake bite. Because neem is regarded as the abode of Sitala, Kali, Mariamman, Yellamma etc, it is considered a remedy for all sickness and bad luck. (9) As mentioned earlier, neem is treated as the manifest form of goddess Neemari Devi. In many parts of India, Neem trees are often associated with small improvised temples where many offer prayers. Haberman presents a study of such neem worship temples in his book People Trees (10).

Earlier, a passing reference was made to tree marriage while discussing the peepal tree. When the tree marriage is practised between neem and peepal, the neem is considered the bride and the peepal the bridegroom. In Rajasthan and Punjab, these roles are reversed, where the neem is considered male and the peepal female. A priest often solemnizes this marriage according to the typical local marriage customs in vogue. For such purposes, neem and peepal trees are grown side by side. When the trees are about eighteen, a marriage is solemnized between these trees. The priest ties a nuptial string on the neem tree on behalf of the bridegroom, peepal. Both trees are decorated with flowers, and the neem tree is adorned with a yellow or red silk saree and flowers to give a bridal look. The peepal tree is dressed in a traditional *dhoti*. The village folk attend the function and bless the 'couple' by throwing sacred rice mixed with vermillion and sandal paste. A sumptuous meal usually follows the tree wedding ceremony. During the past few years, there have been a few reports on such marriages from different parts of India. (11-13). Tree marriage is not unique to India. There is a report from Italy of such a tree marriage between two oak trees. This tree wedding is an annual practice from 1432 onwards.

According to the National calendar of India (Sh*aka* era or *Śaka Samvat* is generally 78 years behind the Gregorian calendar, except January–March, when it is behind by 79 years), the beginning of the New Year is the first day of the first month, *Chaitra*. This day is celebrated with a grand festivity known as *Gudi Padwa Day*, a major festival in Maharashtra and the Konkan regions. It is a spring festival observed on the initial day of Chitra, the first month of the Indian calendar. The significance of this festival is outlined in *Brahma purana*, which suggests that Lord Brahma created the universe on this day. It is considered auspicious for initiating new ventures, as anything commenced on the *gudi padwa* day believed to proper. The general belief among the people is that on this day, Lord Rama returned to his land with Sita and Lakshmana after spending fourteen years in exile. People received him with great jubilation and by putting up 'gudis'. A *gudi* (also spelt *gudhi*) is a long pole, at the top of which a coloured silk cloth is pleated and fixed with a brass pot. It is then decorated with garlands of flowers and twigs of the neem tree – the plant that purifies. This happy occasion is observed as a great festival on that day, and the neem tree plays a role in it. Traditionally the day starts with the consumption of the bitter neem leaves. (14) In recent times the day is being observed an the Neem Day.

Another famous event in which neem plays a vital role is the *Nava kalevara (Nava kalebara)* festival in the Jagannath Temple in Puri, Orissa. In the National calendar, an extra month comes every twelve years; two months of *Ashada* come together (known as *mala masa,* twin month). Such a year will have thirteen months instead of the usual twelve. During this auspicious year, the *Navakalevara* festival is celebrated. It is the 'new incarnation day' of Lord Jagannath of Puri, the day when the wooden idol of Lord Jagannath is replaced with a new one; the old physical form is thus replaced with a new one, and hence it is called *Nava kalevara* (new body). Lord Jagannath's wooden idols, the Balaram and Subhadra deities, and the ancillary deity Sudarshan are carved from specially selected neem trees. The tree selection, cutting, transportation, and carving of the deities all take place according to strict ritual procedures. The carving is done in great secrecy. Later, a blindfolded priest is sent alone to the sanctum sanctorum to remove the *'naabhi brahma'* (the navel portion of the idol of Lord Jagannath) from the old idol, which is placed on the new one. Afterwards, the new idols are installed amidst great ritual functions and celebrations. The old idols are sent to the burial ground and buried according to special rituals. Any neem wood remaining after the carving of the idols is disposed of in great secrecy; such wood should not be allowed to reach the hands of anyone. Thus, neem wood occupies a place of pride in one of India's most sacred ritual festivals. The whole ceremony is very elaborate and complicated, lasting for a hundred or so days. Albertina Nugteren, in her book Belief, Bounty and Beauty, gave an elaborate treatment of *the navakalevara* ceremony. (15)

In Rajasthan, the 'Rathore' sect of Rajputs worships the neem tree as their *'kulavriksha'* (presiding tree), and only its wood is used for making the throne for their *'Kuladevi'* (presiding goddess) (16).

Sometime back, there were newspaper reports from the Reddypettai village in Kanchipuram district of Tamil Nadu that the trunk of a neem had started bulging, resembling a pregnant woman's belly. The village people adorned this tree with flowers and conducted a *'valaikappu'* ceremony. It is a ceremony for a pregnant woman between the seventh and ninth months when she is adorned with bangles and blessed by relatives. This ceremony is for the creation of a pleasant and happy mood for the expecting mother. The villagers performed the same *'valaikappu'* ceremony on the neem tree. The incident indicates this tree's high position in the minds of the rural people of Tamil Nadu."

In his book *People Trees,* Haberman provides a detailed description of the worship of the neem tree as he observed in the Varanasi region. He recorded that the neem trees were all decorated with face masks of the Neem goddess, who is none other than the Mother Goddess (Ma Durga) for the ordinary people. First, there was simply the neem tree, but then people put the face of the goddess on the tree, thinking that the face would help them to be in better communion with the goddess. Such faces on the tree may help the devotees to have a hearty relationship with the Ma as the neem tree. (17)

The neem tree puja involves the following steps:

- Start with Meditation: Stand before the neem tree, take a deep breath, and focus your mind on the divine. Meditate for a few moments to centre your thoughts.
- Offer Prayers to the Neem Tree: Light the earthen lamps and incense sticks, and place them near the tree's base.
- Clean the Base of the Tree: Sprinkle a small amount of water mixed with turmeric and cow dung to purify the base of the tree.
- Offering to the Tree: Apply kumkum on the trunk of the neem tree as a tilak. Offer fresh flowers, especially neem leaves, symbolizing reverence for the goddess. Pour water or milk around the roots of the tree, symbolizing nourishment. Offer fruits, coconut, and raw rice (Akshat) at the base of the tree.
- Recite Mantras and Prayers: Chant simple prayers like *"Om Shakti Namah"* or *"Om Durga Namah"*, invoking the blessings of Goddess Durga, who resides in the neem tree. Another mantra that can be chanted is:

Om Nimbaya Namah |
Om Dhanvantari Namah |

These mantras seek blessings for health, protection, and well-being.

- Circumambulation *(Pradakshina)*: Walk around the tree in a clockwise direction seven times while silently praying for health, strength, and protection.
- After finishing the puja and prayers, sit calmly for a few moments, focusing on gratitude. Bow

down before the tree, expressing respect and thankfulness for its protection and blessings. Distribute the prasad to your family and the poor. Prepare the prasad like sweet Pongal (made with jaggery, rice, and ghee), coconut laddu: (prepared with grated coconut, jaggery, and cardamom), and fruits like banana. They are offered first to the tree and then to the family members and neighbours. (18)

During *Siddhivinayaka vrata pushpa pooja*, neem flowers are offered to Lord Ganesha.

Worshipping the neem tree

Sitala and Sitala Pooja

Sitala is a pre-Aryan goddess worshipped by tribals of North and Central India. Sitala is the goddess of smallpox, as per the reference in the Skanda Purana, which also gives a *Sitalastakam* for worshipping the goddess, Sitala. Legends show Goddess Shitala wearing red attire and riding around on a donkey. She has four arms holding a silver broom, a winnowing fan, a bowl, and an urn with Gangajal. Goddess Shitala protects humanity from deadly diseases and plagues, which can otherwise have adverse effects. According to Hindu mythology, Goddess Katyayani, an incarnation of Shakti, manifested as Shitala Mata to kill the deadly demon Jwarasur, who threatened the world with deadly fever and plague. There are several references to her greatness in the Puranas. The popular folklore depicts that Sitala has seven sisters and may also have one brother who is not as well known. Sitala's sisters are known as Masani, Basanti, Maha Mati, Polamde, Lamkaria, and Agwani, and they are all associated with one of the seven types of fevers prevalent in these regions. Sitala is worshipped during *Phalgun* (February – March). In North India, Sitala is associated with stale or leftover food because she is thought to have been born of the cold ashes of the sacrificial fire. Basora is a festival in her honour, which means "Leftover Food Worship." The people of this region prepare only cold foods on the day before the pujas, offer such foods to Sitala, and eat only cold food themselves. Hence, devotees do not light a fire in the kitchen on the festival day. Instead, they consume food prepared on the previous night. The third region that worships Sitala is the state of Gujarat, where she is no longer associated with disease; instead, she is seen as the giver of good fortune, husbands, and sons. The origin of the Sitala shrine in Gujarat is thought to be identified with Bariha Bapji or Babri Bahan of the Mahabharata. (19)

Legend of Goddess Shitala (Sitala):

According to Puranas (like Skanda Purana), Lord Brahma created Goddess Shitala. She was promised she would be worshipped as a goddess on earth, but she was asked to carry the seeds of lentils with her. Shitala then asked for a companion. Lord Shiva blessed her and created Jwarasura from his sweat. Goddess Shitala and Jwarasura stayed at *Devaloka* (heaven). They used a donkey to transport the lentils to wherever they went. But one day, the lentil seeds became smallpox germs, spreading the deadly disease in *Devloka*. Finally, fed up with this disease, the gods asked her to go and settle on earth, where humans would worship her. Shitala and Jwarasura came down to earth. They started hunting for a place to stay. King Birat (Virat), an ardent devotee of Lord Shiva, agreed to worship her and gave them a place in his kingdom. An angry Shitala demanded supremacy over all other deities. When King Birat refused, she spread different fevers in his kingdom. Finally, the King had to agree to her demands. Soon, the disease and all its ill effects were cured. (For further details on the Sitala cult see 20-22).

Neem tree also played its role in Indian folk songs. In his book on Flowering Trees of India, M S Randhawa quotes lines from a Punjabi ballad.

> 'Father never cut this nim (neem) tree
> The nim offers rest to the sparrows
> Father, never trouble your daughters,
> Daughters are like sparrows.
> All the sparrows will fly away,
> The nim will feel so lonely
> For their fathers-in-law's, will all the daughters leave
> Mother will feel so lonely.'

Randhawa commented on this song: 'The neem tree symbolizes the mother to whom daughters are like sparrows; when they leave it for their new homes, the tree feels lonely like the mother whose daughters leave her one by one, as they get married.' (23).

In his poem on the neem tree, SD Tiwari recollects his association with a tree close to his childhood residence. The concluding lines of this poem are quoted below:

"Cool breeze sway the branches of the tree,
and the birds sitting there sing.
My heart also swings along that pleasant breeze
and to the tune of the bird's pings.
So many dimensions of my life grew
in the shadow of that tree of neem.
Whoever is connected with it, appears my own,
but in the busy life of the city,
now all that looks like a dream." (24)

Titbits on Neem

1. One of the *Dharmasutras* (*Śukranīti* 4.4.105-109) mentions that "The trees (such as *nimba*) are to be watered in the morning and evening in summer, every alternate day in winter, in the fifth part of the day (i.e., afternoon) in spring, never in the rainy season. If trees have their fruits destroyed, the pouring of cold water after being cooked together with *Kulutha, Māṣa* (seeds), *Mudga* (pulse), *Yava*(barley) and *Tila* (oil seed), would lead to the growth of flowers and fruits. Neem tree growth could be improved by applying water with which fishes are washed and cleansed." (*Dharmasutras* contain the instructions (*shastra*) regarding religious conduct of livelihood (*dharma*), ceremonies, jurisprudence (study of law) and more. It is categorized as *smriti,* an essential and authoritative selection of books dealing with the Hindu lifestyle.)

2. In the *Pacharatra* text *Īśvarasaṃhitā, Nimba* refers to neem as a type of vegetable fit for use in oblation offerings (25.121b-125). (*Pancharatra (pāñcarātra)* represents a tradition of Hinduism where Narayana is revered and worshipped; it is closely related to *Vaishnavism*. The *Pancharatra* literature includes various Agamas and tantras incorporating many *Vaishnava* philosophies.)

3. In *Shaktism**, *Nimba* is one of the thirty-six sacred trees, according to the *Ṣaṭsāhasrasaṃhitā*, an expansion of the *Kubjikāmata tantra*: the earliest popular and most authoritative Tantra of the *Kubjikā* cult., "According to the *Kula* teaching (these) (i.e., *Nimba*) are the most excellent *Kula* trees that give accomplishments and liberation. (They are full of) Yoginīs, Siddhas, Lords of the Heroes and hosts of gods and demons. One should not touch them with one's feet or urinate and defecate on them or have sex etc. below them. One should not cut or burn them. Having worshipped and praised them regularly with their flowers and shoots, one should always worship the *Śrīkrama***with devotion with the best fruits and roots...". (*Shaktism represents a tradition of Hinduism where the Goddess (Devi) is revered and worshipped. Shakta literature includes a range of scriptures, including various Agamas and Tantras. ** The Kubjikā cult is called the Śrīkrama; It is the tradition or *krama* of the goddess who bestows well-being and prosperity.)

4. In Shaivism*, *Nimba* refers to one of the nine *kulavṛikṣhas* (*Kula* trees) in which the *Kula Yoginīs* reside, according to the *Kulārṇava-tantra*** (11.66-68.) Accordingly, "*Kula Yoginīs* always live in *kulavṛikṣhas* (Kula trees). Therefore, one should not eat on the leaves of such trees, instead one should worship them. One should neither sleep under the *Kula Vṛikṣhas* nor create any disturbance under them. Otherwise, seeing or hearing about such trees, one should greet them with devotion and never cut them down...". (*Shaivism (śaivism) represents a tradition of Hinduism worshipping Shiva as the supreme being. Closely related to Shaktism, Shaiva literature includes a range of scriptures, including Tantras; ** The "Kularnava Tantra" is a significant text in the Kula tradition of Shaktism and Tantric Shaivism. The main focuses of this Tantra are guru

devotion, the philosophy of Tantrism, the doctrine of duties and the distinctive rituals)

5. In Vajrayana Buddhism (tantric Buddhism), *Nimba* is mentioned in the *Susiddhikara-sūtra*, according to which the fruit of the *tāla* (palmyra) tree, the fruit of the coconut, the fruit of the *bilva*, the fruit of the *nimba* (neem), and other malodorous fruits unpleasant to all should not be offered (to Lord Buddha).

6. In *Kuvalayamala,* the 8th century *Prakrit Champu Kavya*, there is mention of a guild of merchants at Surparka*, where there was a custom to hold receptions to foreign merchants to discuss matters of trade and merchandise. One merchant said: "I went to Ratnadvīpa** with leaves of the *Nimba* tree and brought gems from there ..." (24) (*An ancient port near the Konkan coast, south of Mumbai. It was believed to be the capital of Apranta (an old name for Konkan) and the oldest historical testament of Mumbai in the form of Ashokan Edits. ** Present-day Sri Lanka). (25)

Description and Uses:

Nimba (Neem, *Azadirachta indica* A. Juss. (Syn. *Melia azadirachta* L.) Meliaceae

Margosa tree, Indian lilac, neem (English); nimbi, neem (Hindi);nim, nimbi (Bengali); baevina mara, nimbi (Kannada); aaryaveppu, rajaveppu (Malayalam); veppamaram, veppu (Tamil); nimbamu, vaepa (Telungu).

Neem is a well-known multipurpose tree that became famous due to its insecticidal properties and applications. Its common names include Indian lilac and margosa tree, and it is known by many Sanskrit and local names. It is a native of the semi-arid regions of South Asia, especially of India. It has been introduced into many other tropical and sub-tropical countries. In East Africa, it is known as the Tree of forty (*Muarubaini*) as it is used for treating forty diseases. Neem is a fast-growing tree, reaching 20 25 meters in height with a main trunk that is relatively short, and the branches spread out to provide very thick shade. Leaves are alternate, pinnate; flowers in loose axillary, drooping panicles, bearing many flowers (up to 250 or even more); whitish or with pale lilac colour, faintly fragrant, edible and used in many parts of India (like Andhra Pradesh and Tamil Nadu) for the preparation of certain curries. Fruit is an eval drupe. Oil of neem is an effective insect repellent (including mosquitoes) and has pronounced insecticidal properties and hence seed and leaf extract are used in pest control in crops.

The neem is a native of the Indian subcontinent, it is widely distributed by introduction, mainly in the drier (arid) tropical and subtropical zones of Asia, Africa, the Americas, Australia, and the South Pacific islands. In India, it is widely distributed in many states. In Myanmar, it is common in the central parts of the country. In the South Pacific neem occurs in the Fiji Islands. In Australia, it was first introduced about 60-70 years ago. In Indonesia, neem exists mainly in the low-lying northern and eastern parts of Java and the Islands to the east (Bali, Lombok, Sumbawa). In the Philippines, it was introduced during the seventies and eighties of the last century. In China, neem trees were planted on the subtropical island of Hainan and southern China. In Nepal, neem trees are found in the Southern, low-lying areas (Tarai region). In Sri Lanka, it is widespread in the drier northern parts of the island. In Iran, neem trees grow along the coast up to the Chat el Arab in Iraq on the Arabian Peninsula. In Qatar and Abu Dhabi, neem was planted under irrigation using desalted seawater along avenues and parks. A large plantation was established on the Arafat plains near Makkah to provide shade for pilgrims. (26)

Neem is a remarkable tree, equally impressive are its medicinal properties. Charaka indicated it in various skin diseases; Susrutha recommended it in urinary tract obstruction; Vagbhata used the seed oil for treating grey hair. Neem plant and its oil are indicated in *jvara* (fever), *krimi* (worms), *prameha* (diabetes), *vrana* (ulcers), *kasa* (asthma and other respiratory tract infections), *chardi* (vomiting), *visharoga* (poison-induced ailments), *arsa* (piles), *gulma* (accumulated gas), *netraroga* (eye diseases) etc. Bhavaprakasa mentions that *nimba* is: "cold in potency, light in action, absorbent, pungent in post-digestive effect, and is an appetizer. It is highly bitter and reduces all ailments related to *vata, pitta, kapha,* tiredness, thirst, cough, fever, distaste, and worms; cures ulcers, vomiting, skin diseases, and urinary diseases. Neem leaves are beneficial for the eyes, reduces *pitta* and poisonous effects, and pacifies all types of distaste and skin diseases. Fruit is demulcent, clear skin diseases, intestinal tumours, haemorrhoids, worms, urinary diseases, and glycosuria." (27)

Many chemical constituents have been reported from neem. Leaves contain azadirachtin, azadiractanin, azadirone, nimbandiol, nimbin, nimbolide etc. Stem contains nimbin, nimbidin, nimbinin, kulinone, margosinolide etc. Nimbin and nimbidin are important constituents of roots. Azadirachtin, azdirachtol, nimbol, nimocin etc occur in fruits. Seed oil has tocopherol, azdirone, nimbinin, nimbin, nimbidin etc. Flowers contain azadiradione, margosene etc. Seed extract and seed oil are widely used as pesticides for controlling crop pests. More information is available in reviews on neem tree (28-30).

Citations and notes

1. Elza Kazi, The Neem Tree Poem, http://www.poemsurdu.com/2015/05/27/the-neem-tree-poem-and-summary/.

2. Kumar VS and Navaratnam V (2013) Neem (*Azadirachta indica*): Prehistory to contemporary medicinal uses to humankind. Asian Pacific Journal of Tropical Biomedicine, 3 (7), 505-514.

3. Oyebode O et al. (2016) Use of traditional medicine in middle-income countries: a WHO-SAGE study. Health Policy Plan. 2016 Oct;31(8):984-91. doi: 10.1093/heapol/czw022. PMID: 27033366; PMCID: PMC5013777.

4. Anon. (2014) Neem Foundation – History of Usage https://neemfoundation.org/about-neem/history-of-usage/, accessed on Aug.31, 2024.

5. Ravindran PN (2020) Sacred and Ritual Plants of India. Notion press, Chennai.

6. Neem Worship, retrieved on 28.11.09 from http://www.paghat.com/neemworship.html.

7. Anonymous (2024) Renuka. https://en.wikipedia.org/wiki/Renuka.

8. The legend of Parashuram, https://sladeviper777.wordpress.com/2014/06/16/full-history-of-parashuram/.

9. Ravindran (see 5)

10. Haberman DL (2013) People Trees. Oxford University Press, Oxford, UK..

11. Tree marriage performed to appease rain god in Coimbatore. http://www.theindian.com/ newsportal/

india-news/tree-marriage-performed-to-appease-rain-god-in-coimbatore-2_100204763.html

12. Villagers perform tree 'wedding' to send green message; http://www.thaindian.com/ newsportal/ uncategorized/villagers-perform-tree-wedding-to-send-green-message_10060522.html.

13. 90-yr-old's message by tree marriage http://www.nowpublic.com/strange/90-yr-olds-message-tree-marriage.

14. Gudi padva, http://www.hindu-blog.com/2008/03/gudhi-padwa-maharashtra-new-year-gudi.html Retrieved on 28.11.09; gudipadva, Wikipedia, the free encyclopedia, en.wikipedia.org/wiki/Gudi_Padwa.

15. Nugteren A (2005) Belief, Bounty and Beauty. Brill, UK.

16. Sood SK. et al. (2005) Sacred and Magico-religious Plants of India. 2005.

17. Habermann DL (2013) People Trees. Oxford, New York.

18. Rajendran A. (2024) How to worship neem tree in Hinduism – A comprehensive guide. https://www.hindu-blog.com/2014/12/how-to-worship-neem-tree-in-hinduism.html.

19. Ravindran, see 5.

20. Wadley, S. (1980) Sitala: the cool one. Asian Folklore Studies, 39 (1), 33-62

21. Mukhopadhyay SK (1994) Cult of Goddess Sitala in Bengal: an enquiry into folk culture, Calcutta. Calcutta Firma Pvt. Ltd,

22. Ghatak P (2013) The Sitala Saga: a Case of Cultural Integration in the Folk Tradition of West Bengal. Rupkatha Journal 5(2) ,119 – 131.

23. Randhawa MS (1957) Flowering Trees In India, ICAR, New Delhi.

24. Tiwari SD (2014) That neem tree. https://allpoetry.com/poem/11637679-That-Neem-Tree-by-S.-D.-Tiwari.

25. Anon. (2024) Nimba, Nīmbā: 40 definitions, Wisdom Library, https://www.wisdomlib.org/definition/nimba.

26. Neem Foundation (2014) Introduction to Neem Tree. https://neemfoundation.org/about-neem/introduction-to-neem-tree/

27. Alzohairy MA (2016) Therapeutics role of *Azadirachta indica* (Neem) and their active constituents in diseases prevention and treatment. Evidence Based Complementary and Alternative Medicine, 7382506. doi: 10.1155/2016/7382506.

28. Pratik B et al. (2023) The remarkable neem tree: a comprehensive review of its botanical pharmacological and therapeutic properties. International Res. J. Creative Research Thoughts, 11 (3): 738 – 744.

29. Akhila A and Rani, K. (1999). Chemistry of the Neem Tree (*Azadirachta indica* A. Juss.). In: Herz, W et al (eds) Progress in the Chemistry of Organic Natural Products. vol 78. Springer, Vienna. https://doi.org/10.1007/978-3-7091-6394-8_2.

30. Gupta AC et al. (2017) Neem (*Azadirachta indica*): An Indian traditional panacea with modern molecular basis. Phytomedicine, 34: 14-20.

SUBJECT INDEX

<u>VOLUME – 1</u>

Vilva — **333**

Lotus — **365-500**